BANGOR PROBATE RECORDS

VOL. I : PRE - 1700

N.L.W. PROBATE INDEXES No. 1

LLYFRGELL GENEDLAETHOL CYMRU
THE NATIONAL LIBRARY OF WALES

INDEX
OF THE
PROBATE RECORDS
OF THE
BANGOR CONSISTORY COURT

VOL. I : PRE - 1700

COMPILED BY

NIA HENSON

N.L.W. PROBATE INDEXES No. 1

ABERYSTWYTH
1980

ISBN 0 901833 95 9

ARGRAFFWYD YN
LLYFRGELL GENEDLAETHOL
CYMRU

PRINTED AT
THE NATIONAL LIBRARY
OF WALES

1980

FOREWORD / RHAGAIR

This volume is the first of a series in which it is hoped to provide indices to all the pre-1858 probate records from Welsh dioceses in the National Library of Wales. It need not be emphasised how important probate records are for family, social and economic history, and such indices will be a great convenience to all those working in these fields. This volume, covering the earliest records from the diocese of Bangor, has been compiled by Mrs. Nia Henson, M.A., Assistant Keeper in the Department of Manuscripts and Records, under the general direction of Mr. G. Milwyn Griffiths, M.A., the Keeper of that Department. Further volumes for Bangor and the other Welsh dioceses will follow in due course. The way in which the present volume has been set out is experimental and may be modified in later volumes.

R. GERAINT GRUFFYDD
Librarian
February 1980

Y mae'r gyfrol hon yn gyntaf o gyfres y gobeithir ynddi fynegeio holl gofnodion profeb y cyfnod cyn 1858 a ddaeth i Lyfrgell Genedlaethol Cymru o'r esgobaethau Cymreig. Nid oes angen pwysleisio mor bwysig yw cofnodion o'r fath o safbwynt hanes teuluol, cymdeithasol ac economaidd, a bydd y mynegeion arfaethedig yn ddiau'n hwylustod mawr i bawb sy'n gweithio yn y meysydd hyn. Paratowyd y gyfrol hon, sy'n ymwneud â'r cofnodion cynharaf o esgobaeth Bangor, gan Mrs. Nia Henson, M.A., Ceidwad Cynorthwyol yn Adran y Llawysgrifau a'r Cofysgrifau, dan gyfarwyddyd cyffredinol Mr. G. Milwyn Griffiths, M.A., Ceidwad yr Adran honno. Fe fydd cyfrolau pellach ar gyfer esgobaeth Bangor, ac ar gyfer yr esgobaethau Cymreig eraill, yn dilyn yn eu tro. Arbrofol yw'r dull y gosodwyd allan y gyfrol hon, ac efallai y newidir peth arno mewn cyfrolau diweddarach yn y gyfres.

R. GERAINT GRUFFYDD
Llyfrgellydd
Chwefror 1980

CONTENTS

INTRODUCTION

The pre-1858 probate records of the Consistory Court of the diocese of Bangor were transferred to the Library in 1945 from the probate registry at Bangor following the Direction issued by the President of the Probate Division of the High Court of Justice that all pre-1858 Welsh ecclesiastical probate records housed in the district probate registries be transferred into the custody of the Library. The Bangor records hardly commence before 1635, although a few wills or copies of wills for earlier years have survived. From 1635 they continue in an unbroken run up to 1858, apart from the Interregnum period between 1648 and 1660 when the Bangor court ceased to function. They were arranged in yearly bundles in the district registry, the reckoning employed by the probate courts being from 25 March, and this arrangement was retained after their transfer to the Library. Recently the contents of each yearly bundle were arranged under county and then in alphabetical order of parishes. Between 1961 and 1965 all the documents were treated and repaired in the Library's Bindery.

Four volumes of manuscript indexes compiled at the registry and covering the whole run of documents have hitherto been the only indexes available. The need to prepare new indexes based on the documents themselves has long been recognised and this volume, which is intended to replace the old index for 1635–1699, marks a start on that task. It is hoped, eventually, to publish revised indexes to cover the entire period up to 1858 and similar indexes to the pre-1700 probate records of some of the other Welsh dioceses are in progress.

The old index to the pre-1700 records was unsatisfactory in many ways, one of its main disadvantages being that it was arranged chronologically, unlike the other three volumes which are arranged alphabetically by surname. This revised index is an alphabetical one but, should any reader at the Library wish to consult a chronological rather than an alphabetical index for the 1635–1699 period, a new index arranged under county and then alphabetically by parish is available.[1] This was compiled by xeroxing the card entries for each yearly bundle while preparing this present index before placing them in their appropriate alphabetical positions. Another disadvantage of the old index was its unreliability. The documents relating to each person were originally folded[2] with the name of the deceased, the parish and, in most cases, the date of probate or administration endorsed on the outside, that is, on the back of whichever document happened to be on the outside, or sometimes on a separate piece of paper which was used as a wrapper. The old index appears to have been compiled mainly from these endorsements and, since the deceased person's name or place of abode in the endorsements is often incorrect or incomplete, the index is inaccurate. There are also many instances of the details contained in the endorsements having been copied inaccurately, of the same persons being listed more than once either under different years or under the same year, of wills and administrations being listed under incorrect dates and a number of wills and administrations which are not listed at all.

JURISDICTION.

The Consistory Court at Bangor was responsible for the proving of wills and the granting of administrations in the counties of Anglesey, Caernarfon (except for the parishes of Eglwys-rhos, Llangystennin and Llysfaen, which were in the jurisdiction

1 For anyone whose interest lies in a particular parish rather than person or family, there is also available on cards an index of parishes in which all records from a particular parish are listed by their reference number (year / no. within bundle).

2 Since repair they have been kept open and flat.

of the Consistory Court of St. Asaph) and Merioneth (except for thirteen parishes, also in the jurisdiction of the St. Asaph Court), in the Deanery of Dyffryn Clwyd in the county of Denbigh and the Deanery of Arwystli in the county of Montgomery. Also represented among the pre-1700 records of the court are the Caernarfonshire townships of Tre Eidda and Gwydir or Trewydir which belonged to the Denbighshire parishes of Ysbyty Ifan and Llanrwst respectively. Although these two parishes were in the jurisdiction of the St. Asaph Consistory Court, it appears that the two townships were considered as part of the Bangor diocese, at least during the seventeenth century, and they seem to have been administered by the Bangor Consistory Court for probate purposes.[1] In addition, apart from the parishes normally in the jurisdiction of the Bangor Consistory Court, a few Merionethshire, Montgomeryshire and Denbighshire parishes normally in the jurisdiction of the St. Asaph Consistory Court, one Montgomeryshire parish normally in the jurisdiction of the Consistory Court of the Archdeaconry of Brecon, two or three Shropshire parishes, the parish of Cliffe in Kent, and Dublin are represented among the records.

ARRANGEMENT OF INDEX.

There are two important points which should be borne in mind concerning the arrangement of this revised index:

1. **Forename and Surname Index.** The period covered by this index sees the gradual breakdown of the Welsh naming system, which was a patronymic one, and only a little over a third of the entries in the index are in the form of patronymics. Since the only satisfactory way of dealing with this group was to index them under their forenames, it was necessary to divide the index into two sections, a forename index and a surname index.

The forename index includes all names which contain the word *ap* or *verch* and any name consisting of three or more Welsh Christian name elements. In an example such as the following, the names would be taken as equatable:

Thomas ap David ap John
Thomas ap David John
Thomas David ap John
Thomas David John

Epithets and place-names such as *Glynne*, *Lloyd*, *Vaughan*, *Wynne*, which later became surnames, have been put in italics in the forename index and disregarded, except for the purpose of ordering otherwise equatable names. The following example illustrates the principle adopted in the arrangement of entries containing epithet-names:

Hugh ap Evan
Hugh ap Evan *Gouff*
Hugh ap Evan *Lloyd*
Hugh *Lloyd* ap Evan
Hugh ap Evan Dafudd
Hugh ap Evan Dafudd *Lloyd*

[1] It should be noted that the Caernarfonshire townships of Maenan and Eirias, belonging to the Denbighshire (diocese of St. Asaph) parishes of Eglwys-bach and Llandrillo-yn-Rhos respectively, are not represented among the pre-1700 Bangor records.

Forms such as *Pugh*, *Probert*, *Bevan*, occurring as part of the patronymic, have been equated with *ap Hugh*, *ap Robert*, *ap Evan*. An entry for John Lewis Pugh Parry, for example, is arranged as though it were John Lewis (ap) Hugh (ap) Harry. Where there are entries for two or more persons with equatable names, they are arranged chronologically, that is, according to the year of granting probate or administration, and where two or more equatable names occur within the same year, the entries are arranged alphabetically by parish.

The surname index includes all names consisting of two elements only, whether they be a Christian name and a surname or two common Welsh Christian name elements, even though in the case of the latter the second element might not be an established surname. The same principles of arrangement were adopted as in the forename index in the case of two or more persons with equatable names.

Second entries, rather than cross-references, have been included for the following types of name:

(a) Names in patronymic form containing epithets or place-names, such as *Glynne*, *Vaughan*, *Wynne*, which became surnames. Their arrangement in the forename index has been discussed above; they have also been included in the surname index under the epithet-names.

(b) Names in the forename index which include surnames, such as *Bayly*, *Massey*, *Salusbury*, as the last element of the patronymic are also included in the surname index.

(c) Names with variant forms linked by *alias*. Entries for names such as Alice verch John *alias* Alice Williams appear in both the forename and surname indexes and entries for names such as Frances Brereton *alias* Wynne appear under both surnames in the surname index.

It is important for users of this index to bear in mind that it might be necessary to search in both sections of the index for some persons, the reason for this being evident if one recalls that all entries containing two common Welsh Christian name elements only have been placed in the surname index under the second element. A person called William ap Evan might also be known as William Evan / Evans / Bevan and a person called Humphrey (ap) William Humphrey might also be known as Humphrey William / Williams. The coexistence of primitive and more developed forms of the same name during the period covered by this index is reflected in the records themselves. For example, a person's name is often in Christian name and surname form in the will or administration bond while the patronymic form is found in the accompanying inventory. As will be explained later, the form taken for the index entry was usually that occurring in the will or administration bond.

2. Standardisation of Names. Variant forms of forenames and surnames have been brought together and arranged under the forms which, on the evidence of the documents, were considered to be the most common during the period of the index. Cross-references have been included from the variant forms to the standard forms chosen, unless the entries were adjacent in the index or the variation between the chosen standard form and the other forms was very slight. In the few instances when a name occurred in an uncommon form only and the entry or entries had to be indexed under that form, cross-references have been included from a form which would be more familiar to the searcher, even though it does not occur in the index entries, to the form under which the entry is indexed.

In the forename index, all other elements of the patronymics have been reduced to the same standard spelling as that under which the first elements were indexed. For example, since the standard form chosen for the forename Rhydderch / Rytherch / Rutherch / Roderick was Rhydderch, an entry for Lowrie verch Roderick is arranged before Lowrie verch Richard in the index. Likewise, since the standard form chosen for names such as Kadwaladr, Katherine was the one with the initial letter 'C', an entry for Edward ap Kadwaladr comes before Edward ap David, even though no example of Edward ap Cadwaladr occurs in the index entries. For the sake of consistency Christian names in the surname index have also been arranged according to the standard forms used in the forename index. For example, Roderick Jones was notionally reduced to Rhydderch Jones and Annes William to Agnes Williams and indexed accordingly. Thus, it has sometimes been necessary to include in the surname index cross-references not only from variant to standard forms of surnames but also from variant to standard forms of Christian names.

Another point to note concerns documents relating to the same person filed under different years. Documents produced in later years relating to an estate, the papers of which had already been filed by the court, would nearly always be placed in the current bundle. A bond for the administration of goods left unadministered (*de bonis non*), for example, might be filed several years after the first administration or a will might be proved and filed a year or two after the administration bond had been filed. Whenever documents filed under different years could be identified as relating to the same estate, the references were brought together under the one entry in the index. However, in the few cases where there was uncertainty as to whether or not documents filed under different years related to the same estate, separate entries were made. Therefore in a few instances the index may possibly contain more than one entry for the same person.

It should be mentioned in passing that, in the process of indexing the records, some documents were transferred from one yearly bundle to another because they were found to have been filed under the incorrect year. Also, inventories filed separately from the will or administration bond, probably because they were exhibited either in the year prior to or following that in which probate or administration was granted, were transferred to the same yearly bundle as the will or administration bond.

No documents were traced for a few of the names listed in the old index. Some of these entries were found to have been included in error but those which appear to be genuine entries are listed in an appendix. In addition to the records indexed in this volume, there are a few unidentified fragments belonging to the same period which could not be included in the index.

ABBREVIATIONS AND SYMBOLS.

The general rules adopted in the preparation of entries for the index, and the various symbols and abbreviations used, are explained here under the appropriate column headings used in the arrangement of the index, namely:

Name

The name was taken from the beginning of the will or, in the case of an intestate, from the administration bond, unless a fuller version of the name occurred elsewhere, e.g. at the foot of the will or in the inventory, in which case the fuller form was copied. If for some reason the name could not be taken from the will or administration bond, it was taken from the inventory or, in the absence of an inventory, from any other accompanying document. Failing that it was taken from the endorsement. When the name or any part of it was supplied from any source other than the actual documents, it was placed in square brackets.

The name is given in the spelling found in the documents, an exception being those documents filed in later years relating to persons for whom documents had already been filed. Since the references in such cases have been combined under a single entry, the name appears in the index entry in the form and spelling found in the earliest reference. Abbreviated forms of names have been extended, except when there was uncertainty as to what the extension should be, e.g. *Ric.* which could be an abbreviated form for either *Richard* or *Rice*. In all cases an initial *ff* has been written as a captial *F*, even in Welsh Christian names such as *ffoulk*, and a *u* used as a consonant, e.g. in names such as *Dauid* or *Ieuan*, transcribed as *v*. In the forename index, *ap* and *vch* have been used for *ap* and *verch* or their variants.

† beside a name denotes that a document relating to that particular person is wholly, or partly, in Welsh.

Parish & County

The spelling of parish names has been standardised and generally follows Melville Richards: *Welsh Administrative and Territorial Units* (Cardiff, 1969). Where the name of a township, hamlet or homestead is given in any document, in addition to the name of the parish, it has been included in the index in round brackets after the name of the parish, and in the spelling found in the document. Several of the documents give the name of a township or homestead within a particular county as the place of abode but do not give the name of the parish. The majority of these places have been identified and attributed to their appropriate parish, mainly by reference to the tithe maps and apportionments or the earliest available edition of the O.S. 6-inch maps, although when using the latter one had to take into account some changes in the parish boundaries from those of the old ecclesiastical parishes. In such cases, where the name of the parish has been supplied by the indexer, it has been put in square brackets. Only one or two places remain unidentified and that because of the existence of more than one place of that particular name within a county. A few of the records contain either no mention at all of a place of abode or only the name of the county, but where a place of burial is mentioned in such documents, this has been taken as the name of the parish and included in square brackets.

Within the jurisdiction of the Bangor Consistory Court six names represent two different parishes, each of them in two different counties: Llanfachreth, Llanfihangel-y-Pennant, Llanfwrog, Llangelynnin, Llangwyfan and Llaniestyn. Where the county is not specified in records from these parishes, it has usually been possible to find to which county they belong by examining burial entries in the parish registers or bishops transcripts of parish registers, where entries exist for those parishes for that particular period, or by comparing the signatures of witnesses with those in other records from the same two parishes or by means of other evidence contained in the probate records. However, there still remain a few which could not be attributed with certainty to one county or the other and in such cases both alternatives have been indicated thus: Llanfachreth [A/Mr]. A similar problem of identification arose occasionally with the parishes of Llanbedr-Goch and Llanbedr Niwbwrch / Newborough, both in the county of Anglesey and both of which are sometimes referred to simply as 'the parish of Llanbedr', and also with the parish of Penrhosllugwy in the county of Anglesey, often referred to as 'the parish of Penrhos', which could be confused with Penrhos in the county of Caernarfon where no county is specified.

Most chapelries of the period are referred to as parishes in the probate records and are listed as such in the index, the exceptions being Capel Curig, Tal-y-llyn (Anglesey) and Llanfeirian, chapelries or chapels-of-ease in the parishes of Llandygái, Llanbeulan and Llangadwaladr respectively. Records from these three are listed under the name of the parish followed by the name of the chapelry in round brackets. A person stated in the records to be of Maenol Bangor rather than of the parish of Bangor or Pentir is described as such in the index. It appears that the area covered by Maenol Bangor corresponded with that of the parish of Bangor including Pentir chapelry.

The following abbreviations have been used for the counties:

A	Anglesey
Cn	Caernarfonshire
D	Denbighshire
Mr	Merioneth
Mg	Montgomeryshire
S	Shropshire

Status

All references to a person's rank or occupation in the records have been placed under this heading. Modern standard spelling has been used and all abbreviations have been extended with the exception of *Gent.* and *Esq.* Information supplied from any source other than the documents which relate to that particular person has been put in square brackets.

Documents Filed

The range of documents available for each person listed in the index is shown by using the following code letters for the various types of documents found among the probate records:

Ac Executors' or administrators' accounts.

Al Allegation or articles of the person wishing to establish the validity of a will when it was being proved in form of law rather than in common form.

B Administration bond (including a bond for the administration of goods left unadministered, a bond to administer during the minority of the executor or administrator, a bond to administer *pendente lite*, etc.).

C Commission to administer the oath to the executor, administrator or witnesses (usually containing the form of oath to be administered).

Cd Codicil.

D Deposition of witnesses on being examined by the court.

Db List of debts.

G Memorandum of a grant of administration or of the taking of the oath by the administrator.

I Inventory.

Ir Interrogatories of the person disputing a will.

L Letter.

M	Miscellaneous memoranda.
R	Renunciation by the executor or administrator of his duties.
Rd	Bond for the redelivery of an original will or an inventory.
S	Record of the sentence or decree of the court for the validity or nullity of a will.
W	Will (including copy will).
*	denotes that a document is damaged and imperfect in some way.

Where more than one document of its type exists, the number of copies or differing versions is noted in round brackets after the code letter, e.g. W(2) where a copy will is filed as well as the original will. In listing the range of documents available for each person, the first document listed, if it is filed, is always the will (and codicil where one exists) or the administration bond in the case of an intestate, followed by the inventory and then the other documents in chronological order or in the order in which one assumes they were drawn up.

It should be noted that a codicil appended to a will and a debt list incorporated in a will or appended to a will or inventory are not specified; they are listed only when they occur as separate documents, because of the need to give each individual document a code letter. Similarly a memorandum relating to the grant of administration endorsed on a will or administration bond or on an inventory accompanying either of them is not specified. It is noted only when it occurs as a separate document or as an endorsement on a document, in most cases an inventory, where no other document naming the administrator or next of kin exists. The blank pieces of paper used as covers for the probate records, on which the name of the deceased, his parish and the date of probate or administration was endorsed, have already been mentioned. In a few cases a document unconnected with the records has been used as a covering. Such documents have not been listed under a code letter in the index, since they are unrelated to the probate records, but a typescript list of them is available in the Library.

Date of Probate or Administration

The date of probate usually occurs twice in the records, in the probate act which is endorsed on the majority of the wills and, as has been previously mentioned, in the endorsement on the outside or cover. The date quoted in the index is usually that given in the probate act, the date being taken from the endorsement only when the probate act is not endorsed on the will or when the two dates differ and the documentary evidence indicates that the cover endorsement is the correct one. Where no date of probate / administration is given, the date of the taking of the oath by the executor or administrator is quoted in square brackets if it is endorsed. Where neither date is given, the nearest date to that of granting probate or administration is quoted in a footnote. Depending on the range of documents available, the date quoted in the footnote is usually that of taking the inventory, since it was often taken a few days before the date of probate, or the date of making the will if it happens to be the same year as that under which the will is filed, or occasionally that of the commission to swear the executor or administrator, a renunciation or allegation. Where a will is proved or an administration granted some ten years or more after the taking of the inventory, the date of making the inventory or the date of death, whichever is given in the inventory, is quoted in a footnote. Nearly all instances of this in the index relate to persons who died during the Interregnum period. Several inaccuracies and inconsistencies occur in the dating of the records and some of these are dealt with in footnotes. However, there are so many instances where the date of probate in the cover endorsement does not exactly correspond with that given in the endorsed probate act or, indeed, where other details in the endorsements do not correspond with those in the actual documents that it would not have been practical to note all the variant readings or inaccuracies in footnotes.

The probate court observed the old style of reckoning, taking 25 March as the beginning of the year. A double indication is given in the index for all dates of probate or administration falling between 1 January and 24 March, although it is given only occasionally in the records. Sometimes when dating wills and inventories the year was reckoned from 1 January. Therefore, when the date of a will, inventory, etc. is quoted in a footnote, no double indication of date is given for those dates between 1 January and 24 March unless it occurs in the actual document or unless the dates of accompanying documents or the regnal year indicate which reckoning has been employed.

Reference Number

The reference number consists of the year of the bundle followed by the number of the document within the bundle. The reference number should be used on readers' issue slips and order forms for copies, preceded by the name of the diocese, e.g. Bangor Probate Records 1667/103.

N.H.

PART I
FORENAME INDEX

Name	Parish & County	Status	Docs. Filed	Date of Probate/Admon.	Ref. No.
Agnes vch David	Llanwnda Cn	–	B I	12 April 1692	1692/63
Annes vch Evan	Llanystumdwy Cn	Widow	W I	6 May 1685	1685/59
Annas vch Hugh	Llanidan A	Widow	B	3 May 1681	1681/16
Agnes vch Humphrey	[Llanycil][1] (Amnoedd) Mr	Widow	W*	29 Oct. 1670	1670/193
Agnes vch John	Llanystumdwy Cn	–	W* B*	9 July 1636	1636/38
Agnes vch John	Pentir Cn	Spinster	W	7 Sept. 1648	1648/13
Annes vch John Robert	Llangynhafal D	Spinster	W	22 July 1647	1647/47
Agnesse vch John Tudur	Llanenddwyn Mr	Widow	W	15 April 1641	1641/51
Agnes vch Kynrhig	Llangristiolus A	Widow	W	19 May 1662	1662/26
Agnes vch Pierce	Llangefni A	–	B*	14 Dec. 1670	1670/41
Agnes vch Richard	Clynnog Cn	–	W	23 Feb. 1670/1	1670/86
Agness vch Robert	Llanrhaeadr-yng-Nghinmeirch D	Widow	W	27 May 1690	1690/112
Agnes vch Robert	Maentwrog Mr	Widow	B I	4 Aug. 1696	1696/107
Anes vch Robert ap William	Ffestiniog (Place Mini) Mr	Widow	W I	16 Dec. 1669	1669/117
Agnes vch Rowland	Llannor Cn	–	B	19 July 1682	1682/54
Agnes vch William	Llanddaniel-fab A	Widow	W(2)	2 June 1635	1635/3
Agnes vch William	Llanrhaeadr-yng-Nghinmeirch D	Widow	W	18 Jan. 1682/3	1682/87
Agnes vch William	Llangybi Cn	Widow of Owen William	W I	22 Aug. 1696	1696/74
Agnes vch William David	Llangaffo A	[Wife of John ap William ap Hugh]	B	23 May 1677	1677/14
Ales *see* Alice					
Alice vch Hugh	Llanddeiniolen Cn	Widow	W	13 Dec. 1641	1641/36
Alice vch Hugh	Bangor (Porthaythwy) Cn	Widow	W I	28 June 1662	1662/37
Alice vch Hugh Lewis	Nefyn Cn	Widow	W	18 April 1671	1671/92
Alice vch John	Clocaenog D	–	I/G	[21 June] 1664	1664/108
Alice vch John *alias* Alice Williams	Pentraeth A	Widow	B I	23 Jan. 1666/7	1666/33
Alice vch John Robert	Maentwrog Mr	Widow	W I	14 Jan. 1691/2	1691/96
Ales vch John Thomas	Bangor Cn	Widow	W I	5 March 1678/9	1678/18
Alice vch Tyder[2]	Llanfwrog [D]	Widow of Edward John ap Richard	W I	10 Oct. 1666	1666/103
Ambrose ap Robert	Llanynys (Rhudonnen) D	–	W	[13 Feb. 1671/2]	1671/135
Ann vch Hugh	Dolgellau Mr	Widow	W* I	[3 April 1691]	1691/78
Anne vch John	Llanfechell A	Widow	B*	27 Sept. 1670	1670/36

[1] Normally within the jurisdiction of the St. Asaph Consistory Court.

[2] Described as *sole executrix of Edward John ap Richard* but no will is filed for him. The inventory is of the goods *of Edward John ap Richard and Alice vch Tuder his wife both lately deceased.*

Name	Parish & County	Status	Docs. Filed	Date of Probate/Admon.	Ref. No.
Anne vch John *Wynne*	Aberffraw A	Widow	W I	5 Nov. 1667	1667/1
Anne John Evan	Ffestiniog Mr	Widow	W B	9 May 1698	1698/54
Anne vch John Griffith	Llanfihangel-y-traethau Mr	Widow	W I	18 Nov. 1675	1675/47
Ann vch John ap Hugh	Llangoed A	Widow of Owen Thomas of Heneglwys, gent.	W	20 March 1661/2	1661/21
Anne John Lewis	Llanwnnog Mg	–	B	30 April 1696	1696/139
Anne vch John Thomas	Llandrygarn A	Widow	W*	7 Feb. 1638/9	1638/8
Anne vch Richard John	Carnguwch Cn	Widow	W I	21 Jan. 1696/7	1696/43
Anne vch Richard William	Holyhead A	–	W*	[1 March 1671/2]	1671/10
Annes *see* Agnes					
Arthur ap David	Bryncroes (Manachdu) Cn	Yeoman	W(2) I Rd L	10 July 1668	1668/37
Arthur David ap Hugh	Holyhead A	–	W	23 Jan. 1637/8	1637/3
Arthur David Probert	Aber Cn	–	W I	21 Oct. 1681	1681/22
Cadwaladr David ap Ievan	Llanfachreth [Mr]	–	W*	1 June 1636	1636/46
Kadwaldr ap Hughe Griffith	Clynnog Cn	–	W* B	9 Feb. 1636/7	1636/26
Cadwalader John ap Moris	Llandrygarn A	–	B* I*	15 Jan. 1661/2[1]	1661/14
Cadwalader ap Moris	Rhuthun D	–	W	21 May 1636	1636/62
Kadwaladr ap Richard	Llanystumdwy (Roskill) Cn	Yeoman	W	18 Aug. 1635	1635/32
Cadwalader ap Richard	Llandygái Cn	–	W	[17 Jan. 1672/3]	1672/60
Cadwaladr ap Robert	Llanfachreth Mr	–	B I	12 June 1663	1663/98
Kadwaleder Thomas *Wynne*	Aber (Hafod gelŷn) Cn	Gent.	W	14 Jan. 1646/7	1646/10
Cadwalader ap William	Trawsfynydd Mr	–	W	31 Dec. 1667	1667/111
Cadwalader ap William	Llanrhaeadr-yng-Nghinmeirch D	Yeoman	W	17 April 1699	1699/138
Kadwaleder ap William Gruffyth	Llanwnda Cn	–	B* I*	16 March 1662/3	1662/54
Katheryn vch [ ] *Wynne*	[Clynnog] (Bryn y grô) Cn	Widow of Robert ap Rees Wynne	W*	2 July 1646	1646/14
Katherine vch Cadwalader	Amlwch (Havodonen) A	Widow	W I	4 July 1670	1670/1
Catherine vch Kadwalader	Cricieth Cn	–	B*	7 Feb. 1687/8	1687/46
Catherine vch David	Trawsfynydd Mr	Spinster	W	29 Oct. 1644	1644/36
Katherine vch Ddavidd	Nefyn Cn	Widow	W*	n.d.[2]	1685/61
Catherin vch David *Lloyd*	Llanbedrycennin Cn	–	M	n.d.[3]	1671/63

[1] Inventory taken 18 Sept. 1650.

[2] Will dated 11 July 1685.

[3] Revocation of caveat dated 29 June 1671. Nuncupative will mentioned but not filed.

Name	Parish & County	Status	Docs. Filed	Date of Probate/Admon.	Ref. No.
Katherin vch Evan	Conway Cn	Widow	W	19 March 1660/1	1660/13
Katherine vch Gruffith *Vaughan*	Llanrhaeadr-yng-Nghinmeirch (Trevibychen) D	Widow	W	9 March 1647/8	1647/49
Katherin vch Hugh	Llanfair Mathafarn Eithaf A	–	B	17 July 1667	1667/21
Katherine vch Hugh	Llanrhaeadr-yng-Nghinmeirch D	Widow	W	9 Jan. 1671/2	1671/131
Catherine vch Hugh	Llaniestyn A	Widow	W I	14 April 1696	1696/21
Kathering vch Hugh Bievan	Llangeinwen A	–	I	n.d.[1]	1670/42
Catherin vch Hugh ap William	Llangeinwen A	Widow	B I	31 Aug. 1693	1693/17
Cathrine vch John	Llanaelhaearn Cn	Widow	W	6 Feb. 1696/7	1696/52
Katheringe vch John ap Ievan Lewis	[Aber-erch] Cn	Widow	W*	31 Dec. 1646	1646/11
Cathrin John Griffith	Aber-erch (Llain hen) Cn	Widow	W	24 Aug. 1688	1688/31
Catherine vch John ap Howell ap Owen	Llanaelhaearn Cn	Spinster	W B	2 April 1635	1635/27
Katharine vch John ap Hugh	Llanfechell A	Widow	W*	5 June 1677	1677/10
Catherine vch John ap Ithel	Llanelidan D	–	W I	15 June 1668	1668/108
Cathrine vch John Lewis	Llanwnda Cn	Widow	W	21 July 1640	1640/35
Katherin John Lewis	Llangoed A	Widow [of David ap William David]	B	11 Oct. 1667	1667/32
Catherine vch John Morris	Maentwrog Mr	Widow	W I	8 April 1692	1692/81
Catherine John Pierce	Ffestiniog Mr	–	W	3 Feb. 1692/3	1692/70
Catherine vch Kadwalader *see* Catherine vch Cadwaladr					
Katherine vch Morgan	Llannerch-y-medd A	Spinster	W	2 April 1641	1641/16
Kathering vch Morgan	Llanfihangel-y-traethau Mr	Widow	W* I*	31 May 1666	1666/91
Katherin vch Morys	Llangynhafal D	Widow	W	[ ] 1642[2]	1642/40
Katherin vch Reignald	Clocaenog (Bryn Gwrgi) D	Widow	W* I	7 Jan. 1684/5	1684/86
Katherine vch Rutherch	Llanfachreth Mr	–	B	27 Nov. 1662	1662/65
Catherin vch Richard	Llanfwrog D	Spinster	B	3 May 1666	1666/104
Catherin vch Richard	[Llanbadrig] (Clygyrog) A	Spinster	W I	1 July 1671	1671/13
Catherine vch Thomas	Llanynys (Rhydonnen) D	Widow	W	26 Sept. 1645	1645/41
Katharine vch Thomas	Llanrhaeadr-yng-Nghinmeirch (Lloyn) D	Widow	W I	[30 Dec.] 1664	1664/116
Catharine vch Thomas	Rhuthun D	Widow	B I R	19 March 1666/7	1666/111
Katherine vch Thomas	Llanfair Dyffryn Clwyd (Eyarth) D	Widow	W I	[12 March 1676/7]	1676/90

[1] Died 1 March 1670.
[2] Will dated 20 Feb. 1641.

Name	Parish & County	Status	Docs. Filed	Date of Probate/Admon.	Ref. No.
Katherine vch William	Efenechtid D	Widow	W	[1 March 1671/2]	1671/114
Catharine vch William	Penmachno Cn	Widow	W I	24 May 1698	1698/49
Katherin vch William *feddig*	Llan Sant Cathrin *alias* Cricieth Cn	–	W*	19 April 1641	1641/28
Catherine vch William Bevan	Amlwch A	–	B	31 March 1682	1682/2
Katteringe vch William Lewis	Llanddeiniolen Cn	Widow	W	8 Dec. 1643	1643/20
Catherine vch William Lewis	Llanddeusant A	–	W	8 April 1644	1644/6
Katherin vch William Nicolas	Cricieth Cn	Widow	I/G	2 May 1667	1667/61
Catherine vch William Prees	Penmynydd A	–	B I	27 Nov. 1686	1686/24
Daniell ap John Lewis	Trawsfynydd Mr	Yeoman	W I	n.d.[1]	1687/104
David ap David	Carno Mg	–	W	9 April 1641	1641/69
Davyd ap Davyd *alias* David Clydro	Heneglwys A	–	W	25 Feb. 1644/5	1644/4
David ap Edward Griffith	Llanaber Mr	–	B I	4 Oct. 1667	1667/86
David ap Elis	Conway Cn	Labourer	W I	6 Feb. 1660/1	1660/14
David ap Ellisse	Dolgellau Mr	–	W	15 April 1641	1641/47
David ap Evan Hugh	Llanfihangel-yn-Nhywyn A	–	W	16 Oct. 1689	1689/17
David ap Evan John	Llanaelhaearn (late of Clynnog) Cn	Labourer	W(2)	8 Aug. 1677	1677/35
David ap Ieavan ap Meredydd	Llangïan Cn	–	W	7 Sept. 1636	1636/34
David Evan Morgan	Tywyn (Gwyddellfynydd) Mr	Yeoman	B I	4 April 1666	1666/99
David ap Ievan ap Morrice	Llangurig Mg	–	W I	30 May 1661	1661/136
David Evan Rees	Llangurig Mg	Yeoman	B I	7 July 1698	1698/78
David ap Gruffith	Dolwyddelan Cn	–	W I B	21 May 1635	1635/24
David ap Harry	Llanegryn Mr	–	W*	6 Nov. 1661	1661/95
David ap Hugh	Rhodogeidio A	Miller	W* Al*	23 July 1640	1640/17
David ap Hugh	Holyhead A	–	W	15 Oct. 1670	1670/7
David ap Hugh	Llangelynnin (Tre r morva) Mr	Gent.	W I	15 March 1672/3	1672/96
David ap Hugh	Llanynys D	Yeoman	W I	11 July 1692	1692/104
David ap Hugh	Llaneilian A	Yeoman	B I	16 July 1697	1697/10
David *Lloyd* ap Hugh	Llanynys (Maesmaen Cymro) D	Gent.	W Rd	19 June 1645	1645/42
David ap Hugh David	Trawsfynydd Mr	Yeoman	W B	5 June 1643	1643/38
David ap Hugh George	Conway Cn	Glover/Yeoman	W* I*	8 March 1697/8	1697/21
David ap Hugh Griffith	Llansadwrn A	–	W(2)	14 July 1637	1637/11
David Pugh Gruffith	Llangefni A	Yeoman	W I	22 June 1681	1681/13

[1] Inventory taken 25 Oct. 1687.

Name	Parish & County	Status	Docs. Filed	Date of Probate/Admon.	Ref. No.
David ap Hughe ap John	Llaniestyn Cn	–	W	5 Oct. 1643	1643/26
David ap Hugh Morgan	Llandwrog Cn	–	B I	28 Nov. 1673	1673/34
David Hugh Owen	Tywyn Mr	–	B I	1 June 1670	1670/161
David ap Hugh Probert	Holyhead A	Yeoman	W I	5 Nov. 1670	1670/8
David ap Hugh ap Robert	Rhoscolyn A	–	W I	19 Feb. 1672/3	1672/33
David ap Hugh ap William	Gyffin Cn	–	W B	24 Jan. 1647/8	1647/27
David ap Humphrey	Llangeinwen A	–	W*	9 Jan. 1645/6	1645/8
David ap Humffry	Dolgellau (Dolgleder) Mr	Yeoman	W	26 July 1674	1674/38
David ap Humphrey David	Llanfihangel-y-Pennant Mr	–	B I	12 June 1663	1663/103
David ap Ievan *see* David ap Evan					
David Jenkin Moris	Llangurig Mg	–	B I	27 May 1669	1669/167
David ap John	Efenechtid D	–	W(2) I(2)	10 July 1665	1665/78
David ap John	Caerhun Cn	Yeoman	W*	16 Feb. 1666/7	1666/44
David ap John ap David	Gyffin Cn	–	W*	5 April 1636	1636/28
David ap John ap David	Llandegfan A	–	W I	26 Aug. 1661	1661/13
David John David ap Howell	Llangelynnin (Llwyngoril) Mr	Yeoman	W I	6 June 1661	1661/104
David ap John ap Ievan	Llanwnda Cn	–	W* Al* B*	12 June 1635	1635/31
David ap John Ievan	Llanegryn Mr	–	W B	1 June 1636	1636/45
David John Howell	Llandinam Mg	–	W I*	[3 Aug. 1672]	1672/127
David John Lewis	Llanidloes Mg	Yeoman	W I	24 May 1667	1667/138
David John Lewis	Carno Mg	–	I/G	13 March 1683/4	1683/95
David John ap Meredydd	Carno Mg	–	B	1 Aug. 1661	1661/125
David John Owen	Llangristiolus A	–	B I R	17 Jan. 1680/1	1680/11
David John Rowland	Beddgelert Cn	–	W I	1 Sept. 1666	1666/41
David ap John Thomas	Llaneugrad A	–	W*	13 March 1636/7	1636/10
David ap John Thomas	Llandwrog Cn	–	W I B	8 Nov. 1687	1687/60
David ap John ap William	Clynnog Cn	–	W Rd	3 May 1646	1646/15
David John William	Llanaber Mr	Glover	W	22 Feb. 1674/5	1674/41
David Lewis Cadwalader	Llanidloes Mg	Tailor	W* I	30 Sept. 1661	1661/140
David Lewis Prees	Llangelynnin Mr	Tailor	B I	10 July 1694	1694/91
David Meredith Moris	Llangurig Mg	–	W I	2 July 1685	1685/117
David ap Owen	[Tal-y-llyn] Mr	–	W	4 Oct. 1638	1638/65
David ap Owen	Llanrhychwyn Cn	–	B I	29 Oct. 1666	1666/66
David *Lloyd* ap Owen	Llangurig Mg	–	I	n.d.[1]	1668/135
David ap Rees	Rhuthun D	–	W	26 June 1635	1635/49
David Rees Lewis	Carno Mg	–	I/G	27 July 1667	1667/129

[1] Inventory taken 8 Feb. 1668.

Name	Parish & County	Status	Docs. Filed	Date of Probate/Admon.	Ref. No.
David Rees Meredith	Carno Mg	–	I/G	17 Feb. 1665/6	1665/92
David ap R[ichard]	[Llanbedrycennin Cn][1]	–	W*	30 March 1641	1641/33
David ap Richard	Llangelynnin (Llwyngwril) Mr	–	B I	14 Aug. 1683	1683/74
David ap Richard	Tywyn Mr	Yeoman	W I	[18 April 1684]	1684/82
David ap Richard	Trawsfynydd (Votty bach) Mr	Yeoman	B I	23 Feb. 1690/1	1690/99
David ap Richard ap David	Llanfair-yn-neubwll A	Yeoman	W*[2]	n.d.	1641/11
David ap Richard ap Harry	Llanbeblig (Trefflan) Cn	Gent.	W	3 March 1647/8	1647/28
David Prichard William	Llanbeblig (Treflan) Cn	Yeoman/Weaver	W I	29 Oct. 1683	1683/33
David ap Robert	Llanllechid Cn	–	W	29 May 1643	1643/27
David ap Robert	Efenechtid D	–	W	10 Jan. 1663/4	1663/115
David ap Robert	Llanfair-is-gaer Cn	–	W I	20 Jan. 1680/1	1680/32
David ap Robert	Clynnog Cn	Tailor	W I	12 Nov. 1688	1688/39
David ap Robert ap David	Llandudno (Riwledinge) Cn	–	W	10 Dec. 1645	1645/26
David ap Robert Griffith	Aber Cn	–	B	28 March 1661	1661/34
David ap Robert Owen	Nefyn Cn	–	W*	6 July 1638	1638/49
David ap Robert ap Rees	Llanelidan (Garneath) D	Gent.	W Rd	16 Aug. 1647	1647/46
David ap Robert ap William	Derwen D	–	W I	8 June 1677	1677/71
David ap Thomas	Llanbedr Dyffryn Clwyd D	–	W	6 June 1644	1644/42
David Thomas Gryffyth	Llanrhaeadr-yng-Nghinmeirch D	Yeoman	B	9 April 1692	1692/101
David ap William	Beddgelert Cn	–	B	17 Sept. 1688	1688/33
David ap William	Llanddwywe (Ganllwyd) Mr	–	B I	11 Sept. 1688	1688/75
David ap William David	Llangoed A	–	B	21 Oct. 1667	1667/33
David ap William David	Trawsfynydd Mr	–	W I	11 May[3] 1679	1679/47
David William ap Evan *alias* David Williams	Aberffraw A	Labourer	W	17 Aug. 1689	1689/1
David ap William John	Bodwrog A	–	B	10 Jan. 1661/2	1661/6
David ap William ap Rees	Llanfwrog [A]	–	W	20 Feb. 1636/7	1636/14
David ap William Prichard	Ynyscynhaearn Cn	–	W*	10 May 1666	1666/72
Dorythye vch David	[Maentwrog] (Llech y Cwyn) Mr	Widow	W	[26 Oct.] 1664	1664/100
Dorothy vch Humffrey	[Llanbeblig] (Caernarvon) Cn	Spinster	W B	10 Aug. 1637	1637/21
Dorothy vch John ap Evan	Llanfair-iuxta-Harlech Mr	Widow	W*	12 Oct. 1671	1671/107
Doritie vch Rees	Llanllechid (Talybont) Cn	Widow	W I	12 June 1694	1694/57
Dorithy vch Robert	Llanrhaeadr-yng-Nghinmeirch (Prion) D	Widow	W* I	24 April 1668	1668/123
Dorothy vch Robert	Amlwch A	–	W	31 May 1672	1672/2

[1] Supplied from the will of Gwenhwyvar vch Richard Lewis, his widow.

[2] Mutilated and illegible.

[3] Recte *June*? Will dated 16 May 1679 and inventory taken 5 June 1679.

Name	Parish & County	Status	Docs. Filed	Date of Probate/Admon.	Ref. No.
Dorothy vch Robert	Llanfihangel-y-Pennant Cn	Widow	C[1]	[14 March 1689/90]	1689/49
Dorothy vch Robert	Llanfair Dyffryn Clwyd (Keelan) D	Widow	W I	2 Feb. 1697/8	1697/58
Doulce vch Evan	Llanfwrog (Bodyngharad) D	Widow	W I	n.d.[2]	1672/111
Doulce vch Hugh	Cerrigceinwen A	Widow	W	n.d.[3]	1666/7
Doulce vch James	Derwen D	Widow	W(2)* I	29 Nov. 1662	1662/80
Doulce vch Robert Lewis	Llaneilian A	Widow	W	22 Feb. 1674/5	1674/9
Dowse vch Thomas	[Gyffy]lliog D	–	W* B*	30 [ ][4] 1640	1640/52
Edmund ap David	Llandysilio A	–	W	n.d.[5]	1672/15
Edmund ap Hugh	Bangor Cn	–	B	5 July 1661	1661/42
Edmund John ap Hugh	Dwygyfylchi Cn	–	W	n.d.[6]	1670/94
Edmund John William	Llandecwyn Mr	–	B	2 May 1672	1672/90
Edmund ap William ap Ievan	Derwen D	–	W*	19 June 1643	1643/40
Edmund ap William ap Ivan	Llanbeulan A	Yeoman	W* I*	5 Dec. 1670	1670/18
Edward ap Kadwaladr	Llandegfan A	–	W	19 Jan. 1636/7	1636/7
Edward ap David	Clocaenog D	–	W* I	20 Nov. 1662	1662/78
Edward ap David	Llanfair Dyffryn Clwyd (Llwynynn) D	Yeoman/Servant	W I	21 Feb. 1692/3	1692/99
Edward ap David *Lloyd*	Llanfair-iuxta-Harlech Mr	–	W B	11 Oct. 1637	1637/33
Edward David ap Rees	Llangurig Mg	–	B I	31 July 1663	1663/141
Edward David ap Thomas	Pentraeth A	Yeoman	W I	7 April 1635	1635/11
Edward ap Edward	Llanaelhaearn Cn	–	B I	9 June 1664	1664/63
Edward ap Evan	Dolgellau (Brithdir) Mr	–	W* I*	n.d.[7]	1670/137
Edward ap Evan	Llanrhaeadr-yng-Nghinmeirch D	–	B	27 May 1695	1695/96
Edward Evan John	Carno Mg	Yeoman	W I	5 March 1699/1700	1699/143
Edward Foulke ap Elis	Llanrhaeadr-yng-Nghinmeirch (Llewesog) D	Gent.	W I	16 Feb. 1694/5	1694/110
Edward ap Griffith	Llanfachreth Mr	–	B	31 May 1662	1662/64
Edward Gruffith ap Moris	Llanrhaeadr-yng-Nghinmeirch D	Yeoman	W	24 March 1635/6	1635/46

1 Will mentioned but not filed.
2 Inventory taken 14 May 1672.
3 Will dated 11 Aug. 1666.
4 Will dated 7 April 1640.
5 Witnesses sworn 9 April 1672; endorsed *Adco non conc:*
6 Will dated 24 June 1670. Endorsed *9 May 1671 not proved.*
7 Inventory taken 1 April [1670].

Name	Parish & County	Status	Docs. Filed	Date of Probate/Admon.	Ref. No.
Edward Gruffyth ap Robert	Llanfair Mathafarn Eithaf A	Gent.	W	10 Nov. 1669	1669/25
Edward Gryffith ap William	Llanaber Mr	–	I/G	28 Sept. 1683	1683/64
Edward ap Hugh	Llanfwrog A	–	W	24 Feb. 1638/9	1638/15
Edward ap Hugh	Llanfair Dyffryn Clwyd D	–	I	n.d.[1]	1641/61
Edward ap Hugh	Llangelynnin Mr	Yeoman	I/G	20 June 1667	1667/103
Edward ap Hugh	Llanbedrycennin (Arddau) Cn	Yeoman	W I Al L	25 May 1693	1693/46
Edward ap Humffrey	Penmachno Cn	–	B I	19 June 1667	1667/81
Edward ap John	Llandecwyn Mr	Yeoman	W* B Rd	21 Oct. 1635	1635/34
Edward ap John	Clocaenog D	Yeoman	W I Rd	19 Dec. 1665	1665/76
Edward John *Wynn*	Llanynys (Rhŷd-onnen) D	–	B I	6 Dec. 1672	1672/120
Edward ap John David ap Jeinkin	Llanaber Mr	–	W	12 May 1637	1637/31
Edward John ap Edward	Llanaber Mr	Gent.	W	[8 June 1674]	1674/42
Edward John ap Edward	Llanfair Dyffryn Clwyd (Garthkynnan) D	Carpenter	W I	29 Sept. 1677	1677/79
Edward John ap Edward	Pistyll Cn	Yeoman	B I	3 Nov. 1696	1696/86
Edward ap John ap Hugh	Llanfwrog D	Yeoman	W Rd	20 Nov. 1661	1661/117
†Edward John Prees	Ceirchiog A	–	B I Db C	10 May 1692	1692/6
Edward John ap Richard	[Llanfwrog D]	–	I[2]	n.d.	1666/103
Edward John ap Robert	Cerrigceinwen A	–	{B {B	20 Dec. 1664 16 Aug. 1688	1664/9 1688/8
Edward John ap Robert	Ysbyty [Ifan] (Eidde) Cn	Yeoman	W I B	14 May 1679	1679/32
Edward John William	Llanaber Mr	–	I/G	11 Feb. 1696/7	1696/96
Edward John William	Trefriw Cn	–	I	n.d.[3]	1699/92
Edward ap Kadwaladr *as* Edward ap Cadwaladr					
Edward ap Morice	Gyffylliog (Tâl y cefn) D	Yeoman	W	17 Jan. 1638/9	1638/73
Edward Owen ap Howell	Rhoscolyn A	–	W	27 June 1636	1636/21
Edward Owen ap Rees	Rhoscolyn A	–	W	n.d.[4]	1668/29
Edward ap Richard	Llandanwg (Harleigh) Mr	Gent.	W Rd	2 Oct. 1667	1667/91
Edward ap Richard	Trawsfynydd (Bodyfydde) Mr	Yeoman	I	n.d.[5]	1669/136
Edward ap Richard	Rhuthun D	Butcher	I	n.d.[6]	1684/103

[1] Inventory taken 14 Feb. 1641.
[2] Filed with the will of Alice vch Tuder, under whom see footnote.
[3] Inventory exhibited 17 Oct. 1699.
[4] Will dated 5 March 1668.
[5] Inventory taken 24 Nov. 1669.
[6] Inventory taken 26 March 1684.

Name	Parish & County	Status	Docs. Filed	Date of Probate/Admon.	Ref. No.
Edward ap Richard	Llanynys (Maesmankymro) D	Innholder	W R	[9 June 1688]	1688/96
Edward ap Richard ap Ithell	Llanbedr Dyffryn Clwyd (Lloynedd & Rhiscog) D	–	W I Rd	20 June 1667	1667/120
Edward ap Robert	Llanfair Dyffryn Clwyd D	–	W B	26 Sept. 1643	1643/45
Edward ap Robert	Llangynhafal D	–	W I	7 Jan. 1668/9	1668/118
Edward ap Robert	Derwen D	–	W	[21 July 1670]	1670/162
Edward ap Robert	Llandanwg (Morva) Mr	Yeoman	B I	10 Jan. 1699/1700	1699/109
Edward ap Robert ap John	Llanynys D	–	W	n.d.[1]	1614/1
Edward ap Thomas	Llanynys (Maesmayncymro) D	Gent.	W* Rd*	8 Nov. 1647	1647/53
Edward ap Thomas	Llanynys D	Yeoman	W I	[6 June 1672]	1672/119
Edward ap Thomas	Llanfair Dyffryn Clwyd (Eyarth) D	Yeoman	I Ac	n.d.[2]	1676/91
Edward ap Thomas	Llanrhaeadr-yng-Nghinmeirch (Tre yr Llan) D	Gent.	W I	1 March 1682/3	1682/88
Edward Thomas David	Llanfihangel Ysgeifiog A	–	W	8 May 1666	1666/22
Edward ap Thomas ap Hugh	Llanelidan D	–	W	[18 June 1675]	1675/55
Edward ap William	Llanllechid Cn	–	B I	15 Feb. 1682/3	1682/51
Edward ap William ap Edward	Pistyll Cn	–	W	5 April 1643	1643/30
Edward ap William Pugh	Aberffraw A	–	B	22 July 1685	1685/1
Edward ap William Owen	Beddgelert Cn	–	W B	11 Dec. 1647	1647/20
Edward ap William Owen	Llanbedr (Caer Gynog) Mr	Gent./Yeoman	W I	21 Dec. 1692	1692/73
Edward ap William ap Rytherch	Llandecwyn Mr	Yeoman	W*	1 March 1647/8	1647/40
Edward ap William Probert	Bangor Cn	–	W	24 May 1682	1682/33
Edward ap William Rowland	Llanddyfnan A	–	W*	28 July 1644	1644/7
Ellen vch Edward	Carno Mg	Widow	W I	16 June 1663	1663/132
Ellen vch Eliza	Llanfrothen Mr	Widow	W	26 Feb. 1645/6	1645/38
Ellin vch Evan	Llanfaglan Cn	Widow	W	[26 May 1675]	1675/26
Ellin vch Evan	Dolwyddelan (Penanmen) Cn	Widow	W I	6 Sept. 1681	1681/39
Ellin vch Evan John	Llanbedr Mr	Widow	W/I	12 May 1690	1690/88
Elline vch Evan ap Richard	Llandrygarn A	–	B	8 Oct. 1669	1669/17
Ellen vch Hugh	Trawsfynydd Mr	Widow	B R	4 Oct. 1667	1667/112
Ellin vch Hugh	Llanynys [Maesmankymro] D	Widow [of Tydyr ap Robert Wynne]	W	28 Oct. 1682	1682/92
Ellen vch Hugh	Llanaber Mr	–	B C	17 Nov. 1688	1688/70
Ellen vch Hughe	Maentwrog Mr	Spinster	B	7 Sept. 1693	1693/92
Ellen vch Hugh	Amlwch A	Widow	W I	27 March 1694	1694/6

[1] Commission to overseers to administer during the minority of the executors dated 26 Jan. 1614/5.
[2] Account exhibited 29 June 1676.

Name	Parish & County	Status	Docs. Filed	Date of Probate/Admon.	Ref. No.
Ellin vch Hugh John	[ ] [?Mr]	Widow	W	7 Oct. 1669	1669/138
Ellin vch Hugh Owen	Llanllyfni (Eithinog) Cn	Widow	W* I* Al*	27 Jan. 1686/7	1686/61
Ellin vch Hugh ap Owen	Llanfair-yn-neubwll A	–	B	1 June 1689	1689/15
Elline vch James	Clocaenog D	Widow	W I	21 June 1683	1683/82
Ellin[1] vch John Gruffith	Pentir Cn	Widow	W	3 July 1644	1644/30
Ellin John ap Hugh	Llanfair-yng-Ngwaredog (Mynydd mwyn) A	Widow	W	12 May 1674	1674/10
Ellin vch John ap Prichard	Llangristiolus A	Widow	W	15 Jan. 1676/7	1676/20
Ellin Lewis David	Llanbadrig A	–	B I	18 Nov. 1685	1685/12
Elenn vch Owens	Cricieth Cn	Widow	W	28 Dec. 1699	1699/56
Elin vch Richard	Llanystumdwy Cn	Widow	W Al Ir D	[16 May 1683]	1683/54
Ellin vch Richard	Nefyn Cn	–	W	9 Jan. 1687/8	1687/78
Elin vch Richard	Penmachno (Penbedw) Cn	Widow	W I	16 Dec. 1687	1687/83
Ellin vch Robert	Dolwyddelan Cn	Widow	W*	28 Jan. [1636/7]	1636/27
Elin vch Robert	Caerhun Cn	Widow	W I	4 Aug. 1671	1671/48
Ellen vch Robert	Llanrhwydrys A	Widow	B R	23 Nov. 1699	1699/28
Ellin vch Robert *Wynne*	Derwen D & Gwyddelwern (Beyarth) Mr	Widow	W I(2)	10 Dec. 1680	1680/62
Ellen vch Thomas	Llaniestyn Cn	Widow	B I	11 July 1664	1664/73
Ellin vch Thomas ap Richard	Llanbedr[-goch] A	Widow	W I Rd	18 Jan. 1694/5	1694/13
Ellen vch William	Llanddeiniolen Cn	–	B*	[ ] Aug. 1679	1679/25
Ellen vch William[2]	[ ][3] [Cn]	–	B	6 Aug. 1680	1680/44
Ellin vch William ap Evan	Llangefni A	–	W	7 Nov. 1695	1695/11
Elin vch William Pue	Llanddyfnan A	Widow	W I	15 May 1697	1697/9
Elin vch William Morris	Llanddeiniolen Cn	Widow	B I	20 June 1688	1688/49
Ellen vch William Owen	Penrhos[llugwy] A	Spinster	W	17 April 1637	1637/13
Elis ap Edward	Llanddyfnan / Penrhos-[llugwy] A	–	W I	6 Feb. 1690/1	1690/19
Elice ap Evan	Clocaenog (Bronbanog) D	–	W* I	13 March 1695[4]	1694/99
Ellis ap Howell	Llanaber Mr	–	W* I* R	18 July 1668	1668/86
Elice ap Hugh	Llanbedr Dyffryn Clwyd D	–	I/G	[30 April] 1664	1664/114
Elis ap Hugh ap Morgan	Llangelynnin Cn	–	W	24 May 1644	1644/24
Ellis ap Hugh Morgan	Penmachno (Blaen y Cwm) Cn	–	W	7 June 1664	1664/79
Ellis Humfrey ap Evan	Llanbedr Mr	–	B	19 Oct. 1688	1688/72

1 *Jonet* in cover endorsement and endorsed probate act.

2 Endorsed *Elen vch Evan.*

3 Catherine vch Richard, her daughter, described as being of Aberdaron.

4 *1694/5* or *1695/6*? *13 March 1694* in cover endorsement. Inventory taken 4 March 1694 (7 Wm. III).

Name	Parish & County	Status	Docs. Filed	Date of Probate/Admon.	Ref. No.
Ellis John Griffith	Llanllyfni (Ffrith bala day llyn) Cn	Yeoman	W I	23 Oct. 1672	1672/74
Ellis John Morris	Penmorfa (Pennant) Cn	–	B I	16 Sept. 1684	1684/61
Ellis John Owen	Llanenddwyn Mr	–	B I	13 Nov. 1680	1680/51
Ellis ap John Thomas	[Llanbeblig] (Carnarvon) Cn	–	W	[4 June 1674]	1674/14
Ellis Morris ap Ellis	Beddgelert Cn	–	W I Al	[31 Oct. 1682]	1682/36
Ellis Morris ap Richard	Llanbeblig Cn	Yeoman	B I	6 March 1699/1700	1699/68
Elis ap Robert ap Evan	Gyffylliog D	–	W I	7 Oct. 1691	1691/105
Ellis ap Robert John	Caerhun Cn	–	B I	13 Nov. 1676	1676/38
Ellis ap Robert Pirce	Gyffylliog D	–	W I	31 March 1663	1663/118
Ellisse ap Symond	Clocaenog D	Widower	W I	[ ] April 1696	1696/113
Ellis ap William ap Ellis	Dolwyddelan Cn	Yeoman	B	30 April 1690	1690/52
Ellis William Bevan	Dolgellau Mr	–	I/G	20 Oct. 1696	1696/88
Ellis ap William ap Hugh	Llanelltud Mr	Widower	W I	27 May 1682	1682/71
Ellis ap William Moris	Llangybi Cn	–	I	24 Jan. 1671/2	1671/80
Ellis ap William Morris	Llanrhychwyn Cn	Yeoman	I R	23 May 1672	1672/79
Eliza ap Edward	Llanaelhaearn (Cumkeiliog) Cn	–	W I	23 July 1675	1675/23
Elisa ap Hugh Powell	Beddgelert Cn	–	B	4 July 1662	1662/38
Eliza John ap William	Betws Garmon Cn	Yeoman	W	n.d.[1]	1675/17
Ellisa ap Rutherch Owen	Maentwrog Mr	–	W	31 May 1638	1638/64
Ellisse ap William	Llanelltud (Maes y garnedd) Mr	–	W I	n.d.[2]	1688/77
Elizabeth vch David	Llannor Cn	Widow	W I	23 July 1684	1684/54
Elizabeth vch Edmund	Llanfairfechan Cn	Widow	W* I	6 Oct. 1697	1697/28
Elizabeth vch Edward	Efenechtid D	–	W	1 July 1635	1635/40
Elizabeth vch Edward	Llanfair Dyffryn Clwyd D	–	B I	27 March 1671	1671/123
Elizabeth vch Edward	Llandyrnog D	Widow	W	15 Jan. 1675/6	1675/54
Elizabeth vch Edward	Llanddeiniolen Cn	Widow	B I	9 Nov. 1697	1697/27
Elizabeth vch Evan	Llanystumdwy (Rhoskill) Cn	Widow	W I	2 Nov. 1669	1669/102
Elizabeth vch Evan	Holyhead A	–	W*	15 June 1671	1671/11
Elizabeth vch Evan	Llanynghenedl A	–	B	25 Sept. 1676	1676/24
Elizabeth vch Ievan ap John Tudir	Gyffylliog D	Widow	W*	4 May 1635	1635/41
Elizabeth vch Harry	Gyffylliog (Ffrithoedd) D	Widow	W I	8 Feb. 1667/8	1667/117
Elyzabeth vch Harry[3]	[Rhodogeidio] (Bryngwallan) A	Widow	I	n.d.[4]	1685/29

1 Will dated 4 June 1675.
2 Inventory taken 14 Aug. 1688.
3 Same person as Elizabeth Parry of Rhodogeidio (q.v.)?
4 Inventory taken 9 Nov. 1685.

Name	Parish & County	Status	Docs. Filed	Date of Probate/Admon.	Ref. No.
Elizabeth vch Howell	Llanfihangel-y-Pennant Cn	Widow	W*	13 April 16[40]	1640/29
Elizabeth vch Hugh	Llanrhwydrys A	Widow	W Al	6 Feb. 1670/1	1670/50
Elizabeth vch Hughe	Tywyn (Dyffryn Gwyn) Mr	Widow of Hugh Price, gent.	W I	28 Oct. 1672	1672/98
Elizabeth vch Hugh	Llanbabo A	Widow	W	12 May 1690	1690/13
Elizabeth vch Hugh	Llanbedr Mr	–	B	14 Nov. 1691	1691/83
Elizabeth vch Hugh ap Owen	Llangristiolus A	Widow	W I	2 March 1664/5	1664/36
Elizabeth vch Hugh Thomas	Gyffin Cn	Widow	I G	6 Feb. 1668/9	1668/50
Elizabeth vch Ievan *see* Elizabeth vch Evan					
Elizabeth vch John	Llanegryn Mr	Widow	W	3 May 1644	1644/33
Elizabeth vch John	Llanegryn (Rhytkriw) Mr	Widow	W I	1 Dec. 1671	1671/105
Elizabeth vch John	Trawsfynydd Mr	Widow	G	31 March 1671	1671/111
Elizabeth vch John David	Llangïan Cn	Widow	W	17 June 1670	1670/116
Elsebeth vch John Davydd *Lloyd*	Llanllyfni Cn	Widow	B I W	2 March 1670/1 30 Sept. 1674	1670/120 1674/28
Elizabeth vch John ap Ievan	Aber-erch Cn	–	W	11 Jan. 1635/6	1635/17
Elizabeth vch John ap Evan	Llantrisant A	–	W	22 Aug. 1643	1643/14
Elizabeth vch John Evan	Ysbyty [Ifan] (Tir Evan) Cn	Widow	W	6 May 1684	1684/62
Elizabeth vch John Griffith	Llanfihangel [Glyn Myfyr][1] (Llyssan) D	–	W	n.d.[2]	1666/126
Elizabeth vch John Gruffyth	[Penmon] A	–	B	29 June 1670 28 July 1671	1671/35
Elizabeth John Lewis	Pentraeth A	Widow	B I	25 Nov. 1696	1696/26
Elizabeth vch John Piers	Gyffylliog D	Widow	W I	25 Nov. 1669	1669/143
Elizabeth vch John ap Rees	Rhuthun & Llanarmon[3] D	–	W I	13 July 1680	1680/73
Elizabeth vch John ap William	Penmorfa Cn	Widow	I	n.d.[4]	1682/63
Elizabeth vch Lewis	Llanidloes Mg	Spinster	W*	23 March 1639/40	1639/3
Ellizabeth vch Morgan	Llanrhychwyn Cn	Widow	W I	14 Feb. 1684/5	1684/58
Elizabeth vch Morris	Llanynghenedl (Cliviog) A	Widow	B* I R	12 Feb. 1690/1	1690/32
Elizabeth vch Moris	Llanfair-yng-Nghornwy A	Spinster	W I	27 April 1691	1691/21
Elesbeth Owen Morgan	Llanbedr Niwbwrch A	Widow	I/G	20 Sept. 1664	1664/14
Elizabeth vch Rees	Llanfachreth (Bottan) A	Widow	W I	30 April 1666	1666/15
Elizabeth vch Rees	Rhuthun D	Widow	W	5 June 1694	1694/115

[1] Normally within the jurisdiction of the St. Asaph Consistory Court.

[2] Will dated 31 March 1666.

[3] I *Llanfair Dyffryn Clwyd.*

[4] Inventory taken 26 Jan. 1682.

Name	Parish & County	Status	Docs. Filed	Date of Probate/Admon.	Ref. No.
Elizabeth vch Richard	Llangynhafal D	Widow	W B	8 March 1637/8	1637/43
Elizabeth vch Richard	Llandyrnog D	Widow	W	29 March 1638	1638/76
Elizabeth vch Richard	Llanrhaeadr-yng-Nghinmeirch (Lloyne) D	Widow	W* I	n.d.[1]	1684/98
Elizabeth vch Richard	Llanfrothen (Bwlch-plwm) Mr	Widow	B I	18 Dec. 1685	1685/79
Elizabeth vch Richard	Nefyn Cn	Widow [of John Pugh Davidd]	B I*[2]	25 Nov. 1686	1686/66
Elizabeth vch Richard	Llantrisant A	Widow	W I	11 April 1699	1699/30
Elizabeth vch Robert	Llanfflewin A	Widow	W	22 Feb. 1675/6	1675/7
Elizabeth vch Robert	Llanynys (Maesmyncymro) D	Widow	W I	11 Jan. 1681/2	1681/101
Elizabeth vch Robert	Trefdraeth A	Widow	W I	6 Dec. 1681	1681/21
Elizabeth vch Robert	Llanfair Dyffryn Clwyd (Bacheurig) D	–	B I	10 March 1690/1	1690/107
Elizabeth vch Robert	Dolgellau Mr	Widow	B I	10 Oct. 1693	1693/72
Elizabeth vch Robert Humffrey	Llaneilian A	Widow	W I G	10 April 1664[3]	1665/12
Elizabeth vch Thomas	Llangïan Cn	Widow of William Griffith, gent.	B	30 March 1661	1661/77
Elizabeth vch Thomas	Trawsfynydd Mr	Spinster	W	n.d.[4]	1664/104
Elizabeth vch Thomas Owen	Caerhun Cn	–	W B(2) Al	10 Feb. 1679/80	1679/20
Elizabeth vch Tudder	Dolgellau (Dyffrydan) Mr	Widow	W I	[7 June 1679]	1679/36
Elizabeth vch William Davidd	Llangelynnin (Glynn uchaph) Cn	Widow	W	3 April 1647	1647/33
Elizabeth vch William David	Llanddeusant A	Widow	W/I	[19 Oct. 1675]	1675/3
Elizabeth vch William Madocke ap Ievan	Llanwnda Cn	Widow	W	7 March 1642/3	1642/29
Elisabeth vch William Mredith	Llangelynnin Cn	Widow	W I	6 Nov. 1680	1680/33
Elizabeth vch William Owen	Bangor (Garth) Cn	Widow	W I	24 Nov. 1670	1670/69
Ellen, Ellin *see* Elin					
Ellis, Ellisse *see* Elis					
Ellisa, Ellisse *see* Eliza					
Erlliw vch David	Llannor Cn	–	B	20 Oct. 1680	1680/36
[Ell]iw vch John	Ffestiniog Mr	–	W*	20 July 1668	1668/84
Ellyw vch Morgan	Tywyn (Dolegwynn) Mr	Widow	W	5 May 1648	1648/17
Erlliw *see* Elliw					
Eva vch John ap Rees	Llanbabo A	Widow	W	7 May 1672	1672/9

1 Inventory taken 28 Aug. 1684.

2 An inventory of the goods of both John Pugh Davidd and Elizabeth his wife.

3 Recte *1665*? Memorandum of swearing the executor dated 29 March 1665; testator died 27 Feb. 1664 (old style reckoning?).

4 Will dated 13 Feb. 1664.

Name	Parish & County	Status	Docs. Filed	Date of Probate/Admon.	Ref. No.
Evan David Griffith	Llangurig Mg	Yeoman	W I Al	23 Sept. 1697	1697/65
Evan David ap Hugh	Llaniestyn Cn	–	B G	8 Nov. 1664	1664/74
Evan David Jenkine	Llangurig (Glynbrochan) Mg	–	B I	29 May 1669	1669/168
Evan David Morgan	Carno Mg	–	I/G	22 Jan. 1690/1	1690/116
Evan David Robert	Trefeglwys Mg	–	W	20 May 1677	1677/95
Evan ap Edward	Gyffylliog D	–	W B	20 May 1640	1640/53
Evan ap Edward	Llanynys (Bachymbid) D	–	B I	8 Feb. 1667/8	1667/127
Evan ap Edward	Llanbedr Dyffryn Clwyd D	Yeoman	W I	12 Dec. 1690	1690/104
Evan ap Edward ap Jeffrey	Llanaber Mr	Yeoman	W	10 April 1643	1643/32
Evan ap Ellis	Llanllechid Cn	Yeoman	W I	27 Oct. 1698	1698/38
Evan Ellis Morgan	Penmachno (Moel y Merch-yrrie) Cn	Yeoman	B I	13 May 1698	1698/50
Evan ap Elisha	Clocaenog D	–	B I	21 March 1660/1	1660/24
Evan ap Elisa	Conway Cn	–	B I	10 Aug. 1671	1671/57
Evan ap Eliza	Llanfrothen Mr	Yeoman	I*	n.d.[1]	1679/43
Evan ap Evan John Lewis *alias* Evan Cadlan	Aberdaron (Bodryth) Cn	Gent.	W	2 June 1645	1645/16
Evan ap Hugh	Gyffylliog D	Gent.	B R	24 Sept. 1687	1687/113
Evan ap Hugh	Trefdraeth A	–	B	20 April 1687	1687/29
Evan ap Hugh	Gyffylliog D	–	I	n.d.[2]	1693/100
Evan ap Hugh	Dwygyfylchi Cn	Yeoman	W I	13 May 1698	1698/28
Evan ap Hugh Lewis	Llaniestyn Cn	–	W I C	26 April 1667	1667/77
Evan ap Hugh ap Owen	Llanbedr[-goch] A	Yeoman	W I	22 Oct. 1696	1696/8
Evan ap Hugh Preynallt	Trawsfynydd Mr	Labourer	I/G	8 May 1696	1696/110
Evan ap Humffrey	Llanbedr Mr	Gent.	B* I*	[ ] 1663[/4][3]	1663/89
Evan Jenkyn Robert ap William	Tywyn Mr	–	W B	16 Feb. 1637/8	1637/37
Evan John ap Elissa	Dolgellau (Dolgleder) Mr	–	B I	2 Sept. 1687	1687/92
Evan John ap Evan	Llanbedrog Cn	–	I	n.d.[4]	1670/98
Evan John ap Evan Robert	Llanddwywe Mr	Yeoman	I/G	24 Nov. 1668	1668/89
Evan John Gruffyth	Clynnog (Coyd-y-tynoe) Cn	Yeoman	W Al	29 Nov. 1692	1692/41
Evan John Griffith	Llangurig Mg	Yeoman	W* I B	6 July 1695	1695/106
Evan John Gruffith ap Rees	Dolgellau Mr	–	W* I	18 June 1664	1664/82
Evan John ap Howell Bedo	Llanaber Mr	Labourer	W	18 April 1637	1637/32

1 Inventory taken 30 Dec. 1679.

2 Inventory taken 26 June 1693.

3 Inventory taken 11 Jan. 1663.

4 Inventory taken 29 Sept. 1670.

Name	Parish & County	Status	Docs. Filed	Date of Probate/Admon.	Ref. No.
Evan John Hugh *alias* Evan Jones	Tywyn (Trevreean) Mr	Yeoman	W I	n.d.[1]	1684/81
Ievan ap John Lewes	Llanystumdwy Cn	–	W	26 Feb. 1638/9	1638/48
Ievan ap John Owen	Bangor Cn	–	W	28 Oct. 1638	1638/32
Evan John Owen	Penmachno Cn	–	B I	10 Feb. 1663/4	1663/75
Evan John Reignallt	Pennal Mr	–	W(2) I	[30 June 1676]	1676/82
Evan John ap Robert	Ffestiniog Mr	Yeoman	W I	n.d.[2]	1681/67
Evan John ap Robert	Botwnnog Cn	–	B C	1 Jan. 1688/9	1688/36
Evan John Robert	Llanfair-iuxta-Harlech Mr	–	W I	5 Jan. 1693/4	1693/84
Evan John Thomas	Beddgelert Cn	–	B	12 Feb. 1677/8	1677/24
Evan John ap William	Llanfaelog A	–	I	n.d.[3]	1687/11
Evan Lewis David	Llangelynnin (Peniarth) Mr	Yeoman	W I	25 April 1670	1670/158
Evan Lewis Meredyth	Llanidloes (Manleth) Mg	Gent.	W I	6 Feb. 1678/9	1678/91
Ievan ap Morgan	Llandanwg Mr	–	W	23 Sept. 1643	1643/33
Evan ap Morgan ap Ievan	Edern Cn	–	B	14 March 1660/1	1660/16
Evan Morgan Evan	Tywyn Mr	–	W	n.d.[4]	1673/58
Evan ap Rees ap Ievan ap Morgan	Llangelynnin Mr	–	W	28 Jan. 1637/8	1637/35
Evan Rees Thomas	Llangurig Mg	–	W I	[12 Jan. 1675/6]	1675/65
Evan ap Richard	Llanbedrycennin Cn	Smith	W	14 Aug. 1663	1663/57
Evan ap Richard	Llanynghenedl A	–	B	25 April 1668	1668/25
Evan ap Prichard	Dolgellau Mr	–	W	22 Jan. 1675/6	1675/37
Evan ap Richard	Llangybi Cn	Yeoman	W I	17 Sept. 1698	1698/36
Evan ap Robert	Llangynhafal D	–	W	21 May 1638	1638/81
Evan ap Robert	Llanrhaeadr-yng-Nghinmeirch (Trevibychain) D	–	W I	25 Sept. 1677	1677/83
Evan ap Robert	Llangwnnadl Cn	–	W	1 Aug. 1695	1695/48
Evan ap Robert	Gyffylliog (Vron vawr, Trevor) D	Yeoman	W I*	27 March 1698	1698/62
Evan Roberts James	Heneglwys (Bodwine Isa) A	Gent.	W	27 Feb. 1695/6	1695/2
Evan ap Robert ap John	Aberdaron Cn	–	W	29 May 1638	1638/28
Evan ap Robert Owen	Ceidio Cn	Gent.	W/I*	4 June 1697	1697/19
Evan ap Robert ap Rees	Gyffylliog D	–	W	22 Jan. 1671/2	1671/116
Evan ap Robert ap Rice	Llanwnda Cn	Yeoman	W I	30 June 1699	1699/85

1 Inventory taken 4 July 1684.
2 Inventory taken 6 July 1681.
3 Inventory taken 7 Oct. 1687.
4 Will dated 26 Jan. 1673.

Name	Parish & County	Status	Docs. Filed	Date of Probate/Admon.	Ref. No.
Evan *Lloyd* Rowland	Trawsfynydd Mr	Gent.	W	3 Jan. 1638/9	1638/67
Evan Thomas Lewis	Llangurig Mg	–	B I	20 Dec. 1662	1662/101
Ievan ap William	Llanfaelog A	Yeoman	W*	13 June 1644	1644/8
Evan ap William	Llanystumdwy Cn	–	W*	23 July 1646	1646/24
Evan ap William	Llangïan Cn	–	B I(2) G	14 Feb. 1665/6	1665/46
Evan ap William Davith	Llangelynnin Cn	–	I/G	1 Dec. 1670	1670/114
Evan ap William ap Edward *see* William ap Evan ap Edward	Trawsfynydd Mr				
Evan ap William Bevan	Amlwch A	–	W Al B	27 Jan. 1679/80	1679/2
Evan ap William John	Aberdaron Cn	Freeholder	W I C	[ ] 1689[1]	1689/29
Evan ap William John	Llanllechid Cn	Yeoman	W* I*	21 April 1697	1697/32
Evan ap William Morris	Llanddeiniolen Cn	–	B	30 July 1668	1668/61
Evan ap William Prichart	Dolgellau (Coed myssoglog, Brithdir ucha) Mr	Gent.	I/G	5 April 1698	1698/53
Evan ap William Probert	Llanengan Cn	Yeoman	W	3 Feb. 1647/8	1647/30
Foulke ap Edward	Llanrhaeadr-yng-Nghinmeirch (Prion) D	Yeoman	W	15 Jan. 1682/3	1682/89
Foulke ap Ellis	Llanrhaeadr-yng-Nghinmeirch (Llawessog) D	–	W Rd	9 March 1647/8	1647/50
Foulke ap John ap Rees	Llanhychan D	–	W I	22 Oct. 1669	1669/154
Foulke ap Richard	Llandyrnog (Corvedwen) D	Gent.	W*	13 Aug. 1677	1677/76
Foulke ap Roberte Gronow	Llanrhaeadr-yng-Nghinmeirch D	Yeoman	W	5 April 1641	1641/63
Foulke ap Thomas	Gyffin Cn	–	W	15 June 1633	1633/3
Francis ap William John	Aberdaron Cn	–	B I	3 Feb. 1681/2	1681/23
Gabriel ap Richard	Llangeinwen A	–	W I	28 April 1663	1663/26
Gaynor vch David *Lloyd*	Conway Cn	Widow	W(2) C	[20 June 1684]	1684/39
Gaynor vch Morris	Penmynydd A	Widow	W	5 Nov. 1670	1670/55
Gaynor vch Nicholas ap Hugh	Conway Cn	Widow	B I	31 Aug. 1691	1691/51
Gaynor vch Robert	Llaniestyn Cn	Widow	W Al	5 July 1677	1677/42
Gaynor vch Robert	Gyffin (Merchlyn) Cn	Widow	W I	[20 May 1679]	1679/23
Gainor vch Thomas	Llanengan Cn	Widow	W I	27 Aug. 1688	1688/51

1 Commission to swear executors issued 15 Sept. 1689.

Name	Parish & County	Status	Docs. Filed	Date of Probate/Admon.	Ref. No.
Gaynor vch Thomas Lewis	Beddgelert Cn	Widow	W I Al Ir D B	7 Feb. 1687/8	1687/37
Gaynor vch William Pugh	Aber-erch [Tythyn Yockws] Cn	Widow [of John Lloyd, gent.]	B	10 Oct. 1695	1695/23
Gaynor vch William Prees	Llandudno Cn	[Widow of Thomas John David Lloyd]	B M	4 Nov. 1670	1670/101
Gaynor William Theodyr	[Beddgelert] (Aberglaslyn) Cn	–	W* I*	[2 March 1684/5]	1684/30
George ap Hugh	Gyffin Cn	Gent.	W I Rd	27 Dec. 1661	1661/57
George ap John	Penmynydd A	–	W	23 March 1636/7	1636/20
George ap Prichard	Aber Cn	Yeoman	W	10 Feb. 1645/6	1645/15
Grace vch Hugh	Llanfairfechan Cn	Widow [of David Lewis]	W I*	{11 Feb. 1695/6 {26 May 1696	1696/68
Grace vch John	Llangeinwen (Towr) A	Widow	W	6 Aug. 1635	1635/6
Grace vch John Thomas	Llandwrog Cn	Widow	B I M	25 Oct. 1699	1699/71
Grace vch Richard	Llandyfrydog A	Spinster	W I	9 July 1694	1694/15
Grace vch Robert	Pentir Cn	Widow	W* I	n.d.[1]	1682/64
Grace vch Robert	Llangoed A	Spinster	W(2) I	10 Oct. 1687	1687/19
Grace vch Robert	Llandwrog Cn	–	I/G	21 Sept. 1689	1689/45
Grace vch Robert *Lloide* *alias* Grace Lloyde	Llanfihangel-y-Pennant Cn	Widow	W I	12 May 1669	1669/91
Grace vch William	Llanfwrog D	Widow	B I	25 Sept. 1696	1696/121
Grace vch William Gruffyth	Llandygái Cn	Widow	W	26 April 1668	1668/58
Gruffyth ap David	Llanfaelrhys Cn	–	W	13 April 1648	1648/12
Gruffyth ap David	Aber Cn	–	I/G	1 May 1669	1669/53
Griffith ap David	Llanberis (Cwmbrwunog) Cn	–	B I	17 March 1681/2	1681/45
Griffith ap David	Aber Cn	–	B I	16 Feb. 1686/7	1686/25
Griffyth David ap Evan	Deneio Cn	–	W	18 Oct. 1638	1638/39
Griffith ap Ednevet	Llanaber Mr	–	W*	14 July 1663	1663/87
Griffith *Lloyd* ap Ellissey	Dolgellau Mr	–	W I	21 Nov. 1661	1661/90
Griffith ap Evan	Beddgelert (Havod Riffyth) Cn	–	W I	1 June 1698	1698/22
Gruffith ap Howell	Llandyrnog D	–	W	2 Jan. 1635/6	1635/43
Gruffeth ap Hoell ap David	Dolgellau Mr	Yeoman	W	19 Sept. 1642	1642/32
Griffith ap Hugh	Llanfachreth [A]	–	B*	[ ] 1682	1682/18
Griffith ap Hugh Bowen *alias* Gruffyth Hughes	Llanbeblig Cn	–	B I	16 Jan. 1693/4	1693/45
Griffith ap Hugh Thomas	Tregaean A	Yeoman	W I C	26 April 1661	1661/31
Griffith ap Humphrey	Llanegryn Mr	Yeoman	W I	26 July 1679	1679/39
Griffith ap Humphrey	Llanarmon Cn	–	W I	[17 Aug. 1687]	1687/52

[1] Inventory taken 15 May 1682.

Name	Parish & County	Status	Docs. Filed	Date of Probate/Admon.	Ref. No.
Griffith ap Humphrey	Llanarmon Cn	Yeoman	W I	23 July 1696	1696/54
Griffith John David	Aberffraw (Bodgedwydd) A	Yeoman	W I	19 Aug. 1667	1667/2
Griffith John David	Llangelynnin (Llwyngwrill) Mr	Yeoman	W I	13 March 1667/8	1667/104
Griffith ap John Griffith	Llanfairfechan Cn	–	W	11 April 1637	1637/27
Griffith ap John Griffith	Penmorfa Cn	–	W	9 May 1644	1644/29
Griffith John Griffith	Llanfechell (Bodtenniel) A	Gent.	W I	27 June 1668	1668/15
Griffith John Griffith	Clynnog Cn	Yeoman	B I	26 Jan. 1670/1	1670/87
Griffith John Griffith	Llanberis Cn	Yeoman	W*	4 April 1693	1693/47
Griffith Sion Griffith	Llangwnnadl Cn	Yeoman	W I Rd	3 Feb. 1696/7	1696/73
Griffith ap John ap Hughe	Llanbedr Dyffryn Clwyd (Lloyneth and Rhiscogge) D	–	W B	23 March 1642/3	1642/36
Griffith ap John ap Hugh	Llangïan Cn	Gent.	W	13 March 1643/4	1643/24
Griffith John ap Humphrey	Llanaber Mr	Labourer	W(2) I(2)	20 March 1681/2	1681/69
Griffyth John Lewys	Dolgellau (Brithdir) Mr	Gent.	W R Rd	12 March 1671/2	1671/100
Gruffith John Lewis	Llanaber Mr	Gent.	W I	21 Feb. 1693/4	1693/75
Gruffith John Phyllip[1]	Llandanwg Mr	–	M	25 May 1666	1666/85
Gruffith ap John ap Rees	Aberdaron Cn	–	W	16 Feb. 1638/9	1638/29
Gryffyth ap John ap Rees	Llanllyfni Cn	–	W B	1 July 1642	1642/28
Griffith John Thomas	Llanrhaeadr-yng-Nghinmeirch D	Yeoman	B	19 Aug. 1691	1691/118
Gryffyth ap John ap William	Derwen D	Yeoman	W(2) Rd	27 Sept. 1643	1643/41
Gruffith ap Rees	Llanddwywe Mr	Yeoman	B I	30 Dec. 1663	1663/92
Griffith ap Rees	Clynnog Cn	–	B I	23 Jan. 1676/7	1676/43
Griffith ap Rees	Llanegryn Mr	–	I/G	5 Dec. 1694	1694/82
Gruffith ap Richard	Dolgellau Mr	Gent.	I*	1 June 1636	1636/41
Gruffuth ap Richard	Tywyn (Kevenrhose) Mr	–	W*	1 June 1636	1636/52
Gruffith ap Richard	Efenechtid D	–	W	7 May 1638	1638/72
Gruffyth ap Richard *alias* Griffith Price	Aber-erch Cn	–	W*	30 March 1640	1640/21
Griffith ap Richard	Llanbedr Mr	–	W	4 Oct. 1642	1642/34
Griffith ap Richard	Edern Cn	–	B I	13 June 1661	1661/55
Griffith ap Richard	Llandinam Mg	–	B	1 Aug. 1666	1666/115
Griffith ap Richard	Llanaelhaearn Cn	–	B I	20 Feb. 1678/9	1678/25
Griffith ap Richard	Llangybi Cn	–	W I Al	[26 Jan. 1685/6]	1685/54
Griffith ap Richard	Llangwnnadl (Nant) Cn	Yeoman	W(2) Rd Al	29 July 1687	1687/68
Griffith ap Robert	Llan-rhudd D	Yeoman	W*	22 May 1643	1643/50
Gryffith Sir Robert	Llanfrothen (Clarken-well) Mr	Yeoman	W	21 May 1688	1688/82
Griffith ap Robert	Llanelidan D	–	W I	21 Sept. 1694	1694/103

[1] See also under Robert ap William ap Evan of Llanaber (document L).

Name	Parish & County	Status	Docs. Filed	Date of Probate/Admon.	Ref. No.
Griffith ap Robert Lewis	Dolwyddelan Cn	–	W	4 Feb. 1663/4	1663/47
Griffith ap Robert Owen	Llanfihangel-y-Pennant (Llecheiddior) Cn	Weaver	W	29 June 1643	1643/22
Griffith ap Robert ap Rice	Llanddwywe Mr	Tailor	W I	20 June 1673	1673/54
Gruffyth ap Robert ap Richard	Aberdaron Cn	–	W	4 Oct. 1645	1645/17
Griffith ap Robert ap William	Penmorfa Cn	–	B I	30 Dec. 1661	1661/85
Griffith ap Robert William	Llanenddwyn Mr	–	W I	31 May 1682	1682/72
Gryffith ap Thomas	Tywyn (Errow Porthor) Mr	–	W	23 Sept. 1637	1637/38
Gruffyth Thomas ap Evan	Llanfwrog (Bodynharad) D	–	W	24 Feb. 1669/70	1669/152
Gruffyth ap Thomas ap Hugh	Llanllyfni Cn	–	W B	15 Feb. 1637/8	1637/29
Griffith Thomas Lewis	Bodfean Cn	Drover	B I C	6 May 1661	1661/45
Gruffith Thomas ap Roger	Llanfair Dyffryn Clwyd (Derwen) D	–	W	2 July 1673	1673/62
Griffith ap William Bevan	Aberdaron Cn	–	B I C	30 Nov. 1685	1685/31
Griffith ap William Griffith	Llanfihangel-y-Pennant Cn	–	W	31 Aug. 1643	1643/23
Gruffyth ap William Gruffyth	Cerrigceinwen A	Gent.	W I	24 Oct. 1661[1]	1661/7
Griffith William John	Dolgellau Mr	Yeoman	W I	11 July 1699	1699/104
Griffith ap William Owen	Beddgelert Cn	Yeoman	B*	21 May 1697	1697/17
Gruffuth ap William Prichard	Maentwrog (Garth gwyn) Mr	Yeoman	W I C	[2 July 1687]	1687/102
Grissiel vch Thomas	Coedana A	Spinster	W	22 July 1663	1663/8
Gruffith, Gruffuth, Gruffyth *see* Griffith					
Gryffith, Gryffyth *see* Griffith					
Gwen vch Edward	Llanelidan D	Widow	W I	15 July 1682	1682/84
Gwen vch Evan ap William	Llanfachreth Mr	Widow	W I	[8 March 1680/1]	1680/52
Gwen vch Hugh	Maentwrog Mr	Widow	W	18 Nov. 1674	1674/53
Gwen vch Humphrey	Llandecwyn Mr	Widow	W	23 Sept. 1685	1685/73
Gwen vch John	Llanbedr Dyffryn Clwyd D	Widow	W I*	4 June 1681	1681/89
Gwenne vch John	Aberdaron Cn	–	B	11 Aug. 1683	1683/20
Gwen vch John *Wyne*	Llangïan Cn	Widow	W	2 May 1638	1638/44
Gwen vch John ap Gruiffith	Llanrhychwyn Cn	Widow	W	2 Feb. 1638/9	1638/47
Gwen vch Moris	Llanddwyn A	–	W	9 Nov. 1670	1670/25
Gwen vch Pierce	Llanrhaeadr-yng-Nghinmeirch (Segroit ucha) D	Widow	W	21 Sept. 1691	1691/119
Gwen vch Rees ap Owen	Llanegryn Mr	Widow	W	31 May 1638	1638/58
Gwen vch Robert	Aber-erch Cn	Widow	W	28 Sept. 1635	1635/18
Gwen vch Robert	Llanfihangel-y-Pennant Cn	Widow	B I	9 Sept. 1686	1686/56

[1] Inventory taken 23 Feb. 1648.

Name	Parish & County	Status	Docs. Filed	Date of Probate/Admon.	Ref. No.
Gwen Robert Morgan	Llandanwg (Harleigh) Mr	Widow	W I R	5 Nov. 1689	1689/67
Gwen vch Thomas	Dolwyddelan Cn	–	W I	[18 June 1688]	1688/42
Gwen Thomas David	Llanegryn (Tonfane ucha) Mr	Widow	I/G	27 June 1692	1692/77
Gwen vch Thomas ap Evan	Llanelidan D	Widow	W* I*	14 July 1671	1671/119
Gwen vch William	Gyffylliog D	–	W	8 April 1695	1695/86
Gwen vch William David	Llangefni A	–	W I	n.d.[1]	1667/28
Gwen vch William Morris	Penmynydd A	Widow	B I	16 Nov. 1672	1672/30
Gwen vch William Prees *Wynne alias* Gwen Williams	[Llanfechell] (Bottenniel) A	Widow [of Griffith John Griffith]	W	3 Dec. 1670	1670/11
Gwenhwyvar vch Richard [Lewis]	Llanbedrycennin Cn	Widow [of David ap Richard]	W	8 July 1641	1641/34
Harry ap David *Lloid*	Gyffin (Kymrhyd) Cn	Gent.	W	16 Nov. 1646	1646/18
Henry ap Evan	Conway Cn	–	W	25 March 1647	1647/24
Henry ap Evan	Llanynys D	–	W*	25 June 1662	1662/91
Harry ap Ivan	Nefyn Cn	Yeoman	W* I	4 Feb. 1669/70	1669/104
Harrie ap Ievan *Lloyd*	Llanrhaeadr-yng-Nghinmeirch D	–	W*	11 Nov. 1641	1641/64
Harry Evan Parry *alias* Harry Evans	Llanfihangel-y-Pennant Cn	–	B I	9 March 1693/4	1693/53
Henry Evan ap Lewis	Llangelynnin (Llwyngoril) Mr	Yeoman	W I B* C	25 [Oct.] 1662	1662/71
Harry Griffith *Lloyd*	Dolgellau Mr	–	W I	13 July 1665	1665/61
Harry ap Hugh	Llanaelhaearn Cn	Yeoman	W	25 May 1666	1666/55
Henry Pugh Parry	Nefyn Cn	Yeoman	B I	21 Nov. 1699	1699/86
Harry ap Hugh ap Owen	Gyffin Cn	–	W I B	21 May 1635	1635/26
Harry ap Hugh ap Robert	Llanarmon Cn	–	W	13 July 1640	1640/24
Harry ap Hugh Salisbury	Clocaenog D	Gent.	W I Rd	16 Nov. 1691	1691/103
Harry ap Hugh Tyder	Tudweiliog Cn	Yeoman	W Rd	2 Oct. 1623	1623/1
Harry ap Hugh ap William	Penmynydd A	–	W B	6 Oct. 1638	1638/23
Harry ap Ievan/Ivan *see* Harry ap Evan					
Harry ap John	Llangynhafal D	–	W I B	18 Dec. 1660	1660/28
Harry ap John Blethyn	Llan-rhudd D	Glover	W* Rd	28 Jan. 1668/9	1668/125
Harrie ap John ap Evan	Amlwch (Bryntwrkelyn) A	–	W	9 May 1664	1664/1
Henry John Evan	Llanelidan D	–	W*	1 May 1671	1671/120
Harry ap John Griffith	Llangoed A	Yeoman	W I Rd	22 Feb. 1666/7	1666/25
Henry John ap Humffrey	Llanaber Mr	–	G	31 Aug. 1669	1669/119

[1] Will dated 12 April 1667.

Name	Parish & County	Status	Docs. Filed	Date of Probate/Admon.	Ref. No.
Harry John Lewis	Llanfair Dyffryn Clwyd (Derwen Llannerch) D	Yeoman	W	[18 July 1693]	1693/110
Henery John ap Morice	Llanddona (Cremlin) A	–	W I Db	30 Aug. 1664	1664/19
Harry John ap William	Clynnog Cn	–	B I	14 Feb. 1678/9	1678/24
Harry John ap William	Llanystumdwy Cn	Yeoman	W I	10 Jan. 1693/4	1693/65
Harry ap Rees	Gyffylliog D	–	W B	15 May 1640	1640/54
Harrie ap Rees David	Derwen D	Yeoman	W I	8 Nov. 1669	1669/140
Harry ap Richard	Aber Cn	–	W I*	28 Nov. 1670	1670/63
Henry ap Richard	Llanllyfni Cn	Gent.	W	19 March 1682/3	1682/52
Henry ap Richard Lewys	Caerhun Cn	Yeoman	W* I*	7 Nov. 1671	1671/49
Harry ap Robert	Llangoed A	–	B I*	23 June 1670	1670/43
Harry ap Robert	Dolgellau Mr	–	I/G	2 June 1697	1697/40
Harry Thomas ap William	Llanrhaeadr-yng-Nghinmeirch (Tre parke, Trevi buchin) D	–	W* I	n.d.[1]	1693/116
Henrry ap William Powell	Penmachno (Llaw r Ynus) Cn	Yeoman	W* I* C*	24 Dec. 1696	1696/83
Henery ap William Jeffrey	Llanbedr Niwbwrch A	Yeoman	W I	11 June 1697	1697/4
Harry William John	Llanaber Mr	–	W*	[Aug. 1672]	1672/88
Henry ap William Owen	Penmynydd A	Yeoman	B	3 Nov. 1666	1666/30
			W	[19 Aug. 1673]	1673/17
Henry *see* Harry					
Howell ap David	Llangefni (Trefollwyn) A	–	W I Rd	21 June 1667	1667/29
Howell David *Vaughan*	Carno Mg	Gent.	B I	6 June 1661	1661/126
Howell ap Evan	Llangurig Mg	–	B I	23 April 1663	1663/142
Howel ap Evan	Gyffin Cn	–	G	7 Sept. 1669	1669/68
Howell ap Hugh	Dolgellau Mr	–	I/G	10 June 1668	1668/80
Howell ap Hugh	Tywyn Mr	–	W* I	1 Sept. 1687	1687/109
Howell ap John	Llanfihangel-y-Pennant Cn	–	W B	24 April 1644	1644/23
Howel ap John	Llanfihangel-y-Pennant Cn	–	W	26 Sept. 1695	1695/47
Howell ap John David	Llanfihangel Tre'r-beirdd A	–	W*	16 May 1641	1641/13
Howell ap John Ievan	Dolgellau Mr	–	W	14 Aug. 1638	1638/54
Howel John ap Evan	[Llanfachreth] (Nannau) Mr	–	W I	2 Sept. 1687	1687/100
Howell ap Morris	Dolgellau Mr	–	B I	2 Oct. 1667	1667/83
Howell ap Rees Thomas	Llanfair Mathafarn Eithaf A	–	B	5 Nov. 1668	1668/14
Howell ap Ynner	Llanfaglan (Llwyn ynne) Cn	Yeoman	W I	2 Oct. 1661	1661/73
Hugh ap Arthur	Bangor Cn	Labourer	W*	30 May 1670	1670/70
Hugh ap David	Llantrisant (Bodynolwyn) A	Gent.	W*	28 Sept. 1646	1646/8
Hugh ap David	Aber Cn	–	W* I	27 Feb. 1676/7	1676/34

[1] Will dated 2 Dec. 169[3].

Name	Parish & County	Status	Docs. Filed	Date of Probate/Admon.	Ref. No.
Hugh David *Lloyd*	Dolgellau Mr	Yeoman	B I	18 July 1661	1661/91
Hugh David John	Penmachno (Dulasse) Cn	–	W I B	2 March 1684/5	1684/60
Hugh ap David ap Rees	Llangelynnin Cn	Gent.	W	25 April 1637	1637/28
Hugh David Robertes	Llanfair-is-gaer (Cruge) Cn	Husbandman/ Gent.	W I B	22 Nov. 1676	1676/53
Hugh ap Edmund	Gyffin Cn	Yeoman	W I	8 Feb. 1692/3	1692/47
Hugh ap Ednevett	Llanaber Mr	–	W	n.d.[1]	1663/88
Hugh ap Edward	Trewalchmai A	Yeoman	W	17 Dec. 1673	1673/19
Hugh ap Edward	Llanelidan D	Yeoman	W I	6 May 1693	1693/105
Hugh ap Ellissa	Llanfachreth Mr	–	I/G	6 April 1670	1670/151
Hugh ap Evan	Llanfair Dyffryn Clwyd D	–	W I	10 May 1642	1642/38
Hugh ap Evan	Tal-y-llyn Mr	–	B I	2 Oct. 1662	1662/72
Hugh ap Evan	Rhuthun D	Smith	W I	9 Aug. 1664	1664/122
Hugh ap Evan	Ynyscynhaearn Cn	–	B*	14 Feb. 1670/1	1670/131
Hugh ap Evan	Llanbedrog Cn	Yeoman	W	26 May 1672	1672/56
Hugh ap Evan	Dolgellau (Cefn r Owen) Mr	Gent.	I R	n.d.[2]	1690/85
Hugh ap Evan *Gouff*	Aber-erch Cn	–	W	27 Jan. 1636/7	1636/23
Hugh ap Evan *Lloyd*	Ffestiniog Mr	–	W	31 May 1638	1638/55
Hugh ap Evan *Lloyd*	Nefyn Cn	–	B	1 July 1663	1663/74
Hugh ap Evan Dafudd *Lloyd*	Dolgellau Mr	Yeoman	W I Db	10 June 1668	1668/81
Hugh ap Ievan Lewis	Llanrhaeadr-yng-Nghinmeirch D	–	W B	23 Feb. 1637/8	1637/45
Hugh ap Evan Thomas	Trawsfynydd Mr	Yeoman	W I	12 April 1669	1669/137
Hugh Gruffith ap John	Bodedern A	–	W	29 April 1647	1647/3
Hugh Gruffith ap Lewis	Derwen D	Yeoman	W I	1 Sept. 1680	1680/63
Hugh Griffyth Morgan	Dolgellau Mr	–	B I	12 June 1663	1663/82
Hugh Griffith ap Moris	Llanfair-yng-Nghornwy A	–	W	22 June 1647	1647/12
Hugh Griffith ap Tyder	Llangelynnin [Cregennan][3] Mr	Yeoman	W I	4 April 1666	1666/92
Hugh ap Hugh	Aberffraw (Dyndryfoel) A	Yeoman	W*	3 June 1641	1641/1
Hugh ap Hugh	Gyffylliog D	–	B* I* R*	[ ] 1685	1685/92
Hugh ap Hugh Evan	Llanfihangel-y-Pennant Mr	–	B I	17 June 1664	1664/98
Hugh ap Hugh Prichard	Coedana A	–	B* I	n.d.[4]	1682/6
Hugh ap Humffrey	Dolgellau Mr	–	W B	6 Oct. 1643	1643/31
Hugh ap Humffrey	Llanfihangel-y-Pennant Mr	–	W	25 Sept. 1644	1644/35
Hugh ap Humffrey	Pennal Mr	–	I/G	1 Dec. 1669	1669/135

1 Will dated 20 Jan. 1663.
2 Renunciation dated 16 April 1690.
3 Supplied from the will of Lowry vch John Griffith, his widow.
4 Inventory taken 8 Aug. 1682.

Name	Parish & County	Status	Docs. Filed	Date of Probate/Admon.	Ref. No.
Hugh ap Humffrey	Llangelynnin Mr	Yeoman	W I*	5 April 1671	1671/110
Hugh ap Humphrey	Llanfihangel-y-Pennant Mr	Yeoman	W I	19 May 1691	1691/92
Hugh ap Humffrey ap Rees	Llanfihangel-y-Pennant Mr	–	W I	18 June 1662	1662/67
Hugh ap Ievan *see* Hugh ap Evan					
Hugh ap John	Llanrhaeadr-yng-Nghinmeirch (Havod lome) D	–	W	27 Sept. 1643	1643/48
Hugh ap John	Llanelltud Mr	–	B	12 June 1663	1663/95
Hugh ap John	Ynyscynhaearn Cn	–	B	28 Oct. 1680	1680/43
Hugh ap John ap David	Llanbadrig A	Yeoman	W*	28 March 1636	1636/6
Hugh John David	Llanfachreth Mr	–	W I	10 June 1668	1668/96
Hugh ap John David	Trefdraeth A	–	W* I	13 Dec. 1670	1670/61
Hugh ap John David ap William	Dwygyfylchi Cn	–	W I	21 Dec. 1663	1663/48
Hugh ap John ap Edward	[Llangadwaladr] (Llanfeirian) A	Gent.	W	3 Sept. 1642	1642/11
Hugh John ap Evan	Pistyll Cn	–	B I	12 June 1668	1668/74
Hugh ap John ap Evan	Llanfechell A	–	W I	n.d.[1]	1675/6
Hugh ap John ap Evan	Llanllechid Cn	Petty Chapman	W I	1 June 1681	1681/51
Hugh ap John Harry	Llannor Cn	Yeoman	W I	31 Oct. 1692	1692/59
Hugh John ap Hugh	[Llanbeblig] (Carnarvon) Cn	Smith	W	12 Sept. 1661	1661/49
Hugh John ap Hugh	Llanengan Cn	–	I L	12 Sept. 1670	1670/108
Hugh ap John ap Hugh	Llanegryn (Tu newydd) Mr	–	I/G R(2)	[14 April 1679]	1679/40
Hugh John ap Hugh	Llanbeblig Cn	–	B I	15 Aug. 1688	1688/46
Hugh John ap John ap Rees	Dolgellau Mr	Yeoman	B* I*	2 Oct. 1662	1662/58
Hugh ap John Llewelyn	Trewalchmai A	–	B I	5 April 1661	1661/33
Hugh John Morgan	Llanrhaeadr-yng-Nghinmeirch (Llech) D	–	W I	6 June 1693	1693/117
Hugh ap John Owen	Gyffin Cn	Yeoman	W I	4 May 1677	1677/31
Hugh John Reece	Dolgellau Mr	Gent./Yeoman	B I	4 Aug. 1696	1696/89
Hugh ap John ap Richard	Rhoscolyn A	–	W*	24 May 1641	1641/22
Hugh ap John Thomas	Llanddeusant A	–	I	2 Oct. 1666	1666/12
Hugh Lewis David	Bodedern A	–	W	21 Dec. 1646	1646/2
Hugh Lewes ap Hugh	Llanrhuddlad A	Gent.	W	9 July 1647	1647/19
Hugh Lewis ap Hugh *Lloyd*	Llanidan (Trerdryw) A	Gent.	W	1 Nov. 1647	1647/17
Hugh Lewys ap Rees	Llanfechell A	Yeoman	W*	13 June 1644	1644/10
Hugh ap Morgan	Caerhun Cn	–	W	17 Oct. 1643	1643/18
Hugh Morgan David	Llanfihangel-yn-Nhywyn A	–	W	1 Jan. 1664/5	1664/25

[1] Inventory taken 16 June 1675.

Name	Parish & County	Status	Docs. Filed	Date of Probate/Admon.	Ref. No.
Hugh ap Moris	Trawsfynydd Mr	Yeoman	I/G	[1 April 1678]	1678/56
Hugh ap Owen	Llandinam (Dethienidd) Mg	Gent.	W I	31 July 1663	1663/136
Hugh ap Owen	Aberffraw A	–	W I	12 Feb. 1676/7	1676/1
Hugh Owen *Gwyn*	Llanbedr Niwbwrch A	–	B I	8 Jan. 1693/4	1693/8
Hugh ap Owen Humphrey	Heneglwys A	–	W	17 March 1680/1	1680/3
Hugh Owen Jenkin	Tal-y-llyn Mr	–	B I	17 June 1664	1664/103
Hugh ap Owen John	Aberffraw A	–	W	5 June 1641	1641/2
Hugh ap Owen Thomas	Ceirchiog A	Gent.	W	29 May 1663	1663/7
Hugh ap Owen Tuder	Llantrisant A	–	W B	6 July 1635	1635/9
Hugh ap Rees Gruffith	Llanelidan (Bryncymme) D	Yeoman	W I B	4 Oct. 1677	1677/78
Hugh ap Rees ap Hugh	Llanfachreth (Bottan) A	Yeoman	W B	6 Oct. 1647	1647/9
Hugh Prees ap Owen	Llanegryn Mr	–	W I	12 June 1663	1663/94
Hugh ap Rees ap William	Pentraeth A	Gent.	W	28 Sept. 1637	1637/14
Hugh ap Reinalt	Llanfairfechan (Camernant) Cn	–	B* I	5 Nov. 1670	1670/111
Hugh ap Reignald	Clocaenog (Ffrithoedd) D	Bachelor	W I	[11 May 1674]	1674/55
Hugh ap Rytharch	Penmachno Cn	–	B I	6 May 1679	1679/30
Hugh ap Richard	Pistyll Cn	–	W	20 May 1662	1662/55
Hugh ap Richard	Llangelynnin Mr	–	I/G	20 June 1667	1667/105
Hugh ap Richard	Llangristiolus A	Yeoman	B	9 Feb. 1690/1	1690/28
Hugh ap Richiard David	Llanfechell (Caerdegog) A	–	W	6 Jan. 1647/8	1647/13
Hugh ap Richard Lewis	Llanddwywe (Talybont) Mr	Smith	W* I R	n.d.[1]	1663/93
Hugh ap Prichard Owen	Llanystumdwy Cn	–	B I	16 June 1663	1663/72
Hugh ap Robert	Llanfaglan Cn	–	W Al	14 Jan. 1635/6	1635/30
Hugh ap Robert	Llandwrog Cn	Yeoman	W(2)* I Al*	5 Oct. 1671	1671/65
Hugh ap Robert	Gyffylliog D	Yeoman	W I	26 Jan. 1695/6	1695/87
Hugh ap Robert Gruffith	Llanbedr Niwbwrch A	–	W	3 April 1635	1635/1
Hugh ap Robert ap Howell	[Llanbeblig] (Carnarvon) Cn	–	B	28 Oct. 1676	1676/40
Hugh ap Robert ap Hughe	Llanaelhaearn Cn	–	W	12 Jan. 1642/3	1642/23
Hugh ap Robert John	Holyhead A	–	W*	27 June 1640	1640/3
Hugh ap Robert John	Aber-erch Cn	Yeoman	B I	27 Dec. 1694	1694/37
Hugh Probert Lawrence	Llandygái Cn	Yeoman	B I	1 May 1697	1697/26
Hugh ap Robert Lewes	Llanaelhaearn Cn	–	W	20 Sept. 1637	1637/24
Hugh ap Robert Owen	Gyffin Cn	–	W	10 Oct. 1670	1670/95
Hugh ap Rowland	Llannor Cn	–	B	19 July 1682	1682/55
Hugh Thomas David *Lloyd*	Llanbadrig A	Yeoman	W/I	17 Aug. 1643	1643/4
Hugh ap Thomas ap Evan	Aberdaron Cn	–	W I	6 July 1665	1665/31
Hugh Thomas Moris	Amlwch A	Yeoman	B I	5 May 1686	1686/2

[1] Renunciation dated 28 Sept. 1663.

Name	Parish & County	Status	Docs. Filed	Date of Probate/Admon.	Ref. No.
Hugh ap William	Penmynydd A	–	W B	7 Sept. 1638	1638/24
Hugh ap William	Llanllechid Cn	–	W*	25 Jan. 1640/1	1640/32
Hugh ap William	Llanfair-yng-Nghornwy A	–	I/G	1 Jan. 1664/5	1664/23
Hugh ap William	Llanddwywe Mr	–	W	16 Oct. 1695	1695/73
Hugh ap William David	Llandyfrydog A	–	I L/G	11 Dec. 1665	1665/9
Hugh ap William Davydd	Amlwch (Rhyd-wigir) A	Yeoman	W*	14 Nov. 1671	1671/4
Hughe ap William Davidd	Llandrygarn A	Yeoman	W* I Rd*	2 March 1691/2	1691/16
Hugh ap William Bevan	Llangeinwen A	–	B I	17 Sept. 1687	1687/17
Hugh ap William Griffith	Llanllechid (Tuddin-isaf) Cn	–	I/G	10 May 1692	1692/56
Hugh ap William Powell	Heneglwys A	–	B I	1 May 1677	1677/4
Hugh ap William Pugh	Llanfechell A	Yeoman	W	n.d.[1]	1669/29
Hugh ap William Pugh	Aberffraw A	–	B	24 Nov. 1673	1673/1
Hugh ap William Pugh	Trawsfynydd Mr	–	W I	5 Oct. 1692	1692/92
Hugh ap William John	Amlwch A	–	W	30 Aug. 1642	1642/1
Hugh ap William John	Llangoed A	Yeoman	W I	23 Jan. 1666/7	1666/26
Hugh ap William John	Tudweiliog (Brynodol) Cn	–	W I*	6 Jan. 1676/7	1676/61
Hugh ap William Kenricke *alias* Hugh Kenricke	Coedana A	Gent.	W I Rd	5 April 1662	1662/8
Hugh ap William Mathew	Pentir Cn	–	W*	22 April 1640	1640/36
Hugh ap William Probert	Rhiw Cn	–	W	13 Feb. 1668/9	1668/76
Hugh ap William Probert	Llanddaniel-fab A	–	W I Al	9 March 1670/1	1670/23
Humffrey ap Arthur	Tywyn Mr	Yeoman	W*	24 April 1644	1644/38
Humphrey ap Edward	Llanfihangel-y-Pennant (Maes-yllech) Cn	Yeoman	B I	7 Jan. 1663/4	1663/62
Humphrey ap Ellis	Llanelltud Mr	–	B I	17 June 1664	1664/94
Humffrey ap Ievan	Llanenddwyn Mr	–	W*	4 Oct. 1638	1638/59
Humphrey ap Evan	[ ] Cn	Yeoman	W I	16 March 1675/6	1675/32
Humphrey ap Evan	[Llandanwg] (Harleigh) Mr	–	W I C*	7 Dec. 1686	1686/74
Humphrey ap Evan	Llanddeiniolen Cn	–	B	20 July 1686	1686/53
Humphrey ap Evan	Dolgellau (Dyffrydan) Mr	Yeoman	W I C	21 April 1691	1691/79
Humphrey ap Evan *Lloyd*	Tywyn Mr	–	B	20 April 1678	1678/59
Humffrey ap Evan Griffyth	Llanllyfni Cn	Yeoman	I/G	1 March 1669/70	1669/95
Humphrey ap Evan Jenkin	Tywyn (Doledeheuwydd) Mr	Yeoman	W I	n.d.[2]	1684/83
Humffrey ap Howell ap Jenkin	Tywyn Mr	Yeoman	W	10 July 1640	1640/50
Humphrey Pugh John	Tywyn Mr	Yeoman	W* I* B*	9 Nov. 1699	1699/119
Humphrey ap Hugh Prydderch	Llannor Cn	–	W I	[23 Feb. 1680/1]	1680/37

[1] Will dated 7 June 1669.

[2] Will dated 27 Sept. 1683. Endorsed *1684*.

Name	Parish & County	Status	Docs. Filed	Date of Probate/Admon.	Ref. No.
Humphrey Pugh Thomas	Llanbadrig A	Yeoman	W I G	12 Dec. 1662	1662/10
Humffrey ap Ievan *see* Humffrey ap Evan					
Humphrey Sir John	Llanenddwyn Mr	Yeoman	W I	29 May 1663	1663/96
Humphrey John David	Llanystumdwy Cn	Yeoman	B I	26 March 1690	1690/78
Humffrey John ap Humffrey	Treflys Cn	–	W	[3 April 1674]	1674/33
Humphre John Morgan	Llangoed A	Butcher	W I B	25 April 1671	1671/27
Humphrey John Rowland	Llanddeiniolen Cn	Tailor	W	2 Oct. 1665	1665/45
Humffrey ap Morgan	Maentwrog Mr	–	B	25 April 1661	1661/106
Humffrey ap Rynallt	Llanddeiniolen Cn	–	W*	27 May 1640	1640/26
Humphrey ap Richard	Penystrowed Mg	–	I/G	16 April 1663	1663/152
Humphrey ap Richard Humphrey	Llanfaethlu A	–	W	19 March 1671/2	1671/21
Humphrey ap Richard Lewis	Ffestiniog Mr	Smith	W	[26 Oct.] 1664	1664/87
Humphrey Thomas Richard	Llanddwywe Mr	Yeoman	I/G	15 Dec. 1670	1670/145
Humphrey ap William Bevan	Llanddeiniolen Cn	–	B	10 Jan. 1699/1700	1699/75
Humphrey ap William Humphrey *alias* Humphrey Williams	Llanddeiniolen Cn	Yeoman	W I	30 Sept. 1696	1696/64
Humffrey ap William ap Robert	Maenol Bangor Cn	–	W	1 Aug. 1637	1637/16
Humphrey ap William Rowland	Llanbeblig Cn	–	B I*	5 March 1694/5	1694/48
Ievan *see* Evan					
Ismael ap Rees ap William	Llanfair-yng-Nghornwy A	Yeoman	W	22 July 1638	1638/10
James ap John Thomas	Llanfwrog D	Glover	W	21 May 1636	1636/58
James ap Owen	Efenechtid D	–	W*Rd*	10 Nov. 1637	1637/41
Jane vch David	Gyffylliog D	Widow	W I	6 March 1692/3	1692/96
Jane vch David	Llandyrnog D	–	B	23 Feb. 1696/7	1696/120
Jane vch David *Lloyd*	Dwygyfylchi Cn	Widow	W I	12 May 1635	1635/25
Jane vch David ap Evan	Llandyrnog D	–	B I	8 April 1665	1665/81
Jane vch Edward	Llangynhafal D	Widow	W I	23 Sept. 1685	1685/98
Jane vch Edward	Llanllechid Cn	Widow	I	n.d.[1]	1692/57

[1] Inventory taken 13 Feb. 1692.

Name	Parish & County	Status	Docs. Filed	Date of Probate/Admon.	Ref. No.
Jane vch Ellis	Penmachno Cn	Widow	B I	28 March 1663	1663/76
Jane vch Ellis	Llanfair Dyffryn Clwyd (Vaynoll Quarter) D	Widow of Tudur ap Edward	W	19 Feb. 1683/4	1683/85
Jane vch Evan	Llangybi Cn	Widow	W I	26 Jan. 1663/4	1663/66
Jane vch Evan	Llangelynnin Mr	–	B	29 May 1667	1667/106
Jane vch Evan	Bangor Cn	Widow	W I	29 July 1689	1689/32
Jane vch Evan	Trawsfynydd (Tyddin-gwladis) Mr	Widow	I/G Db	30 April 1694	1694/95
Jane vch Gruffith	Llaniestyn [Cn]	–	W	7 May 1640	1640/31
Jane vch Hugh	Llanengan Cn	Widow	W I	22 July 1678	1678/31
Jane vch Humffrey	Llanddeiniolen Cn	Widow [of John Griffith of Fronoley]	W	n.d.[1]	1672/64
Jane vch Humphry	Llanrhaeadr-yng-Nghinmeirch D	Widow	W I	26 May 1693	1693/118
Jane vch John *see* Nicholas, Hugh	Conway Cn				
Jane vch John	Llandwrog Cn	–	B	10 April 1671	1671/66
Jane vch John	Llangeinwen A	Widow	W	1 March 1691/2	1691/26
Jane vch John David	Derwen D	Widow	W I	n.d.[2]	1689/79
Jane vch John Edward	Llanbedr Mr	Widow	B I*	22 Sept. 1697	1697/44
Jane vch John Morgan	Tregaean A	Widow of Griffuth ap Hugh Thomas	W	14 Feb. 1661/2	1661/32
Jane vch John Owen	Llandygái Cn	Widow	B	23 July 1666	1666/60
Jane vch John ap Richard	Dolgellau Mr	Widow	W	[22 Aug. 1674]	1674/39
Jane vch John ap Robert	Llandecwyn (Mirie-r-Gwyddil) Mr	Widow	W I	7 March 1683/4	1683/66
Jane vch John ap William	Llanelidan D	Widow	W I	16 April 1694	1694/104
Jane Owen Pwlckyn	Penrhos[llugwy] A	Spinster	B	29 Oct. 1666	1666/31
Jane vch Rees	Llanhychan D	–	W	16 April 1640	1640/56
Jane vch Rees	Dolgellau (Brithdir) Mr	Spinster	W I	19 July 1692	1692/68
Jane vch Rees Owen	Cerrigceinwen (Pryssierwerth ucha) A	Widow of Moris Lloyd	W B	23 Sept. 1662	1662/7
Jane vch Rhydderch	Llanddyfnan A	Spinster	W I	17 April 1689	1689/9
Jane vch Richard	Aberffraw A	–	W	6 July 1637	1637/1
Janne vch Richard	Llandysilio A	Widow	W*	17 Dec. 1646	1646/6
Jane vch Robert	Llanfihangel-y-Pennant Cn	–	B	15 July 1667	1667/72

[1] Will dated Nov. 1672.

[2] Inventory taken 2 Sept. 1689.

Name	Parish & County	Status	Docs. Filed	Date of Probate/Admon.	Ref. No.
Jane vch Robert	Clocaenog D	–	B	29 Dec. 1686	1686/87
Jane vch Robert	Llanrhaeadr-yng-Nghinmeirch (Llech) D	Widow	W I B	23 April 1688	1688/93
Jane vch Robert	Llangybi Cn	Widow	W	12 April 1692	1692/53
Jane vch Robert	Llanfachreth Mr	Widow	I*	n.d.[1]	1697/48
Jane vch Robert ap David	Beddgelert Cn	–	W I B	6 April 1671	1671/46
Jane vch Thomas	[Llan-rhudd] (Merllyn) D	–	W* I*	n.d.[2]	1663/125
Jane vch Thomas	[ ]	–	W(2)	n.d.[3]	1669/178
Jane vch Thomas	Llanllechid Cn	–	W* I*	28 May 1672	1672/70
Jane vch Thomas	Rhuthun D	Widow	W I	[10 June 1679]	1679/61
Janne vch Thomas	Llanddaniel-fab A	Widow	W I	31 Dec. 1686	1686/11
Jane vch Thomas *Wynne*	Derwen D	Widow	W B	4 Aug. 1640	1640/51
Jane vch Thomas ap Evan	Llanfwrog D	Widow	W I	25 Nov. 1669	1669/153
Jane vch William David	Dolwyddelan Cn	Widow [of Ellis ap William ap Ellis]	W I	[ ] 1690[4]	1690/53
Jane vch William Jeffrey	Efenechtid D	Widow	W* I	30 Dec. 1696	1696/118
Jane vch William Morgan[5]	[ ]	–	I	n.d.[6]	1690/123
Jane vch William Probert	Llanidan A	Widow	W I B	16 March 1696/7	1696/20
Jeffrey ap William Thomas	Derwen D	–	W I	[20 Oct. 1676]	1676/87
Jenkyn ap Ievan	Llanbeblig Cn	–	W	14 Feb. 1644/5	1644/21
Jenkin ap Evan ap Edward	Llangurig Mg	–	I/G	25 June 1667	1667/134
Jenkin John ap Mredith	Llandinam Mg	Gent.	I/G	18 Feb. 1663/4	1663/137
John David *Lloyd*	Llandecwyn (Moel y geifr) Mr	Gent.	W I	30 Sept. 1667	1667/93
John David ap Edward	Llanfachreth Mr	–	B I	11 June 1689	1689/73
John David ap Evan	Llanfair Mathafarn Eithaf A	–	B I	17 Sept. 1689	1689/14
John David Foulke	Llanrhaeadr-yng-Nghinmeirch D	–	W*	17 April 1640	1640/58
John David ap Griffith	[ ] Mr	–	W I	[ ] 1665[7]	1665/74
John David Powell David	Llanfachreth Mr	–	B I	22 Nov. 1681	1681/74
John David ap Hugh	Llanegryn (Rhydgarneth) Mr	–	W Db	6 July 1680	1680/49
John David ap Hugh	Llanaber Mr	–	B I	19 June 1681	1681/70
John David ap John	Llanfair Dyffryn Clwyd D	–	B I	9 March 1660/1	1660/26

1 Inventory taken 10 May 1697.
2 Inventory taken [ ] Aug. 1663.
3 Will dated 17 Oct. 1669.
4 Inventory taken 12 May 1690.
5 Endorsed *Jane vch Robert*.
6 Inventory taken 2 June 1690.
7 Will dated 16 April 1665.

Name	Parish & County	Status	Docs. Filed	Date of Probate/Admon.	Ref. No.
John David ap John	Gyffin Cn	–	W I Rd	3 July 1677	1677/32
John David Shion	Llanidloes Mg	Labourer	W	14 March 1699/1700	1699/155
John David Lewis	Llanegryn Mr	Yeoman	W I	5 Oct. 1692	1692/78
John David ap Owen	Llanfwrog D	–	W I	28 Jan. 1662/3	1662/87
John Davydd ap Thomas	Holyhead A	–	W	28 Jan. 1669/70	1669/8
John David ap Thomas	Llanfair Dyffryn Clwyd (Derwen Llannerch) D	–	W I	22 Oct. 1669	1669/147
John David ap William	Llangelynnin Mr	–	W*	20 Oct. 1643	1643/37
John Edmund Morgan	Llanfachreth Mr	Fuller	W	2 Aug. 1690	1690/93
John ap Edward	Trefriw (Arthe y Wlad) Cn	–	W*	4 April 1636	1636/39
John ap Edward	Pistyll Cn	–	W I	10 July 1668	1668/75
John ap Edward	Llandecwyn Mr	–	W	[25 May 1674]	1674/43
John ap Edward	Llanelidan (Bryn cymme) D	–	W I B*	27 June 1687	1687/117
John ap Edward Griffith	Llanaber Mr	–	W	11 July 1648	1648/15
John Edward Prichard	Tywyn (Bron y prees) Mr	–	B I	25 Feb. 1683/4	1683/79
John ap Edward ap Thomas	Llanbedr Dyffryn Clwyd D	Yeoman	W	7 March 1638/9	1638/74
John Ellice ap Robert Pierce	Gyffylliog D	–	W I	2 May 1693	1693/101
John ap Eliza	Llanfrothen (Garthllwynog) Mr	Yeoman	W*	18 Jan. 1671/2	1671/108
John ap Ellisae	Dolgellau (Tall y Waen, Dolgleder) Mr	–	W I	6 Feb. 1682/3	1682/65
John ap Ievan	Llannor Cn	–	W	29 June 1641	1641/41
John ap Evan	Llanddona (Cravegoed) A	Yeoman	W	16 Sept. 1642	1642/7
John ap Evan	Trefeglwys Mg	Miller	W I	16 June 1663	1663/155
John ap Evan	Llanelidan D	Yeoman	B I	27 May 1668	1668/109
John ap Evan	Llaneugrad (Bodgunda) A	–	W I	12 May 1684	1684/13
John ap Evan	Llanynys D	Labourer	W	26 Oct. 1699	1699/140
John Evan ap Humphrey	Trawsfynydd (Bodyfydda) Mr	–	W	2 May 1694	1694/96
John ap Evan John	Llangynhafal D	Yeoman	W I	19 Aug. 1671	1671/124
John ap Evan ap Morgan	Llanbedrog Cn	Yeoman	W	29 Feb. 1671/2	1671/61
John ap Evan ap Morgan	Penmachno Cn	–	B	24 April 1682	1682/60
John ap Evan ap Rees	Llangurig Mg	Tailor	W/I	27 Sept. 1667	1667/135
John ap Evan ap Rees	Llangynhafal D	Yeoman	W I	1 Oct. 1668	1668/119
John ap Ievan ap Ric.	Llandudno Cn	–	W	23 May 1637	1637/25
John Evan ap Richard	Llanelltud Mr	Gent.	B I	15 April 1668	1668/93
John Foulke ap Ellis	Llangwyfan D	Miller	W	n.d.[1]	1675/58
John Gryffith David	Dolgellau (Garth-gynvawr) Mr	Yeoman	W I	14 Oct. 1696	1696/90
John Gryffith ap Evan	Dolgellau (Garthgynvor) Mr	Gent.	W I	24 March 1676/7	1676/68

[1] Will dated 8 June 1675.

Name	Parish & County	Status	Docs. Filed	Date of Probate/Admon.	Ref. No.
John Griffith Evan	Llandanwg Mr	Tailor/Yeoman	I/G	5 May 1696	1696/100
John Griffith John	Clynnog (Y Wern) Cn	–	B I	9 Oct. 1663	1663/44
John Griffith ap Moris	Llanfihangel-y-Pennant Cn	–	W	9 May 1663	1663/63
John Gruffith ap Rutherch	Aber-erch Cn	–	B I	7 June 1667	1667/50
John ap Harry	Llanfwrog A	–	W	17 Jan. 1642/3	1642/9
John Parry Griffith	Llangwyfan D	Yeoman	W I B	13 Dec. 1686	1686/99
John *Lloyd* ap Howell Griffith	Clocaenog D	–	B* I	17 Jan. 1662/3	1662/79
John ap Hugh	[Llanbeblig] (Carnarvon) Cn	Smith	W Rd	1 July 1642	1642/21
John ap Hugh	Llanrhaeadr-yng-Nghinmeirch D	Gent.	W I	5 Aug. 1661	1661/120
John ap Pue	Llangaffo A	–	W	29 July 1668	1668/17
John ap Hugh	Llangelynnin Mr	Glazier	I/G	28 Jan. 1669/70	1669/132
John ap Hugh	Aber Cn	Husbandman	W I	11 Dec. 1677	1677/21
John ap Hugh	Llanddeusant A	–	B	21 Oct. 1681	1681/8
John ap Hugh	Llanddwywe (Myvod) Mr	–	W(2) Al	n.d.[1]	1682/69
John ap Hugh	Llanwnda Cn	–	B I	16 May 1682	1682/57
John ap Hugh	Llanengan Cn	–	B	21 May 1683	1683/38
John ap Hugh	Aberffraw A	Yeoman	B	12 May 1690	1690/2
John ap Hugh David	Llannor Cn	Yeoman	W I	21 Oct. 1664	1664/77
John Pugh Davidd	Nefyn Cn	–	I[2]	n.d.	1686/66
John ap Hugh David *Lloyd*	Llanbeblig Cn	Yeoman	W	14 June 1669	1669/72
John ap Hugh ap Elize	Dolgellau Mr	–	W I	10 June 1668	1668/82
John ap Hughe ap Evan	Llanfihangel-y-Pennant Cn	–	W	9 July 1636	1636/33
John ap Pugh ap Ievan	Llanfihangel-y-Pennant Mr	–	W	10 July 1640	1640/46
John ap Hugh Parry	Llechgynfarwy A	Labourer	W I	17 May 1692	1692/27
John ap Hugh Lewys	Trawsfynydd Mr	Gent.	W* I B	17 June 1664	1664/105
John Pugh Morys	Tal-y-llyn Mr	Yeoman	W I	31 July 1690	1690/98
John ap Hugh Owen	Bodfean Cn	Yeoman	B I	5 July 1690	1690/45
John Hugh Philip	Llandinam Mg	Gent.	B I	21 March 1692/3	1692/114
John ap Hugh ap Rees	Llanegryn (Penniarth) Mr	Yeoman	W* I*	[3 Jan.] 1664/5	1664/91
John ap Hugh ap Rees	Clocaenog D	–	W I	n.d.[3]	1669/139
John ap Hugh ap Robert	Llanfechell A	–	W B	15 Feb. 1641/2	1641/12
John ap Hugh Robert	Llandwrog (Nanlley) Cn	Tailor	W I	26 Oct. 1675	1675/25
John ap Hughe ap Robert ap Gruffith	Llanllyfni Cn	–	W*	4 Feb. 1636/7	1636/35
John ap Hugh Thomas	Caerhun Cn	Carpenter/Yeoman	W I R	15 Sept. 1687	1687/43

[1] Will dated 19 March 1671. Endorsed *1681* and *1682*.

[2] Filed with the admon. of Elizabeth vch Richard of Nefyn (q.v.).

[3] Inventory taken 4 Jan. 1669.

Name	Parish & County	Status	Docs. Filed	Date of Probate/Admon.	Ref. No.
John ap Humphrey	Llanbedr Mr	–	W I	17 Aug. 1669	1669/123
John ap Humphrey	Llanarmon Cn	Yeoman	W I	[29 Oct. 1674]	1674/22
John ap Humphrey	Llanarmon Cn	Yeoman	B I(2)	5 May 1685	1685/43
John Humphrey David	Llanfihangel-y-Pennant Mr	–	B I	12 June 1663	1663/104
John ap Ievan *see* John ap Evan					
John ap John	Llangynhafal D	–	W(2)	16 Dec. 1597	1597/1
John ap John	Beaumaris A	Gent.	W/Al* B*	25 April 1638	1638/4
John ap John	Llanrhaeadr-yng-Nghinmeirch D	–	W	6 June 1638	1638/83
John ap John	Llanddeusant A	Yeoman	W I	21 Aug. 1663	1663/15
John ap John	Maenol Bangor Cn	–	W I	31 Aug. 1672	1672/42
John ap John	Llan-rhudd D	Yeoman	W* I	11 Feb. 1672/3	1672/118
John ap John	Llanidloes (Stredynod) Mg	Yeoman	W I	12 March 1674/5	1674/62
John ap John	Aberffraw A	Yeoman	W I	n.d.[1]	1677/1
John ap John	Llanelidan D	Yeoman	W I	3 July 1686	1686/95
John ap John	Aberdaron Cn	Freeholder	W I	3 Oct. 1694	1694/35
John ap John	Llanelidan[2] D	Yeoman	B* I	16 June 1694	1694/105
John ap John	Beddgelert Mr	Yeoman	W I	17 March 1698/9	1698/23
John ap John Griffyth	Llanynys (Bachymbid) D	–	W I	27 Feb. 1666/7	1666/108
John ap John Griffith	Ffestiniog Mr	–	B I* C	28 Feb. 1684/5	1684/67
John ap John a[p] Mredyth	[Llanidan] A	–	W*	27 June 1636	1636/17
John ap John ap Richard	Llangynhafal D	–	W	28 Sept. 1643	1643/46
John ap John Robert	Llanfwrog (Penycoed) D	–	W I	20 June 1667	1667/123
John ap John Rowland	Llanfflewin A	–	W I	17 Oct. 1685	1685/21
John ap John Rowland	Aber-erch Cn	–	B I	31 May 1688	1688/32
John Lewis David ap Owen	Llanidloes Mg	–	W	30 Sept. 1635	1635/53
John Lewis Pugh Parry	Llangwyllog (Tresgawen) A	Gent.	W I Rd	15 June 1680	1680/12
John Lewis Price	Llanfair Mathafarn Eithaf A	Yeoman	W I	8 May 1683	1683/8
John Lewis ap Richard	Pentraeth A	–	B I	16 March 1669/70	1669/50
John Morgan Evan	Llangurig Mg	–	W	[12 Dec. 1674]	1674/61
John Morgan ap Evan Bedow	Llangurig Mg	Gent.	W I	16 June 1663	1663/143
John Morgan Lewis	Llangurig Mg	–	W	27 Sept. 1637	1637/52
John Owen David	Trefdraeth A	Gent.	W	n.d.[3]	1677/19
John Owen ap Evan	Llechgynfarwy A	–	W I	31 March 1690	1690/34
John Owen Gruffyth	Llanddyfnan A	Gent.	W B	29 June 1640	1640/7
John Owen Gruffith	Beddgelert (Nanmor) [Mr]	–	W	30 Oct. 1643	1643/17

1 Inventory taken 19 May [1677].
2 Living at the time of his death at Glothedd [*sic*], parish of Llanrhos, diocese of St. Asaph.
3 Will dated 4 April 1677.

Name	Parish & County	Status	Docs. Filed	Date of Probate/Admon.	Ref. No.
John Owen Griffith	Llanbedr Niwbwrch A	–	W I	25 Feb. 1661/2	1661/12
John Owen Lewis	Tal-y-llyn Mr	–	B I C	3 April 1666	1666/95
John Owen Lewis	Llangwyfan / Llechylched A	Yeoman	W I	1 May 1696	1696/18
John Owen Peirs *alias* John Peirs	Beddgelert Cn	–	W/I	14 April 1637	1637/17
John Owen ap Richard	Llangelynnin Cn	–	W I	20 June 1671	1671/75
John Pierce Salusbury	[Llanrhaeadr-yng-Nghinmeirch] (Astrad) D	Yeoman	W* I	14 Dec. 1685	1685/99
John Rees ap Evan Morgan	Llanegryn Mr	Yeoman	W B	15 April 1641	1641/50
John Price James	Llanfechell (Caerdegog) A	Gent.	B I(2)	19 June 1689	1689/16
John Rees ap John ap Howell	Llanfachreth Mr	–	I/G	12 Oct. 1683	1683/71
John Price Thomas	Dolwyddelan Cn	–	B I(2) R	30 Aug. 1694	1694/46
John ap Rhydderch	Deneio (Pwllhelley) Cn	Mercer	W I	1 Sept. 1666	1666/52
John ap Rytherch Griffith	Ynyscynhaearn (Cwm bach) Cn	–	W I	1 Nov. 1670	1670/132
John ap Richard	Trefeglwys Mg	–	W*	29 Dec. 1646	1646/32
John ap Richard	Gyffylliog (Trevor) D	Miller	W I	12 Aug. 1661	1661/113
John ap Richard	Llanddeiniolen Cn	–	W	3 March 1661/2	1661/70
John ap Richard	Aber Cn	–	B	18 May 1665	1665/30
John ap Richard	Llanrug Cn	–	B*	31 May 1671	1671/86
John ap Richard	[Llandanwg] (Harleigh) Mr	–	W	[17 Oct. 1678]	1678/43
John ap Prichard	Llanfair-yn-neubwll A	Gent.	W	11 April 1683	1683/11
John ap Richiard	Treflys Cn	–	W	n.d.[1]	1685/62
John ap Richard	Clynnog (Hengwm) Cn	Yeoman	B I	13 Oct. 1686	1686/41
John ap Richard	Llanystumdwy Cn	–	B I	7 Dec. 1686	1686/64
John ap Prichard	Llandygái Cn	–	B I	18 Sept. 1694	1694/50
John ap Richard	Llanystumdwy Cn	–	W	n.d.[2]	1696/82
John ap Richard Davide	Llangwnnadl (Hendrevowr) Cn	–	W I	20 July 1669	1669/92
John ap Richard Evan	Trawsfynydd Mr	–	B	27 Oct. 1664	1664/106
John ap Richard Gruffith	Llanenddwyn Mr	–	B I	3 Oct. 1667	1667/99
John ap Richard Griffith	Cricieth (Trevan) Cn	–	W I	6 Dec. 1670	1670/90
John ap Richard Lewis	Holyhead A	–	B I	17 June 1689	1689/7
John ap Richard Morris	Gyffin Cn	Yeoman	I	[24 Jan.] 1664/5	1664/62
John ap Richard Owen	Aberdaron Cn	–	W	[30 Nov. 1675]	1675/14
John ap Richard ap Rytherch	Ffestiniog Mr	Yeoman	W I B	27 May 1635	1635/33
John ap Robert	Llangwyfan A	Labourer	W	1 Jan. 1664/5	1664/38
John ap Probert	Llanfechell A	–	W/I C	7 Jan. 1667/8	1667/24

[1] Will dated 2 Jan. 1685.
[2] Will dated 21 April 1696.

Name	Parish & County	Status	Docs. Filed	Date of Probate/Admon.	Ref. No.
John ap Robert	Botwnnog Cn	Yeoman/Gent.	W Al	n.d.[1]	1670/74
John ap Robert	Llangefni A	–	B I	17 Jan. 1680/1	1680/9
John ap Robert	Llanfair Dyffryn Clwyd (Gartkynnan) D	Yeoman	W* I	2 June 1681	1681/92
John ap Robert	Penmorfa (Ceven coch) Cn	Yeoman	W* I*	14 Aug. 1694	1694/64
John ap Robert David	Llanbedrycennin Cn	Yeoman	W* I* M	3 Sept. 1687	1687/55
John ap Robert ap Ievan	Derwen D	–	W	5 April 1641	1641/55
John Probert Francis	Llanaelhaearn Cn	Yeoman	W I	27 June 1699	1699/62
John Probert Griffith	Ynyscynhaearn Cn	–	B I	10 March 1691/2	1691/74
John Probert Griffith	Penmynydd A	Yeoman	W I	15 June 1698	1698/15
John ap Robert ap Humffrey	Beddgelert Cn	–	B	22 Feb. 1666/7	1666/42
John Robert ap Humphrey	Llan-rhudd D	Yeoman	W I	5 Feb. 1693/4	1693/120
John ap Robert ap John	Llanfair Dyffryn Clwyd & Llanarmon-yn-Iâl D	Gent.	W*	5 Aug. 1640	1640/55
John ap Robert Owen	Nefyn Cn	–	B I/Db	18 Oct. 1687	1687/79
John ap Probert ap Roger	Llanrhaeadr-yng-Nghinmeirch (Bryn yockin, Trefibychain) D	–	W I	[29 May 1683]	1683/90
John Robert Simon	Dolgellau Mr	Yeoman	I/G R	22 Sept. 1694	1694/71
John Robert Thomas	Llanenddwyn Mr	–	I/G	31 March 1670	1670/148
John ap Robert ap William Prees	Caerhun Cn	Yeoman	B I	18 Sept. 1691	1691/45
John Rowland Griffith	Bryncroes Cn	Gent.	B R	19 June 1661	1661/46
John Thomas *Wynne*	Amlwch A	–	W Rd	18 Jan. 1646/7	1646/1
John Thomas ap Ellis	Clocaenog (Llannerch gron) D	–	W	26 May 1673	1673/59
John Thomas Ellish	Llangeinwen A	Yeoman	W I*	7 June 1698	1698/9
John Thomas ap Evan	Llanelidan D	Weaver	W	24 May 1672	1672/107
John Thomas ap Evan	Llanfwrog (Keelygroslwyd) D	–	W I	2 March 1681/2	1681/96
John Thomas ap Hugh	Derwen D	–	W*	26 Sept. 1643	1643/42
John Thomas Jones	Llangwyfan D	–	W	10 June 1642	1642/39
John Thomas John	Llanbadrig A	–	G	6 July 1663	1663/10
John Thomas John	Betws-y-coed Cn	Yeoman	B	6 Jan. 1699/1700	1699/47
John Thomas Lewis	Llanfair-is-gaer Cn	Yeoman	W I	12 April 1689[2]	1690/64
John Thomas ap Morgan	Pentir Cn	–	W* I	27 Sept. 1670	1670/129
John Thomas Owen	Llanfair-yng-Ngwaredog (Mynydd Mwyn) A	Gent.	W	n.d.[3]	1671/24

[1] Allegation dated 15 Dec. 1670.

[2] Recte *1690*? Will dated 19 Feb. 1689/90 and inventory taken 24 Feb. 1689.

[3] Will dated 5 May 1671.

Name	Parish & County	Status	Docs. Filed	Date of Probate/Admon.	Ref. No.
John Thomas ap Richard	Llanfwrog D	–	W*	n.d.[1]	1668/113
John Thomas ap Richard	Llanelidan D	–	W	27 May 1680	1680/65
John Thomas ap Robert	Llanelidan (Garthneuadd) D	–	W I	10 May 1669	1669/145
John Thomas ap Robert	Gyffylliog D	–	B I	13 Feb. 1671/2	1671/117
John Thomas ap William	Clocaenog D	–	W	5 April 1641	1641/54
John Thomas William	Holyhead A	Yeoman	W	[12 April 1672]	1672/8
John Thomas William	Tywyn Mr	Yeoman	W I	[1 June 1675]	1675/50
John Thomas William	Llanidloes Mg	Bachelor	B I	10 May 1688	1688/104
John Watkin ap Pue ap William	Llaneilian A	Yeoman	W	n.d.[2]	1673/7
John ap William	Llanrhaeadr-yng-Nghinmeirch (Llann) D	–	W	24 April 1637	1637/46
John William Bayly	Carno Mg	Yeoman	W I	4 March 1674/5[3]	1674/58
John ap William David	Aber-erch Cn	–	W	1 July 1641	1641/23
John ap William David	Llanbabo A	Yeoman	W Al Ir D	19 Dec. 1672	1672/10
John ap William David	Llaneilian A	Yeoman	B I	8 Dec. 1699	1699/15
John ap William Edmund	Llandrygarn A	Smith	W	23 May 1670	1670/20
John ap William Gruffith	Llanhychan D	–	W* I	4 May 1635	1635/45
John ap William Griffith	Llanllechid Cn	–	W	6 June 1638	1638/46
John ap William Gruffith	Treflys Cn	–	I	n.d.[4]	1669/112
John William Griffith	Llanaber (Bwlch Coch Ucha) Mr	–	W I	11 June 1689	1689/65
John ap William Parry	Llanbeblig (Carnarvon) Cn	–	B	17 Jan. 1666/7	1666/46
John ap William ap Hugh	Llanfflewin (Ycheldre) A	Gent.	W Rd	10 Nov. 1644	1644/11
John ap William ap Hugh	Trefdraeth A	Labourer	W	14 June 1669	1669/52
John ap William ap Hugh	Llanbeblig Cn	–	I/G	3 Oct. 1672	1672/55
John ap William Hughes *alias* John Williams	Llanarmon / Llanystumdwy Cn	–	B* I	2 Feb. 1681/2	1681/43
John ap William James	Llangybi Cn	Yeoman	W I C	[27 Nov. 1682]	1682/50
John ap William John	Llanwnda Cn	Yeoman	B	27 Nov. 1691	1691/68
John ap William ap John Bedo	Dolgellau Mr	–	W*	2 June 1636	1636/42
John ap William Lewis	Holyhead A	Gent.	W	23 Dec. 1646	1646/4
John ap William Massey	Llanelidan D	Yeoman	W	n.d.[5]	1675/56

1 Will dated 4 Jan. 1668 (20 Chas. II). Endorsed *1668 vel 69*.

2 Will dated 1 Sept. 1673.

3 Incorrect? Will dated 3 March 1674[/5]; date of testator's death given as 15 March 1674[/5].

4 Inventory taken 8 Nov. 1669.

5 Will dated 3 June 1675.

Name	Parish & County	Status	Docs. Filed	Date of Probate/Admon.	Ref. No.
John William Morgan	Dolgellau Mr	–	I/G	5 May 1694	1694/72
John ap William Maurice	Llanystumdwy Cn	Corviser	W I	10 April 1677	1677/47
John ap William Morris	Bangor (Perveddgoed) Cn	Gent.	W I	[24 May 1681]	1681/29
John ap William Morris	Penllech Cn	–	I	n.d.[1]	1690/80
John William Owen	Llanegryn Mr	–	W* I	14 Aug. 1683	1683/68
John ap William ap Richard	Llanelltud Mr	Yeoman	W	21 July 1644	1644/34
John ap William Prichard	Llannor Cn	–	I L(2)	9 Dec. 1670	1670/121
John ap William Prichard	Llanengan Cn	–	W	14 March 1672/3	1672/65
John ap William Prichard	Aber (Weeg) Cn	–	B* I*	20 Aug. 1696	1696/30
John ap William Rowland	Llanbedrycennin Cn	–	R	n.d.[2]	1670/100
John ap William Thomas	Llangelynnin (Tan yr Allt) Cn	Yeoman	W I R	21 Oct. 1670	1670/115
Jonet vch David	Gyffylliog D	Widow	W I	17 Nov. 1681	1681/86
Jonett vch David *Lloyd*	Llanbeulan A	Widow	W	29 Dec. 1664	1664/16
Jonet vch Edward	Llanllechid Cn	Widow	W I Al	26 April 1683	1683/48
Jonet vch Edward	Llangynhafal D	Widow	W	1 Dec. 1686	1686/100
Jonet vch Ellice	Llanberis Cn	–	W I	19 March 1669/70	1669/75
Jonnet vch Ellisse	Llanelltud (Tyddyn Bach) Mr	Widow	W I	19 May 1691	1691/89
Jonet vch Evan	Dolwyddelan Cn	–	W	26 Nov. 1647	1647/26
Jonnett vch Griffith *Vaughan*	Llangristiolus A	Widow	W* Al*	10 Feb. 1636/7	1636/15
Jonett vch Hugh Rowland	Llanbeulan (Trevebion Miricke) A	Widow	W	27 Feb. 1665/6	1665/7
Jonett vch John	Pentraeth A	–	B I	2 March 1670/1	1670/57
Jonett vch John	Llandecwyn Mr	Widow	W	12 Aug. 1672	1672/91
Jonet vch John	Trefdraeth A	Widow	B I*	12 July 1688	1688/28
Jonette vch John ap Evan	Llanddeiniolen Cn	–	W	11 July 1668	1668/62
Jonet vch John Gruffith *see* Ellin vch John Gruffith	Pentir Cn				
Sionet John Lewis	Llanfaelrhys Cn	Widow	W* I	6 Oct. 1671	1671/72
Jonet vch John ap Llewelyn	Llanddeusant A	Widow	W I	22 June 1663	1663/16
Jonet vch John Llewelin	Llanynys (Bachymbyd) D	–	W I	26 Sept. 1685	1685/102
Jonett vch John Thomas	Llandyrnog D	–	W I	[5 March 1673/4]	1673/61
Jonette vch John Thomas	Llanbedr Niwbwrch A	Widow	W I	23 July 1680	1680/5
Jonet vch John ap William	Heneglwys A	Widow	W I	7 May 1674	1674/3
Jonet vch Rytherch	Llanrhaeadr-yng-Nghinmeirch (Cader) (late of Nantlgyn) D	Widow	W I	1 May 1688	1688/94
Joned vch Richard	Llanengan Cn	–	W	19 Sept. 1637	1637/26

[1] Inventory taken 22 March 1689.
[2] Renunciation dated 21 Jan. 1670 (22 Chas. II).

Name	Parish & County	Status	Docs. Filed	Date of Probate/Admon.	Ref. No.
Jonet vch Robert	Deneio Cn	Widow of Owen Madrin, gent.	W M	[31 Aug.] 1664	1664/61
Jonett vch Thomas	Llanrhaeadr-yng-Nghinmeirch D	Widow	B I	17 Dec. 1660[1]	1660/29
Jonett vch Thomas	Aber-erch Cn	Spinster	B	19 July 1661	1661/38
Jonet vch Thomas	Aber Cn	Widow	W(2) I*	n.d.[2]	1662/33
Jonet vch Thomas	Trawsfynydd Mr	Widow	B	2 June 1666	1666/96
Jonett vch Thomas	Llanrwst (Trewydyr) Cn	–	B I	9 July 1684	1684/56
Jonet vch William	Llanrhaeadr-yng-Nghinmeirch (Trevybychyn) D	Widow	W I	26 Aug. 1698	1698/68
Jonett vch William Gruffith	Aber Cn	Widow	B	19 Nov. 1667	1667/47
Joseph John David	Aber Cn	Yeoman	W I Al	19 May 1685	1685/30
Julius ap Richard	Llanfair Dyffryn Clwyd (Kaerperson) D	Yeoman	W	19 July 1667	1667/121

Kadwaladr *see* Cadwaladr
Katherine *see* Catherine

Lewis ap David	Llanbedr Dyffryn Clwyd D	–	W	5 April 1641	1641/59
Lewis David ap Hugh	Llangelynnin (Cregennan) Mr	–	W I	8 May 1678	1678/47
Lewis David Robert	Pennal Mr	Miller	W I(2)	[ ][3] 1694/5	1694/93
Lewis ap Edward	Dolgellau (Coed Croes) Mr	Yeoman	B I	27 Sept. 1699	1699/105
Lewis ap Evan	Llanengan Cn	Yeoman	W	24 Oct. 1647	1647/31
Lewis ap Ievan	Dolgellau Mr	–	B* I R	1 Feb. 1660/1	1660/20
Lewis ap Evan David	Llanaber Mr	–	W I	9 May 1670	1670/141
Lewis ap Evan ap Edward	Llangurig Mg	–	B	29 Aug. 1676	1676/101
Lewis ap Evan Lewis	Llangeinwen A	Yeoman	W I/B	21 Dec. 1685	1685/24
Lewis Evan Owen	Llanddwywe Mr	–	I	13 March 1667/8	1667/94
Lewis Griffith Humphrey	Tywyn Mr	Yeoman	B I	27 Sept. 1699	1699/120
Lewis ap Harry	Penrhos[llugwy A]	–	W	31 July 1645	1645/12
Lewis ap Hugh	Dolgellau Mr	Gent.	B I R	10 Feb. 1669/70	1669/115
Lewys ap Hugh Lewys	Llandegfan A	Yeoman	W* I	8 June 1672	1672/13
[?Lewis][4] ap Hugh Owen	Tal-y-llyn Mr	Bachelor	W* I*	29 June 1693	1693/94

1 Inventory taken 2 Dec. 1648.
2 Inventory taken 23 April 1662.
3 Died 4 Jan. 1694.
4 Taken from the bishops transcripts of the parish registers of Tal-y-llyn, 1693.

Name	Parish & County	Status	Docs. Filed	Date of Probate/Admon.	Ref. No.
Lewis ap Hugh ap Rees	Llanbabo (Llannol) A	–	W	8 Aug. 1642	1642/3
Lewis ap Hugh Tydyr	Trefeglwys Mg	–	W I	[2 March 1675/6]	1675/71
Lewis ap Humphrey	Llangwnnadl Cn	Yeoman	B I	25 Feb. 1689/90	1689/52
Lewis ap Ievan *see* Lewis ap Evan					
Lewis ap John	Llanddona A	–	W* B	13 May 1639	1639/2
Lewis ap John ap Jenkin	Tywyn Mr	–	W	14 Oct. 1644	1644/39
Lewis ap John Lewis	Aberdaron Cn	–	W	7 July 1665	1665/32
Lewis ap John Lewis	Llangelynnin (Cregennan) Mr	Gent.	W I B	10 May 1677	1677/62
Lewis ap John Lewis	Llangeinwen A	–	B I	22 July 1679	1679/9
Lewis ap John Owen	Ceirchiog A	–	B I	23 May 1687	1687/2
Lewis ap John Thomas	Llanfachreth Mr	–	W*	27 March 1640	1640/45
Lewis John ap William	Llanbedr Niwbwrch A	–	B	19 Dec. 1664	1664/15
Lewis Meredith Evan	Llanidloes (Manleth) Mg	Gent.	W I	[4 March 1674/5]	1674/63
Lewis ap Owen	Llandrygarn A	–	W	23 June 1645	1645/6
Lewis ap Owen	[ ]	–	I	n.d.[1]	1666/129
Lewis Owen Ellis	Llangelynnin (Tre r Morva) Mr	Yeoman	B I	1 Aug. 1690	1690/97
Lewis ap Rees	Dolgellau (Garthgynvor) Mr	Gent./Yeoman	W I	22 Sept. 1697	1697/41
Lewis ap Rees ap Ievan ap Morgan	Llangelynnin Mr	–	W*	20 July 1637	1637/36
Lewis ap Richard	Caerhun Cn	–	I/G	7 June 1666	1666/45
Lewis ap Richard	Dolgellau Mr	Carpenter	W I	28 July 1691	1691/80
Lewis ap Richard Lewis	Dolgellau Mr	–	B	6 Feb. 1663/4	1663/83
Lewis ap Robert	Eglwys-ael *alias* Llangadwaladr A	–	W*	17 April [ ]	1641/14
Lewis ap Robert ap Rees	Llanynghenedl (Clivioc) A	Gent.	W	10 Nov. 1645[2]	1645/10
Lewis ap William David	Aberffraw A	Yeoman	W*	27 March 1668	1668/2
Lewis ap William Pugh	Ceirchiog A	Yeoman	W* I	n.d.[3]	1671/8
Lewis ap William John	Bangor Cn	–	I	n.d.[4]	1648/8
Lewis ap William Lewis	Aberdaron Cn	–	B	12 Aug. 1673	1673/20
Lewis ap William Owen	Pentraeth A	Gent.	B I	5 March 1666/7	1666/34
Lewis ap William Probert	Derwen D	–	W I	25 Feb. 1694/5	1694/100
Lewis William Rowland	Penrhos[llugwy] A	–	B*	31 May 1671	1671/37
Lowry vch Edward	Llanbedr Mr	Widow	I/G	9 Feb. 1694/5	1694/80
Lowry vch Elissa	Llanelltud Mr	–	W	13 Sept. 1677	1677/58

[1] Inventory taken 11 May 1666.
[2] Incorrect? Will dated 28 Nov. 1645 (21 Chas.I).
[3] Inventory taken 23 Jan. 1671/2.
[4] Inventory taken 7 July 1648.

Name	Parish & County	Status	Docs. Filed	Date of Probate/Admon.	Ref. No.
Lowry vch Evan	Tywyn Mr	Widow	W I	6 May 1685	1685/89
Lowry vch Evan	Clocaenog (Gwaynypyscodlyn) D	–	B	4 April 1687	1687/110
Lowrie vch Evan ap William	Dwygyfylchi Cn	–	W	3 July 1676	1676/49
Lowry vch Howel	Dolgellau Mr	–	W	18 June 1664	1664/83
Lowrie vch Hugh Lewis	Llanfechell A	Widow	W	5 March 1661/2	1661/16
Lowry vch John	[Llandygái] (Capell kirig) Cn	Widow	W I	24 Oct. 1661	1661/67
Lowry John Cadwalader	Dolgellau (Brithdir ucha) Mr	Widow	W I Al	5 Aug. 1696	1696/91
Lowry vch John Evan	Llangybi Cn	Widow	W	2 March 1638/9	1638/45
Lowry vch John Griffith	Llangelynnin [Cregennan] Mr	Widow of Hugh Griffith Tuder of Cregennan	{B I R {W(2) Al C	13 July 1667 1 July 1668	1667/107 1668/100
Lowry vch John Griffith	Penmachno Cn	Widow	I	n.d.[1]	1669/105
Lowry vch John ap William	Aber-erch Cn	Widow	W	n.d.[2]	1686/30
Lowry vch Lewis	Dolgellau Mr	Widow	B	2 Oct. 1662	1662/59
Lowry vch Morgan	Llanfihangel-y-traethau Mr	Widow	W I	23 Oct. 1694	1694/88
Lowrie vch Moris	Aber Cn	Widow	W	27 Feb. 1644/5	1644/17
Lowry vch Moris	Ynyscynhaearn (Cwm mawr) Cn	Widow	W W/Al I	14 Jan. 1674/5	1674/34
Lowrie vch Rees	Llanrug Cn	Widow[3]	W B	8 July 1641	1641/42
Lowry vch Rees	Maenol Bangor Cn	Widow	W I	[19 Feb. 1676/7]	1676/36
Lowrie vch Roderick	Llanidan A	Widow	W I	30 Jan. 1690/1	1690/31
Lowrie vch Richard	Llanbedr Mr	Widow	B	12 June 1663	1663/90
Lowry vch Richard	Tudweiliog (Brynodol) Cn	Widow	B I	13 Aug. 1691	1691/73
Lowry vch Robert	Ynyscynhaearn (Bron-y-gadair) Cn	Widow of John Prichard	W Al Ir	n.d.	1671/96
Lowry vch Robert	Dolbenmaen Cn	–	B	10 June 1689	1689/38
Lowrie vch Roderick *as* Lowrie vch Rhydderch					
Lowry vch Thomas	Llanfaelog A	Widow	W*	18 July 1663	1663/18
Lowry vch Thomas	[Ynyscynhaearn][4] (Garreg Velen) Cn	[Widow of William Moris Evan]	W	9 Jan. 1668/9	1668/77
Lowry vch Thomas Lewis	Llanfair Dyffryn Clwyd (Derwen Llannerch) D	Spinster	B I	28 Dec. 1689	1689/84
Lowry vch William	Ysbyty [Ifan] (Eiddey) Cn	Widow	W I B(2)	24 Jan. 1679/80	1679/33
Lowry vch William Bevean	Llandysilio A	–	I/G	9 April 1672	1672/16

1 Inventory taken 22 Nov. 1669.
2 Will dated 2 Sept. 1686.
3 W *spinster*, although mention is made of the testator's children.
4 Endorsed *Penmorva* (cf. will of William Moris Evan of Ynyscynhaearn).

Name	Parish & County	Status	Docs. Filed	Date of Probate/Admon.	Ref. No.
Lowry vch William John	Llanfair-iuxta-Harlech Mr	Widow	B	22 April 1697	1697/49
Luce vch Hugh	Llanfechell A	Widow	W	16 March 1669/70	1669/30
Madog ap Richard	Gyffylliog D	–	W*	31 Aug. 1641	1641/57
Magdalen vch Rees *Wynne* *alias* Magdalen Thelwall	Llanynys (Maesmaen Cymro) D	Widow [of Thomas Thelwall]	W Al D B[1]	17 Jan. 1677/8	1677/86
Mallt vch Robert	Llanrug Cn	Widow	W I Al	27 Nov. 1687	1687/71
Margeret vch Kadwalader	Aber-erch Cn	–	L	[18 July 1670]	1670/67
Margarett vch David ap Jeffrey	Llangeinwen A	Widow	B* I	9 Dec. 1662	1662/23
Margarett vch Edward	Llanfachreth Mr	Widow	W I	27 July 1667	1667/101
Margarett vch Edward	[Dolgellau] (Dolgleder) Mr	–	W	15 May 1678	1678/39
Margerett vch Ellis	Trawsfynydd Mr	Widow	W B	10 July 1640	1640/47
Margret vch Evan	Llanfairfechan Cn	Widow	W	29 Nov. 1664	1664/69
Margarett vch Evan	Dolgellau Mr	Widow	B	5 Feb. 1672/3	1672/87
Margeret vch Evan	Amlwch A	Widow	W	2 July 1674	1674/1
Margaret vch Evan	Derwen D	–	W/I	24 July 1682	1682/80
Margarett vch Evan	Beddgelert Cn	Widow	W I	12 July 1688	1688/34
Margarett vch Evan	Llanllyfni (Talmignedd ycha) Cn	Widow	W* I	2 March 1690/1	1690/72
Margerett vch Hary	Llangeinwen A	Widow	W Cd	28 Nov. 1667	1667/31
Margeret vch Hugh Shion	Llangelynnin Mr	Old woman	W I	13 April 1697	1697/51
Margerett vch Hugh Lewis	Nefyn Cn	Widow	W I	20 June 1661	1661/84
Margaret vch Humphrey	Llanfaelrhys Cn	Spinster	B	17 June 1691	1691/59
Margaret vch John	Llanidloes Mg	Widow of David Lloyd ap Evan	W*	27 June 1638	1638/90
Margaret vch John Davidd	Llanbeblig Cn	Spinster	B	2 Nov. 1691	1691/55
Margret vch John ap Evan	Penmorfa Cn	Widow	W I	12 Jan. 1669/70	1669/110
Margarett vch John ap Evan	Aberffraw A	Widow	W I	5 July 1689	1689/2
Margaret vch John Foulke	Gyffylliog D	–	W	13 May 1686	1686/89
Margaret vch John Griffith	Llanfair Dyffryn Clwyd D	–	W I	7 Sept. 1681	1681/93
Margret vch John ap Hugh	Gyffylliog D	Widow	W	5 April 1641	1641/58
Margaret vch John Tudyr	Llanddeusant A	–	W*	29 April 1642	1642/6
Margarett vch John ap William	Llanddeiniolen Cn	Widow	W	18 March 1647/8	1647/29
Margeret vch Kadwalader *as* Margeret vch Cadwalader					
Margret vch Morgan	Llanbeulan A	Spinster	W	9 April 1646	1646/5

[1] This could also be a bond for the administration of the goods of Magdalen Thelwall, spinster, daughter of Magdalen Thelwall, widow.

Name	Parish & County	Status	Docs. Filed	Date of Probate/Admon.	Ref. No.
Margeret vch Rytherech	Aber-erch Cn	Widow	W/I	29 March 1661	1661/39
Margarett vch Rhytherch	Llannor Cn	Widow	W Rd	19 April 1672	1672/78
Margarett vch Richard	Llanidan A	–	L	24 Feb. 1668/9	1668/21
Margarett vch Richard	Nefyn Cn	Widow	W	17 Nov. 1670	1670/127
Margeret vch Richard	[Llanrwst] (Trewydyr) Cn	–	W	21 May 1684	1684/57
Margarett vch Richard Evans	Llanengan Cn	Widow	W I Al	[21 June] 1688	1688/52
Margrett vch Richard John	Llanbeulan A	Widow	W	25 Dec. 1674	1674/5
Margret vch Richard ap Lewelyn	Heneglwys A	Widow	W*	9 March 1640/1	1640/2
Margaret vch Richard Owen	Llangïan Cn	Spinster	W	23 Feb. 1670/1	1670/117
Margret vch Robert	Llanfechell A	Widow	W	21 Oct. 1643	1643/9
Margaret vch Robert	Gyffin Cn	Widow	W	14 Nov. 1666	1666/54
Margaret vch Robert	Bryncroes Cn	Spinster	W	27 March 1668	1668/38
Margaret vch Robert	Pistyll Cn	Widow	I*	6 Oct. 1671	1671/95
Margerett vch Robert	Llanfihangel-yn-Nhywyn A	Widow	W I	12 March 1690/1	1690/24
Margaret vch Robert *Lloyd*	Gyffylliog D	Widow	W I	22 Jan. 1672/3	1672/102
Margarett vch Robert *Wynn*	Clocaenog (Bryngwrgi) D	Widow	W	17 April 1638	1638/70
Margaret vch Thomas	Llanynys D	Widow	B	10 Aug. 1663	1663/127
Margaret vch Thomas	Derwen D	Widow	W I	29 July 1696	1696/116
Margaret vch Thomas Davidd	Llanfair-yng-Ngwaredog (Mynudd Mwun) A	Widow	W I	18 April 1688	1688/16
Margaret vch William	Beaumaris A	Widow	W	11 July 1664	1664/6
Margarett vch William	Llangynhafal D	Widow	W I	4 July 1667	1667/125
Margaret vch William ap Roberte	Tregaean A	Widow	W	14 Sept. 1635	1635/13
Margarett vch William Rowland	Llanllibio A	–	B	4 Nov. 1669	1669/40
Margeret vch William Thomas	Holyhead A	–	W	20 June 1667	1667/10
Marsley vch John ap Rhydderch	Llangaffo (Treverwidd) A	Widow	W I	31 Jan. 1698/9	1698/8
Marsley vch Rees	Llanrhaeadr-yng-Nghinmeirch (Astrad) D	Widow	W I	26 Sept. 1687	1687/125
Margerie vch William John	Llanllyfni (Carreg Wen) Cn	Widow of Evan Gryffyth	W I	15 May 1663	1663/69
Margerry vch William Morgan	Clynnog Cn	Widow	W(2)	n.d.[1]	1688/40
Marke ap David	Llanfechell A	–	I G	4 April 1665	1665/16
Marmaduke ap Rees	[?Rhodogeidio] (Bryngwallan) A	Glover	I	[4 June] 1664	1664/27
Marsley *see* Margery					

[1] Will dated 3 July 1688; endorsed *nondum probatum*.

Name	Parish & County	Status	Docs. Filed	Date of Probate/Admon.	Ref. No.
Martha vch Harry	Llanfair Dyffryn Clwyd D	–	W	7 Aug. 1668	1668/110
Mary vch Da[vid] Morgan[1]	Carno Mg	–	W	29 May 1671	1671/141
Mary vch Evan	Llanddona A	Widow	B I	30 Sept. 1678	1678/6
Mary vch Evan	[Llanrwst] (Trewydur) Cn	–	B	28 Oct. 1695	1695/52
Mary vch Evan *Gwynn*	Llangurig Mg	Widow	I	n.d.[2]	1675/66
Mary vch Evan *Lloyd*	Llanfair-iuxta-Harlech Mr	Widow	W	12 May 1674	1674/46
Mary vch Harry	Llanynys (Esceibion) D	Widow	W I	8 April 1679	1679/58
Marie vch Hugh Probert	Holyhead A	Widow of Richiard John ap Prichiard, gent.	B I	26 Aug. 1667	1667/11
Mary vch Humphrey	Llanenddwyn Mr	Widow	W I	9 Sept. 1670	1670/149
Mary vch Humphrey	Rhuthun D	Widow	B I	26 May 1693	1693/127
Mary vch John David *Lloyd*	Trawsfynydd Mr	Widow	W	5 June 1643	1643/39
Mary Lewis John	Dolgellau Mr	Widow	B I	12 Oct. 1666	1666/79
Mary vch Richard Edmund	Llanddeiniolen Cn	Spinster/Widow	W* I	8 Jan. 1690/1	1690/58
Mary Thomas Griffith	Llanddeiniolen Cn	Widow	W I	12 Feb. 1698/9	1698/34
Mary vch William Moris	Llandwrog Cn	Widow	W I	[1 Dec. 1691]	1691/58
Mathew David Lewis	Llangurig Mg	–	I/G	3 Aug. 1665	1665/103
Mathew ap Edward	Rhuthun D	–	I/G	22 June 1663	1663/131
Maude vch John	Llanfair Dyffryn Clwyd (Vaynol quarter) D	Widow	W I	27 May 1680	1680/67
Maurice *see* Morris					
Meredith ap Robert	Llanfair-yn-neubwll A	–	W	6 March 1638/9	1638/11
Meredith ap Thomas	Llanbedr Niwbwrch & [Llangeinwen] (Kelliniog) A	Gent.	W* Rd	10 March 1640/1	1640/4
Mredyth ap William Lewis	Bodedern A	–	W	21 Sept. 1636	1636/4
Morgan David *Lloyd*	Llanelltud Mr	–	W*	6 June 1640	1640/44
Morgan ap Harrye	Llanwnda Cn	–	W	19 Oct. 1576	1576/1
Morgan ap John Gruffith	Caerhun Cn	–	W I B	8 June 1635	1635/20
Morgan John ap William	Aber-erch Cn	–	B	25 July 1667	1667/51
Morgan ap Richard Morgan	Llangeinwen A	Yeoman	W I	14 Aug. 1677	1677/15
Morgan Thomas ap Hugh	Trawsfynydd Mr	–	W	5 Aug. 1647	1647/44
Morgan ap William	Llanfaelog A	–	G*	1 Dec. 1662	1662/17
Morgan ap William Morgan	Llanfihangel-y-traethau Mr	–	W*	19 Feb. 1643/4	1643/35
Morgan ap William Morgan	Clynnog (Derwyn) Cn	Gent.	W I*	1 Aug. 1662	1662/44
Moris David ap Howell	Beddgelert Cn	–	W* I B	18 June 1635	1635/19

[1] Endorsed *Mary Thomas*.

[2] Inventory taken 9 June 1675.

Name	Parish & County	Status	Docs. Filed	Date of Probate/Admon.	Ref. No.
Moris ap Edmund	Clynnog Cn	–	W	14 Feb. 1638/9	1638/37
Morris ap Edward	Llandyrnog D	Gent.	W I	[28 Dec. 1689]	1689/81
Moris ap Ievan ap John	Llandinam Mg	–	W B	27 Sept. 1637	1637/50
Moris ap Evan ap John	Llanwnnog Mg	–	W* B	7 July 1640	1640/61
Morris ap Evan Morgan	Llanwnda Cn	Labourer	W	n.d.[1]	1669/100
Maurice Evan Owen	Ffestiniog (Teilie Mawr) Mr	–	B I	2 Aug. 1690	1690/86
Morrice ap Hugh	Maentwrog Mr	–	B I	11 June 1663	1663/109
Moris ap Hugh	Llanynghenedl A	Gent.	W I Rd	27 May 1667	1667/37
Moris ap Hugh	Carno Mg	–	W I	5 June 1668	1668/127
Moris ap Hugh ap Humffrey	Beddgelert Cn	Gent.	W I	18 March 1666/7	1666/43
Moris ap Ievan *see* Moris ap Evan					
Moris ap John	Llanelidan D	Fuller	W*	12 Oct. 1671	1671/121
Maurice ap John ap Moris	Llanbedr Niwbwrch A	–	W Rd	29 Nov. 1630	1630/1
Morris John ap Richard	Llanfair-iuxta-Harlech Mr	–	B I*	22 Sept. 1685	1685/77
Moris John ap Robert	[Llanrwst] (Glyn llygwy, [Gwydir]) Cn	–	W I	4 July 1665	1665/49
Morris John Thomas	Llanystumdwy (Tŷ Kerrig) Cn	–	I/G	22 Aug. 1683	1683/55
Morris John William	Carno Mg	Gent.	B I	5 June 1668	1668/128
Morris ap Prytherch	Llanrug Cn	Yeoman	B* I	28 Dec. 1684	1684/55
Maurice ap Richard	Llantrisant A	Farmer	B I	27 Sept. 1664	1664/40
Morris ap Richiard	Aber-erch (Penychen) Cn	–	W I	18 Oct. 1681	1681/25
Morris ap Richard	Llandinam Mg	–	B I	4 May 1682	1682/98
Morris ap Richard	Llanegryn Mr	–	I/G	2 May 1693	1693/77
Maurice ap Robert	Llanbeulan A	–	W I	20 Jan. 1669/70	1669/13
Morris ap Robert	Llanrhaeadr-yng-Nghinmeirch D	Yeoman	W	[25 April 1676]	1676/94
Morris ap Robert	Llanelidan D	–	W I	21 April 1680	1680/66
Morris ap Robert	Beddgelert Cn	–	W I	n.d.[2]	1687/38
Morris ap Robert	Amlwch A	Yeoman	B I	22 Nov. 1689	1689/4
Maurice ap Robert Morgan	Llanfihangel-y-traethau Mr	Yeoman	W	11 March 1674/5	1674/51
Moris ap Robert Prydderch	Llanystumdwy Cn	–	B	6 Jan. 1670/1	1670/126
Morris ap Robert William	Llanfihangel Ysgeifiog A	–	B I	11 April 1687	1687/15
Morris Thomas David	Llanddeiniolen Cn	–	B	29 July 1669	1669/85
Maurice Thomas Griffith	Llanidan A	Yeoman	W I	23 April 1689	1689/22
Moris ap William	Dolwyddelan (Penanmen) Cn	–	W	17 May 1645	1645/22
Moris ap William Pugh	Aberffraw A	–	W I	8 July 1685	1685/2

[1] Will dated 22 Oct. 1669.

[2] Inventory taken 6 Jan. 1687/8.

Name	Parish & County	Status	Docs. Filed	Date of Probate/Admon.	Ref. No.
Maurice ap William Morgan	Clynnog Cn	–	B I R(2) M	19 May 1688	1688/41
Moris ap William ap Richard	Penmynydd A	–	W B	9 March 1638/9	1638/25
Morris ap William ap Robert	Llanbeblig Cn	–	B I	25 Jan. 1670/1	1670/96
Moris ap William Thomas	Llanddeiniolen Cn	Yeoman	W Al*	29 Dec. 1671	1671/68
Nicholas ap Ievan	Llanfihangel Bachellaeth Cn	Yeoman	B(2) I	22 Oct. 1661	1661/75
Oliver ap Robert	Llandinam Mg	–	B I	26 Sept. 1667	1667/131
Owen David ap Robert	Aber Cn	–	B I	1 Dec. 1670	1670/64
Owen ap Edmund	Aber Cn	–	W*	14 Aug. 1640	1640/20
Owen ap Evan	Llanfair Mathafarn Eithaf A	Bachelor	W I	16 April 1688	1688/17
Owen ap Evan David *Lloyd*	Dolgellau Mr	Yeoman	B(2) I	12 Oct. 1666	1666/80
Owen ap Evan John	Llangurig Mg	Yeoman	W I R	6 Aug. 1696	1696/133
Owen ap Evan Thomas	Llanelltud Mr	–	W* I	11 Dec. 1661	1661/96
Owen Griffith Meyricke	Llanfair-iuxta-Harlech Mr	Gent.	W	25 Jan. 1674/5	1674/47
Owen ap Hugh	Llanfachreth Mr	–	B I	19 Nov. 1663	1663/99
Owen ap Hugh	Maentwrog Mr	–	I/G	12 Dec. 1667	1667/109
Owen ap Hugh	Penmynydd A	–	W I	24 March 1669/70	1669/49
Owen ap Hugh	Llandwrog (Modryn) Cn	–	Ac	n.d.	1682/44
Owen ap Hugh Bellis	Amlwch A	Yeoman	W I Al	15 Oct. 1690	1690/5
Owen ap Hugh ap Ievan	Llandecwyn Mr	–	W* B*	9 March 1640/1	1640/41
Owen ap Hugh ap Ievan	Llechylched A	–	W B	30 April 1640	1640/16
Owen ap Hugh ap Evan	Amlwch A	–	W*	22 April 1641	1641/4
Owen ap Hugh Bevan	Llangeinwen A	Yeoman	B I	6 Oct. 1697	1697/11
Owen ap Hugh Lewis	Llangaffo (Treverwydd) A	Yeoman	W	22 June 1648	1648/5
Owen Hugh Lewis	Edern Cn	–	W* I	6 June 1699	1699/61
Owen Hugh Owen	Llangelynnin Mr	–	B I	17 June 1664	1664/99
Owen ap Hugh Bowen	Llantrisant A	Yeoman	W I	6 Feb. 1688/9	1688/25
Owen Pugh Rowland	Trefdraeth A	–	B I*	14 Nov. 1694	1694/32
Owen ap Hugh Thomas	Pentraeth A	Labourer	W	n.d.[1]	1675/11
Owen ap John *Lloyd*	Trewalchmai A	–	W	11 June 1666	1666/37
Owen John David	Tal-y-llyn Mr	Slater	W Db	4 Aug. 1696	1696/109
Owen John David	[Deneio] (Pwllhely) Cn	Corviser	W I	14 Jan. 1698/9	1698/27
Owen ap John Ievan	Llanfihangel-y-traethau Mr	–	W	5 March 1647/8	1647/43

[1] Will dated 16 Aug. 1675.

Name	Parish & County	Status	Docs. Filed	Date of Probate/Admon.	Ref. No.
Owen John ap Evan	Llan Sant Catherin *alias* Cricieth Cn	Yeoman	I/G	2 July 1673	1673/32
Owen John Evan	Llanelltud (Maesytryfer) Mr	–	W I	3 July 1695	1695/74
Owen John Moris	Penmachno (Penybont) Cn	Yeoman	W I	10 Dec. 1694	1694/62
Owen ap John Owen	Llanfihangel[-y-Pennant] Cn	–	W*	28 May 1640	1640/30
Owen John Owen	Llechylched A	–	W	31 Jan. 1664/5	1664/42
Owen John Owen	Llanbedrog Cn	–	W	25 July 1666	1666/56
Owen John Owen	Tywyn Mr	Yeoman	W I	20 Sept. 1678	1678/60
Owen John Owen	Tal-y-llyn Mr	–	B	21 Feb. 1681/2	1681/83
Owen John ap Price	Llanddyfnan A	–	W I	n.d.[1]	1669/22
Owen John ap Rytherch	Llanfair-iuxta-Harlech (Cravenant) Mr	Gent.	W I	20 Sept. 1678	1678/46
Owen Lewis Edmund	Llechylched A	–	W I	23 Feb. 1691/2	1691/33
Owen ap Rees	Llaniestyn A	–	W	2 June 1665	1665/20
Owen ap Reignald	Llanbedrycennin Cn	–	B I	2 Feb. 1692/3	1692/49
Owen ap Rudderch	Llanystumdwy Cn	–	W I	16 Jan. 1665/6	1665/52
Owen ap Rytherch	Bangor Cn	Yeoman	B I	14 Feb. 1698/9	1698/20
Owen ap Richard	Clynnog Cn	–	W	8 March 1642/3	1642/22
Owen ap Richard	Llanfflewin A	–	W D	29 April 1647	1647/15
Owen ap Richard	Llanllechid Cn	–	W	6 Jan. 1647/8	1647/35
Owen ap Richard	Llanllyfni (Dôlbebyn) Cn	Gent.	W	1 June 1664	1664/76
Owen ap Richard	Llannerch-y-medd A	Labourer	W	27 May 1668	1668/23
Owen ap Richard	Llanfair-yn-neubwll A	Gent.	W I L	24 April 1669	1669/26
Owen ap Richard	Trefdraeth A	Shopkeeper	W I(2) Db	31 Jan. 1690/1	1690/39
Owen ap Richard	Bangor (Vodol ycha) Cn	–	B I	23 Jan. 1694/5	1694/41
Owen ap Richard ap Hugh ap John *alias* Owen Richards	Llangristiolus A	–	W(2) I Rd	24 Feb. 1664/5	1664/34
Owen ap Richard Lewis	Aberffraw A	Yeoman	W	3 June 1684	1684/3
Owen ap Richard Owen	Llanarmon / Aber-erch Cn	Weaver/Yeoman	B I R	6 Oct. 1693	1693/44
Owen ap Robert	Bodwrog (Mays y llyn) A	–	W	1 Aug. 1636	1636/5
Owen ap Robert	Llanfair-is-gaer Cn	–	B/I	2 Nov. 1666	1666/64
Owen ap Robert Lewis	[Llanfair-y-Cwmwd] A	–	W*	n.d.[2]	1660/4
Owen ap Robert Moris	Llanfair-yng-Nghornwy A	–	W I	18 Feb. 1662/3	1662/20
Owen Thomas Gruffyth	Caerhun Cn	Yeoman	W	28 July 1678	1678/21
Owen Thomas ap Howell	Llanrhychwyn Cn	–	W* Al*	18 July 1641	1641/43
Owen Thomas Meredith	Heneglwys A	–	B M	13 July 1664	1664/10

[1] Inventory exhibited 2 Feb. 1669/70.

[2] Will dated 9 Aug. 1659. Endorsed *1660*.

Name	Parish & County	Status	Docs. Filed	Date of Probate/Admon.	Ref. No.
Owen Thomas Rowland	Llanddyfnan A	–	W B	19 Feb. 1646/7	1646/7
Owen ap William David ap Lewis	Maenol Bangor Cn	–	W	n.d.[1]	1670/71
Owen Bwilliam Bedward	Llanrug (Ceafen tre Seiont) Cn	–	W I	4 May 1693	1693/59
Owen ap William Parry	[Amlwch] (Gweredog) A	–	W* I	n.d.[2]	1691/5
Owen ap William Lewis	Gyffin Cn	Yeoman	W	7 Feb. 1641/2	1641/31
Owen ap William Owen	Llanbedr Mr	Gent.	W I	13 May 1667	1667/89
Owen ap William Owen	Llanbedr / Llandanwg Mr	–	I/G	24 June 1692	1692/74
Owen ap William Prichard	Llechylched A	–	W	n.d.[3]	1669/47
Owen ap William Prichard	Pistyll Cn	–	W	22 Jan. 1680/1	1680/42
Owen ap William Rowland	Ceirchiog A	–	B I	7 April 1687	1687/3
Peirce, Peirs *see* Pierce					
Phillip John Phillip	Llandanwg Mr	–	W	5 July 1678	1678/44
Pierce ap Edward	Llanrhaeadr-yng-Nghinmeirch D	–	W	13 April 1671	1671/132
Peirs ap Evan	Amlwch A	Pedlar	W	14 Jan. 1644/5	1644/1
Peirce ap Evan	Llan-faes A	–	W	9 Jan. 1666/7	1666/16
Piers ap Harry	Rhuthun D	–	W*	23 April 1640	1640/60
Peirs ap Hugh	Llan-rhudd D	Gent.	W* I	1 Oct. 1670	1670/174
Piers ap Hugh	Derwen D	–	W* I	17 Jan. 1684/5	1684/87
Pierce ap John Rowland	Llanllechid Cn	–	W I	19 May 1685	1685/55
Peirc ap Richard	Llanllechid Cn	–	W	[30 July 1674]	1674/27
Piers ap Robert	Llanbedrycennin (Ardde) Cn	–	W	4 June 1663	1663/58
Piers ap William	Llangwyfan D	Yeoman	W I	7 Aug. 1668	1668/115
Randalph ap Humphrey	Gyffin Cn	Yeoman	W I	21 March 1663/4	1663/52
Rebeca vch William ap Edward	Llanrug Cn	Widow	W*	n.d.[4]	1698/44
Rees ap Edward	Llanddeiniolen Cn	–	B I*	27 Oct. 1670	1670/105
Rice ap Edward	Llanfwrog D	Weaver	B I*	11 Aug. 1694	1694/107
Rees ap Edward John	Llanaber Mr	Gent.	W(2) I	23 Aug. 1666	1666/83
Rees ap Evan	[Llangelynnin] (Llwyngoril) Mr	Yeoman	W I Rd	3 April 1666	1666/93
Rees ap Evan David	Llangwnnadl Cn	Weaver	W I	31 July 1689	1689/53

[1] Will dated 26 Sept. 1670.
[2] Inventory taken 10 Nov. 1691.
[3] Will dated 10 April 1669.
[4] Will dated [ ] March 1697/8. Endorsed *not proved but broug[ht] in 1698.*

Name	Parish & County	Status	Docs. Filed	Date of Probate/Admon.	Ref. No.
Rees ap Evan ap John	Carno Mg	Gent.	W I	14 April 1665	1665/93
Rees Gruffith Evan	Llanegryn Mr	Yeoman	B I	17 June 1664	1664/92
Rice Griffith John	Llanddwywe Mr	Yeoman	W I	20 June 1673	1673/55
Rees ap Howell ap Owen	Carno (Pentre'r nef) Mg	–	W	15 July 1636	1636/63
Rees ap Hugh	Llanfihangel-y-Pennant Mr	–	W* Al D	16 July 1674	1674/48
Rees ap Hugh	Llanfachreth (Bottan) A	Gent.	W Cd I	14 Oct. 1675	1675/4
Rees ap Hugh Griffith	Llanegryn Mr	–	W	29 Jan. 1669/70	1669/125
Rice ap Hugh Bowen	Llanidan A	Yeoman	W I	26 Feb. 1693/4	1693/19
Rice ap Hugh ap Rees	Llanfihangel-y-Pennant Mr	–	B I	12 June 1663	1663/105
Reece ap John	Llanrhaeadr-yng-Nghinmeirch (Segroit) D	Yeoman	W I	28 March 1663	1663/124
Rice ap John David	Derwen D	Yeoman	W	1 March 1682/3	1682/81
Rhese John David Prees *alias* Rhese Jones	Llanfaelrhys Cn	–	W* I	14 Jan. 1684/5	1684/44
Rees ap John Gruffyth	Dolgellau (Brithdir) Mr	–	W M	[ ] June 1641	1641/48
Rees ap John Thomas	Bangor Cn	–	W* I	19 Feb. 1671/2	1671/45
Rees Meredith Moris	Llangurig Mg	–	W I	11 Feb. 1685/6	1685/118
Rees Morgan Moris	Llangurig (Llanivyny) Mg	–	W I	[7 July 1687]	1687/131
Rees ap Morres ap Reignald	Llanrhychwyn Cn	–	W	13 May 1636	1636/37
Rees ap Owen John	Llangelynnin (Tyddyn Meirike bach) Mr	Gent.	W	[ ] 1693	1693/91
Rees ap Rees Edward	Llannerch-y-medd A	–	W	19 April 1642	1642/13
Rees ap Richard	Llanrhaeadr-yng-Nghinmeirch (Llan) D	Yeoman	W I	18 Nov. 1672	1672/117
Rees ap Richard	Llandanwg (Harleigh) Mr	–	W* I	8 March 1686/7	1686/75
Rees ap Richard	Llanddeusant A	Yeoman [/Shop-keeper]	B I	17 Aug. 1692	1692/12
Rice ap Richard Rowland	Llanrhuddlad & Holyhead A	Yeoman	W I	7 July 1675	1675/10
Rees ap Robert	Gyffylliog D	–	W	18 May 1686	1686/90
Rees ap Robert ap John	[?Llanrhaeadr-yng-Nghin-meirch] D	–	W*	10 Jan. 1638/9	1638/87
Rees ap William Moris	Llanddeiniolen Cn	Yeoman	B I	16 April 1661	1661/71
Rees William ap Rees	Llangelynnin Mr	Gent.	B I	10 June 1668	1668/101
Rees ap William ap Rees	Llanfair-y-Cwmwd A	Gent.	W Al	n.d.[1]	1675/5
Reignald ap Hugh	Clocaenog (Bryn-Gwrgi) D	–	W	19 Aug. 1671	1671/112
Rignald ap Robert	Caerhun Cn	Yeoman	B I	5 Oct. 1684	1684/32
Reignallt ap William ap Reignallt	Llanegryn Mr	Gent.	W I	3 July 1677	1677/56

[1] Will dated 18 Aug. 1675.

Name	Parish & County	Status	Docs. Filed	Date of Probate/Admon.	Ref. No.
Roderic ap Robert	Tywyn Mr	Yeoman	W	1 Feb. 1637/8	1637/39
Rhytherch ap Thomas	Llanelltud Mr	Gent.	W I B Rd	10 July 1662	1662/61
Rice *see* Rees					
Richard [ ] ap Ellissa	[Llanfachreth Mr]	–	W*	2 July 1638	1638/60
Richard ap David	Conway Cn	–	W	n.d.[1]	1644/20
Richard ap David	Llanllyfni Cn	Yeoman	B	22 July 1690	1690/73
Richard David *Lloyd*	Llanfair-is-gaer (Kreigg) Cn	–	W*	4 Sept. 1645	1645/28
Richard David Lewis	Llangelynnin Mr	Yeoman	W*	1 June 1636	1636/49
Richard David ap Robert	Llangelynnin (Llwyngwril) Mr	Yeoman	W	28 Sept. 1698	1698/57
Richard David ap William	Dolgellau Mr	–	W	24 April 1636	1636/43
Richard David William	Dolgellau Mr	–	I/G*	5 April 1671	1671/101
Richard ap Edward	Llanrhaeadr-yng-Nghinmeirch (Prion) D	–	B I	13 April 1671	1671/133
Richard ap Edward	Llanfachreth (Trenaney) Mr	–	W	n.d.[2]	1676/77
Richard Edward ap David ap Hugh	Llanrhychwyn Cn	–	W	16 May 1640	1640/34
Richard ap Elizey	Ynyscynhaearn Cn	–	B	30 Jan. 1678/9	1678/36
Richard ap Evan	Aber-erch Cn	–	B	28 Aug. 1666	1666/38
Richard ap Evan	Llanfihangel-y-Pennant Cn	Labourer	W Al B	4 Nov. 1676	1676/55
Richard ap Evan	Llandecwyn Mr	Yeoman	B I(2)	29 Aug. 1695	1695/71
Richard ap Ievan *Lloyd*	Llanidloes Mg	–	W M B Rd	5 Nov. 1636	1636/65
Richard Evan Humphery	Carno Mg	–	I/G	16 Oct. 1690	1690/117
Richard Evan John	Trefeglwys Mg	Yeoman	W	[14 Sept. 1688]	1688/107
Richard ap Evan ap Morgan	Edern Cn	Yeoman	W I	15 Feb. 1677/8[3]	1677/30
Richard Griffith David ap Rees	Llanfaethlu A	–	W	20 April 1644	1644/9
Richard Gruffith ap Hugh	Nantgwnnadl *alias* Llangwnnadl Cn	–	W Rd R B	9 April 1646	1646/22
Richard Gruffyth John	Llanenddwyn Mr	Yeoman	I	n.d.[4]	1664/96
Richard Griffith Lewis	Llanddyfnan A	–	W	31 July 1668	1668/12
Richard ap Harry	Llandecwyn Mr	–	W	13 June 1648	1648/16
Richard Howel ap Evan	Llanfachreth (Nanney) Mr	Yeoman	I/G R	30 May 1681	1681/75
Richarde ap Hughe	[Llandygái] (Kapel kirig) Cn	–	W*	[ ] April 1636	1636/32
Richard ap Hugh	Llangaffo (Treasseth) A	–	W	26 April 1669	1669/35
Richard ap Hugh	Llanystumdwy (Rendre) Cn	Freeholder	W I	[22 Feb. 1676/7]	1676/58

1 Will dated 11 April 1644.
2 Will dated 23 Sept. 1675; memorandum of omissions dated 1 June 1676.
3 Inventory taken 4 May 1661.
4 Inventory taken 14 May 1664.

Name	Parish & County	Status	Docs. Filed	Date of Probate/Admon.	Ref. No.
Richard ap Hugh	Llanelltud (Tre Nanney) Mr	Yeoman	W* I*	22 Sept. 1685	1685/75
Richard ap Hugh *Gwyn*	Llanllechid Cn	Yeoman	W I B	16 April 1696	1696/79
Richard ap Hugh *Lloyd*	Llangybi Cn	Shoemaker	W I	10 Feb. 1679/80	1679/26
Richard ap Hugh ap Davydd ap Ievan	Llanddaniel-fab A	–	W* Db*	9 Aug. 1636	1636/9
Richard ap Hugh ap Evan	Llanrhuddlad A	–	W I	6 July 1635	1635/8
Richard ap Hugh John	Dwygyfylchi Cn	–	W	4 Dec. 1663	1663/49
Richard ap Hugh Oliver	Pennal Mr	–	W I	22 July 1635	1635/37
Richard Pugh Bowen	Llangefni A	Yeoman/Gent.	W I	14 June 1692	1692/19
Richard ap Hugh ap Robert	Caerhun Cn	–	W C	13 Jan. 1665/6	1665/35
Richard ap Hugh Salesbury	Gwyddelwern[1] (Boteulog) Mr	Yeoman	W	17 Aug. 1696	1696/142
Richard ap Hugh ap William	Bodferin Cn	–	W	19 July 1644	1644/19
Richard ap Ievan *see* Richard ap Evan					
Richard John *Vaughan*	Trawsfynydd (Brynclynnog) Mr	Gent.	W* I	1 Aug. 1662	1662/74
Richard John ap Edward	Ynyscynhaearn Cn	–	W	2 May 1661	1661/88
Richard ap John ap Ievan	Llandyrnog D	–	W	3 Feb. 1646/7	1646/28
Richard John Evan	Llangwnnadl Cn	–	W Db	17 Oct. 1661	1661/78
Richard John Griffith	Llandwrog Cn	Yeoman/Slater	{B I {W(2) Al	13 Dec. 1695 22 Sept. 1696	1695/42 1696/58
Richard John Hooffe	Llanenddwyn Mr	Blacksmith	W I	29 July 1679	1679/42
Richard John ap Hugh *alias* Richard Jones	Llan-rhudd D	Gent.	W	19 Dec. 1691	1691/121
Richard ap John ap Llewelyn	Holyhead A	–	W*	30 April 1641	1641/8
Richard John Moris	Llanfrothen Mr	Yeoman	W I B	14 Oct. 1686	1686/80
Richard John ap Rees	Llanegryn Mr	Yeoman	W	27 Oct. 1668	1668/91
Richard ap John ap Richard	Llandyrnog D	Yeoman	W I	17 Oct. 1666	1666/100
Richard John ap Richard	Llanenddwyn Mr	–	W I	26 May 1691	1691/91
Richard John Robert *alias* Richard Jones	Aber-erch (Rhosfawr) Cn	Gent.	W* Rd	23 March 1663/4	1663/32
Richard ap John ap Roberte	Llanbeulan A	Yeoman	W I	29 Jan. 1663/4	1663/12
Richard John ap Robert	Llangwyfan A	Labourer	B I C	15 Dec. 1686	1686/20
Richard ap John ap Robert	Llanrhaeadr-yng-Nghinmeirch (Prion) D	Gent.	W	2 Aug. 1688	1688/95
Richard John ap William	Caerhun Cn	–	W	20 July 1640	1640/22
Richard Lewis Stukeley	Holyhead A	Gent./Yeoman	W I	10 Dec. 1698	1698/4

[1] Normally within the jurisdiction of the St. Asaph Consistory Court. Testator bequeaths property in the parish of Derwen, co. Denbigh, within the jurisdiction of the Bangor Consistory Court.

Name	Parish & County	Status	Docs. Filed	Date of Probate/Admon.	Ref. No.
Richard Lewis Thomas	Llanengan Cn	–	W D B	28 Jan. 1662/3	1662/47
Richard ap Morgan	Llanfihangel-y-traethau Mr	Gent.	W I	n.d.[1]	1688/81
Richard Morgan David	Aber-erch Cn	–	W I	6 July 1693	1693/31
Richard Owen *Lloid*	Gyffin (Gweredros) Cn	Gent.	W I	31 Aug. 1669	1669/69
Richard Owen Theodor	Penmynydd A	Esq.	W	10 June 1645	1645/11
Richard Owen Theodor	Penmynydd A	Esq.	B I	26 Feb. 1668/9	1668/28
Richard ap Rees	Llandwrog (Tuddyn Ellen) Cn	–	W I B	10 Jan. 1661/2	1661/65
Richard ap Rytherch	Penmachno Cn	–	W B Rd	22 May 1638	1638/50
Richart ap Rhudderch	Maentwrog Mr	Yeoman	W I	3 Jan. 1692/3	1692/82
Richard ap Richard	[Llanbeblig] (Carnarvon) Cn	–	W Al	19 Dec. 1693	1693/34
Richard ap Robert	Llanbedr Dyffryn Clwyd D	Yeoman	W I	2 June 1685	1685/93
Richard ap Robert ap David	Gyffylliog/[Llanynys] (Esceibion) D	–	W I	26 Jan. 1690/1	1690/113
Richard ap Robert John	Llanenddwyn Mr	Labourer	I/G	18 April 1693	1693/81
Richard ap Robert John	Llanberis Cn	Gent.	B* I*	19 April 1697	1697/24
Richard ap Robert ap Madog	Llanynys D	–	W B	20 April 1636	1636/60
Richard ap Robert Rowland	Llantrisant A	Yeoman	W I	19 Feb. 1693/4	1693/22
Richard ap Thomas	Llanynys (Bringerthel) D	–	W	17 June 1643	1643/52
Richard ap Thomas	Gyffylliog D	–	W I	18 July 1664	1664/111
Richard Thomas David	Llanegryn Mr	–	W I	2 May 1694	1694/83
Richard Thomas Griffith	Bryncroes Cn	Yeoman	W	[4 Sept.] 1669	1669/61
Richard Thomas ap Harry	Aberconway *alias* Conway Cn	–	W*	14 Feb. 1641/2	1641/27
Richard Thomas ap Hugh	Ceidio Cn	–	I/G	22 Jan. 1668/9	1668/40
Richard Thomas ap Hugh	Gyffin Cn	–	W	9 May 1674	1674/21
Richard Thomas Jefrey	Llanedwen A	–	W I	18 June 1689	1689/11
Richard Thomas ap Jenkin	Llandinam (Ma[es] mawr) Mg	–	W	30 Sept. 1635	1635/51
Richard Thomas John	Gyffylliog D	Yeoman	W I	6 June 1677	1677/72
Richard Thomas ap William Jeffrey	Llangristiolus A	–	W I	26 July 1670	1670/45
Richard ap William Andrew	Llangristiolus A	–	B	24 Jan. 1670/1	1670/46
Richard ap William Davyd[2]	Llanddeusant A	–	W	13 April 1674	1674/6
Richard ap William ap Edmond	Llanddeiniolen Cn	–	W*	20 Oct. 1643	1643/21
Richard ap William ap Evan	Bangor Cn	–	B	7 June 1672	1672/43
Richard ap William Parry	Llanynghenedl A	Gent.	W* Cd* Rd*	21 Sept. 1646	1646/9
Richard ap William ap Richard	Llanfihangel-y-traethau Mr	–	W	15 Aug. 1638	1638/62
Richard ap William Prichard	Llanfair-yng-Nghornwy (Cornwyllys) A	–	W	9 July 1672	1672/19

[1] Inventory taken 26 April 1688.

[2] *Richard ap Wm Rowland* in fiat endorsed on will.

Name	Parish & County	Status	Docs. Filed	Date of Probate/Admon.	Ref. No.
Richard ap William Probert	Llanddeusant A	Yeoman	W	[15 July 1674]	1674/7
Robert ap David	Llandanwg (Harlech) Mr	Yeoman	W	15 July 1640	1640/40
Robert ap David	Rhuthun D	[Wea]ver	W* I B	[ ][1] 1686	1686/103
Robert David *Lloyd*	Llanaber Mr	Gent./Yeoman	W I	19 Feb. 1669/70	1669/120
Robert David *Lloyd*	Llanystumdwy Cn	Yeoman	W	[18 May 1672]	1672/81
Robert David *Lloyd*	Llandudwen (Treferwyn) Cn	–	W I	17 May 1687	1687/57
Robert David Parry	Clocaenog D	–	B	25 May 1696	1696/114
Robert ap David ap Rees	Llanrhaeadr-yng-Nghinmeirch (Llewesog) D	Gent.	W	n.d.[2]	1682/90
Robert ap Edward	Llangynhafal D	–	W I	[15 Dec. 1673]	1673/63
Robert ap Edward	Llandanwg / Llandecwyn Mr	Gent.	W I	11 May 1681	1681/71
Robert ap Edward	Caerhun Cn	Yeoman	W I	15 March 1687/8	1687/44
Robert ap Edward	Llan-rhudd D	Yeoman	B I	11 April 1692	1692/102
Robert ap Ellis	Llandygái Cn	–	B	21 April 1669	1669/84
Robert ap Evan	Llandinam Mg	Gent.	W I	9 Jan. 1661/2	1661/132
Robert ap Evan	Llanelidan (Bryncymme) D	Yeoman	W I	2 May 1666	1666/102
Robert ap Evan	Clocaenog D	–	B I	5 March 1698/9	1698/61
Robert ap Evan Hugh	Holyhead A	–	B B	24 Sept. 1670 2 June 1671	1670/9 1671/12
Robert ap Evan Lewis	Aberdaron Cn	–	W	2 Feb. 1636/7	1636/22
Robert ap Evan ap Rees	Rhiw Cn	–	W B	19 May 1648	1648/14
Robert Griffith *Lloyd*	Dolgellau (Brithdir) Mr	Gent.	W I	15 Jan. 1676/7	1676/69
Robert Griffith ap Ivan	Llanfair [ ] A	–	W*	[ ] July 1638	1638/12
Robert ap Harry Butler	Llan-rhudd (Talesarne) D	–	W	19 March 1638/9	1638/84
Robert ap Howell	Llanddeusant A	–	W	29 Jan. 1640/1	1640/6
Robert ap Hugh	Conway Cn	Yeoman	W I C	14 March 1660/1	1660/15
Robert ap Hugh	Penmachno Cn	–	B I/L	21 Sept. 1664	1664/80
Robert ap Hugh	Llandegfan A	Gent.[/Harper]	W I	23 Nov. 1665	1665/8
Robert ap Hugh	Llangeinwen A	–	B	31 Dec. 1666	1666/23
Robert ap Hugh	Rhuthun D	Cook	W* I	10 Dec. 1666	1666/112
Robert ap Hugh	Llanrhaeadr-yng-Nghinmeirch (Prion) D	Yeoman	W	[25 March 1673]	1673/65
Robert ap Hugh	Llanrhuddlad A	Yeoman	W I	31 March 1682	1682/25
Robert ap Hugh	Llangïan Cn	Yeoman	W* I B	5 March 1684/5	1684/48
Robert ap Hugh *Gwynne*	[Llandwrog] (Bryn r Odin) Cn	–	B	8 April 1678	1678/28

1 Died 24 April 1686.
2 Will dated 15 Aug. 1674; endorsed *1682*.

Name	Parish & County	Status	Docs. Filed	Date of Probate/Admon.	Ref. No.
Robert ap Hugh ap David	Llandyrnog D	–	Rd	[23 Oct. 1622][1]	1674/56
Robert ap Hugh ap Evan	Llanarmon Cn	–	I L	27 April 1664	1664/64
Robert ap Hugh Bevan	Llanddyfnan A	–	B I	24 June 1686	1686/12
Robert ap Hugh Lewis	Llaniestyn Cn	–	W I	26 Dec. 1663	1663/67
Robert ap Hugh Morgan	Llandwrog Cn	–	W I	30 Jan. 1683/4	1683/35
Robert ap Hugh ap Robert	Holyhead (Llanvawr) A	Gent.	W I R	n.d.[2]	1669/9
Robert ap Hugh Probert	Llanfwrog A	–	B I	2 Aug. 1687	1687/16
Robert ap Hugh Probert	Pistyll Cn	–	W I	12 June 1694	1694/65
Robert ap Hugh ap Roger	Llanrhaeadr-yng-Nghinmeirch (Llech) D	Yeoman	W I	3 May 1682	1682/91
Robert ap Hugh Salesbury	Clocaenog D	–	W	27 May 1665	1665/77
Robert ap Humphrey	Maentwrog Mr	Gent.	B I	10 March 1663/4	1663/110
Robert John *Wynne*	Holyhead A	Gent.	W I Db	21 April 1677	1677/6
Robert ap John David	Llanrhaeadr-yng-Nghinmeirch D	–	W	17 Dec. 1647	1647/51
Robert John David	Llanfechell A	–	B I	9 Nov. 1685	1685/20
Robert John Edmund	Llanarmon Cn	Miller	I	n.d.	1641/32
Robert John Edward	Llanfrothen Mr	–	W	[10 April 1677]	1677/61
Robert ap John Gruffith	Llanrhaeadr-yng-Nghinmeirch (Myvod) D	–	W	4 June 1635	1635/47
Robert John Gruffyth	Llanrhychwyn (Kynllwyd) Cn	Yeoman	W Al	[8 May 1683]	1683/53
Robert John Griffith	[Gyffylliog] (Ffrithoedd) D	Yeoman	W I	n.d.[3]	1690/103
Robert John Gryffith	Dolgellau (Brithdir ucha) Mr	–	I/G	20 Sept. 1694	1694/73
Robert John ap Hugh	Llanegryn Mr	–	W(2)	3 March 1666[4]	1666/88
Robert John ap Humphrey	Llanberis Cn	–	B I	6 Jan. 1668/9	1668/54
Robert John Lewis	Derwen D	–	W	12 April 1679	1679/50
Robert John Lewis	Derwen D	Yeoman	B I	15 July 1692	1692/94
Robert John Lewis	Llanllechid Cn	Widower/Yeoman	B I	9 May 1693	1693/56
Robert John ap Moris	Cricieth Cn	Gent.	W I	26 Feb. 1669/70	1669/67
Robert John ap Morris	Trawsfynydd Mr	–	W	13 Dec. 1670	1670/160
Robert John ap Maurice	Llanllyfni (Berth) Cn	Yeoman	B I(2)	27 Oct. 1696	1696/81
Robert John ap Rees	Llanfrothen Mr	Yeoman	W*	3 Feb. 1699/1700	1699/113
Robert John ap Rhichard	Tal-y-llyn (Cwmrhwyddor) Mr	Yeoman/Gent.	W I B	22 July 1682	1682/78
Robert John ap Robert	Llanystumdwy Cn	–	W I	31 July 1684	1684/59
Robert John ap Robert	Derwen D	Yeoman	W	21 Sept. 1685	1685/90

[1] No copy filed of the will stated in the redelivery bond to have been proved in 1622.
[2] Inventory taken 27 Oct. 1669.
[3] Inventory taken 23 Oct. 1690.
[4] *3 April 1666* in endorsement on back of will.

Name	Parish & County	Status	Docs. Filed	Date of Probate/Admon.	Ref. No.
Robert John Thomas	Llanddaniel-fab A	–	I	n.d.[1]	1669/19
Robert John Tyddur	Clocaenog D	Yeoman	W	10 July 1671	1671/113
Robert ap John ap William	Ceirchiog A	–	W*	n.d.[2]	1641/5
Robert John Gwilim	Llanfechell A	Tailor	W	n.d.[3]	1669/31
Robert John ap William	Caerhun Cn	–	W Al	6 Nov. 1679	1679/21
Robert John William *alias* Robert Jones	Clocaenog (Waynpyscodlyn) D	Yeoman	W I	[9 July 1684]	1684/84
Robert ap Lowrence	Gyffin Cn	–	W	10 Aug. 1645	1645/23
Robert Morgan Howell	Llanbadrig A	–	B	15 Dec. 1670	1670/14
Robert ap Mores	Llannor Cn	Yeoman	W B	1 June 1647	1647/37
Robert Owen ap Evan	Llanaelhaearn Cn	–	B I R	30 Sept. 1686	1686/46
Robert Owen Lewis	Dolgellau (Brithdir) Mr	Gent.	W I	1 Oct. 1667	1667/84
Robert ap Rees	Llanfihangel Ysgeifiog A	–	W*	15 Jan. 1638/9	1638/13
Robert ap Rees *Wynne*	Llanelidan D	Gent.	W I	17 Jan. 1684/5	1684/92
Robert ap Rees William	Llanwenllwyfo A	–	W I B	25 June 1635	1635/10
Robert ap Rhydderch	Derwen D	–	B	1 Sept. 1669	1669/141
Robert ap Richard	Llanllyfni Cn	–	W*	25 Feb. 1640/1	1640/33
Robert ap Richard	Llandwrog (Talysarn) Cn	–	B I/R	29 April 1661	1661/66
Robert ap Richard	Llanenddwyn Mr	–	B	8 Nov. 1662	1662/62
Robert ap Richard	Llanbedr[?-goch] A	–	W*	n.d.[4]	1667/13
Robert ap Richard	Llanenddwyn Mr	Gent.	I(2)	27 July 1667	1667/100
Robert ap Richard	Ysbyty [Ifan] (Tre Eidde) Cn	–	B C	27 Oct. 1676	1676/62
Robert ap Richard	Llanfaglan Cn	–	B	19 Nov. 1684	1684/45
Robert ap Richard	Llangynhafal D	Gent.	W I	22 July 1689	1689/85
Robert ap Prichart David *Lloyd*	Llandwrog (Llyn y meibion) Cn	–	W M	17 July 1667	1667/68
Robert ap Richard ap Ievan David	Aberdaron Cn	–	W*	12 July 1637	1637/15
Robert ap Richard ap Hugh	Llanystumdwy Cn	–	W I Al Ir D	18 Nov. 1686	1686/65
Robert ap Richard ap John Roger	Llanbedr Dyffryn Clwyd D	Gent.	W(2)* I B	12 Feb. 1671/2	1671/118
Robert ap Richard Owen	Llanfihangel-y-Pennant Cn	Yeoman	W	n.d.[5]	1678/33
Robert ap Richard ap Rees	Llangynhafal D	Yeoman	W I Rd	4 July 1667	1667/126
Robert ap Robert	Llaniestyn Cn	Yeoman	W I	11 Jan. 1660/1	1660/17
Robert ap Robert	Llanynys D	Yeoman	B I	15 June 1661	1661/121
Robert ap Robert	Gyffylliog D	–	B	7 Aug. 1665	1665/79

1 Inventory taken 29 Sept. 1669.
2 Will dated 26 May 1641; endorsed *not proved*.
3 Will dated 16 Nov. 1669.
4 Will dated 27 Dec. 1667.
5 Will dated 6 Aug. 1678.

Name	Parish & County	Status	Docs. Filed	Date of Probate/Admon.	Ref. No.
Robert ap Robert ap Harry	Llanrhaeadr-yng-Nghinmeirch (Caerserwyd) D	–	W I	6 Jan. 1668/9	1668/124
Robert ap Roger	Llanrhaeadr-yng-Nghinmeirch D	–	B I	7 Dec. 1677	1677/84
Robert Symon Owen	Dolgellau Mr	–	W	2 Feb. 1637/8	1637/30
Robert ap Thomas	Llanfaelog A	–	W	9 Sept. 1636	1636/12
Robert ap Thomas	Llan-rhudd D	–	W	26 Sept. 1643	1643/51
Robert ap Thomas[1]	Llanfair Dyffryn Clwyd (Derwen Llanerch) D	–	W	8 Nov. 1670	1670/170
Robert ap Thomas	Llanbedr Dyffryn Clwyd D	Yeoman	W I	10 April 1677	1677/74
Robert ap Thomas	Llanrhaeadr-yng-Nghinmeirch D	Yeoman	W I	7 Dec. 1693	1693/119
Robert Thomas ap Howell	Pentraeth A	–	W*	16 March 1671/2	1671/40
Robert ap William	Llanynghenedl A	Yeoman	W I* B	1 March 1694/5	1694/30
Robert William *Wynne*	Llanaber Mr	–	B* I(2)	9 Oct. 1694	1694/79
Robert ap William ap Edward	Llangybi Cn	–	B I	30 Oct. 1667	1667/75
Robert ap William ap Eignione	Maentwrog Mr	–	W I	8 Aug. 1663	1663/111
Robert ap William ap Evan	Llanaber (Hendremynech) Mr	Gent.	R L[2]	25 May 1666	1666/84
Robert ap William ap Eviean	Gyffin (Boddath) Cn	Yeoman	W I	17 April 1667	1667/62
Robert ap William ap Evan	Holyhead A	Gent.	W I	7 Aug. 1667	1667/12
Robert ap William ap Hugh	Llechylched A	–	W*	8 April 1640	1640/15
Robert ap William Jeffrey	Derwen D	–	B	20 July 1672	1672/101
Robert ap William John	Aberdaron Cn	–	W	25 Oct. 1667	1667/48
Robert ap William ap Owen	Caerhun Cn	Yeoman	B I	[ ][3] 1682	1682/37
Robert ap William Prichard	Penmorfa (Gorllwyn) Cn	–	W I	14 April 1676	1676/59
Robert ap William Prichard	Llanengan Cn	Yeoman	W	15 Dec. 1690	1690/60
Robert ap William Roger	Llanddaniel-fab A	Yeoman	B I	23 April 1695	1695/5
Robert ap William Thomas	Llanfair-yn-neubwll A	–	W	8 Aug. 1684	1684/14
Robert William Thomas	Llaniestyn A	–	B	12 Nov. 1685	1685/25
Robert ap William Thomas	Llangelynnin (Ffrythlas) Cn	Yeoman	W I Db D	25 Sept. 1689	1689/50
Roderick *see* Rhydderch					
Roger ap Ellis	Llanynys D	Yeoman	W I	6 Sept. 1679	1679/59
Rowland ap Edward	Llanrhychwyn Cn	–	W I	15 Nov. 1693	1693/62
Rowland ap Edward	Llanddeiniolen Cn	Yeoman	W I Al Ir D	26 May 1696	1696/65
Rowland ap Hugh	Llanfaethlu A	–	W* Rd M	22 Aug. 1662	1662/19
Rowland Humphrey Gwilim	Amlwch A	–	I	n.d.[4]	1665/1

1 See also under Thomas, Robert, of Clynnog (document I).

2 Also relates to the administration of the goods of Gruffith John Phyllip of Llandanwg (q.v.).

3 Inventory taken 6 Nov. 1682.

4 Inventory taken 24 June 1665.

Name	Parish & County	Status	Docs. Filed	Date of Probate/Admon.	Ref. No.
Rowland John ap Richard	Llanbedr[-goch] A	Yeoman	W	26 Jan. 1660/1	1660/1
Rowland John ap Robert	Llanfair-yng-Nghornwy A	–	W	14 June 1645	1645/7
Rowland Lewis ap Hugh	Dolgellau (Brithdir issa) Mr	–	W Rd	n.d.[1]	1683/61
Rowland Price ap Hugh	Ffestiniog Mr	Yeoman	W	27 June 1668	1668/85
Rowland ap Reignalt	Llanberis Cn	–	B I	25 April 1672	1672/58
Rowland ap Rhytherch	Penmachno Cn	Yeoman	W I	19 June 1667	1667/82
Rowland ap Richard	Llanfachreth Mr	–	W	1 June 1636	1636/47
Rowland ap Richard	Llanddeiniolen Cn	Husbandman	W I	9 July 1664	1664/66
Rowland ap Richard	Llanfaethlu (Ty croes) A	–	B I	18 May 1694	1694/18
Rowland ap Prichard ap Howell	Llangefni A	Yeoman	W I	2 March 1681/2	1681/14
Rowland ap Richard William	Llangybi (Pentyrch) Cn	Yeoman	B I	13 Aug. 1691	1691/63
Rowland ap Robert	Llanbeblig Cn	–	B	20 June 1661	1661/59
Rowland ap Robert	Llangeinwen A	–	B*	4 [ ] 1672	1672/23
Rowland ap Robert	Trawsfynydd Mr	Labourer	W I C	[2 July 1687]	1687/105
Rowland ap Robert ap Ellis	Llandygái Cn	–	B	9 June 1686	1686/51
Rowland ap Robert Gruffithe	Llanbedr Niwbwrch A	–	W* B*	24 June 1637	1637/4
Rowland Thomas David ap Griffith	Llanddeiniolen Cn	–	W	22 April 1640	1640/27
Rowland Thomas Gruffyth	Aber Cn	Yeoman/Widower	W I	[16 Aug. 1679]	1679/16
Rowland ap William ap Edward	Llanbedr Niwbwrch A	–	W	22 Jan. 1635/6	1635/2
Roland ap William ap Hugh	Llaneilian A	–	W*	29 July 1640	1640/9
Rowland ap William James	Llangristiolus A	Yeoman	W I	17 April 1665	1665/18
Rowland ap William John	Caerhun Cn	Yeoman	B I	1 Oct. 1677	1677/27
Rowland ap William Prees	Caerhun Cn	Yeoman	W I	n.d.[2]	1681/34
Samson ap Robert	Llanynys D	Yeoman	W I*	7 April 1662	1662/92
Samuel ap William Morgan	Llandygái Cn	–	B I	10 April 1694	1694/51
Sara vch David ap William	Llandegfan A	Widow	W I*	21 April 1664	1664/17
Sarah vch Richard ap David	Pentraeth A	Widow	W I	18 Jan. 1670/1	1670/58
Sara vch Robert Lewis	Penrhos[llugwy] A	Widow [of John Owen]	W I	4 Feb. 1679/80	1679/14
Symon ap Howell	Llanfachreth [Mr/A]	–	W	30 Nov. 1647	1647/42
Sionet *see* Jonet					
Stukeley ap William Bevan	Llechylched A	Yeoman	B	29 Aug. 1699	1699/35

1 Proved by 23 April 1683 according to bond for redelivery of will.
2 Inventory taken 8 June 1681.

Name	Parish & County	Status	Docs. Filed	Date of Probate/Admon.	Ref. No.
Thomas ap David ap Griffith	Llanrhaeadr-yng-Nghinmeirch D	–	W Rd	12 May 1643	1643/49
Thomas David ap Harry	Llandyrnog D	–	W Rd	24 Feb. 1647/8	1647/45
Thomas David Rees	Llanbedr Dyffryn Clwyd D	–	W Rd	14 June 1643	1643/44
Thomas David ap William	Carno Mg	Yeoman	W I	28 Oct. 1672	1672/124
Thomas ap Edward	Trawsfynydd Mr	Yeoman	W*	11 Feb. 1640/1	1640/48
Thomas ap Ellice	Llanfair Dyffryn Clwyd D	Gent.	W	18 April 1638	1638/78
Thomas ap Ievan	Llanwnda (Rhydynog felen) Cn	Yeoman	W	15 May 1641	1641/44
Thomas ap Evan	Llanfair Dyffryn Clwyd D	Yeoman	W(2) Rd	n.d.[1]	1681/94
Thomas ap Evan	Bangor Cn	–	I	n.d.[2]	1682/34
Thomas ap Evan	Carnguwch Cn	Yeoman	W	23 Nov. 1686	1686/40
Thomas ap Evan	Llanynys (Pant glâs) D	–	W(2)	9 July 1689	1689/87
			B	24 Aug. 1692	1692/105
			B	28 Aug. 1693	1693/121
Thomas ap Evan David	Derwen D	–	W I	25 Feb. 1678/9	1678/64
Thomas ap Evan Griffith	Llangïan (Nanhoron) Cn	Yeoman	W	25 July 1647	1647/34
Thomas ap Ievan ap Ierwerth	Llanfachreth [A]	–	W	28 Jan. 1642/3	1642/8
Thomas ap Evan Lewis	Heneglwys A	Gent.	W* I B Rd	15 Oct. 1667	1667/8
Thomas ap Evan Phillippe	Llanidloes Mg	–	B	3 Oct. 1678	1678/92
Thomas Evan Rees	Llanidloes Mg	–	I/G	27 Sept. 1667	1667/139
Thomas Griffyth ap Richarde	Llangwnnadl Cn	–	W Db	22 Feb. 1643/4	1643/25
Thomas ap Harrie	Llangoed A	–	W/I	23 Oct. 1688	1688/23
Thomas ap Hugh	Llanddeiniolen Cn	Miller	W	[14 June 1673]	1673/37
Thomas ap Hugh	Llandegfan A	–	B I	23 Sept. 1678	1678/4
Thomas ap Hugh Bevan	Llangeinwen A	Yeoman	W(2) I Al Ir	16 June 1691	1691/27
Thomas ap Hugh ap William	Llantrisant A	–	W* I*	18 June 1641	1641/18
Thomas ap Ievan *see* Thomas ap Evan					
Thomas ap John	Llaneilian A	–	W B	31 July 1635	1635/4
Thomas ap John	Dolgellau Mr	–	W	17 June 1664	1664/84
Thomas John *Lloyd alias* Thomas Lloyd	Derwen D	–	W I	18 May 1687	1687/112
Thomas John David *Lloyd*[3]	Llandudno Cn	–	W I R G/R L	20 Oct. 1670	1670/102
Thomas ap John Gruffyth	Aber-erch Cn	–	W*	9 July 1638	1638/31
Thomas John Griffith	Llanddeiniolen (Vachwen) Cn	Yeoman	W I	n.d.[4]	1683/37

1 Will dated 19 March 1680; redelivery bond dated 2 Jan. 1681 (33 Chas. II).
2 Inventory taken 16 Dec. 1682.
3 See also Gaynor vch William Prees (endorsement on document M).
4 Will dated 19 Aug. 1683.

Name	Parish & County	Status	Docs. Filed	Date of Probate/Admon.	Ref. No.
Thomas ap John ap Hughe	Llanfihangel-y-Pennant [Mr]	–	W	1 June 1636	1636/48
Thomas John Lewis	Llanfihangel Tre'r-beirdd A	Yeoman	W*	11 M[ay] 1674	1674/11
Thomas John Owen	Llangïan Cn	–	W	17 Sept. 1644	1644/26
Thomas John ap Rees	Llanfair Mathafarn Eithaf A	Yeoman	W Rd	21 Sept. 1676	1676/14
Thomas John ap Reingnald	Llanelidan (Garthneuodd) D	–	W I	9 April 1681	1681/91
Thomas John ap Rutherch	Llanfair-iuxta-Harlech Mr	Bachelor	B I	17 June 1664	1664/97
Thomas ap John ap Richard	Clynnog Cn	–	W B	3 Sept. 1635	1635/22
Thomas ap John Thomas	Bodwrog A	–	W* I G Rd*	16 Oct. 1662	1662/5
Thomas ap John Thomas	Llanelidan (Garthneuodd) D	–	W I	19 Dec. 1693	1693/106
Thomas ap John ap William	Llanfachreth [Mr]	–	W*	19 July 1641	1641/52
Thomas John William	Llandecwyn Mr	Gent.	W I B	15 May 1688	1688/74
Thomas ap John William	Penllech Cn	Husbandman	B I	n.d.[1]	1689/60
Thomas ap Morys	Pentraeth A	Yeoman	W I	26 May 1635	1635/12
Thomas ap Moris	Gyffylliog D	Yeoman	W I(2)	24 April 1668	1668/106
Thomas Owen John	Llanfair Mathafarn Eithaf A	Yeoman	W I	27 Nov. 1695	1695/7
Thomas ap Rees	Gyffylliog D	–	W	5 Oct. 1637	1637/42
Thomas ap Rees *Wynne*	Llanelidan (Garthneuodd) D	Yeoman	W I	[28 June] 1663	1663/121
Thomas ap Rees ap John ap Jenkyn	Llanfair Dyffryn Clwyd D	–	W*	28 Sept. 1638	1638/79
Thomas ap Rees Lewies	Llanddeiniolen (Dinorwicke) Cn	Yeoman	W/I	29 July 1669	1669/86
Thomas ap Rees Owen	Llanllibio A	–	I	n.d.[2]	1665/21
Thomas Rees Owen	Llanfechell A	–	B	13 Dec. 1667	1667/25
Thomas ap Reignald	Dwygyfylchi Cn	–	B	3 July 1682	1682/40
Thomas ap Richard	Llangristiolus A	–	W	13 March 1636/7	1636/16
Thomas ap Richard	Bangor (Brithtire) Cn	Youngman	W B	3 June 1645	1645/19
Thomas ap Richard	Penystrowed Mg	–	B I	16 June 1663	1663/153
Thomas ap Richard	Llanystumdwy Cn	–	I*	n.d.[3]	1671/90
Thomas ap Richard	Tal-y-llyn / Llanfihangel [-y-Pennant] Mr	–	W I	26 Aug. 1684	1684/76
Thomas ap Richard Lewis	Llangelynnin [Cn/Mr]	–	W I	4 June 1663[4]	1663/65
Thomas ap Richard William	Llangelynnin Cn	–	W Al B	18 Nov. 1642	1642/25
Thomas ap Robert	Llangeinwen (Tre-Bill) A	–	W	28 July 1635	1635/7
Thomas ap Robert	Llanrhaeadr-yng-Nghinmeirch (Segroit) D	Shearman	W* C	29 Nov. 1666	1666/106

1 Inventory taken 17 June 1689.
2 Died 29 April 1665.
3 Inventory exhibited 7 April 1671.
4 Inventory taken 27 April 1650.

Name	Parish & County	Status	Docs. Filed	Date of Probate/Admon.	Ref. No.
Thomas ap Robert	Caerhun Cn	–	W	n.d.[1]	1667/56
Thomas ap Robert	Caerhun (Kefn) Cn	Gent.	W	4 Aug. 1671	1671/50
Thomas ap Robert	Llanbedr Dyffryn Clwyd D	–	W	18 Nov. 1672	1672/104
Thomas ap Robert & Ann Powel his wife	[ ]	–	I	n.d.[2]	1675/74
Thomas ap Robert	Llanfachreth (Vriog, Nanney) Mr	–	B I	27 Aug. 1694	1694/86
Thomas ap Robert Cadwaleder	Caerhun Cn	Yeoman	B* I*	1 May 1699	1699/48
Thomas ap Robert ap Edward	Llanfair Dyffryn Clwyd (Keelan) D	Yeoman	W* I	18 May 1686	1686/97
Thomas ap Robert ap Evan	Llanfaelrhys Cn	–	B* I	10 [ ] 1686	1686/55
Thomas ap Robert ap Hugh	Rhuthun D	Butcher	W I	20 July 1670	1670/178
Thomas ap Robert ap Rees	Gyffylliog D	–	W I	8 Feb. 1672/3	1672/103
Thomas Rowland Owen	[Llanbeulan] (Tal-y-llyn) A	–	W	27 July 1642	1642/5
Thomas ap Thomas	Llanystumdwy Cn	Corviser	B I	14 Dec. 1685	1685/60
Thomas ap Thomas	Llanelidan D	–	W I	3 March 1687/8	1687/118
Thomas ap Thomas	Bodedern (Manaw) A	–	W I	6 Jan. 1690/1	1690/8
Thomas ap William	Penmynydd A	–	W	5 July 1638	1638/26
Thomas ap William	Gyffin Cn	–	W	12 May 1648	1648/10
Thomas ap William Edmond	Rhodogeidio (Pwll y Gynne) A	Gent.	W I	8 Dec. 1693	1693/26
Thomas ap William ap Edward	Llandygái (Penrhyn) Cn	Steward	B I	10 July 1683	1683/36
Thomas ap William ap Ievan	Llangaffo A	–	W*	7 Sept. 1638	1638/17
Thomas ap William Bevan	Llanddeiniolen Cn	–	B I	23 Feb. 1687/8	1687/62
Thomas ap William Bevan	Llanbeblig Cn	–	B	10 Jan. 1694/5	1694/49
Thomas ap William Pue	Llangristiolus A	–	W I	1 Aug. 1673	1673/12
Thomas ap William John	Llanddeiniolen (Tu Mawre) Cn	Yeoman	W I B	17 Feb. 1669/70	1669/87
Thomas ap William Lewis	Llanddeiniolen Cn	–	W I	7 May 1690	1690/59
Thomas ap William Lewis	Llangwyfan A	Yeoman	W* I	30 Jan. 1693/4	1693/18
Thomas ap William Morgan	Llanbeblig Cn	Yeoman	W Rd	17 Oct. 1661	1661/60
Thomas ap William Price	Derwen D	–	W I	27 Feb. 1692/3	1692/95
Thomas ap William Prees	Penmynydd A	Yeoman	W I	23 March 1699/1700	1699/36
Thomas ap William Prichard	Dwygyfylchi Cn	–	B I	3 March 1663/4	1663/50
Thomas ap William ap Rowland	Llandegfan A	–	B I	16 May 1681	1681/6
Thomas ap William Rowland	Amlwch A	–	B	30 April 1689	1689/5
Trevor John ap Hugh	Llandwrog Cn	–	B I	16 May 1673	1673/35
Tydyr ap Robert *Wynne*	Llanynys (Maesmonkymro) D	Yeoman	W	7 July 1682	1682/93
Tudor ap Robert William	Llanfihangel-y-traethau Mr	–	I	8 April 1695	1695/77

1 Will dated 15 Feb. 1667.

2 Inventory exhibited July 1675.

Name	Parish & County	Status	Docs. Filed	Date of Probate/Admon.	Ref. No.
William ap Arthur	Llanegryn Mr	Yeoman	W/I	18 Oct. 1678	1678/45
William ap Arthur	Llanllechid Cn	–	B I	18 Dec. 1680	1680/34
William ap Arthur	Tywyn Mr	–	I/G	18 Sept. 1694	1694/98
William ap Arthyr	Llanbeblig Cn	Yeoman	B I	2 Sept. 1695	1695/35
William David *Lloyd*	Llanfachreth Mr	–	I/G	10 Aug. 1669	1669/128
William David *Lloyd*	Bangor Cn	–	W I	12 May 1680	1680/20
William David ap Ievan	Llan[ystumdwy] Cn	–	W*	19 May 1642	1642/30
William David ap Bivan	Llanrhuddlad A	Yeoman	W Rd	30 Sept. 1686	1686/21
William David ap Hugh	Llaneilian A	Yeoman	W I	n.d.[1]	1667/18
William David ap John	Llanbabo A	–	W	4 March 1672/3	1672/11
William David John	Tywyn (Bron y prys) Mr	Yeoman	W(2) I(2)	6 May 1680	1680/61
William David Lewis	Carno Mg	Gent.	W I	21 Sept. 1665	1665/94
William David ap Nicholas	Penmachno Cn	–	W*	16 Feb. 1638/9	1638/51
William David ap Robert	Coedana A	Yeoman	W*	29 April 1641	1641/7
William ap Edward	Llanfachreth [Mr]	–	W*	25 Sept. 1635	1635/35
William ap Edward	Tregaean A	Weaver	W I	5 May 1670	1670/62
William ap Edward	Llanberis (Llwynbedw) Cn	–	B I	11 Feb. 1690/1	1690/54
William ap Edward	Llangelynnin Cn	Yeoman	W I	17 May 1692	1692/52
William ap Edward ap David	Llangefni A	–	W	31 Dec. 1638	1638/18
William ap Edwart John	Llangefni A	Gent.	W I	n.d.[2]	1685/23
William ap Ellice	Maenol Bangor Cn	Yeoman	W	1 Oct. 1661	1661/43
William ap Elis	Beaumaris A	Carpenter	W I	11 May 1664	1664/7
William ap Ellis	Llanbedrycennin (Arthey) Cn	–	W I	9 July 1668	1668/52
William ap Ellis	Llangelynnin Mr	–	W I	25 Nov. 1679	1679/45
William ap Eliza	Dolgellau Mr	–	B I	26 July 1661	1661/92
William ap Elisha	Beddgelert Cn	–	W	17 June 1675	1675/16
William ap Elisa	Ffestiniog (Glanypwll) Mr	–	W I	[7 April 1677]	1677/51
William ap Ellisse	Llanelltud Mr	–	W I	19 April 1693	1693/79
William ap Evan	Tywyn Mr	–	W	13 Sept. 1635	1635/39
William ap Evan	Tywyn Mr	–	W B	2 July 1638	1638/69
William ap Evan	Llanrhaeadr-yng-Nghinmeirch D	Husbandman	W B	28 Sept. 1641	1641/65
William ap Evan	[Llangelynnin] (Llwyngwrill) Mr	–	W	20 June 1667	1667/108
William ap Evan	Llanrug (Cau poyth) Cn	Gent.	W* I Rd	6 Oct. 1670	1670/122
William ap Evane	Trefdraeth A	–	W	9 Aug. 1675	1675/12

[1] Inventory taken 17 Sept. 1667.

[2] Inventory taken 28 Sept. 1685.

Name	Parish & County	Status	Docs. Filed	Date of Probate/Admon.	Ref. No.
William ap Evan	Ffestiniog Mr	–	W	n.d.[1]	1677/52
William ap Evan	Llanenddwyn Mr	–	B* I	17 April 1677	1677/59
William ap Ievan *Lloyd*	Derwen D	–	W	n.d.[2]	1641/56
William ap Evan Edmund	Llangeinwen A	–	W	19 Feb. 1637/8	1637/8
William ap Evan ap Edward[3]	Trawsfynydd Mr	–	B	13 Feb. 1666/7	1666/97
William ap Evan ap Edward	Llanaber Mr	–	W*	7 Aug. 1672	1672/89
William Bevan Meredith	Llanrug Cn	–	B I	2 June 1682	1682/56
William ap Evan Morgan	Llanfrothen (Ynusffordd) Mr	Yeoman	W I B	6 Feb. 1679/80	1679/44
William ap Evan ap Morgan	Botwnnog Cn	–	W I Rd	n.d.[4]	1683/23
William ap Ievan ap Moris	Aberffraw A	–	W	9 March 1638/9	1638/2
William ap Ievan ap Robert	Llanbadrig A	–	W B	11 May 1642	1642/4
William ap Ievan Thomas	Llangelynnin Mr	–	W B	25 Sept. 1635	1635/36
William Griffith John	Llanarmon Cn	–	W I	[ ] March 1699/1700	1699/64
William Gruffyth Lewis	Llanfihangel-y-Pennant Cn	–	I*	11 Feb. 1670/1	1670/112
William Parry David	Llanbadrig (Rhydcroes) A	–	B	5 July 1689	1689/8
William ap Harry Gruffith	Llanfaglan Cn	–	W* B*	21 July 1640	1640/28
William Parry Owen	Amlwch A	–	W	13 July 1672	1672/3
William Parry Thomas	Aber Cn	Yeoman	B I	19 Feb. 1696/7	1696/31
William ap Hugh	Llanbedrycennin Cn	Miller	W	30 May 1636	1636/30
William ap Hugh	Llangeinwen A	Yeoman	W I	22 Feb. 1663/4	1663/27
William ap Hugh	Llanfair-yng-Nghornwy A	Yeoman	B	1 June 1691	1691/22
William ap Hugh Parry	Coedana A	–	W I B	23 March 1666/7	1666/8
William Pugh ap Harry	Aberdaron Cn	Yeoman	W I	27 Jan. 1686/7	1686/26
William Pue ap Hugh ap Rhydderch	Llanrhwydrys A	–	W	n.d.[5]	1673/14
William ap Hugh John	Llangristiolus A	–	B I	15 April 1668	1668/20
William Pugh Lewis	Llangoed A	–	B I	16 June 1668	1668/19
William Pugh Lewis	Amlwch A	–	W I B	17 Aug. 1688	1688/3
William Pugh ap Owen	Caerhun Cn	Gent.	W* I* B	14 July 1671	1671/51
William Hugh Thomas	Llanarmon Cn	–	B I	21 April 1668	1668/51
William Pugh Thomas	Llangeinwen A	–	B I	28 May 1687	1687/18
William ap Hugh ap William & Ellen Owen his wife	Llanfechell A	–	B	13 Aug. 1661	1661/17

[1] Will dated 16 Feb. 1677.
[2] Will dated 25 Nov. 1641.
[3] Endorsed *Evan ap William ap Edward.*
[4] Inventory taken 14 July 1683.
[5] Will dated 20 Oct. 1673.

Name	Parish & County	Status	Docs. Filed	Date of Probate/Admon.	Ref. No.
William ap Hugh ap William	Llanfihangel Dinsylwy A	Yeoman	I R	n.d.[1]	1695/9
William ap Humffrey	Llanfairfechan Cn	–	B	17 Feb. 1668/9	1668/64
William ap Humffrey	Llanddeiniolen Cn	–	W*	21 [?April] 1670	1670/106
William ap Humphrey	Llanengan Cn	–	W I	18 Dec. 1670	1670/109
William ap Humphrey	Llanenddwyn Mr	Yeoman	W I	6 Aug. 1670	1670/150
William ap Humphrey	[Llanfihangel-y-traethau] (Plâs ucha) Mr	–	W*	n.d.[2]	1676/80
William ap Humphrey	Llanllyfni Cn	–	B	14 June 1677	1677/43
William ap Humffrey	Trawsfynydd (Goppa) Mr	–	W I B	27 Jan. 1679/80	1679/48
William Bumfrey ap [ ]	Llanrhaeadr-yng-Nghinmeirch (Brynbagle) D	Drover	W*	7 [ ]ember 1684	1684/99
William ap Ievan *see* William ap Evan					
William ap Sir John	Llangoed A	–	W* B*	3 Dec. 1641	1641/15
William ap John	Llanfair Dyffryn Clwyd (Vaynol) D	Tailor	W I Al B	5 June 1668	1668/111
William John *Lloyd*	Dolgellau Mr	Carpenter/ Yeoman	W I	10 June 1668	1668/83
William John *Vaughan*	Bryncroes Cn	–	W I	28 June 1661	1661/47
William John ap David ap Hughe	Bangor Cn	–	W	5 April 1643	1643/15
William John David ap Rees	Tywyn Mr	Yeoman	W	13 April 1637	1637/40
William John ap Evan	Llechgynfarwy A	–	W	23 April 1641	1641/19
William John Ivan	Llaneugrad A	–	W I	20 March 1660/1	1660/3
William John ap Ievan	Llanaber Mr	–	B I*	2 Oct. 1662	1662/60
William John ap Evan	Trawsfynydd Mr	Yeoman	W	6 Feb. 1667/8	1667/113
William John ap Evan	Llanllechid (Tythyn y fedw) Cn	–	W I	15 March 1672/3	1672/72
William John ap Evan	Holyhead A	–	B I R	14 Feb. 1687/8	1687/4
William John Griffith	Tywyn Mr	–	B I	10 Sept. 1661	1661/110
William John Gruffith	Llanllechid Cn	–	{W	n.d.[3]	1662/51
			{W	n.d.	1672/71
William John Griffith	Rhoscolyn A	–	W	21 May 1667	1667/44
William John Griffith	Llandyfrydog A	–	B	16 Dec. 1682	1682/12
William ap John ap Harry	Trewalchmai A	–	W*	30 April 1633	1633/2

[1] Renunciation dated 3 Feb. 1695.

[2] Will dated 15 Feb. 1676.

[3] Will filed under 1662 not dated, but a copy of the same nuncupative will, filed under 1672, is dated Allsaints 1670, witnessed 3 April 1672 and endorsed *Wills not proved*.

Name	Parish & County	Status	Docs. Filed	Date of Probate/Admon.	Ref. No.
William ap John ap Hoell	Llanrhaeadr-yng-Nghinmeirch (Myvod) D	–	W Rd	9 March 1647/8	1647/52
William John ap Hugh	Heneglwys A	–	B* I*	5 Aug. 1662	1662/9
William John ap Hugh	Llanfairfechan Cn	–	B I	26 Jan. 1664/5	1664/70
William John ap Hugh	Aber-erch Cn	–	W	23 May 1672	1672/40
William John ap Hughe	Tywyn Mr	Yeoman	B I	7 April 1677	1677/67
William John ap Hugh	Llanbedr (Mochres) Mr	–	W I	13 Feb. 1689/90	1689/66
William *Wynne* ap John ap Humffrey	Ffestiniog Mr	–	B	3 June 1661	1661/94
W[illiam] John Lewis	[ ] A	Smith	W*	n.d.[1]	1640/18
William John Lewis	Dolgellau Mr	–	W/I	28 May 1669	1669/116
William John ap Morgan	Aberffraw A	Gent.	B I L	4 Sept. 1666	1666/1
William John Morgan	Maenol Bangor[2] Cn	Yeoman	W I Al	[4 Nov. 1681]	1681/30
William John Moris	Clynnog Cn	–	W I	1 March 1672/3	1672/50
William John Owen	Llangïan Cn	–	W I	29 Dec. 1676	1676/57
William John Prees	Llandegfan A	–	B I	23 May 1699	1699/13
William John ap Rees *Wyn*	Aberffraw A	–	W	11 Aug. 1638	1638/3
William John ap Richard	Llanddeiniolen (Llys) Cn	Yeoman	W* I* C*	2 May 1696	1696/66
William John Robins	Llanfair Pwllgwyngyll A	Yeoman	B I	1 May 1693	1693/12
William John Rowland	Llangeinwen (Mossoglen) A	Yeoman	W I C	22 Oct. 1661	1661/20
William John Rowland	Llanllechid Cn	Yeoman	B I	29 Jan. 1696/7	1696/80
William ap John Simon	Llanrhaeadr-yng-Nghinmeirch D	–	W B	11 Feb. 1637/8	1637/47
William John Simond	Dolgellau Mr	Yeoman	B I*	16 June 1664	1664/85
William John Thomas	Penrhosllugwy A	–	B	31 Dec. 1689	1689/26
William John Thomas	Llanidan (Pentre Berow) A	–	B I	13 Dec. 1693	1693/20
William John Wattkin	Amlwch A	–	B I	2 July 1688	1688/4
William ap John ap William	Llanbadrig A	Yeoman	W	n.d.[3]	1674/4
William John William	Llanaber Mr	–	W I	[31 Jan. 1675/6]	1675/39
William Morgan ap Evan	Llanberis Cn	Yeoman	W	23 Nov. 1636	1636/31
William Morgan ap William Gwilim	Llandwrog Cn	–	I C	2 March 1669/70	1669/81
William Moris Evan	Ynyscynhaearn (Garegvelen) Cn	Yeoman	W I	17 April 1665	1665/58
William Moris Evan	Llanbeblig Cn	–	B I	2 Nov. 1692	1692/48
William Morris James	Maenol Bangor Cn	Gent.	W I	9 Feb. 1692/3	1692/34
William Morris John	Dolbenmaen Cn	Yeoman	W I	29 Dec. 1692	1692/44

1 Will dated [ ] July 1640.

2 Endorsed *Pentir*.

3 Will dated 18 March 1674 (27 Chas. II).

Name	Parish & County	Status	Docs. Filed	Date of Probate/Admon.	Ref. No.
William Moris ap Llewelin	Llanddeiniolen Cn	Gent.	W Rd	28 April 1641	1641/37
William Moris ap Rudderch	Llanfihangel-y-Pennant [Cn]	–	W* I	[31 May 1673]	1673/40
William Owen *Wynne*	Llanbedr Niwbwrch A	–	B* I	23 Oct. 1685	1685/14
William Owen David	Llanddwywe (Ffrith y brin coch) Mr	Yeoman	W I	29 Dec. 1691	1691/87
William Owen ap Howell	Bodedern (Treyngharad) A	–	W	24 Nov. 1646	1646/3
William Owen Humphrey	Pentraeth A	Yeoman	W* C	[9 Sept. 1670]	1670/59
William Owen John	Llandysilio A	Yeoman	W I	27 April 1698	1698/5
William Owen Mredith	Llanfflewin A	–	W(2)	13 March 1633/4	1633/1
William Prees David	Llanenddwyn Mr	–	I/G	22 June 1693	1693/82
William ap Prees Lewis	Llanwenllwyfo A	–	G	26 Oct. 1666	1666/28
William ap Rees ap Llewelyn	Llanfair-y-Cwmwd A	–	W L	22 Nov. 1667	1667/22
William Price Williams	Pennal Mr	–	I/G	16 April 1694	1694/94
William ap Reinald	Llanbedrycennin (Ardde) Cn	–	B I	26 May 1663	1663/59
William ap Reginald	Llanfairfechan Cn	Yeoman	W I	30 March 1696	1696/69
William ap Richart	Llanegryn Mr	–	W	13 July 1665	1665/65
William ap Richard	Penrhos[llugwy] A	Fuller	W I	9 June 1665	1665/24
William ap Richard	Llantrisant A	–	B*	2 Oct. 1676	1676/22
William ap Prichard	Llandygwnning Cn	–	B	28 April 1681	1681/48
William ap Richard	Aber Cn	–	B I	7 Jan. 1684/5	1684/26
William ap Richard	Tywyn Mr	Labourer	W* Al Ir D	[16 Feb.] 1686/7	1686/85
William ap Richard	Llangristiolus A	Yeoman	B	3 June 1692	1692/23
William ap Richard *Glyn*	Llanarmon Cn	–	W B	18 Feb. 1636/7	1636/29
William ap Richard Griffyth	Penmynydd A	–	W	28 April 1637	1637/12
William Prichard ap Hugh	Llanwnda Cn	Labourer	W	n.d.	1660/18
William Prichard John	Llanwnda (Havod y Wern) Cn	Yeoman	B I	15 July 1669	1669/101
William Prichard Jones	Holyhead A	Yeoman	W	24 March 1685/6	1685/11
William Prichard John	Dolgellau (Brithdir ycha) Mr	Gent.	W I Rd	11 July 1694	1694/74
William ap Richard ap Morgan	Pentir Cn	–	W	15 May 1638	1638/52
William Prichard Morgan	Llangeinwen A	–	B*	16 Oct. 1662	1662/24
William Prychard Morgan	Bodwrog (Cors-r-eira) A	–	I	n.d.[1]	1672/6
William Prichard ap Rees	Llanfaethlu (Borthwen) A	Yeoman	W I	28 Oct. 1670	1670/35
William Prichard ap Rees	Llanddeiniolen Cn	–	W I	6 Nov. 1678	1678/29
William ap Richard ap Robert	Llanbeblig Cn	–	W I R	13 May 1635	1635/28
William ap Richard ap Robert	Llanbeblig Cn	–	B I*	10 Sept. 1663	1663/53
William ap Richard Thomas	Rhoscolyn A	Yeoman	W	n.d.	1660/9
William ap Roberte	Cerrigceinwen	Yeoman	W	8 May 1641	1641/6

1 Inventory taken 14 June 1672.

Name	Parish & County	Status	Docs. Filed	Date of Probate/Admon.	Ref. No.
William ap Robert	Llanllechid Cn	–	W/I	9 June 1669	1669/94
William ap Robert	Llanfachreth A	–	W I*	24 May 1672	1672/18
William ap Robert	Gyffin (Tan r allt) Cn	–	W I	14 June 1689	1689/40
William ap Robert	Ceirchiog A	Yeoman	W R Rd	[c. 23 Feb. 1691/2]	1691/11
William ap Robert	Gyffylliog (Ffrithoedd) D	Yeoman	B I	26 Aug. 1695	1695/88
William Probert ap Edward	Llanddwywe Mr	–	W I	n.d.[1]	1688/76
William Probert Edward	Llanbadrig A	Yeoman	W* I R	15 Nov. 1694	1694/12
William ap Robert ap Ievan	Llanbeblig (Castellmay) Cn	–	W	7 May 1645	1645/24
William Probert Griffith	Llanwnda (Pengwern) Cn	Gent.	B I	14 Jan. 1691/2	1691/69
William ap Robert ap Hugh	Llanfihangel Ysgeifiog (Keint) A	–	B	16 July 1677	1677/11
William Probert ap John *Wynne*	Clocaenog (Llannerch Gronn) D	–	W I	5 June 1677	1677/70
William ap Robert Watkin	Llanrug Cn	–	W	1 March 1669/70	1669/97
William ap Robert ap William	Llanbedrycennin Cn	Gent./Yeoman	W I	28 March 1661	1661/63
William Thomas David	Llanbedr Niwbwrch A	–	B I	18 April 1678	1678/3
William Thomas ap Evan	Llanddeiniolen Cn	Yeoman	W Al	21 Feb. 1670/1	1670/107
William Thomas ap Evan	Gyffylliog (Ffrithoedd) D	–	W I	26 June 1686	1686/91
William Thomas ap Hugh	Llanelidan D	–	W	[ ] 1690	1690/105
William Thomas Humphrey	Llanddeusant A	Gent.	W	16 Feb. 1687/8	1687/7
William Thomas ap John	Llanbeblig (Coedallin) Cn	–	W	11 Jan. 1669/70	1669/73
William Thomas Lewis	Llannor Cn	–	W I	[12 Jan. 1675/6]	1675/29
William Thomas ap William Jeffrey	Llangristiolus A	–	W I B	26 Nov. 1661	1661/22
William ap William	Trawsfynydd Mr	Gent.	W*	27 March 1640	1640/49
William ap William	Rhoscolyn A	–	Rd	n.d.[2]	1661/29
William ap William	Llanfihangel Dinsylwy A	–	W	2 June 1664	1664/24
William ap William	Llanfachreth (Maes y Crymach uchaf) Mr	–	B I R	27 Feb. 1690/1	1690/94
William ap William ap Evan	Trefdraeth A	–	W	28 March 1642	1642/17
William ap William Owen	Llangristiolus A	Yeoman	B I*	11 May 1697	1697/13
William ap William Piers	Llandygái (Kellu y Manach) Cn	–	I	n.d.[3]	1666/61

[1] Inventory taken 10 Sept. 1688.
[2] Will proved but not filed; bond for its redelivery dated 4 Dec. 1661.
[3] Inventory taken 7 March 1666/7.

PART II
SURNAME INDEX

Name	Parish & County	Status	Docs. Filed	Date of Probate/Admon.	Ref. No.
Agleby, John	Llanfair-yn-neubwll A	–	W I M	3 Nov. 1666	1666/17
Andrew, Alice	Llandudno Cn	Spinster	B	20 Feb. 1691/2	1691/56
Andrew, William	Penmynydd A	–	W(2) Al	[17 April 1684]	1684/22
Anwyll, Anne	Penmachno (Hafodwyryd) Cn	Spinster	I*	n.d.	1697/38
Anwill, Emanuel	Penmorfa (Geaste) Cn	Gent.	W	29 Dec. 1646	1646/25
Anwyl, Jane	Beddgelert (Dolfriog) Mr	Widow	B I	10 Feb. 1693/4	1693/32
Anwill, John	Llanfachreth A	Clerk (Rector of Llanfachreth)	W I	12 June 1699	1699/16
Anwill, Maurice	Deneio Cn	–	B	12 Dec. 1687	1687/47
Anwill, Owen	Llanfrothen (Penrhyn) Mr	Esq.	W	25 May 1695	1695/78
Arthur, Ellin	Bangor Cn	Widow	W I	27 June 1699	1699/41
Arthur, Elizabeth	Holyhead A	Widow	B I	11 June 1690	1690/9
Arthur, Henry	Maenol Bangor Cn	Gent.	W Al	[24 Feb. 1691/2]	1691/40
Arthur, Hugh	Bryncroes (Manachdu) Cn	Gent.	W I	28 June 1687	1687/40
Arthur, Humphrey	Tywyn Mr	–	B	5 June 1683	1683/77
Arthyr, John	Beaumaris A	Gent.	B	27 July 1664	1664/2
Arthur, John	Llaniestyn Cn	–	B I	24 July 1668	1668/68
Arthur, John	Llanwnnog Mg	Blacksmith	B I	1 March 1696/7	1696/137
Arthyr, Richard	Llanynghenedl A	Gent.	I/G	16 May 1682	1682/28
Arthur, Thomas	Maenol Bangor Cn	[Gen]t.	W*	13 April 1686	1686/31
Arthur, William	Llandwrog Cn	–	B	20 Oct. 1669	1669/78
Arthur, William	Maenol Bangor Cn	Esq.	W* Cd* I R B	29 Jan. 1684/5	1684/28
Arthur, William	Bangor Cn	Gent.	W Al	19 Aug. 1685	1685/32
Arundell, John	Beaumaris A	Gent.	W I	11 Feb. 1696/7	1696/1
Ashton, John	[Deneio] (Pwllhely) Cn	–	I/G*	13 Jan. 1670/1	1670/91
Banes, Joseph	Rhuthun D	–	B I	7 June 1698	1698/69
Barlow *alias* Hanson, Jane	Llannor (Bodvell) Cn	Wife of John Barlow, esq.	B I	21 Nov. 1698	1698/41
Barry, Elizabeth	Bangor Cn	–	B	23 Aug. 1694	1694/38
Barry, William	Bangor Cn	Gent.	W I	22 Feb. 1681/2	1681/26
Baxter, Mary	Llanwnnog Mg	Widow of William Baxter	B I	20 April 1699	1699/156
Baxter, William	Llanwnnog Mg	–	B I	22 April 1697	1697/69
Bayly, John William	Carno Mg	Yeoman	W I	4 March 1674/5[1]	1674/58

[1] Incorrect? Will dated 3 March 1674[/5]; date of testator's death given as 15 March 1674[/5].

Name	Parish & County	Status	Docs. Filed	Date of Probate/Admon.	Ref. No.
Bayly, William	Llanwnnog Mg	Clerk (Vicar of Llanwnnog)	I/G	7 Feb. 1670/1	1670/187
Beane, Gabriell	Beaumaris A	Gent.	B	4 July 1666	1666/2
Bean, Gabriel	Beaumaris A	Mercer	B* I*	9 Nov. 1697	1697/1
Beane, Margaret	Beaumaris A	Widow	W	[ ] 1686/7	1686/3
Bedmond, William	Llanidan A	Yeoman	W I	8 Jan. 1695/6	1695/14
Bedward, William	Llaneilian A	Smith	W	4 Feb. 1695/6	1695/6
Beingan (Beinion), John	Llan-faes A	Yeoman	W I	29 May 1685	1685/17
Benion, William	Llanynys D	–	W	26 Nov. 1666	1666/107
Bellis, Hugh	Clynnog Cn	Yeoman	W I	20 Dec. 1695	1695/28
Bembow *see* Benbow					
Benbowe, Anne	Trefeglwys Mg	Spinster	W/I	21 April 1684	1684/118
Bembow, Edward	Trefeglwys Mg	–	I/G	10 April 1666	1666/124
Bembowe, Edward	Trefeglwys Mg	Clerk (Vicar of Trefeglwys)	W I	[30 Jan. 1673/4]	1673/71
Benbowe, John	Trefeglwys Mg	Clerk (Vicar of Llangurig and Trefeglwys)	W I	11 Oct. 1669	1669/176
Bembowe, John	Trefeglwys (Glyntrefnant) Mg	Innkeeper	W I B	2 June 1677	1677/93
Bembowe, Lowry	Llanwnnog Mg	Widow	W I	16 Jan. 1668/9	1668/140
Bembow, Mary	Llanwnnog / Trefeglwys Mg	Spinster	W I*	26 Jan. 1699/1700	1699/157
Benion *see* Beingan (Beinion)					
Bennet, Edward	Llangurig Mg	Yeoman	B I	31 March 1663	1663/138
Bennett, Edward	Trefeglwys (Glyntrefnant) Mg	–	W I	27 Sept. 1667	1667/142
Bennett, Nicholas (the elder)	Trefeglwys (Dolegoodden) Mg	Yeoman	W	16 Jan. 1668/9	1668/145
Bennett, Thomas	Trefeglwys Mg	–	W* I	15 April 1675	1675/67
Bennet, William	Trefeglwys (Maesmorrynnion) Mg	Gent.	B I	17 Nov. 1692	1692/128
Bennett, William	Trefeglwys (Glyntrefnant) Mg	–	W* I	17 May 1697	1697/71
Bevan, Hugh	Llanynghenedl (Cleifiog ucha) A	–	W	[24 July 1676]	1676/23
Bevan, William	Llandinam Mg	–	W	28 Nov. 1668	1668/129
Bevan, William	Llanddeiniolen Cn	Yeoman	B I	3 May 1699	1699/73
Beversley, Ann	Trefeglwys Mg	Spinster	W I	29 Aug. 1684	1684/119
Biddle, Nathaniel	Trefeglwys Mg	–	W	20 Dec. 1671	1671/146
Bidle, Richard	Llanidloes Mg	Yeoman	W	9 April 1641	1641/74
Blayney, Robert	Llanwnnog (Caersoosse) Mg	Tanner	B I	8 May 1679	1679/66
Bless, Humphrey	Llanwnnog Mg	Yeoman	B	23 July 1691	1691/133
Bless, Margaret	Llanwnnog Mg	–	B I	9 Dec. 1698	1698/80

Name	Parish & County	Status	Docs. Filed	Date of Probate/Admon.	Ref. No.
Bodurda, Ellin	[Aberdaron] (Bodurda) Cn	Spinster	W* C G	4 April 1671	1671/41
Bodurda, Henry	Llanfrothen Mr	Clerk (Rector of Llanfrothen)	W	20 June 1643	1643/36
Bodurda, Hugh	Aberdaron (Bodurda) Cn	Esq.	W I Rd	1 Nov. 1694	1694/34
Bodurda, John	[Aberdaron] (Bodurda) Cn	Esq.	B I	24 April 1672	1672/37
Bodvell, Alexander	[Deneio] (Pwlhely) Cn	Gent.	B I(2)	7 June 1661	1661/52
Bodvell *alias* Lewis, Anne	Llanfair-yn-neubwll (Trefleske) A	Widow	W(2) Al	7 June 1682	1682/20
Bodvell, Elizabeth	Llandwrog Cn	Widow	B I	12 May 1681	1681/46
Bodvell, Lazarus	Llangybi Cn	Gent.	W	12 Aug. 1671	1671/78
Bodvell, Robert	Llangïan Cn	Gent.	B I	29 March 1661	1661/76
Bodvell, Thomas	Deneio Cn	–	W	[11 Aug. 1683]	1683/29
Bodwrda *see* Bodurda					
Bold, Florence	Llechgynfarwy (Tre yr ddole) A	Widow	W I Ac	14 Nov. 1676	1676/25
Bold, Margarett	[Llanbeblig] (Carnarvon) Cn	Widow	W	9 Nov. 1663	1663/37
Bold, Rice	Beaumaris A	Gent.	W I(2)	15 June 1685	1685/3
Bold, Thomas	[Llanbeblig] (Carnarvon) Cn	Gent.	B I*	12 Aug. 1662	1662/40
Bold, William	Llechgynfarwy (Treyrddole) A	Esq.	{W {B	3 Jan. 1669/70 16 July 1683	1669/45 1683/16
Bold, William	[Llanbeblig] (Carnarvon) Cn	Gent.	W* Rd	n.d.[1]	1684/33
Bold, William	[Llechgynfarwy] (Tre-yr-ddole) A	Gent.	W Rd	6 Feb. 1688/9	1688/26
Bolton *see* Boulton					
Bomford *see* Bounford					
Boulton, Hannah	Bangor Cn	Minor	{B {B	14 May 1669 18 Oct. 1678	1669/57 1678/16
Bolton, Jonett	Beaumaris A	Widow	W(2) I	18 March 1663/4	1663/2
Boulton, Richard	Bangor Cn	Ironmonger	W	5 Nov. 1668	1668/32
Bound, Mary	Llangurig Mg	Widow	W* I	7 July 1698	1698/74
Bownd, Thomas	Llangurig Mg	Yeoman	W I	[10 Sept. 1662]	1662/98
Bound, Thomas	Llandinam Mg	Bachelor	B I	21 April 1681	1681/103
Bound, William	Llandinam Mg	Yeoman	W I	6 March 1678/9	1678/81
Bomford, Katherine	Trefeglwys Mg	Widow [of Oliver Bomford]	W I	[25 March 1674[2]]	1675/68
Bomford, Oliver	Trefeglwys Mg	–	W	[13 Jan. 1674/5]	1674/65

[1] Proved by 26 April 1684 according to bond for redelivery of will.

[2] Recte *1675*. Will dated 3 March 1674[/5] and the will of her husband, Oliver Bomford, dated 7 Dec. 1674.

Name	Parish & County	Status	Docs. Filed	Date of Probate/Admon.	Ref. No.
Bounford, Phillip	Trefeglwys Mg	–	W I	16 March 1689[1]	1689/97
Bowen, Evan	Trefeglwys (Maestregymer) Mg	Gent.	W	[15 March 1675/6]	1675/69
Bowen, Hugh	Aber Cn	–	B	20 June 1695	1695/19
Bowen, Morris	Trefeglwys (Maestre-gummer) Mg	Gent.	W	11 July 1691	1691/140
Bowen, Richard	Llangurig (Havod-wenn) Mg	Gent.	W(2) I(2)	[15 Nov. 1689]	1689/89
Bowens, Robert	Holyhead A	Mariner	W	28 Oct. 1665	1665/4
Bowser, John	Holyhead A	Mariner	B I	25 Sept. 1696	1696/4
Bradbury *alias* Jones, Jane	Llanrhaeadr-yng-Nghinmeirch (Lloyne) D	Widow	W I Rd	[18 March 1691/2]	1691/114
Brabery, John	Llanrhaeadr-yng-Nghinmeirch (Lloyne) D	–	B I	12 Jan. 1690/1	1690/109
Bradshaw, John	[Penmon][2] (Lleiniog) A	Gent.	B I	16 Oct. 1668	1668/26
Bradshawe, Margaret	Penmon A	–	B	16 Feb. 1682/3	1682/29
Brainton, Braynton *see* Brinton					
Brereton *alias* Wynne, Frances	Llandegfan A	–	W	26 April 1694	1694/14
Brereton, Owen	Llanwnda Cn	Gent.	W I Rd	n.d.[3]	1689/58
Brinkir *see* Brynkir					
Brynton, Catherine	Trefeglwys Mg	Widow	W I	6 July 1680	1680/82
Brinton, Evan	Carno Mg	–	B C	7 June 1684	1684/104
Brinton, Humphrey	Trefeglwys Mg	–	W I	27 Dec. 1662	1662/110
Brynton, Humphrey	Trefeglwys Mg	Yeoman	W*	26 Sept. 1671	1671/147
Brainton, John	Trefeglwys Mg	Yeoman	W I	23 Oct. 1679	1679/68
Brynton, John	Llandinam Mg	Gent./Yeoman	W I	n.d.[4]	1695/100
Broadhead, David	Llanbedr[-goch] A	Yeoman	B I G	[4 April] 1665	1665/5
Broadehead, Watkin	Llanbedr-goch A	–	W*	17 Sept. 1638	1638/7
Browne, Owen	Llanidloes Mg	Yeoman	W I	16 Feb. 1664/5	1664/134
Browne, Thomas	Llanidloes Mg	–	I/G	6 Oct. 1668	1668/136
Brwynog *alias* Williams, Sarah	Llantrisant A	Widow	W	25 Sept. 1671	1671/34
Brinkir, Ellis	[Llanfihangel-y-Pennant] (Brinkyr) Cn	Esq.	W I Rd*	18 May 1671	1671/74
Brynkir, Jane	Llanbeblig (Carnarvon) Cn	Widow	W	4 April 1692	1692/39
Brinkir, John	Llanenddwyn Mr	Gent.	I/G	7 Oct. 1670	1670/146
Brynton *see* Brinton					

1 *1688/9* or *1689/90*? Endorsed *1688*; inventory taken 16 Feb. 1687.
2 Endorsed *Llangoed*.
3 Inventory taken 11 Jan. 1688[/9]; bond for redelivery of will dated 5 Nov. 1689.
4 Inventory taken 20 March 1695[/6].

Name	Parish & County	Status	Docs. Filed	Date of Probate/Admon.	Ref. No.
Bubb, Humffrey	Llandinam Mg	Yeoman	I/G	10 Oct. 1663[1]	1663/133
Bubbe, William	Llandinam Mg	Yeoman	W I	26 April 1693	1693/129
Bulkley, Arthur	Llanbadrig A	–	W	23 April 1670	1670/12
Bulkeley *alias* Humphreys, Katherine	Rhosbeirio A	Widow	W	n.d.	1692/28
Bulkeley, Doulce	Llanfair-yn-neubwll A	Widow of John Aglebie	W I	29 May 1667	1667/23
Bulkeley, Edward	Llanfachreth (Bottan) A	Gent.	W I Rd(2)	[25 Aug. 1680]	1680/7
Bulkley *alias* Wynne, Elen	[Trewalchmai] (Bodwiney) A	Widow	W* I	17 March 1666/7	1666/36
Bulkley *alias* Walley, Elen	Llanddona (Cremlin) A	Widow	W*	13 Jan. 1669/70	1669/20
Bulkeley *alias* Lloyd, Ellin	Llanfair Mathafarn Eithaf A	Widow	W	23 April 1696	1696/14
Bulkeley, John	Conway Cn	Gent.	W Rd	6 Aug. 1635	1635/23
Bulkeley, John	Bangor Cn	Innkeeper/Gent.	B I	18 April 1696	1696/34
Bulkeley, Katherine *as* Bulkeley, Catherine					
Bulkeley, Margaret	Llanllechid (Coetmor) Cn	Widow [of William Bulkeley]	W I	10 Dec. 1686	1686/58
Bulkeley *alias* Glynne, Mary	Llangristiolus A	Widow	B*	24 Feb. 1662/3	1662/25
Bulkeley, Mary	Llanfechell A	Spinster	W I	16 Nov. 1695	1695/8
Bulkeley *alias* Williams, Dame Penelope	[Bangor] (Vaynol) & [Eglwys Rhos] (Bodescallan) Cn	Wife of Hugh Wynne, esq.	W	[28 May 1673]	1673/23
Bulkeley, Richard	Llanfachreth A	–	B	10 Feb. 1670/1	1670/29
Bulkeley, Richard	[Llanidan] (Porthamal) A	Esq.	Rd	n.d.[2]	1684/16
Bulkley, Rowland	[Llan-faes] (Kickley) A	Gent.	W	23 Sept. 1662	1662/18
Bulkeley, William	Beaumaris A	Gent.	W Db	17 May 1647	1647/2
Bulkeley, William	Llangristiolus A	Gent.	W B	21 Feb. 1647/8	1647/16
Bulkeley, William	Llanddeusant (Cnewchdernog) A	Gent.	W	10 June 1679	1679/6
Bulkeley, William	[Llanfechell] (Coydan & Brynddu) A & Llanllechid (Coytmor) Cn	Esq.	W Rd	n.d.[3]	1683/12
Burchesse, David	Conway Cn	Gent.	W	19 June 1693	1693/37
Burches, Hugh	Conway Cn	Gent.	W	1 Oct. 1646	1646/16
Butler, Robert ap Harry	Llan-rhudd (Talesarne) D	–	W	19 March 1638/9	1638/84

[1] Died 22 Dec. 1641.

[2] Bond for redelivery of inventory dated 26 April 1684.

[3] Proved by 1 Aug. 1683 according to bond for redelivery of will.

Name	Parish & County	Status	Docs. Filed	Date of Probate/Admon.	Ref. No.
Cadlan, Evan, *alias* Evan ap Evan John Lewis	Aberdaron (Bodryth) Cn	Gent.	W	2 June 1645	1645/16
Cadwalader, Annest	Llangurig Mg	Spinster	W	7 April 1666	1666/116
Cadwaladr, Andrew	Maentwrog Mr	Yeoman	W I	n.d.[1]	1681/77
Cadwalader, Annest *as* Cadwaladr, Agnes					
Cadwalader, Ellen	Llanfair-is-gaer Cn	–	W	8 June 1661	1661/74
Kadwalader, Ellin	Llanfihangel Bachellaeth Cn	Widow	W I	12 April 1694	1694/55
Kadwalader, Ellis	[Deneio] (Pwllhely) Cn	Mercer	W	17 April 1661	1661/53
Cadwalader, Evan	Gyffylliog D	–	W I	[13 March 1675/6]	1675/51
Cadwalader, Hugh	Aber-erch (Penuchen) Cn	–	B I	29 May 1688	1688/30
Cadwalader, Humphrey	Maentwrog (Gyfynis) Mr	Gent.	B I R	4 Aug. 1696	1696/105
Cadwalader, Jenkin	Llanidloes Mg	–	B I	29 Aug. 1661	1661/137
Cadwalader, John	Maentwrog (Penanllyw) Mr	Yeoman	W I	25 July 1668	1668/102
Cadwalader, John	Dolgellau Mr	–	I/G	19 June 1669	1669/113
Kadwalader, John	Dolgellau Mr	Yeoman	W I	2 July 1673	1673/45
Kadwaldr, John	Llanaber (Hirgwm) Mr	–	W I	18 Dec. 1673	1673/48
Cadwalader, John	Llandygái (Cappelkirrig) Cn	Yeoman	W I	25 March 1685	1685/46
Cadwallader, John	Llangian Cn	Tailor	W I	23 Nov. 1687	1687/65
Kadwalader, John	Llanllechid Cn	–	W/I E	5 June 1689	1689/55
Cadwalader, Rees	Bangor Cn	–	W	29 Sept. 1669	1669/58
Kadwallader, Robert	Clynnog Cn	Gent.	W I Ed	24 April 1666	1666/47
Cadwalader, Robert	Gyffylliog D	–	W I	[22 Jan. 1671/2]	1671/115
Cadwalader, Robert	Llanystumdwy Cn	–	W I	28 June 1677	1677/46
Cadwallader, Thomas	Llandinam (Trewythen) Mg	Gent.	B I	29 May 1669	1669/158
Cadwalader, Thomas	Llandudno (Gogarth) Cn	–	W I	8 Nov. 1676	1676/51
Cadwalader, Thomas	Cricieth Cn	–	B I	18 Nov. 1691	1691/52
Kadwalader, William	Llanystumdwy Cn	Yeoman	W I*	27 April 1671	1671/88
Carre *alias* Swift, Margaret	Holyhead A	Widow	W	14 May 1664	1664/11
Carreg, Katherine	Llanffinan (Hiredrevaige) A	Widow	W I B	12 July 1677	1677/12
Carreg, Evan	Aberdaron (Carreg) Cn	Gent.	B I	8 Nov. 1671	1671/42
Carreg, Jane	Aberdaron Cn	Widow	B I C	27 Nov. 1691	1691/38
Carreg, Katherine *as* Carreg, Catherine					
Carreg, William	Aberdaron (Cadlan) Cn	Gent.	W I	27 July 1696	1696/32
Charter, Thomas	Llanddwyn A	Gent.	W I	13 June 1674	1674/8

[1] Inventory taken 26 Jan. 1680.

Name	Parish & County	Status	Docs. Filed	Date of Probate/Admon.	Ref. No.
Chedle, Sir Thomas	Penmon (Lleiniog) A	Knight	W Rd/B	8 Feb. 1668/9	1668/27
Clarke, Ann	Llanwnnog (Escob & Castle) Mg	Widow	B C	12 April 1686	1686/106
			W Al Al/Ir/C Ir D(4) L S	[17 June 1687]	1687/133
Clarke, Robert	Llandinam Mg	Paper-maker	W I	10 Jan. 1693/4	1693/130
Clarkson, Dorothy	Llangristiolus A	Widow	W I	10 March 1697/8	1697/12
Clarkson, Thomas	Llangristiolus A	Chapman	W	2 Dec. 1687	1687/20
Clarksone, William	Llanfwrog [D/A]	Gent.	I	n.d.[1]	1684/94
Cleaton, Christopher	Trefeglwys (Dolegooden) Mg	Yeoman	W I	23 April 1697	1697/72
Cleaton, Edward	Llanidloes Mg	Yeoman	W I	2 May 1682	1682/102
Cleaton, Henry	Trefeglwys Mg	Yeoman	W I	17 Jan. 1678/9	1678/94
Cleaton, Thomas	Llandinam Mg	Yeoman	W I	[17 Nov. 1692]	1692/109
Cleaton, Thomas	Carno Mg	Blacksmith	W I	20 July 1696	1696/124
Clydro, David, *alias* Davyd ap Davyd	Heneglwys A	–	W	25 Feb. 1644/5	1644/4
Coetmor *see* Coytmor					
Conway, John	Llandwrog Cn	–	W	21 Feb. 1644/5	1644/22
Cooper, Anne	Bodedern A	Widow	G	30 June 1684	1684/6
Corbett, Vincent	Tywyn (Ynisymaengwine) Mr	Esq.	B C	13 Feb. 1679/80	1679/49
Coytmor, Katherine	Caerhun Cn	Widow	W	7 Oct. 1648	1648/9
Coytmor, Ellin	Dwygyfylchi (Ty mawr) Cn	Widow	W I(2) Rd	18 Feb. 1695/6	1695/31
Coytmor, Lewis	Eglwys-ael *alias* Llangadwaladr A	Clerk (Rector of Eglwys-ael)	W	[7 Nov. 1676]	1676/17
Coytmor, Owen	Llanfairfechan Cn	Gent.	B	14 Jan. 1691/2	1691/60
Coytmore, Richard	Llanfairfechan Cn	Gent.	W	18 Feb. 1669/70	1669/90
Coetmor, Robert	Dwygyfylchi [Tu Mawr] Cn	Esq.	B I	12 Feb. 1685/6	1685/41
Curver, Elizabeth	Dublin[2]	–	B	20 Sept. 1694	1694/125
Dakin, Eleanor	Llangurig Mg	Widow	W I	5 Feb. 1689/90	1689/90
Dakyn, George	Llangurig Mg	–	I/G	24 May 1667	1667/132
Dackin, Richard	Llangurig Mg	Yeoman	W I	6 Oct. 1690	1690/118
Daniel, Grace	Aberffraw A	Spinster[3]	W Al	8 May 1669	1669/1
Daniel, Robert	Penystrowed Mg	Traveller	B I	16 June 1663	1663/151
David *see* Davies					

1 Inventory taken 18 July 1684.
2 Margaret Curver, her sister and administratrix, described as being of the parish of Amlwch.
3 Al *Widow.*

Name	Parish & County	Status	Docs. Filed	Date of Probate/Admon.	Ref. No.
David, Ann	Llanegryn Mr	–	B	9 Dec. 1671	1671/103
David, Ann	Llandinam Mg	Spinster	W I	[16 Sept. 1675]	1675/61
David, Anthony	Llanenddwyn Mr	Alehouse keeper	I/G	16 Dec. 1669	1669/126
Davis, Katring	Llanfair Dyffryn Clwyd (Vaynal) D	Widow	W*	19 Aug. 1671	1671/122
Davies, David	Llandinam (Dethienith) Mg	Gent.	W I	[12 Jan.] 1664/5	1664/126
Davies, Dorythie	Llanfair Dyffryn Clwyd D	Spinster	W I	28 May 1669	1669/146
David, Dorothy	Trefriw Cn	Widow	B I	26 Oct. 1686	1686/68
David, Edward	Llanegryn Mr	Yeoman	W	1 June 1636	1636/44
David, Edward	Llangurig Mg	Yeoman	W	[6 April 1664]	1664/133
Davies, Edward	Llandinam (Maesmawr) Mg & Westbury (Venington) S	Gent.	W I	10 March 1669/70	1669/159
David, Ellin	Bodfaen Cn	Widow	W	13 Aug. 1642	1642/20
David, Ellen	Carno Mg	Spinster	W I	9 July 1674	1674/57
Davies, Ellis	Llandyrnog D	–	B I	28 July 1668	1668/107
David, Ellis	Llanllechid Cn	Yeoman	W I	20 April 1671	1671/82
David, Ellis	Dolgellau Mr	–	B* I*	19 Oct. 1688	1688/64
David, Elizabeth	Llandanwg (Harleigh) Mr	Spinster	G	18 May 1669	1669/124
Davies, Elizabeth	Clocaenog D	–	B I	28 Aug. 1686	1686/86
David, Elizabeth	Tywyn Mr	Spinster	I/G	1 May 1697	1697/55
David, Elizabeth	Tywyn Mr	Spinster	B I	14 Sept. 1699	1699/116
David, Ellen/Ellin *as* Davies, Elin					
Davies(David), Ellis *as* Davies, Elis					
David, Ievan	Llandwrog Cn	Clerk	W	14 Jan. 1635/6	1635/29
David, Evan	Aberdaron Cn	–	B I	2 April 1662	1662/34
David, Evan	Conway Cn	–	W I	21 March 1663/4	1663/45
David, Evan	Tudweiliog Cn	Yeoman	W I	n.d.[1]	1687/85
David, Evan	Eglwysael *alias* Llangadwaladr A	Corviser	W I	11 July 1688	1688/20
David, Evan	Carno Mg	Yeoman	W I	[7 Sept. 1692]	1692/107
David, Evan	Llanidloes (Kilmachar) Mg	Yeoman	W* I*	22 April 1697	1697/66
David, Francis	Pentir Cn	–	B I	13 May 1680	1680/41
Davies, Gaynor	[Llangadwaladr] (Bodeon) A	–	B	5 June 1694	1694/23
Davies, Godffrey	Botwnnog Cn	Clerk	B	23 July 1670	1670/73
Davies *alias* Lloyd, Grace	Beaumaris A	Wife of John Davies [formerly widow of John Lloyd, mercer]	B G B C	8 Aug. 1679 24 March 1680/1	1679/3 1680/2

[1] Died 24 Nov. 1687.

Name	Parish & County	Status	Docs. Filed	Date of Probate/Admon.	Ref. No.
David, Gryffith	Dolgellau (Garthgynvor) Mr	–	W	4 March 1674/5	1674/35
David, Griffith	Llanenddwyn Mr	–	B	11 Oct. 1681	1681/73
David, Griffith	Llanelltud Mr	–	W I	n.d.[1]	1686/78
David, Gwen	Penystrowed Mg	Widow	W I	[26 Sept. 1674]	1674/64
David, Gwenllian	Llangurig Mg	Spinster	W I	2 May 1698	1698/75
Davies, Henry	Llandyfrydog A	–	B I	12 Jan. 1688/9	1688/13
David, Henry	[Llanbeblig] (Carnarvon) Cn	Slater	B* I C	26 Jan. 1699/1700	1699/49
Davies, Hugh	Llanfihangel-y-Pennant Mr	Gent.	B I	10 March 1663/4	1663/100
Davies, Hugh	Holyhead A	–	W	27 Jan. 1669/70	1669/7
David, Hugh	Llanfair-is-gaer Cn	–	B I	22 April 1687	1687/63
Davies, Hugh	Llanbeulan (Treban Meyrick) A	Gent.	B I C	22 May 1690	1690/16
David, Hugh	Pennal (Ffreeth) Mr	–	I/G	16 May 1699	1699/114
David, Ievan *see* Davies, Evan					
David, Jenkin	Llanidloes Mg	–	B I	1 June 1695	1695/107
David, John	Pistyll Cn	–	W B	16 July 1641	1641/45
David, John	Rhuthun D	Dyer	W B Rd	18 Dec. 1660	1660/31
David, John	Llangybi Cn	Yeoman	W I	29 Dec. 1665	1665/48
David, John	Llanidloes Mg	–	W I	9 April 1666	1666/118
David, John	Llangwyfan D	Smith	B I	1 Feb. 1668/9	1668/114
David, John	Aber (Weege) Cn	–	W	30 Oct. 1675	1675/13
David, John	[Aber] Cn	–	W	[27 Dec. 1676]	1676/29
David, John	Llandinam Mg	–	B	1 July 1683	1683/96
David, John	Trewalchmai A	–	B	27 April 1683	1683/19
Davis, John	Llanfwrog [D/A]	–	I	n.d.[2]	1684/95
David, John	Llangurig Mg	Yeoman	B I	22 May 1684	1684/111
David, John	Tywyn Mr	Yeoman	W I	26 Aug. 1684	1684/78
David, John	Ffestiniog (Dolewen) Mr	–	W I	5 Dec. 1687	1687/93
Davies, John	Bodwrog (Maes y llan) A	Gent.	W I Rd	6 July 1688	1688/6
David, John	Holyhead A	Yeoman	W I	16 June 1690	1690/10
Davidd, John	Aber Cn	–	B I	25 March 1691	1691/37
David, John	Trawsfynydd Mr	–	B	21 Nov. 1695	1695/82
David, John	Trawsfynydd (Twr maen) Mr	Yeoman	W	22 Sept. 1697	1697/53
David, John	Trefeglwys (Talgarth) Mg	Gent.	W	3 Sept. 1698	1698/81
Davies, John	Llechylched A	Smith	W I	12 Sept. 1699	1699/33
Davis, Katring *as* Davies, Catherine					

[1] Inventory taken 9 Feb. 1685.
[2] Inventory taken 12 Aug. 1684.

Name	Parish & County	Status	Docs. Filed	Date of Probate/Admon.	Ref. No.
David, Lewis	Trawsfynydd Mr	Weaver	W*	1 Aug. 1636	1636/50
David, Lewis	Penystrowed Mg	–	B	15 May 1662	1662/108
David, Lewis	Dolgellau Mr	Yeoman	W I	13 Jan. 1676/7	1676/63
Davies, Lewis	[Llanbeblig] (Carnarvon) Cn	Gent.	B I	12 Aug. 1678	1678/22
Davies, Lewis	Llan-faes (Tourne hill) A	Carpenter	W I	16 Aug. 1688	1688/15
David, Lewis	Llangelynnin (Tre yr morva) Mr	–	W I	2 May 1693	1693/88
David, Llewelyn	Llangelynnin Mr	Yeoman	I/G	28 Jan. 1669/70	1669/129
Davies, Magdalen	Llangefni A	Widow	W	24 May 1673	1673/10
David, Margaret	Llanidloes Mg	Widow of Richard David	W	n.d.[1]	1683/102
David, Margaret	Llandinam Mg	–	B	7 May 1694	1694/116
David, Maurice *see* Davies, Morris					
David, Mredith	Llandinam Mg	Gent.	W I	3 June 1665	1665/95
David, Mredith	Llandinam (Dithhen[y]dd) Mg	Yeoman/Gent.	W I	15 Jan. 1684/5	1684/108
Davies, Michael	Penmon A	–	B	17 Aug. 1664	1664/43
David, Michael	Ceirchiog A	Yeoman	B I	25 March 1699	1699/8
David, Morgan	Llanfihangel-yn-Nhywyn A	–	B G	30 Sept. 1663	1663/20
David, Morgan	Llangurig Mg	–	W	18 Dec. 1671	1671/144
David, Morgan	Tywyn Mr	Yeoman	W I Db	26 April 1687	1687/106
David, Morgan	Carno Mg	Yeoman	W I	[3 Sept. 1690]	1690/114
David, Maurice	Llangurig (Glynhaveren vchcoyd) Mg	Yeoman	B I	24 Sept. 1661[2]	1661/133
David, Moris	Penmorfa Cn	–	I*	16 June 1671	1671/93
David, Maurice	Llanengan Cn	Labourer	W I	[18 Feb. 1678/9]	1678/30
Davies, Moris	Derwen D	Yeoman	W	n.d.[3]	1689/78
Davies, Morris	Trefeglwys (Maestre-gymmer) Mg	Gent.	W I	29 Jan. 1697/8	1697/73
David, Nicholas	Llandinam (Blayn y Glyn) Mg	Gent.	W*	12 July 1643	1643/53
David, Nicholas	Gyffin Cn	–	B I	25 May 1663	1663/51
David, Oliver	Dolgellau Mr	Mason	W I	12 June 1663	1663/78
David, Owen	Derwen D	Gent.	W I	20 June 1661	1661/112
David, Owen	Dolgellau (Garthgynfor) Mr	–	W I	11 Aug. 1671	1671/97
David, Owen	Deneio Cn	Yeoman	W I	20 April 1686	1686/43
David, Phillip	Llandinam Mg	–	B I(2) R	28 Sept. 1682	1682/94

[1] Will dated 6 May 1683.
[2] Inventory taken 10 July 1646.
[3] Will dated 12 July 1689.

Name	Parish & County	Status	Docs. Filed	Date of Probate/Admon.	Ref. No.
David, Rees	Llangurig (Glyngunwydd) Mg	–	I/G	3 May 1682	1682/99
Davies, Rice	Llanynys (Berth) D	Yeoman	W I	14 Oct. 1691	1691/122
David, Rees	Penmorfa (Keven Coch) Cn	Yeoman	I	n.d.[1]	1692/64
David, Rodericke	Tal-y-llyn Mr	–	B	22 March 1679/80	1679/46
Davies, Rice *see* Davies, Rees					
Davies, Richard	Llangelynnin Cn	–	W*	1 April 1641	1641/39
David, Richard	Pentraeth A	–	W	7 July 1648	1648/6
David, Richard	Penystrowed Mg	Yeoman	W I	n.d.[2]	1673/70
David, Richard	Llanidloes Mg	Carpenter	W I	n.d.[3]	1683/102
David, Richard	Llaneugrad A	Yeoman	W I Al D	[3 May] 1688	1688/14
Davidd, Richard	Llanrhaeadr-yng-Nghinmeirch D	Yeoman	B R	17 Aug. 1690	1690/110
David, Richard	Llandygái Cn	Yeoman	B	31 May 1693	1693/49
David, Robert	Llandygwnning Cn	Yeoman	W I L M(2)[4]	19 June 1668	1668/59
Davies, Robert	Caerhun (Caerhun) Cn	Gent.	W I Al	25 July 1681	1681/32
David, Robert	Dolgellau (Garthgynvor) Mr	Yeoman	W I	23 Sept. 1685	1685/65
David, Robert	Ynyscynhaearn Cn	–	W I	20 Jan. 1686/7	1686/69
Davies, Robert	Caerhun [Caerhun] Cn	Gent.	W I Rd	[c. 29 April 1687]	1687/41
David, Robert	Llanllyfni Cn	Yeoman	W	25 March 1690	1690/71
David, Robert	Llanfair Dyffryn Clwyd (Eyarth) D	Yeoman	W I	8 April 1693	1693/107
David, Rodericke *as* Davies, Rhydderch					
David, Roger	Llanfwrog (Keelygroeslwyd) D	–	W	[27 July 1675]	1675/57
Davies, Roger	Llanfihangel-y-Pennant Cn	Curate of Llanfihangel-y-Pennant	W	27 Sept. 1684	1684/47
David, Rowland	Llandegfan A	–	B	7 July 1670	1670/19
David, Rowland	Efenechtid D	–	W I	8 Oct. 1696	1696/117
David, Thomas	Beddgelert Cn	–	B	2 Nov. 1661	1661/44
David, Thomas	Llangelynnin Mr	–	B	2 Oct. 1662	1662/69
David, Thomas	Llanbedr Niwbwrch A	–	W I	19 Feb. 1669/70	1669/12
David, Thomas	Llanfair Mathafarn Eithaf A	Labourer	W	16 March 1669/70	1669/24
Davies, Thomas	Caerhun Cn	Gent.	B I	4 July 1678	1678/19
David, Thomas	Penllech Cn	Yeoman	W I	[5 May 1681]	1681/60

1 Inventory dated 6 Oct. 1691 but 4 William & Mary [1692]; endorsed *1692*.

2 Inventory taken 4 Feb. 1673[/4].

3 Inventory taken 1 May 1683.

4 Also relates to William Williams of Llandygwnning (q.v.).

Name	Parish & County	Status	Docs. Filed	Date of Probate/Admon.	Ref. No.
Davies, Thomas	Llangybi / Llanarmon Cn	Clerk (Rector of Llangybi)	B	26 Sept. 1687	1687/69
Davies, Thomas	Llanrhuddlad A	Clerk (Rector of Llanrhuddlad)	I	n.d.[1]	1689/23
David, Thomas	Llanfwrog (Bodyngharad) D	Yeoman	W I	27 Feb. 1699/1700	1699/124
David, Thomas	Llangristiolus A	Yeoman	B I	15 Jan. 1699/1700	1699/23
David, William	Amlwch A	Yeoman	W	30 March 1641	1641/3
David, William	Gyffylliog D	–	B	7 April 1664	1664/110
Davies, William	Llanbeblig Cn	Clerk (Vicar of Llanbeblig)	W	2 June 1664	1664/65
David, William	Llangurig Mg	Gent.	W I	20 Oct. 1665	1665/101
David, William	Llanwnda Cn	–	W	11 Dec. 1667	1667/80
David, William	Trawsfynydd Mr	–	B	9 July 1667	1667/110
David, William	Llandyrnog D	–	I/G	15 Jan. 1670/1	1670/164
Davies, William	Llanfaethlu A	–	W	n.d.[2]	1670/31
David, William	Llanegryn Mr	–	W	[8 Aug. 1672]	1672/93
David, William	Llanfair-yn-neubwll A	–	B I	8 June 1678	1678/9
David, William	Dolgellau (Cefnyrowen) Mr	–	W I	15 Aug. 1683	1683/59
David, William	Caerhun / Llanfairfechan Cn	–	B I	12 March 1684/5	1684/31
David, William	Dolgellau (Garthmailan) Mr	–	W I	22 Sept. 1685	1685/66
David, William	[Llanfihangel-y-Pennant] (Tyddyn mawr) Cn	Yeoman	W	28 Sept. 1685	1685/51
David, William	Trawsfynydd Mr	–	B I	26 June 1685	1685/80
David, William	Aber-erch Cn	–	B I	7 Nov. 1687	1687/33
David, William	Mellteyrn Cn	–	I*	n.d.[3]	1697/37
David, William	Coedana A	Yeoman	B I	24 July 1699	1699/9
Davies, William	Llangynhafal D	–	B I	30 Nov. 1699	1699/132
Davis *see* Davies					
Daviston, Anne	[Llanbeblig] (Carnarvon) Cn	Widow	B I	4 June 1664	1664/56
Daviston, John	[Llanbeblig] (Carnarvon) Cn	Gent.	B I(2)	11 July 1663	1663/38
Deane, Sydney	Beaumaris A	Widow	B I[4]	1 [ ] 1664	1664/3
Dolben, Jane	[Llantrisant] (Nantanog) A	Spinster	B	3 Jan. 1677/8	1677/17
Dolben, William	Llanrhaeadr-yng-Nghinmeirch (Segroyt) D	Esq.	W*	4 May 1643	1643/47

1 Inventory taken 28 Jan. 1688.
2 Will dated 18 Aug. 1670.
3 Inventory taken 6 May 1697.
4 In two parts – 10 Feb. 1664 and 17 April 1665.

Name	Parish & County	Status	Docs. Filed	Date of Probate/Admon.	Ref. No.
Doughty, Ralph	Beaumaris A	Gent.	W I	4 Feb. 1672/3	1672/4
Draycott *alias* Jones, Ellin	Dolgellau Mr	Wife of Maurice Jones, clerk	B C	16 Nov. 1699	1699/97
Dunganon, Marke Lord Viscount	[ ]	–	B	6 March 1670/1	1670/194
Eare, John (the elder)	Llanfwrog D	–	B I	2 April 1698	1698/64
Eaton *see* Eyton					
Edmond *see* Edmund					
Edmund, Cadwaladre	Llandecwyn (Llennurch) Mr	–	W I	21 Oct. 1689	1689/68
Edmund, Elen	Llanrhychwyn Cn	Widow	W*	1 May 1698	1698/45
Edmond, Elisha	Holyhead A	Corviser	W	n.d.[1]	1647/6
Edmund, John	Beddgelert Cn	–	W	n.d.	1686/33
Edmund, John	Aberffraw A	Gent.	W I Rd	11 July 1688	1688/1
Edmund, Joned	Llanystumdwy Cn	Widow [of Robert Owen]	W	22 March 1674/5	1674/29
Edmund, Morgan	Bodedern A	Shepherd	W I	[25 May 1693]	1693/3
Edmond, Richard	Bangor Cn	–	W	24 June 1644	1644/18
Edmunds, Richard	Amlwch (Eskellog) A	Gent.	W I G	15 Aug. 1663	1663/1
Edmond, Thomas *See also* Bedmond	[Bodfari][2] (Aberchwiler) D	Yeoman	W*	7 March 1660/1	1660/33
Edmunds *see* Edmund					
Ednevett, Edward	Llanaber Mr	Yeoman	W I	4 May 1680	1680/48
Ednyfed, John	Llanfwrog A	–	B	29 Oct. 1679	1679/8
Ednyved, William	Llanfaethlu A	–	W	26 July 1670	1670/32
Edward *see* Edwards					
Edward, Anne	[Llandanwg] (Harlech) Mr	Widow	B I	7 Aug. 1691	1691/84
Edwards, Bridgett	Llanwnnog Mg	Widow	I/G	11 Dec. 1666	1666/122
[Edward *alias*] Evans, Dorothy	Carno Mg	Widow [of Edward Evan John]	W	n.d.[3]	1699/142
Edwards, Edward	Llanaber (Cell fechan) Mr	Gent./Yeoman	W I(2) Al	6 July 1693	1693/73
Edwards, Edward	Llanenddwyn Mr	Aleseller	I/G	20 May 1693	1693/80
Edward, Ellin	Llanaber Mr	–	I/G*	9 April 1694	1694/75

[1] Will dated 30 March 1647; endorsed *non adhuc probat.*

[2] Normally within the jurisdiction of the St. Asaph Consistory Court.

[3] Will dated 6 March 1699[/1700].

Name	Parish & County	Status	Docs. Filed	Date of Probate/Admon.	Ref. No.
Edward, Ellis	[Guilsfield][1] (Llanerch-vrochwell) Mg	Yeoman	W Db	21 Feb. 1675/6	1675/73
Edwardes, Ellis	Llanaber (Llwyn dû) Mr	–	W*	[14 [ ] 1678]	1678/40
Edward, Evan	Trefeglwys Mg	–	I/G	10 May 1665	1665/110
Edward, Evan	Ysbyty [Ifan] Cn	–	I/G	11 April 1683	1683/58
Edward, Evan	Beddgelert Cn	Yeoman	W I B	25 Oct. 1699	1699/44
Edwards, Hugh	Tywyn (Dyffryngwyn) Mr	Gent.	W I	26 Feb. 1682/3	1682/79
Edward, Hugh	Dolgellau Mr	–	B I	26 Aug. 1684	1684/63
Edward, Hugh	Carno Mg	–	W I	[15 Oct. 1688]	1688/98
Edwards, Hugh	Llangynhafal D	–	B I	31 March 1699	1699/133
Edwards, Hugh	Llanynghenedl (Cleiviog) A	Yeoman	W I B	26 July 1699	1699/31
Edward, Humffrey	Llanaber Mr	Gent.	W I	n.d.[2]	1688/68
Edwards, Jane	Llanaber (Llwyn-Du) Mr	Widow	W I	23 Aug. 1692	1692/71
Edwards, John	Llanbedr Dyffryn Clwyd D	Clerk	W	6 June 1644	1644/41
Edward, John	Llanrhychwyn Cn	–	B	2 Aug. 1667	1667/79
Edward, John	Llantrisant A	Yeoman	W	n.d.[3]	1669/41
Edward, John	Cerrigceinwen A	–	B I	22 Dec. 1670	1670/5
Edwards, John	Llanfair Dyffryn Clwyd D	–	B I	31 Dec. 1672	1672/108
Edwards, John	Llanbedr Dyffryn Clwyd D	Yeoman	W I	[16 March 1676/7]	1676/88
Edward, John	Llanidan A	–	B I	20 Jan. 1679/80	1679/11
Edward, John	[?Llanidloes] Mg	–	I/G	4 May 1682	1682/103
Edwards, John	Trefeglwys Mg	Yeoman	I/G	19 June 1682	1682/107
Edwards, John	Llanfair-yng-Nghornwy A	Clerk (Rector of Llanddeusant)	B I C	27 Aug. 1687	1687/13
			B	26 Nov. 1692	1692/14
Edwards, John	Rhuthun D	Tailor	W I	26 Aug. 1687	1687/126
Edwarde, John	Llandinam Mg	Yeoman	W I	[14 Sept. 1688]	1688/100
Edward, John	Llanfachreth Mr	–	B I	15 July 1689	1689/72
Edward, John	Llanwnnog Mg	Yeoman	W I	11 Nov. 1691	1691/134
Edward, John	Llangurig (Dyffryn-gwy) Mg	Gent.	W I	13 Oct. 1693	1693/136
Edwards, John	Llandygái Cn	–	W I	6 Dec. 1695	1695/43
Edwards, John	Llandygái Cn	Yeoman	B	29 July 1696	1696/59
Edwards, Lewes	Trefeglwys (Glyntrefnant) Mg	–	W I	21 June 1664	1664/137
Edward, Mallt	Llangelynnin Mr	Spinster	W I	28 Feb. 1682/3	1682/74
Edward, Margarett	Pennal (Bryn y Palme) Mr	Widow	W I	9 Nov. 1695	1695/81
Edward, Margeret	Tal-y-llyn (Comere) Mr	Widow	W* I	5 May 1697	1697/52

[1] Normally within the jurisdiction of the St. Asaph Consistory Court.
[2] Died 5 March 1687.
[3] Will dated 9 July 1667; endorsed *probat. fuit 68 or 69.*

Name	Parish & County	Status	Docs. Filed	Date of Probate/Admon.	Ref. No.
Edward, Mathew	Bangor Cn	Yeoman	B	6 Aug. 1691	1691/41
Edward, Maurice *see* Edwards, Morris					
Edward, Morgan	Llanwnnog (Pant y ?crasdy) Mg	Yeoman	W I*	4 July 1684	1684/115
Edward, Moris	Llanwnnog Mg	–	W	16 May 1661	1661/141
Edward, Maurice	Llandanwg Mr	Gent.	W I	7 Jan. 1675/6	1675/40
Edwards, Morris	Llandinam (Maesmawr) Mg	Gent.	B I	29 Aug. 1684	1684/109
Edward, Owen	Llangelynnin (Llwyngwril) Mr	Yeoman	W I	n.d.[1]	1688/83
Edward, Rees	Llanbeulan A	–	W I	6 Dec. 1670	1670/16
Edwards, Roderick	Carno Mg	–	B I	15 July 1695	1695/98
Edward, Richard	Llangoed A	Labourer	W	23 Feb. 1640/1	1640/14
Edward, Richard	Dolgellau Mr	Yeoman	W	13 Nov. 1675	1675/33
Edward, Richard	Llanegryn Mr	Shoemaker	B I	4 Aug. 1696	1696/101
Edwards, Robert	Rhuthun D	Tanner	W	22 Jan. 1635/6	1635/48
Edward, Robert	Llanrhychwyn Cn	–	W*	15 April 1643	1643/28
Edward, Robert	Llanaber Mr	Gent.	B I	11 March 1663/4	1663/85
Edward, Robert	Llanaber Mr	–	I/G	15 Dec. 1683	1683/63
Edward, Robert	Llanfaelog A	–	B I	30 Aug. 1690	1690/21
Edward, Robert	Llanaber (Hendre r Coed) Mr	Gent.	I/G	17 May 1695	1695/67
Edwards, Roderick *as* Edwards, Rhydderch					
Edwards, Samuel	Rhuthun D	Innkeeper	W	21 Jan. 1683/4	1683/92
Edward, Thomas	Llanfachreth Mr	–	B I R	11 Dec. 1661	1661/98
Edwards, Thomas	Conway Cn	–	W	26 Feb. 1684/5	1684/35
Edwards, Thomas	Llangadwaladr A	–	B I	2 Dec. 1686	1686/15
Edwards, Thomas	Llandinam Mg	Husbandman	W I	5 Sept. 1687	1687/128
Edwards, Thomas *see* Nicholas, Ellyn (n 2)	Llangybi Cn				
Edward, Thomas	Llangybi Cn	–	B	14 Nov. 1699	1699/79
Edward, William	Llanaber Mr	–	W I Rd	22 Sept. 1685	1685/69
See also Bedward					
Elice, Elis *see* Ellis					
Elisey, Agnes	Dolgellau Mr	Widow	W I	1 Sept. 1687	1687/86
Liza, David	Rhoscolyn A	Yeoman	W Al D	12 Dec. 1689	1689/27
Liza, Elin	Aber-erch Cn	Widow [of John Owen, weaver]	W/I C	23 Aug. 1661	1661/36
Eliza, Elizabeth	Llangeinwen A	Widow	B	6 Oct. 1684	1684/15

[1] Inventory taken 10 May 1688.

Name	Parish & County	Status	Docs. Filed	Date of Probate/Admon.	Ref. No.
Elissa, Hugh	Llanegryn Mr	Labourer	W B	3 Dec. 1674	1674/44
Ellisey, Lewis	Llanfachreth Mr	–	W I	n.d.[1]	1688/78
Eliza, Margarett	Gyffin Cn	Widow	W	26 May 1637	1637/22
Elysa, Owen	[Llanbeulan] (Tal-y-llyn) A	–	W* I(2) M	28 June 1671	1671/15
Ellis, Katharine	Aber (Bodsilin) Cn	Spinster	W R	16 Nov. 1693	1693/28
Ellis, David	Dolgellau (Gwanas) Mr	Gent.	W	2 June 1670	1670/134
Ellis, David	Ffestiniog Mr	–	B	21 Feb. 1681/2	1681/64
Ellis, Elin	Trawsfynydd Mr	–	W I	8 Nov. 1681	1681/84
Ellis *alias* Reynallt, Elizabeth	Llanystumdwy Cn	–	B	16 May 1688	1688/57
Ellis, Francis	[Deneio] (Pwllhely) Cn	–	W I	1 Feb. 1670/1	1670/92
Ellis, George	Llandinam Mg	–	I/G	6 June 1668	1668/130
Ellis, Gruffyth	Dolbenmaen Cn	–	W I Rd	10 July 1668	1668/49
Ellis, Gryffith	Tywyn Mr	–	B	5 June 1683	1683/78
Ellis, Griffith	Dolgellau (Brithdir ucha) Mr	Gent.	B I	15 Sept. 1692	1692/66
Ellis, Griffith	Dolgellau (Garthgynvor) Mr	–	B* I* R	3 June 1695	1695/62
Ellis, Gwen	Mellteyrn (Bodnithoedd) Cn	Widow	W I Rd	4 Nov. 1664	1664/78
Ellis, Gwenn	Ynyscynhaearn (Esteddfa) Cn	Spinster	{B* C* {B*	21 Oct. 1698 23 Sept. 1699	1698/51 1699/93
Ellis, Jane	Ynyscynhaearn [Eisteddfa] Cn	Spinster	W* I*	6 July 1698	1698/52
Ellice, Joan	Llandinam (Gwerneryn) Mg	Widow	W I	3 May 1666	1666/114
Ellis, John	Dolgellau Mr	Clerk (Rector of Dolgellau)	W I Rd	15 Dec. 1665	1665/59
Ellis, John	Llandanwg (Harleigh) Mr	–	W	9 Nov. 1673	1673/50
Ellis, John	Llanfachreth Mr	–	W	24 Oct. 1674	1674/45
Ellis, John	Dolwyddelan (Penrhiw) Cn	Yeoman	W I	4 Sept. 1679	1679/22
Ellis, John	Trawsfynydd Mr	–	B I R(4)	26 June 1685	1685/81
Ellis, John	Beddgelert Cn	Yeoman	B* I	2 Sept. 1697	1697/15
Elice, John	Gyffylliog D	–	W I	26 March 1699	1699/121
Ellis, Jonett	Llanarmon Cn	Widow	B I	24 May 1688	1688/44
Ellis, Katharine *as* Ellis, Catherine					
Ellis, Lowry	Carno Mg	Spinster	I/G	[27 March 1679]	1679/62
Ellis, Owen	Dolgellau (Dyffrydan) Mr	–	W*	6 April 1636	1636/40
Ellis, Owen	Dolwyddelan Cn	–	W*	15 May 1641	1641/30
Ellis, Owen	Llanrug Cn	–	B	28 June 1671	1671/85
Ellis, Owen	Llandecwyn Mr	–	W I	[12 Oct. 1681]	1681/72

[1] Inventory taken 30 April 1688.

Name	Parish & County	Status	Docs. Filed	Date of Probate/Admon.	Ref. No.
Ellis, Owen	Llanddwywe Mr	–	W I	n.d.[1]	1689/69
Ellis, Owen	[Cricieth] (Stymllyn) & [Penmorfa] (Llystynrhudd uchaf) Cn	Gent.	W	21 Oct. 1691	1691/53
Ellis, Richard	Llanelltud Mr	Innkeeper	W I	22 Sept. 1685	1685/74
Ellis, Richard	Aber-erch (Cay yr Berech) Cn	–	W I	1 March 1687/8	1687/34
Ellis, Robert	Llanarmon Cn	–	B	21 Sept. 1688	1688/45
Elis, Robert	Ynyscynhaearn (Stedfa) Cn	Gent.	W I*	21 July 1688	1688/63
Ellis *alias* Smyth, Trephena	Llanarmon Cn	Widow[2]	W M	3 May 1689	1689/41
Ellis, William	Dolwyddelan (Ddanhadog) Cn	Yeoman	W I	18 Feb. 1695/6	1695/30
Ellisey *see* Eliza					
Evan *see* Evans					
Evans, Anne	Ffestiniog Mr	Spinster	B	12 Sept. 1661	1661/93
Evans, Anne	Trefeglwys Mg	–	W* I R	[29 May 1690]	1690/120
Evans, Katherine	Llanidloes Mg	Widow	W I	26 Aug. 1668	1668/137
Evans, Catherin	Ffestiniog (Havod y llynn) Mr	Widow	W I	12 Nov. 1675	1675/38
Evans, Catherine	Bangor Cn	Widow	W	22 Jan. 1696/7	1696/35
Evans, Katherine	Llangurig Mg	–	W I	5 Aug. 1699	1699/148
Evan, David	Llanidloes (Carowlam, Stredunod) Mg	–	W I	21 June 1676	1676/102
Evan, David	Llangurig Mg	Yeoman	W I	9 April 1683[3]	1684/112
Evans, Dorothy	Llangynhafal D	Widow	W I	4 Oct. 1677	1677/80
Evans [*alias* Edward], Dorothy	Carno Mg	Widow [of Edward Evan John]	W	n.d.[4]	1699/142
Evans, Edward	Llanrhaeadr-yng-Nghinmeirch D	Carpenter	W I	[1 Jan. 1673/4]	1673/64
Evans, Edward	Llangurig (Glyngynwidd) Mg	–	I/G	18 April 1683	1683/99
Evan, Edward	Llangurig (Travel Gwynn) Mg	–	W I	5 Sept. 1687	1687/130
Evans, Edward	Llangurig Mg	–	B I	9 Feb. 1692/3	1692/115
Evan, Edward	Trefeglwys Mg	Yeoman	B I	10 May 1694[5]	1694/124
Evans, Ellin	Beaumaris A	Widow	W I B	30 Jan. 1668/9	1668/3
Evans, Ellis	Deneio (Pwlhely) Cn	–	W Rd	26 Feb. 1641/2	1641/29
Evans, Ellis	Ffestiniog Mr	Gent.	W	14 March 1642/3	1642/33
Evans, Elis	Llandecwyn Mr	Gent.	W I	4 Aug. 1677	1677/55
Evans, Ellis	Llanrwst (Gwyder) Cn	Servant	B L	10 April 1677	1677/44

1 Died 28 Oct. 1688. Inventory endorsed *1689*.

2 W *spinster*, although it contains a reference to *my Late Husband's goods*.

3 Recte *1684*? Date of probate on back of will is 1 May 1684; will dated 14 Feb. 1683 and inventory taken 20 Feb. 1683 (old style reckoning?).

4 Will dated 6 March 1699[/1700].

5 Or *1695*? 1 May 1695 given as date of swearing administrator; *1695* corrected to *1694* or vice versa in endorsement on cover.

Name	Parish & County	Status	Docs. Filed	Date of Probate/Admon.	Ref. No.
Evan, Ellis	Llanegryn Mr	Miller	B I	31 July 1690	1690/91
Evan, Ellis	Trefriw Cn	Shoemaker	B I	6 Jan. 1699/1700	1699/91
Evans, Elizabeth	Beaumaris A	Widow	W	22 April 1645	1645/1
Evan, Elissapeth	Tywyn Mr	Widow	W B	11 July 1694	1694/97
Evan, Elizabeth	Ffestiniog Mr	[Wife of William Pugh]	B	17 March 1695/6	1695/65
Evans, Ellin *as* Evans, Elin					
Evans, Ellis *see* Evans, Elis					
Evans, Evan	[Ffestiniog] (Tanybwlch) Mr	–	B	24 Feb. 1681/2	1681/65
Evans, Evan	[Llanbeblig] (Carnarvon) Cn	Gent.	I/G	29 Aug. 1692	1692/40
Evans, Henry	Holyhead (Treyarddyr) A	Gent.	B I*	4 Nov. 1685	1685/9
Evans, Henry	Llanaber (Hendre Forion) Mr	Gent.	W I Al B	1 Sept. 1687	1687/94
Evans, Harry, *alias* Harry Evan Parry	Llanfihangel-y-Pennant Cn	–	B I	9 March 1693/4	1693/53
Evans, Hugh	Deneio Cn	–	B	2 Jan. 1664/5	1664/60
Evan, Hugh	Llanwnnog Mg	–	W I	[11 Nov. 1691]	1691/135
Evans, Hughe	Llanidloes Mg	Yeoman	B I	5 July 1692	1692/123
Evans, Hugh	Deneio / [Llannor] (Bryn-hyno[g]) Cn	Gent.	I	n.d.[1]	1696/46
Evan, Humphrey	Llanllyfni (Talmignedd uchaf) Cn	Yeoman	W I	10 March 1684/5	1684/51
Evan, Humphrey	Llandinam Mg	–	B	4 June 1685	1685/109
Evan, Humphrey	Penmorfa Cn	Yeoman	B	3 Jan. 1699/1700	1699/89
Evans, Jane	Llangristiolus (Cerricgwyddil) A	Widow	W I	n.d.[2]	1676/19
Evan, Jenkin	Llangurig (Llaniwared) Mg	–	W I	5 Sept. 1676	1676/99
Evans, John	Bodfean Cn	–	W I C	18 Dec. 1660	1660/10
Evans, John	Gyffin (Boddeetha) Cn	Yeoman	W I	16 Jan. 1661/2	1661/56
Evans, John	Conway Cn	Yeoman	B* I*	19 March 1662/3	1662/45
Evans, John	Clynnog (Berth du) Cn	Gent.	W I B	3 Nov. 1663	1663/42
Evan, John	Carno Mg	Husbandman	I/G	[12 Jan.] 1664/5	1664/123
Evans, John	Llanengan (Cim) Cn	Yeoman	W I	29 Aug. 1667	1667/69
Evan, John	Clocaenog D	–	W I	15 May 1672	1672/99
Evan, John	Rhuthun D	Labourer	W	18 July 1672	1672/121
Evan, John	Tywyn (Gwaen-Dasse) Mr	–	B I	7 Jan. 1677/8	1677/66
Evan, John	Trefeglwys Mg	–	B	29 May 1684	1684/120
Evan, John	Llangynhafal (Llidiart y Pwll) D	Yeoman	W* I	23 Oct. 1685	1685/96

[1] Inventory taken 1 April 1696.

[2] Inventory taken 11 Dec. 1676.

Name	Parish & County	Status	Docs. Filed	Date of Probate/Admon.	Ref. No.
Evans, John	Dolbenmaen Cn	Clerk (Rector of Penmorfa and Dolbenmaen)	I	n.d.[1]	1686/44
Evans, John	Llangelynnin Cn	Gent.	W I*	28 June 1686	1686/57
Evan, John	Llanwnnog Mg	–	B	7 April 1687	1687/134
Evans, John	Llanllyfni Cn	–	B I(2) C	13 May 1689	1689/56
Evans, John	Mellteyrn Cn	Yeoman	B I	1 March 1691/2	1691/72
Evans, John	Llangurig (Glyngynwidd) Mg	Feltmaker	B I	9 Feb. 1692/3	1692/116
Evans, John	Llanidloes Mg	Gent.	B I	20 March 1693/4	1693/139
Evans, John	[Llanbeblig] (Carnarvon) Cn	Gent.	W	24 Sept. 1696	1696/39
Evan, John	Llandinam Mg	–	W* I*	15 July 1696	1696/127
Evans, Katherine *see* Evans, Catherine					
Evans, Lettice	Bangor Cn	–	W I*	n.d.[2]	1670/68
Evan, Lewis	Trawsfynydd Mr	Yeoman	W I	n.d.[3]	1678/52
Evan, Lewis	Llangelynnin Mr	–	B* I	28 Feb. 1682/3	1682/75
Evans, Lewis	Heneglwys A	–	B	1 Feb. 1691/2	1691/12
Evans, Margarett vch Richard	Llanengan Cn	Widow	W I Al	[21 June] 1688	1688/52
Evan, Mary	Llanaber Mr	Widow	B C	27 Oct. 1686	1686/72
Evan, Maurice *see* Evans, Morris					
Evans, Michael	Llanbeulan A	Clerk (Rector of Llanbeulan)	W Rd	12 Sept. 1670	1670/17
Evans, Michael	Llanbadrig A	–	B	24 Dec. 1672	1672/12
Ievan, Morgan	Tywyn Mr	–	W	31 May 1638	1638/68
Evan, Morgan	Llangelynnin Mr	–	W*	1 May 1671	1671/109
Evans, Morgan	Carno Mg	Gent.	W* L	21 Feb. 1673/4	1673/67
Evan, Morgan	Dolgellau (Dyfrydan) Mr	–	W I L Rd	5 June 1679	1679/34
Evan, Moris	Llanenddwyn Mr	Yeoman	I/G	23 July 1668	1668/94
Evan, Morris	Llanwnnog Mg	Clerk	W I	8 Aug. 1672	1672/129
Evans, Morris	Betws-y-coed Cn	–	B	27 June 1681	1681/31
Evan, Maurice	Llanwnda Cn	–	B I	7 July 1693	1693/63
Evans, Owen	[Llaniestyn][4] (Penunllys) A	Gent.	W	19 Aug. 1662	1662/30
Evans, Owen	Llanddona A	Clerk	W	9 Nov. 1664	1664/18

1 Inventory taken 3 Sept. 1686.
2 Inventory taken 10 Nov. 1670.
3 Inventory taken 11 March 1678.
4 Endorsed *Llanvaes*.

Name	Parish & County	Status	Docs. Filed	Date of Probate/Admon.	Ref. No.
Evans, Owen	Llanddeiniolen Cn	Clerk (Rector of Llanbedrycennin and vicar of Caerhun)	W I	26 Jan. 1666/7	1666/62
Evan, Owen	Llanfair-iuxta-Harlech Mr	Yeoman	W I	30 Jan. 1675/6	1675/45
Evan, Owen	Llanaber Mr	–	W I	3 Feb. 1695/6	1695/68
Evans, Rees	Carno Mg	Gent.	W*	20 March 1671/2	1671/139
Evan, Rhees	Llanidloes (Hirieth) Mg	Yeoman	W I	9 July 1680	1680/79
Evan, Rice	Dolgellau (Garthgynvor) Mr	–	W	13 Oct. 1685	1685/67
Evans, Rees	Llangurig Mg	–	B	10 May 1698	1698/76
Evan, Rinallt	Llanwnnog Mg	–	W	8 Nov. 1672	1672/130
Evans, Richard	Ffestiniog Mr	Gent.	W(2)	10 Sept. 1647	1647/39
Evan, Richard	Llanfachreth Mr	–	W I	11 Dec. 1661	1661/99
Evans, Richard	Ffestiniog Mr	–	B Db	15 July 1665	1665/62
Evans, Richard	Llanidloes Mg	Gent.	I/G	2 April 1668	1668/138
Evan, Richard	Penegoes[1] Mg	–	W	6 Aug. 1672	1672/133
Evan, Richard	Llanidloes (Cefen Croeslybr) Mg	–	W I	28 April 1682	1682/104
Evan, Richard	Dolwyddelan Cn	–	W	[14 June 1683]	1683/31
Evans, Richard	Llanddaniel-fab A	Yeoman	B	22 Oct. 1695	1695/3
Evan, Richard	Trawsfynydd Mr	Bachelor/Yeoman	W I	2 July 1695	1695/83
Evans, Richard	Llanddyfnan A	Yeoman	W I*	17 May 1698	1698/6
Evans, Richard	Trefeglwys Mg	Gent.	B I	28 Feb. 1699/1700	1699/159
Evans, Robert	Botwnnog Cn	–	W	9 Nov. 1641	1641/24
Evans, Robert	Ffestiniog (Tan y bwlch) Mr	Gent.	B I C	29 June 1664	1664/86
Evans, Robert	[Llanbeblig] (Carnarvon) Cn	–	W I	16 Sept. 1664	1664/57
Evans, Robert	Llaniestyn Cn	Gardener	W	[5 Dec. 1674]	1674/24
Evans, Robert	Llanynghenedl A	Gent.	W I	12 April 1684	1684/21
Evans, Robert	Llanllyfni Cn	–	I	n.d.[2]	1687/70
Evan, Robert	Dolgellau Mr	–	W I	12 Sept. 1688	1688/65
Evans, Robert	Llanfihangel Bachellaeth Cn	Yeoman	B I C	4 Jan. 1690/1	1690/65
Evans, Roger	Llanbedr[-goch] A	Labourer	W I	22 April 1690	1690/14
Evan, Rowland	Llanaber Mr	–	W	4 Nov. 1674	1674/40
Evans, Rowland	Llanbedr[-goch][3] A	Yeoman	W Ir D	[22 March 1682/3]	1682/8
Evan, Rowland	Llanidloes Mg	Yeoman	B I	16 Sept. 1699	1699/154
Evans, Stephen	Llanwnnog Mg	–	B	22 Oct. 1669	1669/174

1 Normally within the jurisdiction of the St. Asaph Consistory Court.

2 Inventory taken 3 Nov. 1687.

3 Reading of Ir, *Llanbeder in Newborough*, incorrect. See burial entry in the bishops transcripts of the parish register of Llanbedr-goch, 1682/3.

Name	Parish & County	Status	Docs. Filed	Date of Probate/Admon.	Ref. No.
Evan, Thomas	Trawsfynydd Mr	–	B	11 Sept. 1661	1661/107
Evanes, Thomas	Llanrhaeadr-yng-Nghinmeirch (Klickied) D	–	W	14 Sept. 1668	1668/120
Evans, Thomas	Llanfaelog A	–	W*	7 Nov. 1670	1670/30
Evans, Thomas	Llangynhafal D & Trawsfynydd Mr	Clerk (Rector of Trawsfynydd)	W I	9 Oct. 1672	1672/113
Evans, Thomas	Rhuthun D	Tailor	W I	19 Aug. 1679	1679/60
Evan, Thomas	Tywyn Mr	Yeoman	W* I	n.d.[1]	1685/85
Evans, Thomas	Trefriw Cn	Corviser	W	4 Aug. 1687	1687/84
Evans, William	Llandyfrydog (Hendre) A	Gent.	W*	10 Jan. 1660/1	1660/2
Evans, William	Beaumaris A	–	W*	11 July 1662	1662/2
Evanes, William	Llangïan Cn	–	W	14 Aug. 1671	1671/76
Evans, William	Maentwrog Mr	Gent.	W I	19 June 1673	1673/57
Evans, William	Carno Mg	–	W W/Al	31 March 1676	1676/96
Evans, William	Llangurig Mg	Gent.	W I	9 Sept. 1680	1680/75
Evans, William	Llandygwnning Cn	–	B	8 July 1684	1684/43
Eyton, Elizabeth	Llan-rhudd D	Widow	W I	21 Aug. 1686	1686/101
Eaton, George	Llandinam Mg	–	W* B	10 April 1641	1641/70
Eyton, Richard	Llanfair [Dyffryn Clwyd D]	Vicar of Llanfair [Dyffryn Clwyd]	I	n.d.[2]	1684/93
Farmer, Jane	Rhuthun D	Widow	W* I*	[ ] 1697/8	1697/60
Fazakerley, John	Llangelynnin (Brynmadryn) Mr	Gent.	W I Rd	[24 Oct. 1691]	1691/94
Fields, John	Beaumaris A	Corviser	W* I B	31 May 1671	1671/5
Fletcher, Anne	Carno (D[e]rowloyne) Mg	Widow	W I Rd	2 May 1683	1683/94
Fletcher, Margarett	Bangor (Treborth Issa) Cn	Widow	W I	21 Sept. 1664	1664/52
Fletcher, Thomas	Bangor (Treborth) Cn	Gent.	W	7 Aug. 1648	1648/7
Fletcher, Thomas	Bangor (Treborth) Cn	Gent.	B	29 Aug. 1680	1680/18
Foulkes *alias* Wynne, Edward	Llanrhaeadr-yng-Nghinmeirch (Llewesog) D	Gent.	B I	14 March 1691/2	1691/112
Foulke, Elizabeth	Llanrhaeadr-yng-Nghinmeirch (Meyfod) D	Widow	W*	4 Sept. 1699	1699/134
Foulke, Evan	Llangynhafal D	–	W I	28 May 1668	1668/116
Foulke, Henry	Llandyrnog D	Yeoman	W* I* Db	25 April 1694	1694/101
Foulke, Hugh	Llanfwrog (Bodyngharad) D	–	I/G*	[19 Aug. 1676]	1676/92

[1] Inventory taken 7 Nov. 1685.
[2] Inventory taken 2 Jan. 1684 (36 Chas. II).

Name	Parish & County	Status	Docs. Filed	Date of Probate/Admon.	Ref. No.
Foulke, Jane	Llanrhaeadr-yng-Nghinmeirch D	Spinster	W B	30 Jan. 1640/1	1640/57
Foulke, John	Llanrhaeadr-yng-Nghinmeirch (Trefibychain) D	–	I	n.d.[1]	1689/86
Foulks, John	Betws-y-coed Cn	–	B	28 Feb. 1692/3	1692/35
Foulke, Margrett	Llanrhaeadr-yng-Nghinmeirch D	Widow	W*	10 Jan. [1638/9]	1638/82
Foulke, Robert	Llanynys D	–	W	5 May 1637	1637/48
Fowlke, Robert	Llangynhafal D	–	W I Rd B	6 March 1678/9	1678/71
Foulkes, Thomas	Conway Cn	–	B I	17 Feb. 1684/5	1684/36
Foulke, William	Llangynhafal D	–	B*	20 Sept. 1670	1670/171
Foulkes, Foulks *see* Foulke					
Foxwist, Robert	Llanystumdwy Cn	Yeoman	W* I	19 Aug. 1698	1698/46
Foxwist, Rondle	[Llanbeblig] (Carnarvon) Cn	Minor	B	7 May 1672	1672/47
Foxwist, William	[Llanbeblig] (Carnarvon) Cn	Mercer/Gent.	W I	22 Jan. 1672/3	1672/48
Foxwist, William	[Llanbeblig (Carnarvon) Cn] & St. Albans	Esq.	W*	n.d.[2]	1673/24
Francis, Evan	Llanynys (Plas y Warde) D	–	B I	1 March 1685/6	1685/100
Franciss, Hugh	Llanarmon Cn	–	W I	26 Nov. 1680	1680/27
Frannces, John	Llandinam Mg	–	W I	11 Oct. 1669	1669/160
Francis, John	Llanarmon Cn	Yeoman	W I B	26 Nov. 1687	1687/51
Francis, Thomas	Llanidloes Mg	–	B I	17 Dec. 1698	1698/79
Gabriel, Owen	Cricieth Cn	–	I	23 Nov. 1670	1670/88
Gabriel, William	Bodedern A	–	B I	4 July 1688	1688/5
Galloway, Hugh	Beaumaris A	Shoemaker	B* I*	1 May 1699	1699/3
Gardner, Richard	Llandinam Mg	–	B I	25 Feb. 1661/2	1661/127
Gardner, Robert	Trefeglwys Mg	–	W I	6 Dec. 1670	1670/190
Garnons, Hugh	Llanllyfni (Pantdû) Cn	Gent.	W	17 Aug. 1698	1698/39
George, Elizabeth	Penmynydd A	Widow	W* I	8 Oct. 1669	1669/48
George, Lowry	Llanidloes Mg	Widow	W	n.d.[3]	1671/145
George, Robert	Aber (Crymlyn) Cn	Yeoman	B* I	29 July 1696	1696/27
George, Thomas	Aber Cn	Yeoman	B I	4 Feb. 1696/7	1696/28
George, William	Beaumaris A	–	B I	21 April 1685	1685/4
George, William	Llanfairfechan Cn	–	B I	28 Nov. 1685	1685/49
Gethinge, Edward	Llandyrnog (Corvedwen) D	Gent.	W Rd	30 Aug. 1661	1661/114

1 Died 16 July 1689.
2 Will dated 25 March 1673.
3 Will dated 24 April 1671.

Name	Parish & County	Status	Docs. Filed	Date of Probate/Admon.	Ref. No.
Gibbs, Hugh	Carno Mg	–	W	n.d.[1]	1685/107
Gilbert, Thomas	[Llanfflewin] (Brwynog) A	–	B I	1 Aug. 1692	1692/17
Gittins, Margery	Llandinam (Gwerneryn) Mg	Widow	W I	28 Sept. 1669	1669/161
Glynne, Edmund	Llanwnda (Hendre) Cn	Esq.	B I	4 Aug. 1685	1685/58
Glyn, Henry	Llandwrog (Penhegell) Cn	Gent.	W I	27 Aug. 1672	1672/59
Glynne, Jane	Llandwrog (Plas Newidd) Cn	Widow	B I Db	6 Nov. 1668	1668/55
Glynne, Jane	Clynnog Cn	Widow	W	n.d.[2]	1669/64
Glynne, Jeffrey	[Llannor] (Gunfryn) Cn	Gent.	W(2) Rd	19 April 1672	1672/75
Glynne, John	Llandwrog (Placenewydd) Cn	Gent.	W Rd	[26 Sept. 1681]	1681/47
Glynne, John	[Llandwrog] (Glynnllifon) Cn	Esq.	W Rd C	14 Jan. 1685/6	1685/45
Glynne, Kilmine	Llandygái Cn	Clerk	W	[2 June 1677]	1677/37
Glynn, Margarett	Llanfihangel-y-Pennant (Brinkyr) Cn	Widow	W*	10 Feb. 1641/2	1641/38
Glynne *alias* Bulkeley, Mary	Llangristiolus A	Widow	B*	24 Feb. 1662/3	1662/25
Glynne, Richard	Llanllyfni (Bryn y gwdion) Cn	Gent.	W Rd	4 Nov. 1642	1642/27
Glynn, Rowland	Llanidloes Mg	Gent.	W	31 Oct. 1696	1696/134
†Glynne, William	Clynnog (Lleyar) Cn	Esq.	B I	28 Feb. 1660/1	1660/12
Glynne, William	Aber-erch Cn	Gent.	B I	9 Sept. 1686	1686/27
Glynne, William	Llanaelhaearn (Elernion) Cn	Esq.	W I	3 Aug. 1695	1695/33
Glyn, William ap Richard	Llanarmon Cn	–	W B	18 Feb. 1636/7	1636/29
Godfrey, William	Tywyn Mr	–	B I Db	31 July 1690	1690/100
Gooden, Richard	Rhuthun D	Apothecary	W* I	[20 March 1677/8]	1677/88
Goodman, Anne	Beaumaris A	Widow	W B	12 Feb. 1685/6	1685/5
Goodman, Charles	Llanelidan (Glanhespin) D	Esq.	W I	13 Nov. 1693	1693/102
Goodman, Gawen	Rhuthun D	Gent.	W I	10 March 1685/6	1685/103
Goodman, Hugh	Bodedern A	Gent.	W I	4 May 1671	1671/6
Goodman, John	Beaumaris A	Gent.	W* I	7 Oct. 1673	1673/2
Goodman, Richard	[Llanbeulan] (Tal-y-llyn) A	Gent.	W* I* C	4 Sept. 1688	1688/11
Goodwyn, Edward	Trefeglwys Mg	–	W	[15 Aug. 1661]	1661/146
Goodwyn, Edward	Trefeglwys Mg	Yeoman	W I	18 June 1677	1677/94
Gouff, Hugh ap Evan	Aber-erch Cn	–	W	27 Jan. 1636/7	1636/23
Gray, Rowland	Llanfair-yng-Nghornwy A	Cooper	W/I	11 Jan. 1664/5	1664/22
Greene, Ales	Rhuthun D	Widow	W	19 Sept. 1687	1687/127
Greene, Edward	Rhuthun D	Gent.	W	29 March 1670	1670/175
Green, Godfrey	[Llanbeblig] (Carnarvon) Cn	Gent./Apothecary	W* I	26 April 1699	1699/50
Greenwood, Joseph	Beaumaris A	Tanner	W Rd	10 Aug. 1676	1676/2

[1] Will dated 22 June 1685.
[2] Will dated 30 Oct. 1669.

Name	Parish & County	Status	Docs. Filed	Date of Probate/Admon.	Ref. No.
Gregory, Anthony	Llangurig Mg	–	W I	20 Sept. 1666	1666/117
Gregory, Harry	Llanidloes Mg	Yeoman	W	28 Nov. 1676	1676/103
Gregory, Robert	Llangurig Mg	–	W	25 Sept. 1697	1697/63
Griffith, Agnes	Llangelynnin Mr	Widow	W	6 June 1661	1661/103
Griffith, Agnes	Llanllechid Cn	–	B I	14 April 1694	1694/56
Griffith, Alice	Trefdraeth A	Widow	{W {W(2)	4 Oct. 1665 26 Oct. 1667	1665/27 1667/45
Griffith, Anne	Llanarmon Cn	Widow	W	14 Feb. 1667/8	1667/63
Gruffyth, Anne	Dolwyddelan Cn	Widow	W	7 Sept. 1696	1696/49
Griffith, Anthony	Llanfair Dyffryn Clwyd D	–	B I	20 May 1665	1665/83
Griffith, Arthur	Holyhead A	Gent.	W	17 Sept. 1698	1698/3
Griffith, Kadwalader	Penmorfa Cn	Gent.	B I	6 July 1694	1694/63
Griffith, Catherin	Llanfair-yng-Nghornwy A	Widow	W	29 April 1647	1647/11
Griffith, Katherin	Dolgellau Mr	Spinster	B	3 April 1665	1665/60
Griffith, Katherine	Llanbedr Dyffryn Clwyd D	Widow	B I L	1 April 1667	1667/118
Gruffith, Katherine	Llanfihangel[-y-Pennant] Cn	Widow	W I	24 March 1674/5	1674/23
Griffith, Catherine	Llandwrog (Llwyn y gwalch) Cn	Widow	W B	19 Sept. 1688	1688/48
Griffith, David	Llanllyfni Cn	–	B	4 July 1661	1661/79
Griffith, David	Aber Cn	Smith	B I	20 Jan. 1684/5	1684/24
Griffith, David	Llanllyfni Cn	Yeoman	W	16 July 1695	1695/51
Griffith, David	Llanaelhaearn Cn	Yeoman	W I	4 May 1698	1698/30
Griffith, Dorothy	Llandwrog Cn	–	B	2 Aug. 1667	1667/66
Gruffith, Doulce	Llansadwrn A	Widow	B I	11 Jan. 1667/8	1667/36
Griffith, Edward	Llanaber Mr	–	W	2 July 1638	1638/56
Griffith, Edward	Llanystumdwy Cn	–	B I	16 June 1663	1663/70
Gruffyth, Edward	Caerhun Cn	–	W I G	1 July 1669	1669/62
Griffith, Edward	Llanaber Mr	–	B	3 June 1670	1670/138
Griffith, Edward	Llanelltud Mr	–	W I	25 April 1693	1693/78
Gryffyth, Edward	Llanelidan D	–	B I	7 Oct. 1695	1695/90
Griffith, Elenor	Llanegryn Mr	Widow of Rees ap Evan of Llwyn-goril, yeoman	W I*	3 April 1666	1666/86
Griffith, Ellen	Llanllyfni Cn	–	B	21 Feb. 1661/2	1661/80
Gruffith, Ellin	Llanynghenedl (Cleiviog) A	Widow	W I G	14 May 1661	1661/26
Griffith, Ellin	[Llanaelhaearn] (Llether-du) & Llanllyfni Cn	Widow [of Robert Griffith]	W I R D B Al	30 April 1691	1691/66
Griffith, Elin	Amlwch (Gwredog) A	Spinster	W I(2) B Rd	15 Feb. 1694/5	1694/3

Name	Parish & County	Status	Docs. Filed	Date of Probate/Admon.	Ref. No.
Griffith, Ellen	[Llanbeblig] (Carnarvon) Cn	Widow	R	n.d.[1]	1696/40
Griffith, Ellin	Ynyscynhaearn Cn	Widow	W	12 March 1699/1700	1699/94
Gruffith, Ellis	Gyffylliog D	–	W I	24 April 1668	1668/104
Gruffith, Elizabeth	Clynnog Cn	Spinster	W Al	25 Sept. 1668	1668/41
Gruffuth, Elizabeth	Llangoed A	Widow	W I	8 Jan. 1668/9	1668/18
Griffith, Ellen/Ellin *see* Griffith, Elin					
Gruffith, Ellis *as* Griffith, Elis					
Griffith, Erlliw	Llannor Cn	Spinster	W I	[8 May 1675]	1675/28
Griffith, Evan	Aberdaron Cn	–	B I	17 Nov. 1669	1669/54
Griffyth, Evan	Aberdaron Cn	Freeholder	W I	16 Feb. 1693/4	1693/29
Griffyth, Evan	Dolwyddelan Cn	Yeoman	W	11 Feb. 1696/7	1696/50
Griffith, Frances	Trefdraeth (Marian) A	Widow	W	1 March 1679/80	1679/15
Griffith, George	Llanidloes Mg	Yeoman	W	[17 Nov. 1692]	1692/124
Griffith, Grace	Llangwnnadl (Treigwraig) Cn	Widow	W R	8 July 1672	1672/68
Griffith, Harry	Llanidan A	–	B	27 March 1682	1682/23
Griffith, Henry	Bryncroes Cn	Weaver	W	[11 May 1692]	1692/37
Griffith, Hugh	[Llandudwen] (Madrin Isaph) Cn	Esq.	W	8 Nov. 1662	1662/46
Gruffith, Hugh	Llangybi Cn	Carpenter/Millwright	W I	10 April 1662	1662/50
Gryffith, Hughe	Llaniestyn Cn	–	I	n.d.[2]	1670/118
Griffith, Hugh	Derwen D	Yeoman	I/G	3 July [ ][3]	1676/86
Griffith, Hugh	Llanfwrog A	–	W	n.d.[4]	1676/16
Griffith, Hugh	Llanfair Dyffryn Clwyd (Llainwen, Derwen) D	– –	W I	[16 June 1679]	1679/53
Griffith, Hugh	Llanfair Pwllgwyngyll A	Clerk	B	15 March 1681/2	1681/11
Gruffeth, Humffrey	Dolgellau Mr	–	W*	7 March 1640/1	1640/38
Griffith, Humphrey	Llanenddwyn (Stymgwern) Mr	Yeoman	W* I	21 Nov. 1699	1699/112
Gryffyth, Jane	[Llanbeblig] (Caernarvon) Cn	Spinster	W	2 Aug. 1647	1647/21
Gruffyth, Jane	[Llanbeblig] (Carnarvon) Cn	Widow of William Gruffydd, esq.	W*	16 Jan. 1662/3	1662/41
Griffyth, Jane	Llanaelhaearn Cn	Widow	W	14 Sept. 1675	1675/22
Gruffith, Jane	Penmorfa Cn	Widow	W* L B	20 Oct. 1677	1677/49

1 Renunciation dated 15 Sept. 1696.
2 Inventory taken 10 Dec. 1670.
3 *1676* or *1677*, depending on the reckoning used in dating the inventory (taken 6 March 1676).
4 Will dated 13 April 1676.

Name	Parish & County	Status	Docs. Filed	Date of Probate/Admon.	Ref. No.
Griffith, Jane	Llanarmon Cn	Widow	W I	15 June 1681	1681/41
Griffith, Jane	Llandwrog Cn	Widow	W* I*	12 Oct. 1689	1689/44
Griffith, Jane	Clynnog Cn	Widow of Thomas ap William Morris	W I	15 May 1696	1696/44
Griffith, Jenkin	Llangurig Mg	Gent./Yeoman	W I	20 Jan. 1693/4	1693/137
Griffith, Jenkin	Tywyn Mr	Yeoman	B I*	2 Aug. 1697	1697/56
Gryffith, Sir John	Llanfair-iuxta-Harlech Mr	Clerk	W	31 May 1638	1638/61
Griffyth, John	Llanllyfni Cn	–	W	14 June 1644	1644/28
Griffith, John	Aber-erch Cn	–	W	21 Oct. 1645	1645/18
Griffith, John	Llanfaethlu A	Clerk (Rector of Llanfaethlu and Llanbeulan)	W	12 July 1648	1648/3
Griffith, John	[Llantrisant] (Chwaen) & Llanddyfnan A	Gent.	B	7 March 1661/2	1661/24
Griffith, John	Llanrhuddlad A	Yeoman	B G	23 Feb. 1664/5	1664/39
Griffith, John	[?Penmorfa] (Kilfach) Cn	Yeoman	B I R	5 Aug. 1668	1668/73
Griffith, John	[Llanddeiniolen] (Fronoley) Cn	–	I/G	12 Nov. 1670	1670/133
Griffith, John	Rhuthun D	–	B I	17 Jan. 1678/9	1678/79
Griffith, John	Llandinam Mg	Yeoman	W I	3 Oct. 1681	1681/104
Griffith, John	Llandecwyn (Hendre Inion) Mr	Yeoman	B I	5 March 1685/6	1685/72
Griffith, John	Penllech (Kevnamwlch) Cn	Esq.	W Rd	17 Jan. 1688/9	1688/59
Griffith, John	Llanidloes Mg	Yeoman	W I	19 July 1689	1689/92
Griffith, Shon	Beddgelert (Bool[ch] Mwrchan) Cn	Yeoman	W I B	4 April 1690	1690/44
Griffith, John	Llandygái Cn	–	W	9 Feb. 1690/1	1690/57
Griffith, John	Llangurig (Glyngunwidd) Mg	Yeoman	W I Al	5 July 1692	1692/117
Griffith, John	[Penmorfa] (Llystyn Rhydd) Cn	–	I	n.d.[1]	1693/67
Griffith, John	Clynnog Cn	Yeoman	B I	24 Aug. 1695	1695/29
Griffith, John	Llantrisant (Penhesgin) A	Gent.	B I	25 Aug. 1696	1696/22
Griffyth, John (the elder)	Llechylched A	Esq.	W I(2)	11 May 1696	1696/23
Griffith, John	Bodedern A	Gent.	B I	13 June 1699	1699/5
Griffith, John	Dolgellau (Dyffrydan) Mr	Gent./Yeoman	B I	11 July 1699	1699/98
Griffith, John	Llechylched A	Gent.	W I Rd	20 Oct. 1699	1699/34
Griffyth, Jonett	Holyhead A	Widow	B* I	4 Nov. 1670	1670/6
Griffith, Kadwalader *as* Griffith, Cadwaladr					

[1] Inventory taken 30 Jan. 1693/4.

Name	Parish & County	Status	Docs. Filed	Date of Probate/Admon.	Ref. No.
Griffith, Katherine *see* Griffith, Catherine					
Gruffith, Lewis	Derwen D	–	W*	30 April 1636	1636/53
Griffith, Lewis	Llanfachreth A	–	B	17 Sept. 1689	1689/12
Gruffyth, Lowrance	Aber-erch Cn	–	W B	7 June 1638	1638/30
Gruffuth, Lowry	Llandecwyn Mr	Widow	W* B*	23 Aug. 1641	1641/49
†Gryffyth, Margaret	Llanfair Dyffryn Clwyd (Tre yr faenol) D	Widow	W* I	14 Nov. 1663	1663/122
Griffithes, Margaret	Llangurig (Glyngunwidd) Mg	Widow	W I	17 Sept. 1694	1694/120
Griffith, Margerett	Llanberis Cn	Widow [of Richard Rowland]	W Al	1 Aug. 1695	1695/37
Griffith, Margarett	[Llanbeblig] (Carnarvon) Cn	[Wife of Hugh Griffith]	B	27 Jan. 1696/7	1696/41
Griffith, Margery	Dolgellau (Brithdir ysa) Mr	Widow	W I R	[27 Oct.] 1687	1687/87
Gruffith, Martha	Bangor (Pen r allt) Cn	Widow	W I	25 May 1674	1674/13
Griffith, Maurice *see* Griffith, Morris					
Griffith, Morgan	Llandudwen (Madrin Isaph) Cn	Gent.	W R(2)	20 March 1669/70	1669/77
Griffith, Morgan	Tywyn Mr	–	B	16 Sept. 1680	1680/59
Griffith, Morgan	Llanwnnog Mg	–	B	9 April 1684	1684/116
Griffith, Morgan	Llanwnnog Mg	–	B	25 Sept. 1685	1685/121
Griffith, Maurice	Llanfwrog D	–	B I	12 April 1667	1667/122
Griffith, Morris	[Llanfihangel-y-Pennant] (Fach-goch) Cn	–	W I	[28 April] 1669	1669/106
Griffith, Moris	Maentwrog Mr	–	W/I	[5 Aug. 1672]	1672/97
Griffith, Morice	Llanfair-iuxta-Harlech (Tyddun du) Mr	Yeoman	W I Al Ir D	18 April 1684	1684/72
Griffith, Maurice	Aberdaron (Methlem) Cn	Gent.	W I* B*	29 Feb. 1687/8	1687/32
Griffith, Maurice	[Llanbeblig] (Carnarvon) Cn	Gent./Ironmonger	W I Rd	27 Nov. 1699	1699/51
Griffeth, Owen	Gyffin Cn	–	W	5 Feb. 1637/8	1637/23
Griffith, Owen	Llanfairfechan Cn	–	B I	4 Feb. 1664/5	1664/68
Gruffith, Owen	Llanbedr Mr	–	W	28 Jan. 1669/70	1669/121
Griffith, Owen	[Llanfihangel-y-Pennant] (Fach-goch) Cn	–	I*	n.d.[1]	1669/107
Griffith, Owen	Clynnog Cn	–	L	20 Aug. 1673	1673/26
Griffyth, Owen	Llanfair Mathafarn Eithaf A	Gent.	W* I	10 Nov. 1680	1680/8
Griffith, Owen	Llanfairfechan Cn	–	W I	16 Dec. 1693	1693/50

[1] Inventory taken 5 April 1669.

Name	Parish & County	Status	Docs. Filed	Date of Probate/Admon.	Ref. No.
Griffith *alias* Owens, Penelope	Llanddwywe Mr	Widow	W I	6 Oct. 1675	1675/42
Griffith, Piers	Gyffylliog D	Yeoman	W* I*	24 [ ][1]	1679/51
Gruffith, Rees	Cricieth Cn	–	W	2 Aug. 1647	1647/25
Griffith, Rees	Bangor Cn	Gent.	W I	n.d.[2]	1681/27
Griffith, Rees	Tywyn (Brwinllis) Mr	Yeoman	W* I*	1 Aug. 1690	1690/101
Griffith, Richard	Llanfaethlu A	Gent.	W	24 July 1640	1640/10
Griffith, Richard	Llanwnnog (Uchlawrecoid) Mg	Gent.	W	12 April 1641	1641/76
Griffith, Richard	Beddgelert (Wennallt) Cn	Gent.	W	5 Feb. 1646/7	1646/12
Gryffyth, Richard	Llanddeiniolen Cn	Yeoman	W B	9 Jan. 1661/2	1661/69
Griffithes, Richard	Llanidloes Mg	Mercer	W*	18 Aug. 1662	1662/102
Gruffith, Richard	Llanenddwyn (Talwrn) Mr	–	B I	25 May 1665	1665/66
Griffith, Richard	Llanenddwyn Mr	Yeoman	B I	3 April 1666	1666/89
Griffyth, Richard	Ceidio Cn	Yeoman	W	22 July 1668	1668/39
Griffith, Richard	Llanwnnog Mg	–	I/G	19 Oct. 1668	1668/141
Griffith, Richard	Dolbenmaen Cn	–	I	18 Jan. 1670/1	1670/93
Griffith, Richard	Llanllyfni (Taleithin fynydd) Cn	Gent.	W I Rd	30 Oct. 1679	1679/27
Griffith, Richard	Trefeglwys Mg	–	B C	5 July 1679	1679/69
Griffith, Richard	Llanfair-is-gaer Cn	Esq.	W* I* Rd*	5 Aug. 1681	1681/49
Gruffith, Richard	Llanfwrog D	Yeoman	W I	27 May 1681	1681/95
Gruffyth, Richiard	Llanystumdwy Cn	–	B I	13 Sept. 1681	1681/57
Gryffith, Richard	Dolgellau (Gar[thgyn]vor) Mr	Shoemaker	I/G	14 Sept. 1694	1694/67
Griffith, Richard	Llandanwg Mr	Yeoman	W* I*	18 May 1697	1697/45
Gruffyth, Robert	Beddgelert Cn	–	W*	17 July 1638	1638/33
Gryffyth, Robert	Llanddwywe Mr	–	W	20 May 1664	1664/89
Gruffyth, Robert	Cricieth (Bach y Sainte) Cn	–	W I	6 Nov. 1667	1667/60
Griffith, Robert	[Llanfaethlu] (Careg-lwyd) A	Gent.	W I Rd	4 May 1667	1667/19
Griffith, Robert	Beddgelert (Sygyn) Mr	Gent.	B	18 June 1670	1670/72
Gruffyth, Robert	Beddgelert Cn	–	W I	20 March 1672/3	1672/44
Griffith, Robert	Llanddwywe Mr	–	W	[7 Aug. 1672]	1672/92
Griffith, Robert	Llanaelhaearn (Lletherdû) Cn	Gent.	W I Rd	1 Oct. 1677	1677/33
Griffith, Robert	[Llanbeblig] (Carnarvon) Cn	–	W I	n.d.	1681/35
Griffyth, Robert	Dolwyddelan (Brunmoile) Cn	Yeoman	W I B	15 Aug. 1687	1687/48
Griffith, Robert	Dolgellau Mr	Gent.	I/G	19 Jan. 1696/7	1696/87
Griffith, Robert	Llanarmon (Kefnpencoed) Cn	Yeoman	W I	22 Aug. 1696	1696/53
Griffith, Roger	Llanynys (Rhydonen) D	–	W* Rd*	10 Nov. 1638	1638/85
Griffith, Rowland	Llanllechid Cn	–	W	10 July 1645	1645/31

[1] Will dated 27 June 1679.

[2] Inventory taken 18 July 1681.

Name	Parish & County	Status	Docs. Filed	Date of Probate/Admon.	Ref. No.
Gruffyth, Rowland	Aber (Bodsilin) Cn	Gent.	W Rd	7 Feb. 1667/8	1667/46
Gruffyth, Rowland	Penrhos[llugwy] A	–	B I	29 Oct. 1667	1667/40
†Gruff[ith], Rowland	Llandygái Cn	–	I/G I[1]	8 May 1669	1669/82
Griffith, Rowland	Llanllechid Cn	Tailor	W Al B	30 April 1696	1696/75
Griffith, Sabell	Llanddona A	Widow	B I	23 Nov. 1670	1670/24
Griffith, Sarah	Penllech [Cefn Amwlch] Cn	Minor	B	17 Jan. 1688/9	1688/60
Griffith, Simon	Clocaenog (Llannerchgron) D	Gent.	W I	8 Feb. 1667/8	1667/115
Griffith, Thomas	Llanfwrog D	?Yeoman	W	14 Dec. 1638	1638/80
Gruffith, Thomas	Llanfihangel [Bachellaeth] Cn	–	B	22 Nov. 1667	1667/71
Gruffith, Thomas	Bryncroes Cn	Miller	W I	[8 Jan. 1675/6]	1675/18
Griffith, Thomas	Dolbenmaen (Dolwgan) Cn	–	W	28 Feb. 1680/1	1680/25
Griffith, Thomas	Gyffylliog (Ffrithoedd) D	–	W I	11 Oct. 1680	1680/64
Gruffith, Thomas	Llanelidan D	–	W Cd I	15 July 1684	1684/91
Griffith, Thomas	Edern Cn	–	B I*	16 April 1687	1687/50
Griffith, Thomas	Nefyn Cn	–	B	30 May 1687	1687/74
Gryffith, Ursula	Dolgellau Mr	Widow	W	19 June 1676	1676/64
Griffith, William	Llangïan Cn	Gent.	W Rd	6 Nov. 1645	1645/30
Griffyth, William	Llanllechid (Tû Gwyn) Cn	Gent.	W	4 Aug. 1645	1645/32
Griffith, William	Llanystumdwy (Ffrithlwyd) Cn	–	B I	12 Jan. 1660/1	1660/19
Griffith, William	Bangor (Penrallt) Cn	Gent.	W I Rd	13 Feb. 1663/4	1663/34
Gruffyth, William	Llanwnda Cn	Carpenter	W Cd I	1 March 1669/70	1669/98
Griffyth, William	Holyhead A	Gent.	I/G	29 March 1673	1673/5
Griffith, William	Bangor (Pen'rallt) Cn	–	B	13 April 1686	1686/32
Griffith, William	Llanberis Cn	–	B I	29 Feb. 1687/8	1687/56
Griffith, William	[Penllech] (Kefnamwlch) Cn	Esq.	W* I	26 Nov. 1688	1688/61
Griffith, William	Llangristiolus A	Yeoman	B I	15 April 1691	1691/29
Griffith, William	Bodfean Cn	–	B	3 July 1692	1692/36
Griffith, William	Llandudwen (Madryn Issa) Cn	Esq.	W I	17 Jan. 1693/4	1693/48
Griffith, William	Llanelltud (Havod fedw) Mr	–	W* I	7 Aug. 1694	1694/84
Griffith, William	Bangor Cn	Yeoman	B I	1 Feb. 1696/7	1696/36
Griffiths, Gruffith, Gryffith etc. *see* Griffith					
Gwnnys, Griffyth	Llanengan Cn	–	W* I L*	16 May 1671	1671/69
Gunnys, Griffith	Llandygwnning Cn	Gent.	W I	28 May 1672	1672/61
Gunnis, John	Llanengan Cn	Clerk (Rector of Llanengan)	W I Rd	26 Feb. 1686/7	1686/54

[1] A list in Welsh of household goods only, individually priced. The items are not listed individually in the other inventory but grouped together as *houshold stuffes*.

Name	Parish & County	Status	Docs. Filed	Date of Probate/Admon.	Ref. No.
Gunnis, Richard	Llandygwnning (Neugwl) Cn	Gent.	W* Cd I	17 Dec. 1673	1673/36
Gwyn, Evan	Llangurig (Dernoll) Mg	–	W I	7 Sept. 1678	1678/83
Gwynn, Hugh	Llanfechell (Cromlech) A	Gent.	W	8 Jan. 1635/6	1635/5
Gwyn, Hugh Owen	Llanbedr Niwbwrch A	–	B I	8 Jan. 1693/4	1693/8
Gwynne *alias* Wynne, Lewis	Dolgellau Mr	Gent.	B I*	24 Oct. 1662	1662/57
Gwynn, Mary vch Evan	Llangurig Mg	Widow	I	n.d.[1]	1675/66
Gwynne, Owen	[Ceirchiog][2] (Bodveddan) A	–	W	9 Oct. 1644	1644/3
Gwyn, Richard ap Hugh	Llanllechid Cn	Yeoman	W I B	16 April 1696	1696/79
Gwynne, Robert ap Hugh	[Llandwrog] (Bryn r Odin) Cn	–	B	8 April 1678	1678/28
Gwynne, Thomas	[Llanbadrig] (Rhyt Croes) A	Esq.	B* I(2)	28 Nov. 1687	1687/5
Hall, Abraham	Llangurig Mg	–	I/G	10 Oct. 1663	1663/139
Hall, Christopher	Trefeglwys Mg	–	W	9 April 1641	1641/78
Hall, John	Holyhead A	Gent.	W	9 Sept. 1678	1678/1
Hall, Thomas	Trefeglwys (Maestregymer) Mg	–	B I	5 June 1668	1668/146
Hammer, Abraham	Llanidloes Mg	–	B I	16 Feb. 1694/5	1694/122
Hamer, Adam	Llanidloes Mg	–	W I	27 Sept. 1667	1667/136
Hamer, Charles	Llangurig Mg	Yeoman	W I	[31 May 1688]	1688/102
Hamer, Ezekiell	Llandinam Mg	Gent./Yeoman	W I	7 July 1693	1693/131
Hammond, Elizabeth	Llanegryn Mr	Widow	W I	31 July 1690	1690/92
Hampton, Edwarde	Beaumaris A	Gent.	W/I	n.d.[3]	1600/1
Hampton, William	[Llan-faes] (Henllys) A	Esq.	W I	19 Oct. 1665	1665/13
Hanson *alias* Barlow, Jane	Llannor (Bodvell) Cn	Wife of John Barlow, esq.	B I	21 Nov. 1698	1698/41
Harbert *see* Herbert					
Harkman, Edward	Rhuthun D	–	W I Rd	n.d.[4]	1681/102
Harper, Thomas	Llanidloes Mg	Mercer/Gent.	W I	[24 April] 1696	1696/135
Harrison, Anthony	Beaumaris A	Mercer	W I B	18 Feb. 1685/6	1685/6
Harry, Agnes (Ann)	Trawsfynydd Mr	Widow	W I	12 Feb. 1686/7	1686/84
Harry, Ellin	Dolgellau Mr	Spinster	W B	19 June 1676	1676/65
Harry, Humphrey	Ffestiniog (Teilie bach) Mr	Yeoman	W I C	[15 ?Sept. 1691]	1691/81
Harry, Jane	Dolgellau Mr	Widow	W B	19 June 1676	1676/66
Harry, John	Llanfachreth Mr	–	B I L	10 May 1666	1666/90

1 Inventory taken 9 June 1675.
2 Endorsed *Llanbeulan*.
3 Will dated 16 May 1600.
4 Will dated 3 Sept. 1681.

Name	Parish & County	Status	Docs. Filed	Date of Probate/Admon.	Ref. No.
Harry, Morris	Llanfihangel-y-traethau Mr	Yeoman	I/G	11 Sept. 1693	1693/85
Harwarr, Robert	Beaumaris A	Gent.	I	n.d.[1]	1682/3
Hastings, Edward	[Llanbeblig] (Carnarvon) Cn	Gent.	W	[15 Aug. 1682]	1682/38
Hatfeeld, Gyles	Llandinam Mg	–	W I	10 Feb. 1698/9	1698/70
Heb, Thomas	Pennal Mr	Yeoman	W I	4 March 1664/5	1664/101
Herbert, Anne	Trefeglwys Mg	Spinster	W	28 March 1698	1698/82
Herbart, Charles	Rhuthun D	Innkeeper	W I	22 Nov. 1683	1683/93
Herbert, Edward	Llandinam [Dethienith] Mg	Gent.	I/G	[12 Jan.] 1664/5	1664/127
Herbert, John	Llanidloes (Kefn pennarth) Mg	–	I/G	21 Feb. 1666/7	1666/119
Herbert, Morgan	Llanidloes (Kevenpenarth) Mg	Gent.	W*	27 June 1638	1638/88
Harbert, William	Llandinam (Dethienith) Mg	Gent.	B I	28 July 1664	1664/128
Herbert, William	[Trefeglwys] (Ffrith) Mg	Esq.	W	30 May 1670	1670/191
Herbert, William	Trefeglwys (Ffrithe) Mg	Gent.	W* I*	22 May 1697	1697/74
Heynes *alias* Roger, Evan	Carno Mg	–	I/G	17 Feb. 1665/6	1665/89
Holland, Doritie	Conway Cn	Widow of Hugh Hooks	W	21 April 1638	1638/38
Holland, Edward	[Bodedern] (Maes y wrach) A	Gent.	W	n.d.[2]	1661/5
Holland, Hugh	Llanidan A	Gent.	B*	25 Nov. 1691	1691/30
Holland, Jane	Bodedern (Cymynod) A	Widow	I G	6 Nov. 1669	1669/5
Holland, Richard	Conway Cn	Burgess of Conway	W B	2 July 1645	1645/21
Holland, Sir Thomas	[Llanidan] (Berrowe) A	Knight	W(2)*	17 Oct. 1643	1643/11
Holland, Trustan	Llanfihangel Ysgeifiog A	Gent.	B	4 March 1661/2	1661/18
Holland, William	Conway Cn	Gent.	W I Rd*	27 Feb. 1667/8	1667/59
Hooffe, Richard John	Llanenddwyn Mr	Blacksmith	W I	29 July 1679	1679/42
Hookes, Catherine	Llanegryn Mr	–	B C	30 July 1686	1686/76
Hookes, Elizabeth	Conway / [Gyffin] (Llechen) Cn	Spinster	B I G	8 April 1668	1668/45
Hookes, Margarett	Conway Cn	Widow	B R	17 Nov. 1693	1693/38
Hookes, Nicholas	Conway Cn	Gent.	B I	6 June 1661	1661/50
Hookes, William	Conway [& Gyffin (Llechan)][3] Cn	Esq.	W I	n.d.[4]	1669/66
Hoomes, Thomas	[Llanbeblig] (Carnarvon) Cn	–	B	20 Nov. 1663	1663/39
Howell, David	Llanwnnog Mg	–	B I	11 Oct. 1663	1663/147
Howell, David	Carno Mg	Yeoman	W I	17 Feb. 1672/3	1672/123
Howel, David	Tywyn Mr	Yeoman	W I* Db	18 June 1684	1684/79

1 Inventory taken 1 March 1682 (35 Chas. II).

2 Will dated 6 Oct. 1659; endorsed *probatum fuit in anno 1660 vel 1661.*

3 Supplied from the admon. of Elizabeth Hookes.

4 Inventory taken 7 March 1669[/70]. Will uncompleted and endorsed *not finished or proved.*

Name	Parish & County	Status	Docs. Filed	Date of Probate/Admon.	Ref. No.
Howell, Elizabeth	Dolgellau (Brithdir) Mr	Widow	W I	n.d.[1]	1689/64
Howel, Gruffyth	Tywyn Mr	–	W	23 April 1635	1635/38
Howell, Jane	Llanaber Mr	Spinster	W D	23 Aug. 1666	1666/81
Howell, Jenkin	Llangurig (Llanyvuny) Mg	–	W I	5 July 1692	1692/118
Howell, John	Llanwnnog Mg	–	B	8 May 1679	1679/67
Howell, John	Llanaber Mr	–	B I	23 Sept. 1685	1685/70
Howel, Margaret	Dolgellau Mr	–	I	12 Oct. 1666	1666/73
Howell, Margery *alias* Marsley	Llanaber Mr	Widow	W I	9 June 1687	1687/95
Howell, Mary	Llangurig Mg	Widow	I/G	17 Feb. 1665/6	1665/102
Hugh *see* Hughes					
Hughes, Abraham	Holyhead A	Mariner	W I	6 July 1694	1694/9
Hughes, Ales	Rhuthun D	Spinster	W* Rd*	4 Aug. 1640	1640/59
Hughes, Andrew	Llanrhaeadr-yng-Nghinmeirch (Segroyt) D	–	W I	16 Feb. 1662/3	1662/90
Hughes, Ann	Carno Mg	–	B I	16 March 1685/6	1685/108
Hughes, Anne	[Llanfaethlu] (Trevadog) A	Spinster	Rd	n.d.[2]	1685/18
Hughes, Anne	Llanbedrog (Wernfawr) Cn	Spinster	W	5 Feb. 1696/7	1696/56
Hughes, Kathering	Llanrhaeadr-yng-Nghinmeirch D	Widow	W I	[4 March 1688/9]	1688/92
Hugh, David	Llanidloes Mg	Labourer	W(2) I	17 Feb. 1665/6	1665/104
Hughes, David	Llannor (Pempris) Cn	–	W I C	9 April 1672	1672/76
Hughes, David	Llanrhaeadr-yng-Nghinmeirch (Brynllearth) D	–	B I	25 Feb. 1672/3	1672/115
Hughes, David	Llangristiolus A	Yeoman	W I	15 March 1686/7	1686/18
Hughes, David	Dolwyddelan Cn	–	B I	9 Oct. 1694	1694/45
Hughes, Dorothy	Llangeinwen A	Spinster	B	26 Dec. 1664	1664/30
Hughes, Edmond	Llanrhuddlad A	Yeoman	B I	13 March 1684/5	1684/19
Hughes, Edward	Llandyrnog D	–	B I	20 July 1692	1692/97
Hughes, Ellin	[Bodedern] (Cymynod) A	Widow	W Rd	15 May 1637	1637/2
Hughes *alias* Williams, Ellin	Beaumaris A	Widow	B I	18 Feb. 1669/70	1669/2
Hughes, Ellin	Beaumaris A	Spinster	W	15 Feb. 1691/2	1691/6
Hughes, Ellis	Tywyn (Aberdovey) Mr	Gent.	W C	28 April 1676	1676/85
Hughes, Ellis	Llanllechid (Wynllan) Cn	Yeoman	B I	7 Jan. 1692/3	1692/55
Hughes, Ellis	Bangor Cn	Gent.	B I	2 Oct. 1699	1699/42
Hughes, Elizabeth	Llanbedrog (Wernfawr) Cn	Widow	W	15 June 1677	1677/36
Hughes, Evan	Deneio (Pullhelie) Cn	Tanner	I/G	30 Aug. 1681	1681/37
Hughes, Evan	Bodfean Cn	–	B I	15 June 1687	1687/39

[1] Inventory taken 25 March 1689.

[2] Will proved but not filed; bond for its redelivery dated 3 April 1685.

Name	Parish & County	Status	Docs. Filed	Date of Probate/Admon.	Ref. No.
Hughes, Evan	Llanfaelog A	Clerk (Rector of Llanfaelog)	B I	10 Oct. 1694	1694/16
Hugh, Evan	Tal-y-llyn Mr	–	I/G*	9 June 1696	1696/108
Hughes, Foulk	Llanrhaeadr-yng-Nghinmeirch (Segroit) D	Yeoman	W I	13 Nov. 1691	1691/113
Hughes, Grace	Llanystumdwy (Keven) Cn	–	W	[24 Jan. 1682/3]	1682/58
Hughes, Griffyth	Llanfrothen Mr	Clerk	I L	14 March 1665/6	1665/69
Hughes, Gruffyth, *alias* Griffith ap Hugh Bowen	Llanbeblig Cn	–	B I	16 Jan. 1693/4	1693/45
Hughes, Hennery	Conway Cn	Mercer	W	n.d.[1]	1676/44
Hughes, Henry	Aberffraw (Cerrig Eingan) A	–	B I	23 Aug. 1686	1686/1
Hughes, Henry	Beaumaris A	Mariner	B I	30 March 1687	1687/1
Hughes, Henry	Llanfihangel Bachellaeth Cn	–	B	29 March 1687	1687/64
Hughes, Henry	Llanfairfechan Cn	Bachelor	B I R	9 March 1695/6	1695/46
Hughes, Henry	Llanrhaeadr-yng-Nghinmeirch (Llech) D	Smith	W I	12 June 1695	1695/93
Hughes, Howell	Maentwrog (Brynrodyn) Mr	Gent.	W Rd	27 Feb. 1678/9	1678/48
Hughes, Hugh	Beaumaris A	Gent.	W	7 June 1642	1642/2
Hughes, Hugh	Beaumaris A	Tanner	W I B	12 Dec. 1663	1663/3
Hughes, Hugh	[Llanedwen] (Plascôch) A	Esq.	B	28 May 1666	1666/13
Hughes, Hugh	Heneglwys A	Clerk (Rector of Heneglwys)	W	18 April 1668	1668/6
Hughes, Hugh	Llanfaelog A	–	W	25 June 1690	1690/22
Hugh, Humfrey	Llangelynnin Mr	Miller	W I	4 July 1670	1670/154
Hughes, Jane	[Llanedwen] (Plas Coch) A	Widow	W	5 Jan. 1668/9	1668/13
Hughes, Jane	Llangynhafal D	Widow of John ap Evan ap Rees	B I	7 Aug. 1678	1678/72
Hughes, John	Derwen D	Yeoman	W	20 June 1638	1638/71
Hughes, John	Llanbedrog (Wernvawr) Cn	Gent.	W	25 March 1646	1646/19
Hugh, John	Carno Mg	–	I*	n.d.[2]	1662/95
Hughes, John	Llanidloes Mg	–	B* I*	22 June 1662	1662/103
Hughes, John	Rhuthun D	Butcher	W I	8 Oct. 1663	1663/128
Hughes, John	Llanfechell A	–	I	n.d.[3]	1669/27
Hughes, John *see* Hughes, Owen	Llanddaniel-fab A				

[1] Will dated 10 Nov. 1676.

[2] Inventory taken 29 June 1662.

[3] Inventory taken 9 Oct. 1669.

Name	Parish & County	Status	Docs. Filed	Date of Probate/Admon.	Ref. No.
Hugh, John	Llanfihangel-y-Pennant Mr	–	I/G	[22 June 1676]	1676/78
Hughes, John	Llan-faes (Henllys) A	Gent.	W	8 Feb. 1682/3	1682/19
Hughes, John	Rhuthun D	Butcher	W	7 Dec. 1684	1684/100
Hughes, John	Llanfihangel-y-Pennant Cn	Yeoman	B	2 April 1685	1685/52
Hughes, John	Llangwyllog A	–	B	23 Feb. 1687/8	1687/22
Hughes, John	Holyhead A	Mariner	B I	16 March 1690/1	1690/11
Hughes, John	Penrhosllugwy (Lligwy) A	Gent.	B I	11 Dec. 1690	1690/36
Hugh, John	Llanelltud Mr	–	B I	2 April 1691	1691/88
Hughes, John	Trefdraeth (Marian) A	Gent.	W I	3 Aug. 1691	1691/36
Hugh, John	Tal-y-llyn Mr	Yeoman	W I	28 Jan. 1692/3	1692/85
Hughes, John	Clynnog Cn	Yeoman	B I	17 Jan. 1693/4	1693/35
Hughes, John	Bangor (Aber y pwll) Cn	Smith	W	10 March 1694/5	1694/39
Hughes, John	Rhuthun D	Glover	W I	20 July 1694	1694/111
Hughes, John	Gyffin Cn	–	B I	4 July 1695	1695/32
Hughes, John	Llantrisant A	Gent.	B I	25 Oct. 1695	1695/16
Hughes, John	Llanfaelog A	Yeoman	B	30 Oct. 1696	1696/13
Hughes, John	Bangor Cn	Gent.	B* I*	26 March 1697	1697/14
Hughes, John	Llanddaniel[-fab] A	Labourer	W I	20 July 1697	1697/6
Hughes, Jonete	Llanrhwydrys (Kemlyn) A	Spinster	W	11 March 1644/5	1644/14
Hughes, Kathering *as* Hughes, Catherine					
Hughes, Lewis	Llangwyfan A	–	B I	31 Jan. 1664/5	1664/37
Hughes, Lewis	Llanfihangel-yn-Nhywyn (Towyn) A	Gent.	W R	2 Sept. 1691	1691/25
Hughes *alias* Lloyd, Margaret	Llaniestyn A	–	B*	15 Nov. 1670	1670/49
Hugh, Margaret	Llanddwywe Mr	Spinster	W I	[ ] June 1673	1673/53
Hughes, Margarett	Llaniestyn A	Widow	B	29 Aug. 1682	1682/24
Hughes, Margaret	Llandegfan A	Widow	B I	6 Nov. 1684	1684/9
Hughes, Mary	Holyhead A	Widow	B I	19 Oct. 1691	1691/13
Hughes *alias* Jones, Mary	Bangor Cn	Wife of Elice Hughes, gent.	B	23 Dec. 1692	1692/33
Hugh, Mary	Llandinam Mg	Widow of Hugh Robert	W I	6 Sept. 1695	1695/101
Hughes, Michael	Llangwyllog A	Yeoman	W I B	21 April 1698	1698/10
Hughes, Morgan	Beddgelert (Wernastêg) Cn	Gent.	W I	21 Dec. 1698	1698/21
Hughes, Morris	Beddgelert Cn	Gent.	I/G	10 May 1694	1694/42
Hughes, Owen	Llanfachreth (Bodlasan) A	Gent.	W	25 Sept. 1636	1636/11
Hughes, Owen	Llanbedr Niwbwrch A	Gent.	W	24 Feb. 1644/5	1644/5

Name	Parish & County	Status	Docs. Filed	Date of Probate/Admon.	Ref. No.
Hughes, Owen[1]	Llanddaniel-fab A	Tailor	W I B R	17 July 1669	1669/18
Hughes, Owen	Llangefni A	Clerk (Rector of Llangefni)	B	16 Dec. 1669	1669/36
Hughes, Owen	Llanwnda (Bodaden) Cn	–	W*	n.d.[2]	1670/123
Hughes, Owen	Aberffraw A	Smith	W I	15 May 1679	1679/1
Hughes, Owen	Trewalchmai (Hendre) A	Gent.	W I	3 May 1692	1692/32
Hughes, Owen	Trefdraeth A	–	B	21 April 1693	1693/27
Hughes, Owen	Ynyscynhaearn (Cefn y meusudd) Cn	–	W I	24 Dec. 1695	1695/61
Hugh, Owen	Aber Cn	–	W I M	28 Nov. 1696	1696/29
Hughes, Peter	Llanfwrog D	Yeoman	W* I	29 Jan. 1686/7	1686/98
Hughes, Rees	Llanbedrog (Cefn Llanvair) Cn	Esq.	W I	13 May 1663	1663/54
Hughes, Rees	Heneglwys A	–	B I	13 Nov. 1683	1683/2
Hughes, Richard	Llangoed A	Yeoman	B I	2 Jan. 1660/1	1660/7
Hughes, Richard	Llanddyfnan A	Yeoman	B I	17 Feb. 1662/3	1662/14
Hughes, Richard	Holyhead A	–	B	1 Aug. 1668	1668/7
Hughes, Richard	Beaumaris A	–	B	19 April 1669	1669/3
Hughes, Richard	Llangwyllog A	Gent.	B I	14 Jan. 1670/1	1670/48
Hughes, Richard	Llanwnda Cn	–	B I C	10 May 1680	1680/39
Hughes, Richard	Tywyn Mr	–	B I	31 [?July] 1690	1690/102
Hughes, Richard	Llandyrnog (Rhywbebill) D	Gent.	W	15 Oct. 1691	1691/106
Hughes, Richard	Llanfair-yng-Nghornwy A	Clerk (Rector of Llanddeusant)	B	18 Jan. 1693/4	1693/13
Hughes, Richard	Amlwch A	–	B I R	9 March 1694/5	1694/4
Hughes, Richard	Llanwnda (Bod-aden) Cn	Gent.	B I	3 June 1695	1695/53
Hughes, Richard	Llanddyfnan A	Yeoman	W* I*	27 Nov. 1699	1699/14
Hughes, Robert	Llangïan (Llansoch) Cn	–	C	12 July 1664	1664/71
Hughes, Robert	Trefdraeth A	–	G	13 Feb. 1664/5	1664/45
Hughes, Robert	Deneio Cn	–	B	11 Aug. 1668	1668/48
Hughes, Robert	Derwen D	–	W I	18 Nov. 1672	1672/100
Hughes, Robert	Holyhead (Tre-ddaniel) A	–	B I	8 Feb. 1676/7	1676/6
Hughes, Robert	[Llanrwst] (Gwyder) Cn	–	W	16 Nov. 1680	1680/38
Hughes, Robert	Llangynhafal D	Yeoman	W/I	28 May 1681	1681/98
Hughes, Robert	Bryncroes Cn	–	B I	18 June 1692	1692/38
Hughes, Robert	Aber-erch Cn	–	B	6 July 1693	1693/30

[1] B, I *John*.
[2] Will dated 17 Sept. 1670.

Name	Parish & County	Status	Docs. Filed	Date of Probate/Admon.	Ref. No.
Hughes, Robert	Llanfair Dyffryn Clwyd (Derwen Llannerch) D	Yeoman	I	n.d.[1]	1693/108
Hughes, Robert	Llangwyfan A	Weaver	W Al	4 Dec. 1694	1694/25
Hughes, Robert	Llanrhaeadr-yng-Nghinmeirch (Trevybychyn) D	Yeoman	W* I* B	17 Feb. 1697/8	1697/59
Hughes, Robert	Llanfwrog A	Yeoman	B I	7 March 1698/9	1698/7
Hughes, Rowland	Llanbedr Niwbwrch A	–	B I	10 May 1678	1678/2
Hughes, Rowland	Tywyn Mr	–	B I	18 Sept. 1678	1678/57
Hughes, Rowland	Llanfair-is-gaer (Werne) Cn	Yeoman	B I R	2 Jan. 1690/1	1690/62
Hughes, Sarah	Bodwrog (Cors-r-Eira) A	Widow	W	18 July 1676	1676/4
Hughes, Screeven	Tywyn (Dyffryn Gwyn) Mr	Gent.	I/G	17 Jan. 1698/9	1698/59
Hughes, Sydney	Llaneugrad (Bodgunda) A	Widow [of John ap Evan]	W I	3 June 1684	1684/12
Hughes, Thomas	Llanwnda Cn	–	W* B	13 July 1646	1646/23
Hughes, Thomas	Rhuthun D	–	B*	4 March 1662/3	1662/93
Hughes, Thomas	Llandyfrydog (Clorach) A	Gent.	W I	10 Nov. 1663	1663/13
Hughes, Thomas	Llanfwrog A	–	W*	9 Dec. 1663	1663/21
Hughes, Thomas	Nefyn (Morfa Nevin) Cn	–	W	n.d.	1668/72
Hughes, Thomas	Ceidio Cn	Yeoman	W I	11 Feb. 1670/1	1670/83
Hughes, Thomas	Llanrhaeadr-yng-Nghinmeirch (Brynbagle) D	Gent.	W*	13 June 1671	1671/125
Hughes, Thomas	Llanrhaeadr-yng-Nghinmeirch (Segroyt) D	Yeoman	W	26 May 1684	1684/97
Hughes, Thomas	[Llanrhaeadr-yng-Nghinmeirch] D	–	B I	23 May 1693	1693/114
Hughes, William	Holyhead A	–	W	14 Nov. 1645	1645/4
Hughes, William	Llangoed A	Gent.	W	17 Dec. 1669	1669/39
Hughes, William	Llaniestyn (Penhwnllys) A	Gent.	{ B { B	20 Dec. 1681 28 May 1683	1681/17 1683/15
Hughes, William	Pentraeth A	Gent.	W I	1 April 1687	1687/28
Hughes, William	Bodedern A	–	B I*	27 April 1692	1692/3
Hughes, William	Llanfihangel-yn-Nhywyn A	Gent.	W I Rd(2)	22 Feb. 1695/6	1695/10
Hugh, William	Carno Mg	–	I	n.d.[2]	1696/125
Hugh, William	Carno Mg	Yeoman	W	29 March 1697	1697/61
Hughes, William	Llannor Cn	Gent./Yeoman	W B	13 Aug. 1698	1698/42
Hugh, William	Tywyn (Escair gevele, Keven Rose) Mr	Yeoman	W* Cd* I*	16 April 1698	1698/60

[1] Inventory taken 9 Sept. 1693.
[2] Inventory taken 2 March 1696.

Name	Parish & County	Status	Docs. Filed	Date of Probate/Admon.	Ref. No.
Humphrey, Ales	Llandyfrydog A	Spinster	B	6 Feb. 1663/4	1663/14
Humphrey, Ann	Tywyn (Nant Maney) Mr	Widow	W I	2 Sept. 1687	1687/107
Humffrey, Arthur	Tywyn Mr	–	B I	10 March 1663/4	1663/112
Humphrey, Arthyr	Llanfihangel-y-Pennant Mr	Yeoman	W I	n.d.[1]	1688/79
Humphrey, Barbarah	Llanfihangel-y-Pennant [Cn]	Spinster	B	24 April 1696	1696/70
Humffrey, Catherin	Llangelynnin Mr	Widow	W*	3 June 1670	1670/155
Humphrey, Catherine	[Deneio] (Pwllhely) Cn	Widow	W Al	[30 April 1683]	1683/30
Humphreys *alias* Bulkeley, Katherine	Rhosbeirio A	Widow	W	n.d.	1692/28
Humphrey, David	[ ]	–	W* I*	n.d.[2]	1681/109
Humphrey, Edmund	Llanfair Dyffryn Clwyd D	Yeoman	B R	12 July 1695	1695/91
Humffrey, Edward	Dolgellau Mr	Yeoman	W	27 Feb. 1644/5	1644/30
Humffrey, Edward	Dolgellau Mr	–	W	27 Aug. 1684	1684/64
Humphrey, Edward	Llandyfrydog A	–	B I	24 June 1684	1684/10
Humphrey, Edward	Llanaber Mr	Yeoman	B I	20 Oct. 1688	1688/69
Humphrey, Edward	Llanddwywe Mr	–	I/G	1 Feb. 1695/6	1695/72
Humphrey, Edward	Llanllyfni Cn	Yeoman	B* I*	4 Sept. 1699	1699/82
Humphrey, Elin	Trawsfynydd Mr	Spinster	W	29 June 1678	1678/53
Humphreyes, Ellis	Clynnog Cn	Clerk	W I	3 April 1683	1683/27
Humphrey, Elisabeth	Tal-y-llyn Mr	–	I/G R	4 July 1693	1693/93
Humphrey, Elizabeth	Llanbadrig A	Widow	B I M	7 Dec. 1699	1699/10
Humffreys, Evan	Trefeglwys (Glintrefnant) Mg	Gent.	B I	29 Aug. 1661	1661/147
Humphrey, Evan	Dolgellau Mr	–	B*	17 Nov. 1684	1684/65
Humphrey, Evan	Tywyn Mr	–	I/G*	18 April 1699	1699/117
Humphrey, Griffith	Llanenddwyn Mr	Yeoman	I/G	[9 Oct. 1667]	1667/96
Humphreys, Hugh	Trefdraeth A	Clerk (Rector of Trefdraeth)	W B	19 Jan. 1680/1	1680/15
Humffreys, John	[Tref]eglwys Mg	–	W*	27 July 1640	1640/62
Humffreys, John	Llanenddwyn Mr	–	B	2 Oct. 1667	1667/97
Humffrey, John	Ffestiniog Mr	Yeoman	W* I* M*	16 Jan. 1681/2	1681/66
Humphreyes, John	Llanwnda Cn	–	W* Al* R	16 May 1694	1694/59
Humphrey, John	Llanfair-yng-Nghornwy A	Yeoman	B/I	25 Aug. 1696	1696/15
Humphrey, John	Llanfair-yng-Nghornwy A	Yeoman/Labourer	W I Al	21 March 1699/1700	1699/18
Humphreys, Katherine *see* Humphrey, Catherine					
Humphreys, Lewis	Llanwnnog Mg	–	B I	29 Aug. 1684	1684/117

[1] Inventory taken 10 Sept. 1688.
[2] Inventory taken 8 April 1681.

Name	Parish & County	Status	Docs. Filed	Date of Probate/Admon.	Ref. No.
Humphrey, Mallt	Tal-y-llyn (Cwmcelli) Mr	Widow	W I	12 March 1699/1700	1699/115
Humphrey, Mary	Llanddeiniolen Cn	Widow	W I	7 May 1680	1680/29
Humphrey, Marie	Llanaber Mr	Widow	W I	24 Feb. 1690/1	1690/87
Humphery, Marri	Dolgellau (Deffrudan) Mr	Widow	W I	19 May 1694	1694/68
Humphreys, Mathew	Llanidloes Mg	Corviser	W	10 Dec. 1679	1679/65
Humffrey, Morris	Llanfihangel-y-traethau Mr	–	B*	9 Dec. 1662	1662/68
			W	19 Sept. 1663	1663/106
Humphrey, Owen	Llanbedrog Cn	–	B I	19 March 1663/4	1663/55
Humphrey, Rees	Dolgellau (Dolgleder) Mr	Yeoman	B I	1 Sept. 1687	1687/88
Humphrey, Rice	Llanllyfni Cn	Yeoman	B I*	29 April 1697	1697/33
Humphrey, Richard	Carno Mg	–	I/G	27 Sept. 1666	1666/113
Humphrey, Richard	[Dolgellau] (Garthgynfawr) Mr	Gent.	W Rd	5 April 1666	1666/74
Humphrey, Richard	Llanfaethlu A	Yeoman	B I	5 April 1670	1670/33
Humphreys, Robert	Llandwrog Cn	Yeoman	B	5 March 1668/9	1668/56
Humffrey, Robert	Llanfaethlu A	–	B I	10 Nov. 1670	1670/34
Humphrey, Robert	Llandwrog (Tyddun Elen) Cn	Yeoman	W I*	29 Dec. 1691	1691/57
Humphrey, Robert	Llanarmon Cn	Yeoman	B I	4 Aug. 1699	1699/63
Humphreys, Rowland	Tregaean A	–	B I	9 May 1683	1683/18
Humffreys, Thomas	Clynnog Cn	Gent.	W* Rd*	13 Aug. 1640	1640/23
Humphrey, Thomas	Llanaelhaearn Cn	–	B I R	11 Oct. 1677	1677/34
Humphrey, William	Llanynys (Sceibion) D	Yeoman	B I(2)	4 Jan. 1678/9	1678/77
Humphreys *see* Humphrey					
Hunt, William	Llangurig Mg	Yeoman	B I	24 July 1691	1691/131
Ievan *see* Evans					
Ingram, Richard	Trefeglwys Mg	Yeoman	W* I	19 March 1668/9	1668/147
Ingram, Richard	Llanidloes (Manleth) Mg	–	I/G	12 Oct. 1680	1680/80
Ingram, Richard	Trefeglwys Mg	Yeoman	W I	23 July 1691	1691/141
Ingram, Stephen	Trefeglwys (Glyntrefnant) Mg	Yeoman	B I	20 Jan. 1691/2	1691/142
Ingram, Thomas	Llandinam Mg	–	I/G	20 Aug. 1668	1668/131
Ingram, Thomas	Trefeglwys (Maestre-gummer) Mg	Gent.	W I	26 Oct. 1691	1691/143
Ireland, Catherine	Nefyn Cn	–	B* R	21 May 1687	1687/75
Ireland, Robert	Nefyn Cn	–	I	n.d.[1]	1687/76
Isacke, Esay	Llanddwywe Mr	Grocer	B I	20 May 1687	1687/97

[1] Inventory taken 12 May 1687.

Name	Parish & County	Status	Docs. Filed	Date of Probate/Admon.	Ref. No.
James, Evan	Llangurig (Keveneyvodey) Mg	Gent.	W I	15 May 1678	1678/84
James, Jenkin	Llangurig Mg	Bachelor	W I	2 July 1685	1685/112
James, Llewelyn	Heneglwys (Bodwine) A	Gent.	B I	12 March 1693/4	1693/5
James, William	Llanfachreth Mr	–	W I L	[6 Feb. 1676/7]	1676/76
Jarman, Arthur	Llangurig Mg	Gent.	B I	10 Sept. 1662	1662/99
Jerman, Awdrey	Llangurig Mg	Widow	W I	[27 Jan. 1675/6]	1675/64
Jerman, Giles	Llandinam Mg	Yeoman	W I	[26 May 1693]	1693/132
Jarman, Griffith	Llanidloes Mg	Single man	I/G	22 May 1682	1682/105
Jarman, Richard	Llanidloes Mg	–	B I	5 Sept. 1687	1687/132
Jarman, William	Llanidloes Mg	–	I/G	6 Feb. 1678/9	1678/87
Jaspart, John	Llandygái Cn	–	I	n.d.[1]	1696/60
Jeffrey, Arthur	Llanidan (Berow issa) A	–	W	14 March 1643/4	1643/12
Jeffreyes, Hugh	Caerhun (Tal y Cafn) Cn	Gent.	W(2) I G	14 May 1668[2]	1669/63
Jeffrey, Margaret	Llangeinwen A	Widow	W	19 Feb. 1686/7	1686/17
Jeffreyes, Richard	Llanllechid Cn	Clerk (Rector of Llanllechid)	W I Rd	25 Sept. 1664	1664/75
Jeffery, Richard	Llanffinan A	Yeoman	W	4 Nov. 1669	1669/33
Jeffrey, Thomas	Llangeinwen A	–	W	16 Nov. 1642	1642/12
Jeffreyes, William	Pentir Cn	Gent.	W	19 Jan. 1642/3	1642/31
Jeffreyes *see* Jeffrey					
Jehue, Evan	[Llanwnnog Mg]	–	W	14 Feb. 1670/1	1670/188
Jenkin, David	Llandinam Mg	–	B	7 March 1670/1	1670/179
Jenkin, David	Llangurig (Llanywared) Mg	Gent.	W I	15 May 1685	1685/113
Jenkin, Edward	Llandinam Mg	Yeoman	W I	8 July 1698	1698/71
Jenkin, Elizabeth	Llandinam Mg	Spinster	W* I	10 May 1699	1699/144
Jenkin, Evan	Llanidloes Mg	–	B I	1 Dec. 1669	1669/169
Jenkin, Evan	Trefeglwys Mg	–	W	[24 April 1673]	1673/72
Jenkins, Hugh	Llanbadrig A	–	B	24 Oct. 1683	1683/3
Jenkins, Hugh	Llandygwnning Cn	Clerk (Rector of Rhiw)	W* Rd B	19 Nov. 1685	1685/47
Jenkin, Humphrey	Tywyn Mr	–	B I R	22 Jan. 1684/5	1684/80
Jenkins, Mary	Llandygwnning Cn	Widow of Hugh Jenkins, clerk	W I(2) Al D C	[26 Oct. 1686]	1686/52
Jenkin, Morgan	Llanidloes (Eskyr y blywty) Mg	–	W I	1 May 1669	1669/170
Jenkin, Morgan	Llandinam (Henganydd) Mg	Gent.	W	20 Dec. 1671	1671/142

1 Inventory taken 16 March 1695/6.

2 Nuncupative will confirmed by witnesses 9 Nov. 1669.

Name	Parish & County	Status	Docs. Filed	Date of Probate/Admon.	Ref. No.
Jenkins, Moris	Llandinam (Maesmawre) Mg	Gent.	I/G	30 May 1670	1670/180
Jenkin, Owen	Llangurig Mg	–	B*	2 Oct. 1662	1662/100
Jenkins, Richard	Llangurig Mg	–	I/G	17 March 1680/1	1680/76
Jenkins, Simon	Llangristiolus A	–	W I	24 Nov. 1670	1670/44
Jenkin, Thomas	Tywyn Mr	Yeoman	W	[6 May 1685]	1685/86
Jenkin, Thomas	Llanidloes Mg	Glover	W I	22 Feb. 1686/7	1686/105
Jenkins *see* Jenkin					
Jenkinson, Michaell (senior)	Beaumaris A	Mariner	W I Rd	n.d.[1]	1691/7
Jerman *see* Jarman					
John, Johnes, Johns *see* Jones					
Johnson, Elizabeth	Llanidan A	Spinster	W I	28 Oct. 1698	1698/12
Johnson, Hugh	Clynnog Cn	Gent.	W I	22 Jan. 1667/8	1667/58
Johnson, Hugh	Bangor Cn	Clerk (Vicar of Bangor)	B I	15 Oct. 1695	1695/24
Johnson, Richard	Llanidan A	Gent.	W I B	7 April 1690	1690/30
Jones, Alice	Beddgelert Cn	Minor	B	17 Dec. 1667	1667/52
			B	23 March 1668/9	1668/35
Jones, Alce	Llandyrnog D	Widow	W	n.d.[2]	1675/52
Jones, Andrew	Llanfair Dyffryn Clwyd (Garthconan) D	Yeoman	W I	14 Aug. 1689	1689/83
Jones *alias* Owen, Anne	Llangïan (Ty yn y Caye) Cn	Widow of John Jones	W I	24 Dec. 1668	1668/66
Jones, Anthony	Llangynhafal D	–	B I M	8 Oct. 1663	1663/123
John, Arthur, & Elinor his wife	Llandinam Mg	Butcher	B I R	3 Sept. 1692	1692/110
Jones, Benjamin	Beaumaris A	Merchant	W* R* B*	4 April 1690	1690/6
Jones, Bold	[Bodwrog] (Erianell) A	–	B	18 Feb. 1664/5	1664/8
John, Cadwaleder	Aber-erch Cn	–	W	n.d.	1683/21
John, Cadwalader	Maentwrog Mr	Yeoman	B I R	18 Dec. 1696	1696/106
John, Cadwalder	Clynnog (Derwin fawr) Cn	–	W I	16 Aug. 1698	1698/25
Jones, Catherine	Llandinam Mg	Widow	B* I*	10 May 1662[3]	1662/96
Jones, Cathrin	Aber-erch (Penychen) Cn	Widow	W* I	11 April 1684	1684/27
John, Katharin	[Llangelynnin] (Bodgadvan) Mr	Widow	I/G	19 May 1691	1691/95
John, Catherine	Llangurig Mg	Widow	B	6 Feb. 1696/7	1696/129
John, Catherine	Ffestiniog Mr	Spinster	B	4 Aug. 1697	1697/42
John, Catherine	Llandygái Cn	Widow	B	26 Oct. 1697	1697/25

[1] Proved by 27 May 1691 according to bond for redelivery of will.
[2] Will dated 30 June 1675.
[3] Inventory taken in 1652.

Name	Parish & County	Status	Docs. Filed	Date of Probate/Admon.	Ref. No.
Jones, Catherine	Llanfwrog D	Widow of Richard ap Hugh Salisbury of Boteulog, Gwyddelwern	W* I	15 May 1699	1699/125
Jones, Charles	Penmorfa Cn	–	B I	18 June 1688	1688/62
Jones, Daniel	Llanwnnog Mg	Tailor	W I	5 July 1695	1695/112
Jones, David	Llangurig Mg	Gent.	B I	6 June 1661	1661/134
John, David	Trefdraeth A	–	B	29 May 1666	1666/35
John, David	Llanegryn Mr	–	W* I*	12 May 1671	1671/104
John, David	Llandinam Mg	Yeoman	I/G	11 Nov. 1680	1680/74
John, David	Llanelltud Mr	Gent.	W I	23 Dec. 1682	1682/70
Jones, David	Llanfaglan Cn	–	B	21 July 1683	1683/39
Jones, David	Llanrhaeadr-yng-Nghinmeirch (Segroit) D	Yeoman	I	n.d.[1]	1690/111
Jones, Dorothy	Llanrhaeadr-yng-Nghinmeirch (Llech) D	Widow	W I	26 Sept. 1678	1678/73
Jones, Dorothy	[Llansadwrn] (Trephos) A	Spinster	W	8 March 1694/5	1694/27
Jones, Doulce	Llanfihangel-yn-Nhywyn A	Widow	B G	13 Sept. 1666	1666/21
Jones, Doulce	Llangoed (Tû yn y Wern) A	Widow	W I	28 Aug. 1679	1679/10
Jones, Edmund	Bangor Cn	–	W*	25 April [1661]	1661/40
Jones, Edward	Llandudno Cn	–	B	12 Aug. 1667	1667/65
John, Edward	Llanfair-yng-Nghornwy (Cornwy llys) A	Yeoman	W I	6 Oct. 1671	1671/23
Jones, Edward	Bangor Cn	Carrier	R	n.d.[2]	1677/22
Jones, Edward	Llandrygarn (Glan-yr-Afon) A	–	W I	n.d.[3]	1677/8
Jones, Edward	[Llanynys] (Trefechan) D	Gent.	W I Rd	24 March 1678/9	1678/78
John, Edward	Llanelltud Mr	Weaver	W I	[9 June 1679]	1679/41
John, Edward	Llangurig Mg	–	I/G	8 Dec. 1683	1683/100
John, Edward	Llanaber Mr	–	W I	22 Feb. 1691/2	1691/82
Jones, Edward	Llanfair Dyffryn Clwyd D	Smith	W I	18 Sept. 1693	1693/109
Jones, Edward	Llangynhafal D	Gent.	W I	16 Jan. 1693/4	1693/113
John, Edward	Aberffraw A	Yeoman	W* B	4 May 1694	1694/1
Jones, Ellin	Llanwnda Cn	–	B	8 March 1670/1	1670/124
John, Ellen	Llandrygarn A	Widow	W(2) I	23 Nov. 1678	1678/5
Jones, Ellin	Tudweiliog Cn	Spinster	W	10 July 1685	1685/64

[1] Inventory taken 14 April 1690.
[2] Renunciation dated 5 Jan. 1677.
[3] Inventory taken 1 March 1676[/7].

Name	Parish & County	Status	Docs. Filed	Date of Probate/Admon.	Ref. No.
John, Ellen	Llanllechid Cn	Widow	B I	9 Nov. 1686	1686/59
John, Ellen	Llangwyfan A	Widow of Richard John [ap Robert]	W I B	28 May 1687	1687/21
Jones *alias* Draycott, Ellin	Dolgellau Mr	Wife of Maurice Jones, clerk	B C	16 Nov. 1699	1699/97
Jones, Elizabeth	Rhuthun D	Widow	B	28 July 1665	1665/88
Jones *alias* Marsh, Elizabeth	Conway Cn	Widow	W I M	25 Nov. 1666	1666/49
John, Elizabeth	Llangelynnin Mr	–	B	25 April 1668	1668/98
Jones, Elizabeth	Gyffylliog D	Spinster	W I	10 May 1669	1669/142
Jones, Elizabeth	Llanfflewin A	Spinster	W	12 April 1677	1677/13
Jones, Elizabeth	Llan Sant Cathrin *alias* Cricieth Cn	Widow	B I	9 April 1684	1684/40
Jones,[1] Elizabeth	Beaumaris A	–	B	2 Sept. 1685	1685/7
Jones, Elizabeth	Nefyn Cn	Widow	B I	26 May 1687	1687/77
Jones, Elizabeth	Llanddwywe Mr	Spinster	I	n.d.[2]	1690/90
Jones *alias* Owens, Elizabeth	Pennal Mr	Wife of Robert Owen of Machynlleth, gent.	B C	8 March 1691/2	1691/97
Jones, Elizabeth	Llanfwrog [Galchog] D	Widow of Edward Pierce of Galchog	W	13 Jan. 1699/1700	1699/126
Jones, Ellen/Ellin *as* Jones, Elin					
John, Evan	Llandwrog Cn	–	B I	13 Aug. 1663	1663/60
Jones, Evan	Llangelynnin (Ddol) Cn	Yeoman	W I	26 Nov. 1663	1663/64
John, Ievan	Llangelynnin (Pryske issa) Mr	–	W I	12 July 1665	1665/70
Jones, Evan	Dolgellau (Garthgynfor) Mr	–	B I R	25 April 1678	1678/37
John, Evan	Tregaean A	–	I	n.d.[3]	1682/31
Jones, Evan, *alias* Evan John Hugh	Tywyn (Trevreean) Mr	Yeoman	W I	n.d.[4]	1684/81
Jones, Evan	Clynnog (Cae hir) Cn	Yeoman	B I	7 April 1685	1685/36
Jones, Evan	Llanidloes Mg	–	B	4 June 1685	1685/119
Jones, Evan	Trefriw Cn	Gent.	W C	25 Aug. 1685	1685/63
Jones, Evan	Llanbedrog Cn	Clerk	W(2)	21 Nov. 1688	1688/47
John, Evan	Aberdaron Cn	–	B I	28 Oct. 1689	1689/28

1 Endorsed *Williams*.
2 Died 9 Nov. 1689. Inventory endorsed *1690*.
3 Inventory taken 17 Nov. 1682.
4 Inventory taken 4 July 1684.

Name	Parish & County	Status	Docs. Filed	Date of Probate/Admon.	Ref. No.
Jones, Evan	[Llandyrnog] (Bankar) D	–	I	n.d.[1]	1692/98
Jones, Evan	Llangaffo A	–	B	15 Jan. 1693/4	1693/15
John, Evan	Llanbeblig Cn	Yeoman	B I	18 Aug. 1699	1699/65
Johnes, Foulke	Llanrhaeadr-yng-Nghinmeirch D	–	W I	12 Dec. 1668	1668/121
Jones, Frances	Tudweiliog (Hirdre) Cn	Gent.	W	9 May 1681	1681/62
Jones, Gaynor	[Llanbeblig] (Carnarvon) Cn	Widow	W* Rd	11 Sept. 1696	1696/42
Jones, George	[Llanbeblig] (Carnarvon) Cn	Gent.	W I	2 Feb. 1665/6	1665/36
Jones, Grace	Llantrisant A	Widow	B	[ ]3 [Feb./March] 1685/6	1685/26
John, Gruffith	Penmorfa Cn	Yeoman	I	n.d.[2]	1669/108
Jones, Griffith	[Llangïan] (Castellmarch) Cn	Esq.	W	28 Sept. 1671	1671/77
Johnes, Griffith	Llanrhaeadr-yng-Nghinmeirch (Llwyn) D	Gent.	W* I*	3 April 1671	1671/126
Jones, Griffith	Aber-erch (Tŷ yn y Coed) Cn	Yeoman	W I	19 March 1673/4	1673/21
John, Griffith	Clynnog Cn	–	W	[5 June 1674]	1674/16
Jones, Griffith	Aber (Cambwll) Cn	Yeoman	B I	2 Dec. 1676	1676/30
Jones, Griffith	Aber-erch Cn	–	I	n.d.[3]	1676/35
Jones, Griffyth	Llanfaelrhys Cn	–	I/G	7 Feb. 1680/1	1680/31
Jones, Griffith	Llechgynfarwy A	Weaver	W I	17 Nov. 1687	1687/27
Jones, Griffith	Ceirchiog A	Yeoman	B	28 March 1692	1692/4
Jones, Griffith	Aber-erch (Tanyrallt) Cn	Tanner	W I	9 Jan. 1694/5	1694/36
Jones, Henry	Bangor Cn	Yeoman	B	21 June 1690	1690/42
Jones, Henry	Llangoed A	Gent./Esq.	W I Rd	[c. 29 Dec. 1690]	1690/27
John, Howell	Dolgellau Mr	–	W I	[3 April 1691]	1691/75
John, Howel	Llanaber (Ceilwart) Mr	Gent.	W I	5 Oct. 1692	1692/72
Jones, Hugh	Gyffylliog D	–	I/G	1 May 1663	1663/116
Jones, Hugh	[Llanbeblig] (Carnarvon) Cn	–	B	9 May 1663	1663/40
Jones, Hugh	[ ] [Mr]	–	I	n.d.[4]	1665/75
Jones, Hugh	Dolwyddelan Cn	Gent.	W I	6 May 1665	1665/40
Jones, Hugh	Llandwrog Cn	–	B	7 March 1669/70	1669/79
Jones, Hugh	Llanffinan A	–	B	7 Feb. 1672/3	1672/21
Jones, Hugh	Pentraeth A	Gent.	W	25 Oct. 1672	1672/31
Jones, Hugh	Llandwrog Cn	Gent.	W I B	28 Nov. 1673	1673/33

[1] Inventory taken 16 May 1692.
[2] Inventory taken 9 Aug. 1669.
[3] Inventory taken 15 April 1676.
[4] Inventory taken 6 April 1665.

Name	Parish & County	Status	Docs. Filed	Date of Probate/Admon.	Ref. No.
†John, Hugh	Betws-y-coed (Pen rhiw ddolion) Cn	–	W I	10 May 1677	1677/25
Jones, Hugh	Llanrhaeadr-yng-Nghinmeirch (Prion) D	–	W I	3 March 1677/8	1677/81
John, Hugh	Llanbedr (Tythin du) Mr	Yeoman	B I	14 Aug. 1683	1683/65
John, Hugh	Llanidloes Mg	Carpenter	W I	2 July 1685	1685/120
John, Hugh	Llanengan Cn	–	B I	27 Aug. 1689	1689/47
Jones, Hugh	[Llandyrnog] (Rhiwbebill) D	Yeoman	B I	23 Dec. 1691	1691/107
John, Hugh	Llanfihangel-y-Pennant (Nant Carvan) Cn	–	W I	30 May 1693	1693/52
John, Hugh	Llangelynnin (Talygarreg) Mr	Yeoman	W* I	9 Oct. 1694	1694/89
Jones, Hugh	[Llanbeblig] (Carnarvon) Cn	–	B I	29 March 1695	1695/25
Jones, Hugh	Llanystumdwy (Plas hen) Cn	Clerk	W I Rd	[5 July 1695]	1695/56
Jones, Hugh	Llanllechid Cn	Yeoman	W* I M	22 June 1697	1697/31
Jones, Hugh	Aberdaron (Tu yn y lone) Cn	Yeoman	W Al*	26 Jan. 1698/9	1698/17
Jones, Hugh	Penmachno (Plas yn Glasgwm) Cn	Yeoman	B I	29 Dec. 1699	1699/88
John, Humphrey *see* Humphrey Sir John	Llanenddwyn Mr				
Jones, Humphrey	Llanwnnog Mg	–	B I	5 Nov. 1669	1669/175
Jones, Humphrey	Llan Sant Catherin *alias* Cricieth Cn	Gent.	W I Rd	9 June 1673	1673/30
Jones, Humphrey	Clocaenog D	Gent.	W I	[6 April 1678]	1678/61
Jones, Humphrey	Llanbedr Mr	–	B I	11 Sept. 1688	1688/71
John, Humphrey	Llangelynnin Mr	Labourer/Yeoman	I/G	1 Nov. 1696	1696/104
John, Ievan *see* Jones, Evan					
John, Isaac	Dolwyddelan Cn	–	W Db*	4 Dec. 1685	1685/39
Jones, James	Llanengan ([ ] newydd) Cn	Gent.	W* I Rd	21 Sept. 1694	1694/53
Jones, Jane	Trefdraeth A	Widow	W	26 Nov. 1661	1661/30
Jones, Jane	Llanwnnog Mg	Widow	W I	22 Sept. 1670	1670/189
Jones, Jane[1]	Llangristiolus A	Widow	W	19 March 1671/2	1671/28
Jones, Jane	Llanrhaeadr-yng-Nghinmeirch (Prion) D	Widow of Richard ap Edward	W I	19 Aug. 1671	1671/127
Jones *alias* Bradbury, Jane	Llanrhaeadr-yng-Nghinmeirch (Lloyne) D	Widow	W I Rd	[18 March 1691/2]	1691/114
Jones, Jane	Llanbeblig (Treflan) Cn	Widow	B I	21 July 1696	1696/55

[1] See also under Jones, William, of Llangristiolus (document R/G).

Name	Parish & County	Status	Docs. Filed	Date of Probate/Admon.	Ref. No.
Jones, Jespart	Llandygái Cn	Fuller	W I	n.d.[1]	1687/61
Jones, John	Llangïan (Tû yn kae) Cn	Gent.	W	17 Nov. 1644	1644/25
Jones, John	Rhuthun D	Dyer	W*	n.d.[2]	1662/94
Jones, John	Llanelidan D	Gent.	B	30 Oct. 1663	1663/119
Jones, John	[Llanystumdwy] (Trefan) Cn	Gent.	W* I Rd	17 Sept. 1663	1663/71
Jones, John	Llanfwrog D	Tailor	W I	31 Oct. 1664	1664/115
Jones, John	Llaniestyn Cn	Rector of Llaniestyn	W I	10 Feb. 1667/8	1667/76
Jones, John	Llannor Cn	–	W/R I	8 Oct. 1672	1672/77
Jones, John	Llandecwyn Mr	Yeoman	W I	[28 Aug. 1673]	1673/52
Jones, John	[Penmorfa] (Clenenney) Cn	Gent.	W I Rd	25 Nov. 1679	1679/31
Jones, John	Llangwyfan D	Labourer	W	27 Nov. 1684	1684/96
Jones, John	[Llanbeblig] (Carnarvon) Cn	Dyer	B I*	6 April 1686	1686/37
Jones, John	Llechylched (Cefn-ysgwyd) A	–	B I	6 Oct. 1690	1690/35
Jones, John Thomas	Llangwyfan D	–	W	10 June 1642	1642/39
Jones, Judith	Llanidan (Coch y Powell) A	Widow	W Al	n.d.[3]	1699/27
John, Katharin *see* Jones, Catherine					
John, Lewis	Llanelltud Mr	Gent.	W* I*	n.d.[4]	1664/93
Jones, Lewis	Pennal Mr	–	I/G	13 Dec. 1669	1669/133
Jones, Lewis	Llanfrothen Mr	Gent.	W* I*	[6 April 1680]	1680/53
Jones *alias* Morris, Lewis	Aberffraw A	–	B I	24 Feb. 1684/5	1684/1
John, Lewis	Llanfachreth (Carleg) Mr	–	B I	25 April 1684	1684/70
Jones, Lewis	Llanwnda (Rhydynog felen) Cn	Clerk (Rector of Llandwrog)	W* I	24 Jan. 1692/3	1692/62
Jones, Margarett	Amlwch A	Wife of Edward Price, gent.	W	27 March 1643	1643/1
John, Margarett	Carno Mg	Widow	W I	28 Sept. 1664	1664/124
Jones *alias* Williams, Margarett	[Llanbeblig] (Carnarvon) Cn	Widow	W* Rd	17 Jan. 1671/2	1671/52
Jones, Margarett	Derwen D	–	B	25 March 1695	1695/85
John, Margarett	Llandanwg Mr	–	I/G	11 June 1696	1696/97
Jones, Mary	Ceri[5] Mg	Wife of Edward Morgan, gent.	I/G*	27 Sept. 1662	1662/111

1 Inventory taken 5 July 1687.
2 Will dated 17 Jan. 1662.
3 Will dated 14 April 1699.
4 Inventory taken Oct. 1664.
5 Normally within the jurisdiction of the Consistory Court of the Archdeaconry of Brecon.

Name	Parish & County	Status	Docs. Filed	Date of Probate/Admon.	Ref. No.
John, Mary	Dolgellau Mr	Spinster	W I	16 Feb. 1675/6	1675/34
Jones, Mary	Trefeglwys Mg	–	I/G	14 Oct. 1680	1680/83
Jones, Mary	Llanddyfnan A	–	B	19 Nov. 1683	1683/5
Jones, Mary	Llanegryn Mr	Widow	B I	26 Aug. 1684	1684/69
John, Mary	Llandwrog Cn	Spinster	B	10 March 1686/7	1686/48
Jones, Mary	Llanfwrog (Kil-y-groeslwyd) D	Widow	W I	12 June 1688	1688/90
Jones *alias* Hughes, Mary	Bangor Cn	Wife of Elice Hughes, gent.	B	23 Dec. 1692	1692/33
John, Mary	Dolgellau Mr	–	B I	11 July 1694	1694/69
Jones, Maurice *see* Jones, Morris					
John, Meredith	Llandinam Mg	Gent.	W I	29 Aug. 1684	1684/110
John, Michael	Llanfihangel-y-Pennant Mr	–	B	12 June 1663	1663/101
John, Morgan	Beddgelert Cn	–	W	29 Jan. 1638/9	1638/34
John, Morgan	Llandinam Mg	–	I	n.d.[1]	1678/82
John, Morgan	Llanddeiniolen Cn	Yeoman	W R S	2 Nov. 1694	1694/52
Jones, Maurice	Llanenddwyn Mr	–	W	5 July 1642	1642/35
Jones *alias* Keytley, Mauris	Llannerch-y-medd A	–	I	n.d.[2]	1671/32
Jones, Maurice	Penmorfa (Werne) Cn	Gent.	B I G	4 April 1672	1672/83
Jones, Moris	Dolgellau Mr	Bailiff	I	n.d.	1687/89
Jones, Morris	Llanidan A	Gent.	B	11 Feb. 1689/90	1689/20
Jones, Maurice	Llanystumdwy (Bettus) Cn	–	B I	30 Jan. 1691/2	1691/70
Jones, Maurice	Rhuthun D	–	B I	4 Dec. 1694	1694/112
Jones, Nicholas	Llangurig Mg	Bachelor/Yeoman	W I	[9 Feb. 1692/3]	1692/119
Jonnes, Owen	Llanfechell A	–	W*	5 Feb. 1640/1	1640/11
Jones, Owen	Rhiw Cn	Clerk (Rector of Rhiw)	W* I M	6 July 1665	1665/54
John, Owen	Llangelynnin Mr	Yeoman	W I	10 June 1668	1668/99
Jones, Owen	Pentraeth A	–	W I* B	3 April 1671	1671/38
Jones, Owen	Llanllibio A	–	B	21 April 1673	1673/13
Jones, Owen	Clynnog Cn	–	B	4 March 1683/4	1683/28
Jones, Owen	Llantrisant (Rhiwgoch) A	Shoemaker	W I	17 Feb. 1686/7	1686/22
Jones, Owen	Llanbadrig (Vodol voyle) A	–	B I/R M	11 Feb. 1688/9	1688/9
John, Owen	Dwygyfylchi Cn	Yeoman	W I Al	15 Feb. 1693/4	1693/40
Jones, Owen	Llanegryn Mr	Clerk & Schoolmaster	B I	10 Oct. 1693	1693/76
Jones, Owen	Pentraeth A	Gent.	W I	29 Oct. 1695	1695/17

[1] Inventory taken 4 July 1678.

[2] Inventory taken 26 April 1671.

Name	Parish & County	Status	Docs. Filed	Date of Probate/Admon.	Ref. No.
John, Owen	Llechylched (Gwenfynydd) A	Yeoman/Gent.	W I	25 Aug. 1696	1696/24
Jones, Owen	Llanfihangel-y-Pennant (Braich-y-bîb) Cn	Gent.	W* I* C Rd	[12 Dec. 1698]	1698/35
Jones *alias* Williams, Penelope	Llanfaelog A	Widow	W I	15 June 1687	1687/10
Johnes, Perce	Llanrhuddlad A	–	W	21 April 1674	1674/12
Johnes, Rees	Carno Mg	Yeoman	W I	6 June 1661	1661/123
Jones, Rees	Penmynydd A	–	B I	28 Jan. 1667/8	1667/39
Jones, Rice	[Bodwrog] (Maes y llan) A	Clerk	W	n.d.	1670/4
Jones, Rees	Trefdraeth & Llangristiolus A	Yeoman	W Cd	[15 Jan. 1676/7]	1676/27
Jones, Rice	Llanddaniel-fab (Rosbothan) A	Gent.	B I	25 Feb. 1679/80	1679/5
Jones, Rees	Llanrhwydrys A	Yeoman	W	n.d.[1]	1682/26
Jones, Rhese, *alias* Rhese John David Prees	Llanfaelrhys Cn	–	W* I	14 Jan. 1684/5	1684/44
Jones, Rice	Llantrisant A	Yeoman	B I	25 Jan. 1687/8	1687/26
Jones, Rice	Llanfair Dyffryn Clwyd D	Clerk (Vicar of Llanfair Dyffryn Clwyd)	W	1 June 1691	1691/109
Jones, Reignallt	Rhuthun D	Innkeeper/Butcher	W* I	20 July 1694	1694/113
John, Rodericke	Llanbedrycennin Cn	Yeoman	B I	17 Feb. 1663/4	1663/56
Jones, Roderick	Llangeinwen (Rhyddgar) A	Yeoman	W I R B	7 May 1690	1690/26
Jones, Rice *see* Jones, Rees					
Jones, Richard	Trewalchmai A	–	W	14 April 1635	1635/14
Jones, Richard	Ffestiniog (Brynkyfergid) Mr	–	W	20 April 1640	1640/39
Jones, Richard	Llanfair Dyffryn Clwyd D	Esq.	W(2) I Rd	15 Oct. 1660	1660/25
Jones, Richard, *alias* Richard John Robert	Aber-erch (Rhosfawr) Cn	Gent.	W* Rd	23 March 1663/4	1663/32
John, Richard	Heneglwys A	Miller	B	13 Oct. 1663	1663/9
John, Richard	Penrhos[llugwy] A	–	W/I B	18 Nov. 1665	1665/23
Jones, Richard	Tudweiliog (Hiredre) Cn	Joiner	W	9 June 1665	1665/56
Johns, Richard	Llanaber Mr	–	I L	8 June 1667	1667/85
Jones, Richard	Cricieth Cn	–	B	4 March 1671/2	1671/58
Jones, Richard	Nefyn Cn	Clerk	W I	14 Aug. 1671	1671/91
Jones, Richard	Rhuthun D	Tailor	W* I*	12 Oct. 1671	1671/136
Jones, Richard	Llandinam Mg	–	W* I*	8 June 1672	1672/125
Jones, Richard	Ffestiniog Mr	–	W	[13 Oct. 1676]	1676/70
Jones, Richard	Holyhead A	Yeoman	W I	21 April 1677	1677/5

[1] Will dated 22 March 1681/2.

Name	Parish & County	Status	Docs. Filed	Date of Probate/Admon.	Ref. No.
John, Richard	Dolgellau (Garthgynvoure) Mr	–	B I	10 Aug. 1678	1678/38
Jones, Richard	Llandyrnog D	Widower	W I	26 Nov. 1681	1681/90
John, Richard	Llanwnda Cn	–	B R	1 Dec. 1681	1681/56
Jones, Richard	Trawsfynydd Mr	Gent.	W I	13 Nov. 1683	1683/75
Jones, Richard	Llanllechid (Cychwillan) Cn	–	W I B	15 July 1686	1686/60
Jones, Richard	Llangwyfan D	–	W I B	22 June 1687	1687/120
John, Richard	Llanidloes Mg	Yeoman	I/G	8 Aug. 1689	1689/93
Jones, Richard	Llangefni (Carrog) A	Gent.	B I	21 May 1690	1690/25
Jones, Richard	Llanhychan D	–	I	n.d.[1]	1691/111
Jones, Richard, *alias* Richard John ap Hugh	Llan-rhudd D	Gent.	W	19 Dec. 1691	1691/121
Jones, Richard	[Llanbeblig] (Carnarvon) Cn	Gent.	W I	26 Dec. 1695	1695/26
Jones, Richard	Ynyscynhaearn Cn	Gent.	B	11 March 1699/1700	1699/95
John, Robert	[Llanfair-yn-neubwll][2] (Treflisk) A	Yeoman	W*	22 May 1641	1641/10
Jonnes, Robert	Derwen D	Gent.	W	6 June 1644	1644/40
Jones, Robert	Bangor Cn	Gent.	W*	25 April 1661	1661/41
Jones, Robert	Clocaenog D	Yeoman	W I	26 April 1662	1662/76
John, Robert	Aber-erch Cn	–	B	4 July 1665	1665/33
Jones, Robert	Llanelidan (Garthneuadd) D	Gent.	W I	2 May 1666	1666/101
Jones, Robert	Llandwrog Cn	Clerk (Rector of Llandwrog)	B I	29 Nov. 1667	1667/67
Jones, Robert	Gyffylliog D	–	W* I	22 March 1668/9	1668/105
John, Robert	Llanaber Mr	–	W	3 July 1671	1671/102
John, Robert	Coedana A	–	W	[8 April 1672]	1672/7
Jones, Robert	Rhuthun D	Smith	I/G	10 June 1673	1673/66
Jones, Robert	Llanelidan D	Gent.	W I R	[16 May 1678]	1678/68
Jones, Robert, *alias* Robert John William	Clocaenog (Waynpyscodlyn) D	Yeoman	W I	[9 July 1684]	1684/84
Jones, Robert	Llantrisant A	–	B I	9 May 1684	1684/20
Jones, Robert	[Llanbeblig] (Carnarvon) Cn	Gent.	W I Rd	16 April 1686	1686/38
Jones, Robert	Rhiw Cn	Weaver	W I B M	22 May 1690	1690/81
Jones, Robert	Llanrhaeadr-yng-Nghinmeirch (Llewesog) D	Gent./Yeoman	W I(2) B	25 Jan. 1691/2	1691/115
Jones, Robert	Rhuthun D	Surgeon	W I	1 May 1693	1693/122

1 Inventory taken 15 Dec. 1691.
2 Endorsed *Rhoskolyn*.

Name	Parish & County	Status	Docs. Filed	Date of Probate/Admon.	Ref. No.
Jones, Robert	Llanbedr Dyffryn Clwyd (Lloyneth) D	Gent.	W Rd	24 Jan. 1695/6	1695/89
Jones, Roderick *as* Jones, Rhydderch					
Jones, Roger	Clocaenog D	–	B	15 July 1662	1662/77
John, Rowland	Llangristiolus A	–	W	1 July 1663	1663/28
Jones, Rowland	Amlwch (Bryn-Twrkelyn) A	Smith	W	21 June 1680	1680/1
John, Rowland	Llanbeulan A	–	W I	[7 June 1686]	1686/9
Jones, Rowland	Llanddaniel-fab A	Yeoman	B	15 Oct. 1695	1695/4
Jones, Samuel	Llanrhaeadr-yng-Nghinmeirch (Llech) D	–	W/I*	9 April 1683	1683/88
Jones, Sara	Bangor Cn	–	I/G	11 July 1671	1671/43
Jones, Scipio	Llandudno Cn	Gent.	W I	n.d.[1]	1675/24
Jones, Simon	Llandyrnog (Banckar) D	Smith	W	8 Aug. 1677	1677/75
Jones, Thomas	Llandyrnog D	–	W	20 April 1636	1636/55
Jones, Thomas	Llandyrnog / Denbigh D	–	W	7 Sept. 1646	1646/27
Jones, Thomas	Llanwnnog Mg	–	B I	30 April 1661	1661/142
John, Thomas	Bangor (Treborth) Cn	–	W	25 Feb. 1663/4	1663/35
John, Thomas	Llangelynnin (Llwyngoril) Mr	Labourer	W	12 June 1663	1663/107
Jones, Thomas	Rhuthun D	Gent.	W	24 March 1663/4	1663/129
Jones, Thomas	Llanbedr Dyffryn Clwyd D	–	B I	20 June 1667	1667/119
John, Thomas	Llanelltud Mr	–	W I	10 June 1668	1668/92
Jones, Thomas	Cricieth Cn	Clerk (Rector of Cricieth)	W I	24 Feb. 1674/5	1674/18
Jones, Thomas	Holyhead A	Yeoman	W*	[3 Jan. 1676/7]	1676/7
Jones, Thomas	Llangïan Cn	Yeoman	W I	9 Oct. 1676	1676/56
Jones, Thomas	Llanrhaeadr-yng-Nghinmeirch (Llewesog) D	–	I	n.d.[2]	1679/55
Jones, Thomas	Llanffinan A	–	B I	25 Oct. 1688	1688/19
Jones, Thomas	Llandyrnog (Spethyd) D	Tailor	W I	12 July 1689	1689/80
Jones, Thomas	Trawsfynydd (Orsedd las) Mr	Gent.	W I	9 April 1692	1692/89
Jons, Thomas	Llanfwrog (Bodyngharad) D	Yeoman	W* I* B	2 Feb. 1694/5	1694/106
Jones, Thomas	Llanwnda (Tythin bache) Cn	Gent.	W I	23 April 1695	1695/54
John, Wattkin	Llanegryn Mr	–	W	29 May 1665	1665/64
Jones, William	Pentraeth A	Gent.	W	27 July 1644	1644/15
Jones, William	Conway Cn	–	W	8 Oct. 1647	1647/23

[1] Inventory taken 24 June 1675.

[2] Inventory taken 25 Aug. 1679.

Name	Parish & County	Status	Docs. Filed	Date of Probate/Admon.	Ref. No.
Johns, William	Derwen D	–	B I R	7 Sept. 1663	1663/114
John, William	Dolgellau (Gwengraig) Mr	–	B I	12 June 1663	1663/79
Jones, William	Llanengan Cn	–	I L	6 April 1671	1671/70
Jones, William	Llangristiolus A	–	R/G[1]	11 Jan. 1671/2	1671/29
Jones, William	Efenechtid D	Gent.	W I	[6 April 1678]	1678/65
Jones, William	Derwen D	–	I	n.d.[2]	1687/111
Johnes, William	Llandrygarn (Serie) A	Smith	W I*	6 July 1688	1688/12
Jones, William	Pentraeth A	Gent.	W I B	4 Jan. 1688/9	1688/27
Jones, William	Conway Cn	Gent.	B I	27 Nov. 1689	1689/37
Jones, William	Llanbedrycennin Cn	–	I	n.d.[3]	1689/42
Jones, William	Rhuthun D	–	B	13 June 1693	1693/123
Jones, William	Llanllechid Cn	Gent.	W(2) I Rd	14 May 1696	1696/76
John, William	Llanberis Cn	Yeoman	W* I	30 Aug. 1697	1697/23
Jones, William	Llanbedr[-goch] A	Gent./Yeoman	W* I* Al(2) Rd	[27] Sept. 1699	1699/11
Jones, William Prichard	Holyhead A	Yeoman	W	24 March 1685/6	1685/11
Jones, Wythen (the elder)	[Llandinam] (Trewythen) Mg	Gent.	W I	29 June 1665	1665/96
Josiah, John	Llechgynfarwy A	Labourer	W	30 April 1691	1691/32
Josua, William	Llanbedr Niwbwrch A	Yeoman	W I	21 Dec. 1696	1696/9
Jukes, Thomas	Tywyn Mr	Dyer	W I	5 Oct. 1692	1692/93
Junall, John	Llangurig (Toluch) Mg	Dyer/Gent.	W I	5 June 1668	1668/133
Jushnip, Thomas	Llanrhaeadr-yng-Nghinmeirch D	–	W I	4 May 1691	1691/116
Kadwaladr *see* Cadwaladr		–			
Kenricke, Hugh, *alias* Hugh ap William Kenricke	Coedana A	Gent.	W I Rd	5 April 1662	1662/8
Kenrick, Owen	Llaniestyn A	Yeoman	B I	3 Sept. 1668	1668/22
Kerver, Richard	Rhosbeirio A	Gent.	W(2)	2 Nov. 1665	1665/26
Ketle, John	Rhuthun D	–	B I	13 March 1675/6	1675/59
Key, Richard	Rhuthun D	Tanner	B I	24 Jan. 1666/7	1666/109
Keytley *alias* Jones, Mauris	Llannerch-y-medd A	–	I	n.d.[4]	1671/32
Kingson, Francis	Llanynys D	Clerk (Vicar of Llanynys)	B I	10 March 1685/6	1685/101

1 Also relates to Jane Jones of Llangristiolus (q.v.).

2 Inventory taken 23 Nov. 1687.

3 Inventory taken 11 June 1689.

4 Inventory taken 26 April 1671.

Name	Parish & County	Status	Docs. Filed	Date of Probate/Admon.	Ref. No.
Kinsey, John	Llandinam Mg	Yeoman	W*	20 Dec. 1671	1671/143
Kinsey, John	Llandinam Mg	–	B	4 May 1682	1682/95
Kinsey, Thomas	Llandinam (Dithienith) Mg	Gent.	W I	19 Feb. 1675/6	1675/62
Knight, Joshuah	[Llanbeblig] (Carnarvon) Cn	Mercer	B I	31 Jan. 1695/6	1695/27
Knight, Richard	Llanidloes Mg	Yeoman	W I	30 May 1670	1670/186
Knight, Thomas	Llanidloes Mg	–	W I	5 June 1668	1668/139
Knight, Thomas	[Llanbeblig] (Carnarvon) Cn	Ironmonger	B I	8 July 1670	1670/75
Knowsley, Robert	Llanrhaeadr-yng-Nghinmeirch (Cliffirio) D	Gent.	W Rd	4 Feb. 1646/7	1646/29
Knowsley, Robert	Rhuthun D	Gent.	W I	21 July 1694	1694/114
Kyffin *alias* Stodart, Grace	Conway Cn	Widow	W	15 June 1691	1691/48
Lambe, William	Llanbeblig Cn	Mariner	W	6 Oct. 1687	1687/53
Langford, George	Rhuthun D	Gent.	B C	4 March 1664/5	1664/119
Laurance, John	[Llanbeblig] (Carnarvon) Cn	–	B	16 Aug. 1667	1667/57
Laurence, Morgan	[Llanbeblig] (Carnarvon) Cn	–	B I R	29 March 1664	1664/58
Ledsham, Edward	Llanfair Dyffryn Clwyd D	Mason	W	30 Nov. 1672	1672/109
Ledsham, Edward	Llanfair Dyffryn Clwyd D	Gent.	W*	13 July 1683	1683/84
Leeke, George	Trefeglwys Mg	Yeoman	B I	7 March 1670/1	1670/192
Lewis, Agnes	Llannor Cn	Widow	W	1 June 1647	1647/36
Lewis, Anne	[Llanddeusant][1] (Llynon) A	Widow	W*	21 May 1640	1640/5
Lewis *alias* Bodvell, Anne	Llanfair-yn-neubwll (Trefleske) A	Widow	W(2) Al	7 June 1682	1682/20
Lewis, Anne	[Llanrhwydrys] (Cemlin) A	Widow	W I B	24 March 1695/6	1695/15
Lewis, Cadwalader	Edern Cn	Yeoman	W M	16 Aug. 1699	1699/60
Lewis, Katherine	Penllech Cn	Widow	W	28 April 1683	1683/56
Lewis *alias* William, Catherine	Llanidloes Mg	–	B	11 Oct. 1697	1697/68
Lewis, David	Llanegryn Mr	Shoemaker	W I	3 April 1666	1666/87
Lewis, David	Penrhos[llugwy] A	Yeoman	W I Al	18 May 1680	1680/14
Lewis, David	Pennal Mr	–	B	11 Oct. 1681	1681/78
Lewis, David	Llanbeulan A	–	B I	7 May 1687	1687/6
Lewis, Ebule	Llangelynnin / [Llanegryn] (Bron y Clwdwr) Mr	Clerk	I/G	16 Aug. 1669	1669/130
Lewis, Edward	Trefeglwys Mg	–	W	12 April 1641	1641/79
Lewis, Edward	[Llangelynnin] (Tonfane) Mr	Gent.	W I	3 Oct. 1662	1662/70
Lewis, Edward	Amlwch (Gweredogg) A	Gent.	W I R	26 Jan. 1693/4	1693/2

[1] Endorsed *Bodederne*.

Name	Parish & County	Status	Docs. Filed	Date of Probate/Admon.	Ref. No.
Lewis, Edward	Llandinam Mg	–	B I	17 May 1694	1694/117
Lewis, Edward	Llanidloes Mg	–	B I	15 July 1696	1696/136
Lewis, Edward	Llangurig (Glynnbrochan) Mg	Husbandman	B I	4 Feb. 1698/9	1698/77
Lewis, Edward	Llangurig (Glynbrochan) Mg	Yeoman	B I	29 Dec. 1699	1699/149
Lewis, Ellen	Trefeglwys Mg	Widow	W*	27 June 1638	1638/92
Lewis, Ellen	Bodedern (Ty-yn-y-Cay) A	Widow	W Db	9 Nov. 1663	1663/5
Lewis, Elin	[Llechylched] (Cefnysgwyd) A	–	I	n.d.[1]	1669/46
Lewis, Ellen	Coedana A	Widow	W	10 Dec. 1696	1696/3
Lewis, Ellis	Dolgellau (Brithdir) Mr	Gent.	I/G	4 Jan. 1670/1	1670/135
Lewis, Elizabeth	Llangefni A	Widow of Morgan Rowland, yeoman	W* I	25 Jan. 1670/1	1670/40
Lewis, Elizabeth	Llangïan Cn	Widow	W I	20 May 1690	1690/66
Lewis, Ellen *see* Lewis, Elin					
Lewis, Ellis *as* Lewis, Elis					
Lewis, Ievan	Botwnnog Cn	–	W	3 Jan. 1636/7	1636/24
Lewis, Evan	Llangeinwen (Maes y porth) A	Gent.	W	17 Aug. 1640	1640/13
Lewis, Evan	Llanwnnog Mg	Yeoman	W*	12 April 1641	1641/77
Lewis, Evan	Gyffylliog D	Yeoman	W I	27 May 1667	1667/116
Lewis, Evan	Llanfihangel Ysgeifiog A	Yeoman	W(2)	n.d.[2]	1670/37
Lewis, Evan	Bryncroes Cn	Yeoman	W	n.d.[3]	1679/19
Lewis, Evan	Rhiw Cn	Yeoman	W* I	16 April[4] 1694	1694/66
Lewis, Evan	Trefeglwys (Dolgooden) Mg	Yeoman	W I	14 Sept. 1697	1697/75
Lewis *alias* Roberts, Gaynor	Llanrhwydrys A	–	W	[12 March 1672/3]	1672/28
Lewis, Grace	Pentraeth A	Widow	W* I*	21 June 1671	1671/39
Lewis, Grace	Holyhead A	Widow	W I	31 March 1693	1693/6
Lewis, Gryffeth	Trefdraeth A	–	W	19 Oct. 1644	1644/16
Lewis, Griffith	Trefeglwys Mg	Yeoman	W* I	[12 Jan. 1675/6]	1675/70
Lewis, Griffith	[Llandanwg] (Harlech) Mr	Labourer	W	20 Feb. 1690/1	1690/89
Lewes, Gwen	Llanidloes Mg	Widow	I/G	29 Aug. 1661	1661/138
Lewis, Henry	Deneio (Pwllhely) Cn	Corviser	B I	30 July 1696	1696/47
Lewis, Howell	Llangelynnin (Tre r Morva) Mr	–	W I Rd	28 April 1663	1663/108
Lewis, Howell	Llanfair Mathafarn Eithaf A	–	B	12 July 1671	1671/22
Lewis, Howell	Amlwch (Gwredog) A	Esq.	W I Rd	[c. 24 Nov. 1683]	1683/1
Lewis, Howel	Amlwch (Gwredog) A	Gent.	W I	9 Jan. 1699/1700	1699/1

1 Inventory taken 18 March 1669.
2 Will dated 18 April 1670.
3 Will dated 20 April 1679.
4 Incorrect? Codicil dated 22 June 1694 and inventory taken 3 July 1694. Reading of endorsed probate act obscure; *Septembris* written above *Aprilis*?

Name	Parish & County	Status	Docs. Filed	Date of Probate/Admon.	Ref. No.
Lewys, Hugh	Maentwrog Mr	–	W R B	25 Nov. 1638	1638/63
Lewis, Hugh	Pentraeth A	Yeoman	W	26 March 1666	1666/32
Lewis, Hugh	Llanidloes Mg	Carpenter/ Bachelor	B I	5 July 1695	1695/108
Lewis, Humphrey	Llanengan Cn	–	B	26 Aug. 1682	1682/45
Lewis, Humphrey	Tywyn / Pennal Mr	Gent.	I/G* L*	[27 July 1699]	1699/118
Lewis, Ievan *see* Lewis, Evan					
Lewis, James	Llanelltud Mr	–	W I	10 Dec. 1696	1696/102
Lewis, Jane	Clynnog Cn	–	W*	21 Aug. 1641	1641/26
Lewis, Jane	Beaumaris A	Widow	W	10 May 1686	1686/4
Lewis, Jane	Llangoed A	Spinster	W	4 Nov. 1692	1692/21
Lewis, Jane	Llangelynnin Mr	Wife of John Pugh	B	22 Aug. 1698	1698/55
Lewis, John	Llangurig Mg	–	W I	30 Sept. 1635	1635/52
Lewes, John	Trefeglwys Mg	–	W/I	30 Sept. 1635	1635/54
Lewis, John	Dolgellau Mr	Yeoman	W*	3 Oct. 1662	1662/56
Lewis, John	Gyffylliog (Ffrithoedd) D	–	B I*	24 May 1662	1662/81
Lewis, John	Llanbedr[-goch] A	–	W	17 Dec. 1669	1669/11
Lewis, John	Llanfihangel Tre'r-beirdd A	Gent.	W	22 April 1669	1669/32
Lewis, John	Pennal Mr	–	I/G	8 April 1670	1670/159
Lewis, John	Cerrigceinwen A	–	W	[27 Nov. 1676]	1676/5
Lewis, John	Llanrug (Glanravon) Cn	–	B I	20 Jan. 1685/6	1685/57
Lewis, Katherine *see* Lewis, Catherine					
Lewis, Margarett	Amlwch (Penboll) A	Widow	W I Al	2 May 1661	1661/1
Lewis, Mary	Llanbedr Niwbwrch A	Spinster	B*	31 Dec. 1662	1662/12
			B	29 July 1663	1663/11
Lewis, Mary	Dolgellau Mr	Widow	W I	24 Aug. 1688	1688/66
Lewis, Marie	Llangeinwen A	Spinster	B	24 May 1689	1689/19
Lewis *alias* Thomas, Mathanwy *see* Lewis, William	Llaneilian A				
Lewis, Morgan	Llangurig Mg	–	W	28 Sept. 1637	1637/51
Lewis, Moris	Llangurig (Glinbrochan) Mg	Husbandman	W D Rd	21 May 1669	1669/166
Lewis, Maurice	Amlwch (Truscklwyn) A	Esq.	W(2)* Rd	28 Sept. 1699	1699/2
Lewis, Owen	[Dolgellau] (Garthgynvor) Mr	–	W*	n.d.[1]	1686/70
Lewis, Owen	Llanynghenedl A	Gent.	W	30 Oct. 1693	1693/24
Lewes, Perse	Cliffe, Kent	Curate of Cliffe	W	29 May 1666	1666/127
Lewis, Pierce	Llanfihangel Tre'r-beirdd A	Gent.	W(2)*	1 Nov. 1679	1679/7

[1] Will dated 5 March 1685.

Name	Parish & County	Status	Docs. Filed	Date of Probate/Admon.	Ref. No.
Lewis, Pierce	Bangor Cn	Clerk	W I	29 July 1699	1699/43
Lewys, Rice	Aber-erch Cn	–	W	13 May 1635	1635/15
Lewis, Rees	Dolgellau (Dyffrydan) Mr	–	B I	12 Oct. 1666	1666/75
Lewis, Rhees	Bodedern A	–	W* I	n.d.[1]	1670/2
Lewis, Richard	Llangefni A	–	W	10 Jan. 1637/8	1637/7
Lewis, Richard	Llanwnnog Mg	–	B	30 May 1661	1661/143
Lewis, Richard	Llanfihangel-y-Pennant (Hendref, Llecheiddior) Cn	Gent.	W	10 July 1668	1668/65
Lewis, Richard	[Trewalchmai] (Bodwiney) A	Gent.	W(2)* I	n.d.[2]	1668/31
Lewis, Richard	Trefeglwys (Dolegooden) Mg	Yeoman	W I	5 Sept. 1687	1687/135
Lewis, Richard	Llanbadrig (Cemais) A	Yeoman	W I	13 Aug. 1697	1697/3
Lewis, Robert	Llanbeulan A	–	B I	12 April 1677	1677/7
Lewis, Robert	Llanfair-yn-neubwll (Treflesk) A	Gent.	W Al Rd	3 Feb. 1686/7	1686/13
Lewis, Robert	[Llanfflewin] (Ucheldre) A	Gent.	W* I* Rd*	6 Dec. 1693	1693/14
Lewis, Robert	Llanaber Mr	Yeoman	B I	30 May 1699	1699/107
Lewis, Roger	Llanynys (Rhydonnen) D	–	W I	[19 May] 1664	1664/117
Lewis, Stuckley	Llanfachreth [Mr/A]	–	B	4 May 1685	1685/76
Lewis, Thomas	Beddgelert (Berthlwyd) Cn	–	W	8 April 1643	1643/16
Lewis, Thomas	Llandrygarn A	–	B I*	4 Feb. 1668/9	1668/11
Lewis, Thomas	Penystrowed Mg	–	B I	7 Dec. 1678	1678/93
Lewis, Thomas	[Llanegryn] Mr	–	W I	n.d.[3]	1689/70
Lewis, Thomas	Llanidan (Trefarthin) A	Yeoman	B I	7 Jan. 1689/90	1689/21
Lewis, Thomas	Gyffylliog D	–	B I	11 Dec. 1691	1691/104
Lewis, Thomas	Llanfihangel Ysgeifiog (Gaerwen) A	–	B I	4 May 1694	1694/20
Lewis, Thomas	Llandegfan A	Yeoman/ Husbandman	B I	27 Aug. 1696	1696/11
Lewys, William	Llanallgo A	–	W	12 Feb. 1638/9	1638/6
Lewis, William	Llanbedr Niwbwrch (Abermenay) A	Ferryman	B I	9 Feb. 1664/5	1664/13
			B	21 March 1676/7	1676/9
			B Ac	31 May 1682	1682/9
			B	13 April 1693	1693/7
Lewis, William	Llandinam (Dethienith) Mg	Weaver	W I	3 Aug. 1665	1665/97
Lewis, William	[Trewalchmai] (Cefncaerfôr) A	Gent.	W	6 Jan. 1665/6	1665/28

[1] Died 20 Oct. 1670.
[2] Inventory exhibited 1 Oct. 1668.
[3] Will dated 15 March 1688. Endorsed *1689*.

Name	Parish & County	Status	Docs. Filed	Date of Probate/Admon.	Ref. No.
Lewis, William	Llanystumdwy Cn	–	B I	21 April 1666	1666/67
Lewis, William	Pentraeth A	Gent.	W I	22 Jan. 1667/8	1667/42
Lewis, William, & Mathanwy Thomas his wife	Llaneilian A	Yeoman	W	26 Oct. 1670	1670/28
Lewis, William	Llanfaethlu A	Clerk (Rector of Llanfaethlu)	B	9 May 1671	1671/20
Lewis, William	Llanbeblig Cn	Labourer	W	[24 Oct. 1676]	1676/50
Lewis, William	Llanfaelog A	Yeoman	W	19 March 1676/7	1676/11
Lewis, William	[Llanrhwydrys] (Cemlyn) A	Gent.	W	16 Jan. 1676/7	1676/21
Lewis, William	Llannor (Tû dy) Cn	Gent.	W I Rd	14 April 1690	1690/74
Lewys, William	Llanelidan D	Miller	W I	12 June 1693	1693/103
Lewis, William	Llanfachreth A	Shopkeeper	W I	30 Oct. 1699	1699/17
Liza *see* Eliza					
Llewelin, Owen	Llandyfrydog A	Gent.	W	25 Jan. 1638/9	1638/9
Lloyd, Ales	Llanddaniel-fab A	Widow	W B	23 June 1637	1637/5
Lloyd, Alice	Trewalchmai (Bodwine) A	Widow	W	28 March 1665	1665/29
Lloyd,[1] Ales	Rhuthun D	–	B	29 April 1671	1671/137
Lloyd, Alse	Llaniestyn Cn	–	W I	24 April 1677	1677/41
Lloyd, Andrew	Penmynydd (Bryngo ucha) A	Gent.	B I G	6 March 1671/2	1671/36
Lloyd, Anne	Llangwyfan D	–	W I	13 March 1681/2	1681/97
Lloyd, Anne	Clynnog Cn	Widow	B I	20 March 1690/1	1690/48
Lloyd, Anne	Llangaffo A	Widow	B I	12 April 1692	1692/18
Lloyd, Catherine	Aber-erch (Llwyndyrus) Cn	Widow	W I	19 May 1670	1670/65
Lloyd, Catherine	[Llantrisant] (Chwaen hên) A	Widow	W	n.d.[2]	1673/16
Lloyd, Catherin vch David	Llanbedrycennin Cn	–	M	n.d.[3]	1671/63
Lloyd, Charles	Llanrhuddlad (Botteth) A	–	W* Rd*	13 Nov. 1643	1643/13
Lloyd, Charles	Penmorfa Cn	Gent.	W Rd	1 March 1647/8	1647/38
Lloyd, David	Llanfair Dyffryn Clwyd D	–	W Rd	19 March 1638/9	1638/77
Lloyd, David	Llaniestyn (Penwynllys) A	Gent.	W	4 April 1644	1644/13
Lloid, David	Llanfihangel Bachellaeth Cn	Gent.	W*	25 July 1646	1646/21
Lloyd, David	Llandanwg (Erw-wen) Mr	Gent.	B I R	18 Sept. 1663	1663/91
Lloyd, David	Llannor Cn	–	B I	4 Jan. 1669/70	1669/96
Lloyd, David	Llanbabo A	Gent.	B	[ ] 1670	1670/10
Lloyd, David	Llanrhaeadr-yng-Nghinmeirch (Llwyn) D	Gent.	W I*	18 April 1671	1671/128

1 Endorsed *Jones*.

2 Nuncupative will set down to writing 10 Jan. 1673; executor sworn 10 Jan. 1670 according to endorsement on will. For *1670* read *1673*?

3 Revocation of caveat dated 29 June 1671. Nuncupative will mentioned but not filed.

Name	Parish & County	Status	Docs. Filed	Date of Probate/Admon.	Ref. No.
Lloyd, David	Llanllyfni Cn	–	B	27 Nov. 1672	1672/73
Lloyd, David	Llandrygarn (Clegir Gwnion) A	–	B	1 March 1676/7	1676/10
Lloyd, David	[ ] (Penrhyn) Mr	Gent.	W I	7 April 1677	1677/68
Lloyd, David	[Llanwenllwyfo] (Llysdulas) A	Gent.	W I* Rd	13 May 1679	1679/13
Lloyd, David	Llanrhaeadr-yng-Nghinmeirch (Segroit) D	Gent.	W I	23 July 1687	1687/122
Lloyd, David	Llangelynnin Mr	Gent.	B I	21 July 1690	1690/96
Lloyd, David	Trefeglwys (Talgarth) Mg	Gent.	W I	7 Aug. 1690	1690/121
Lloyd, David	Llanfechell ([Kefn] Coch) A	Clerk	W* I(2)* Rd*	27 March 1691	1691/23
Lloyd, David	Gyffin (Cymrhyd) Cn	Gent.	B I R	22 April 1692	1692/46
Lloyd, Davidd	Bodedern (Sybylltir) A	–	B I	29 March 1694	1694/7
Lloyd, David	Gyffin (Ty yn y Coed) Cn	Gent.	W* I	29 April 1698	1698/29
Lloyd, David	Bodedern (Sybylltir) A	Clerk (Rector of Llanrhuddlad)	W* I*	n.d.[1]	1699/6
Lloyd, David, ap Hugh	Llanynys (Maesmaen Cymro) D	Gent.	W Rd	19 June 1645	1645/42
Lloyd, David, ap Owen	Llangurig Mg	–	I	n.d.[2]	1668/135
Lloyd, Diana	Llanynys D	Widow	B I	21 Jan. 1664/5	1664/118
Lloyd, Dorothy	Llanelidan D	Widow	W I	2 Nov. 1689	1689/82
Lloyd, Dorothy	Penmorfa Cn	–	B I	18 Oct. 1693	1693/68
Lloyd, Edward	Llangelynnin (Garthmon) Cn	–	W	12 Jan. 1647/8	1647/32
Lloyd, Edward	[Llanidloes] (Berth-lloyd) Mg	Knight	W I	10 March 1665/6	1665/105
Lloyd, Edward	Llangwyfan D	Gent.	W	19 Sept. 1667	1667/124
Lloyd, Edward	Llangurig Mg	–	W*	[21 May 1673]	1673/68
Lloyd, Edward	Rhuthun D	–	B	7 April 1685	1685/104
Lloyd, Edward ap David	Llanfair-iuxta-Harlech Mr	–	W B	11 Oct. 1637	1637/33
Lloyd *alias* Bulkeley, Ellin	Llanfair Mathafarn Eithaf A	Widow	W	23 April 1696	1696/14
Lloyd, Ellis	Llandegfan A	Gent.	B I R	6 Nov. 1669	1669/14
Lloyd, Ellis	Llanfair Dyffryn Clwyd (Plas Eynion) D	–	B I	4 July 1678	1678/69
Lloyd, Elizabeth	Llanynys D	Widow	W	24 March 1646/7	1646/30
Lloyd, Elizabeth	Llanynys (Maesmaynkymro) D	Widow	W I	25 Feb. 1663/4	1663/126
Lloyd, Ellizabeth	Llandinam Mg	–	W I	4 Aug. 1670	1670/181
Lloyd, Elizabeth	Maentwrog Mr	–	B R	7 Sept. 1689	1689/75
Lloyd, Elizabeth	[ ] [?D]	Widow	B	26 Sept. 1691	1691/124
Lloyd, Elizabeth	Trewalchmai A	–	B	27 May 1695	1695/18

1 Inventory taken 3 April 16[99].
2 Inventory taken 8 Feb. 1668.

Name	Parish & County	Status	Docs. Filed	Date of Probate/Admon.	Ref. No.
Lloyd, Elsebeth vch John Davydd	Llanllyfni Cn	Widow	B I W	2 March 1670/1 30 Sept. 1674	1670/120 1674/28
Lloyd, Evan	Rhoscolyn A	Clerk (Rector of Rhoscolyn)	B C	8 July 1661	1661/28
Lloyd, Evan	Penystrowed Mg	Gent.	I/G	20 Aug. 1662	1662/109
Lloyd, Evan	Llandwrog (Tryfan) Cn	–	W	5 Aug. 1668	1668/57
Lloyd, Evan	Llangefni A	Yeoman	W I	11 March 1669/70	1669/37
Lloyd, Evan	Trawsfynydd (Rhiwgoch) Mr	Gent.	W Rd	n.d.	1691/99
Lloyd, Evan	[Aber-erch][1] (Bryntanni) Cn	Gent.	W	9 May 1695	1695/21
Lloyd, Evan, Rowland	Trawsfynydd Mr	Gent.	W	3 Jan. 1638/9	1638/67
Lloyd, Foulke	Rhuthun D	Yeoman	B I	6 March 1660/1	1660/32
Lloyd, Franncis	Llanidloes (Berth-lwyd) Mg	Spinster	W*	10 April 1641	1641/75
Lloyd, Francis	[Llanffinan] (Hirdrevaig) A & Penllech Cn	Esq.	W Rd	27 Oct. 1694	1694/22
Lloyd, Grace	Llanbabo A	–	B	26 Nov. 1661	1661/9
Lloyd, Grace	Conway Cn	Widow	B	23 April 1664	1664/59
Lloyde, Grace, *alias* Grace vch Robert Lloide	Llanfihangel-y-Pennant Cn	Widow	W I	12 May 1669	1669/91
Lloyd, Grace	Clocaenog D	Widow	W I	2 April 1677	1677/69
Lloyd *alias* Davies, Grace	Beaumaris A	Wife of John Davies [formerly widow of John Lloyd, mercer]	B G B C	8 Aug. 1679 24 March 1680/1	1679/3 1680/2
Lloyd, Gryffith	[?Llanarmon Cn][2]	–	W	27 Feb. 1629/30	1629/1
Lloyd, Griffith	Aber-erch (Bryntannie) Cn	–	W	27 June 1635	1635/16
Lloyd, Gruffyth	Llanfechell A	Gent.	W*	11 Nov. 1640	1640/12
Lloyd, Griffith	Llandecwyn Mr	Esq.	B	15 April 1667	1667/92
Lloyd, Griffith	[Llangaffo] (Treasseth) A	Gent.	W	5 June 1671	1671/25
Lloyd, Gruffyth	Penmachno (Dugoyd) Cn	–	W*	26 Nov. 1694	1694/61
Lloyd, Griffith, ap Ellissey	Dolgellau Mr	–	W I	21 Nov. 1661	1661/90
Lloyd, Grissiel	Dwygyfylchi (Graige Lloyd) Cn	Widow [of Hugh Lloyd]	W*	24 Oct. 1676	1676/48
Lloyd, Henry	[Trewalchmai] (Bodwiney) A	Esq.	B I	29 Sept. 1664	1664/50
Lloyd, Henry	Llandyrnog D	–	B*	[ ] 1670	1670/165
Lloyd, Henry	Rhoscolyn A	Clerk	W	[12 April 1672]	1672/32

[1] Endorsed *Bryntanni alias Denio*.

[2] A tenement called *llwyn-hulkin* and the lease of a tenement called *tythin y felin* mentioned among the bequests.

Name	Parish & County	Status	Docs. Filed	Date of Probate/Admon.	Ref. No.
Lloyd, Henry	Llanrhaeadr-yng-Nghinmeirch (Pennant Cader) D	–	B I	7 Sept. 1696	1696/122
Lloid, Harry ap David	Gyffin (Kymrhyd) Cn	Gent.	W	16 Nov. 1646	1646/18
Lloyd, Harrie ap Ievan	Llanrhaeadr-yng-Nghinmeirch D	–	W*	11 Nov. 1641	1641/64
Lloyd, Harry Griffith	Dolgellau Mr	–	W I	13 July 1665	1665/61
Lloyd, Howell	Llanidloes Mg	Cooper	W I	[31 May 1688]	1688/103
Lloyd, Howell	Llandecwyn Mr	–	B I	22 May 1699	1699/110
Lloyd, Hugh	Dwygyfylchi [Graiglwyd] Cn	Gent.	W I	14 June 1661	1661/54
Lloyd, Hugh	Llanbedr[-goch] (Rôs-y-Gâd) A	Gent.	W* I Rd	5 June 1662	1662/11
Lloyd, Hugh	Llangurig Mg	–	W I	5 June 1668	1668/134
Lloyd, Hugh	Llantrisant (Nantanog) A	Gent.	W I Rd	15 July 1679	1679/12
Lloyd, Hugh	Deneio (Pwllhely) Cn	Mercer	I/G*	3 Feb. 1680/1	1680/24
Lloyd, Hugh	Llanddyfnan (Hendrehowell) A	Gent.	W I	18 May 1682	1682/16
Lloyd, Hugh	Llanddyfnan (Marrian) A	Gent.	B I	23 April 1682	1682/15
Lloyd, Hugh	Trawsfynydd (Pantmawr) Mr	–	B I C	30 Sept. 1683	1683/76
Lloyd, Hugh	Ffestiniog (Dduallt) Mr	Gent.	W I Rc	23 Oct. 1685	1685/68
Lloyd, Hugh	[ ] ([ ]line) Cn	Gent.	W* I*	12 March 1690/1	1690/83
Lloyd, Hugh	Ffestiniog (Caie Canol) Mr	–	I/G	20 June 1691[1]	1692/69
Lloyd, Hugh David	Dolgellau Mr	Yeoman	B I	18 July 1661	1661/91
Lloyd, Hugh ap Evan	Ffestiniog Mr	–	W	31 May 1638	1638/55
Lloyd, Hugh ap Evan	Nefyn Cn	–	B	1 July 1663	1663/74
Lloyd, Hugh ap Evan Dafudd	Dolgellau Mr	Yeoman	W I Db	10 June 1668	1668/81
Lloyd, Hugh Lewis ap Hugh	Llanidan (Trerdryw) A	Gent.	W	1 Nov. 1647	1647/17
Lloyd, Hugh Thomas David	Llanbadrig A	Yeoman	W/I	17 Aug. 1643	1643/4
Lloyd, Humffrey	Pentraeth A	Gent.	W	21 June 1645	1645/13
Lloyd, Humphrey	Llanfwrog (Coed-y-Gawen) D	–	B I	2 June 1679	1679/54
Lloyd, Humphrey	Penllech Cn	Yeoman	W I C	[27 June 1687]	1687/80
Lloyd, Humphrey	Llanfihangel [Bachellaeth] (Bodlas) Cn	Yeoman	W I	3 Sept. 1689	1689/48
Lloyd, Humphrey ap Evan	Tywyn Mr	–	B	20 April 1678	1678/59
Lloyd, Jane	Trawsfynydd (Rhiwgoch) Mr	Widow	B* I* C*	28 May 1662	1662/73
Lloyd, Jane	Pentraeth A	Widow	W	n.d.[2]	1663/31
Lloyd, Jane	Maentwrog Mr	Widow	W	16 July 1674	1674/52
Lloyd, Jane	[Tal-y-llyn] (Maesypandy) Mr	Widow of John Lloyd, esq.	W C*	17 April 1691	1691/98
Lloyd, Jane vch David	Dwygyfylchi Cn	Widow	W I	12 May 1635	1635/25

[1] Recte *1692*? Buried [ ] Dec. 1691 (see bishops transcripts of the parish registers of Ffestiniog). Inventory taken 1692.
[2] Will dated 9 Feb. 1663.

Name	Parish & County	Status	Docs. Filed	Date of Probate/Admon.	Ref. No.
Lloyd, Jenkin	Llangurig (Clochvaen) Mg	Gent.	B I	15 Aug. 1696	1696/130
Lloyd, John	Llanffinan (Hirdrevaige) A	Gent.	W*	6 July 1638	1638/16
Lloyd, John	Pentraeth A	–	W	24 Feb. 1638/9	1638/27
Lloyd, John	Trawsfynydd Mr	Gent.	W	8 Feb. 1638/9	1638/66
Lloyd, John	Llanbadrig (Kemais) A	–	W B	26 Oct. 1647	1647/7
Lloyd, John	Llangaffo A	–	B	27 Dec. 1662	1662/22
Lloyd, John	Nantgwnnadl *alias* Llangwnnadl Cn	Esq.	W I	15 March 1665/6	1665/47
Lloyd, John	Beaumaris A	Ironmonger	W I	12 Jan. 1666/7	1666/3
Lloyd, John	Llandegfan A	Esq./Gent.	I	n.d.[1]	1666/10
Lloyd, John	Beaumaris A	Mercer	B	3 Dec. 1668	1668/4
			B G	18 July 1679	1679/4
Lloyd, John	Llandinam Mg	–	W I	28 Sept. 1669	1669/162
Lloyd, John	Llandecwyn Mr	Gent.	W I M Rd*	24 March 1670/1	1670/142
Lloyd, John	Llanrhaeadr-yng-Nghinmeirch (Segroit) D	Carpenter	B I	29 June 1672	1672/116
Lloyd, John	Llangelynnin Mr	Clerk	B I	6 July 1680	1680/54
Llooyd, John	Llanarmon Cn	–	W	n.d.[2]	1681/42
Lloyd, John	Llanbedr Mr	–	B	3 June 1684	1684/68
Lloyd, John	Derwen D	–	W I	26 April 1693	1693/97
Lloyd, John	Aber-erch (Tythyn Yockws) Cn	Gent.	B	5 June 1695	1695/22
Lloyd, John	Ellesmere (Trench) S	Servant	W R	n.d.[3]	1696/143
Lloyd, John	Llanddyfnan A	Gent.	B I*	17 May 1697	1697/7
Lloyd, John	Llanfihangel Bachellaeth Cn	Gent.	B I	1 Feb. 1699/1700	1699/77
Lloyd, John David	Llandecwyn (Moel y geifr) Mr	Gent.	W I	30 Sept. 1667	1667/93
Lloyd, John, ap Howell Griffith	Clocaenog D	–	B* I	17 Jan. 1662/3	1662/79
Lloyd, John ap Hugh David	Llanbeblig Cn	Yeoman	W	14 June 1669	1669/72
Lloyd, Jonett	Llangwyfan D	–	W	29 April 1672	1672/112
Lloyd *alias* Poole, Jonett	Botwnnog Cn	Widow	W L	10 Jan. 1693/4	1693/33
Lloyd, Jonett vch David	Llanbeulan A	Widow	W	29 Dec. 1664	1664/16
Lloyd, Lewis	Llanidloes Mg	Gent.	B I	9 April 1666	1666/120
Lloyd, Lewis	Llangybi Cn	–	G	5 Aug. 1683	1683/45
Lloyd, Margarett	Llanwnnog (Caresowes) Mg	Widow	W I	1 Nov. 1662	1662/105
Lloyd *alias* Hughes, Margaret	Llaniestyn A	–	B*	15 Nov. 1670	1670/49
Lloyd *alias* Wynne, Margaret	Llanedwen A	Widow	W I	28 March 1671	1671/19

1 Inventory taken 6 Nov. 1666.

2 Will dated 27 March 1681.

3 Endorsed *never proved ye Executor renounceing*. Renunciation of David Lloyd of Derwen, co. Denbigh, the testator's brother, dated 20 Aug. 1696.

Name	Parish & County	Status	Docs. Filed	Date of Probate/Admon.	Ref. No.
Lloyd, Margarett	Pennal Mr	Widow	B I	12 Nov. 1681	1681/79
Lloyd, Margaret	Penystrowed Mg	Widow	W I	5 July 1683	1683/107
Lloyd, Margarrett	Llangurig (Keven[ ]) Mg	Widow	W* I	10 July 1684	1684/113
Lloyd, Margarett	Trawsfynydd (Rhiw-goch) Mr	Widow	W I	20 Oct. 1692	1692/90
Lloyd, Margarett	Llanwnda (Kefn) Cn	Widow	W I	29 Nov. 1693	1693/64
Lloyd, Margaret vch Robert	Gyffylliog D	Widow	W I	22 Jan. 1672/3	1672/102
Lloyd, Margery	Rhuthun D	Spinster	B I	8 Feb. 1667/8	1667/128
Lloyd, Martha	[Llanfair Dyffryn Clwyd] (Bacheirig) D	Spinster	W	6 Aug. 1685	1685/94
Lloyd, Mary	Derwen D	Spinster	W	22 Oct. 1678	1678/62
Lloyd, Mary	Maentwrog (Penbryn) Mr	–	W I	2 Sept. 1689	1689/76
Lloyd, Mary vch Evan	Llanfair-iuxta-Harlech Mr	Widow	W	12 May 1674	1674/46
Lloyd, Mary vch John David	Trawsfynydd Mr	Widow	W	5 June 1643	1643/39
Lloyd, Maurice *see* Lloyd, Moris					
Lloyd, Morgan	Llandinam (Rhydvaes) Mg	Gent.	W* I	[5 Sept. 1676]	1676/97
Lloyd, Morgan	Llanidloes (Heol y Bont Hir) Mg	Gent.	W I	15 May 1678	1678/88
Lloyd, Morgan	Llanidloes (Heol y Derwen vawr) Mg	Gent.	W I	13 July 1694	1694/123
Lloyd, Morgan David	Llanelltud Mr	–	W*	6 June 1640	1640/44
Lloyd, Moris	Cerrigceinwen A	–	W Rd	15 Nov. 1647	1647/4
Lloyd, Maurice	[Llanystumdwy] (Chwilog) Cn	–	B	12 Sept. 1661	1661/83
Lloyd, Maurice	[Llanaber] (Hendre vrian) Mr	–	I	n.d.[1]	1673/49
Lloyd, Moris	Maentwrog Mr	Gent.	W I	n.d.[2]	1686/82
Lloyd, Owen	Llanengan Cn	Clerk (Rector of Llanengan)	B	8 Aug. 1662	1662/48
Lloyd, Owen	Gyffin Cn	Gent.	W	4 Aug. 1672	1672/52
Lloyd, Owen	Llanllyfni Cn	Gent.	B I	20 Feb. 1698/9	1698/40
Lloyd, Owen ap Evan David	Dolgellau Mr	Yeoman	B(2) I	12 Oct. 1666	1666/80
Lloyd, Owen ap John	Trewalchmai A	–	W	11 June 1666	1666/37
Lloyd, Pierce (the younger)	[Penrhosllugwy] (Lligwy) A	Esq.	W	2 July 1673	1673/18
Lloyd, Pierce	Llanidan & [Penrhosllugwy] (Lligwy) A	Esq.	{B I R {B R	30 Aug. 1680 24 April 1684	1680/13 1684/17
Lloyd, Rice	Llanrhaeadr-yng-Nghinmeirch D	–	W I	21 July 1687	1687/123
Lloyd, Rees	Llangurig (Clochvan) Mg	Gent.	B R	5 Jan. 1699/1700	1699/150
Lloyd, Rhytherech	Llanidan A	Yeoman	W* I*	6 Dec. 1662	1662/27

[1] Inventory taken 21 Nov. 1673.
[2] Inventory taken 9 Aug. 1686.

Name	Parish & County	Status	Docs. Filed	Date of Probate/Admon.	Ref. No.
Lloyd, Richard	Dublin[1]	–	B	1 Aug. 1667	1667/145
Lloyd, Richard	Rhuthun D	Gent.	W	n.d.[2]	1675/60
Lloyd, Richard	Llangadwaladr A	–	W I	12 July 1688	1688/21
Lloyd, Richard	Bangor Cn	Gent.	W I	30 April 1696	1696/37
Lloyd, Richard David	Llanfair-is-gaer (Kreigg) Cn	–	W*	4 Sept. 1645	1645/28
Lloyd, Richard ap Ievan	Llanidloes Mg	–	W M B Rd	5 Nov. 1636	1636/65
Lloyd, Richard ap Hugh	Llangybi Cn	Shoemaker	W I	10 Feb. 1679/80	1679/26
Lloid, Richard Owen	Gyffin (Gweredros) Cn	Gent.	W I	31 Aug. 1669	1669/69
Lloid, Robert	Llanrhaeadr-yng-Nghinmeirch (Brynllyarth) D	–	W*	2[ ] April 1636	1636/59
Lloyd, Robert	Llanynys (Mayse Anod) D	–	W	6 June 1644	1644/44
Lloyd, Robert	Llanrhaeadr-yng-Nghinmeirch (Lloyn) D	Gent.	W(3)	27 Dec. 1670	1670/172
Lloyd, Robert	Llannor Cn	–	B	27 Aug. 1690	1690/75
Lloyd, Robert	Llanddyfnan (Marian) A	–	B	27 Oct. 1691	1691/18
Lloyd, Robert	Llanrhaeadr-yng-Nghinmeirch (Plas y Captaine) & Denbigh D	Gent.	W	28 April 1699	1699/135
Lloyd, Robert David	Llanaber Mr	Gent./Yeoman	W I	19 Feb. 1669/70	1669/120
Lloyd, Robert David	Llanystumdwy Cn	Yeoman	W	[18 May 1672]	1672/81
Lloyd, Robert David	Llandudwen (Treferwyn) Cn	–	W I	17 May 1687	1687/57
Lloyd, Robert Griffith	Dolgellau (Brithdir) Mr	Gent.	W I	15 Jan. 1676/7	1676/69
Lloyd, Robert ap Prichart David	Llandwrog (Llyn y meibion) Cn	–	W M	17 July 1667	1667/68
Lloyd, Rowland	Llanbedr Niwbwrch (Brynne) A	Clerk	W I	23 May 1690	1690/15
Lloyd, Thomas	Maentwrog (Hendre yr Mur) Mr	Gent.	W	23 Jan. 1661/2	1661/105
Lloyd, Thomas	Llanwnnog Mg	–	B I	16 June 1663	1663/148
Lloyd, Thomas	Llangristiolus A	Yeoman	W I	6 June 1664	1664/33
Lloyd, Thomas	Llanhychan D	Gent.	W	6 May 1666	1666/105
Lloyd, Thomas, *alias* Thomas John Lloyd	Derwen D	–	W I	18 May 1687	1687/112
Lloyd, Thomas	Derwen D	Yeoman	W I	18 March 1696/7	1696/115
Lloyd, Thomas John David[3]	Llandudno Cn	–	W I R G/R L	20 Oct. 1670	1670/102
Lloyd, William	Llanrhuddlad (Botthedd) A	–	W Rd	17 Jan. 1637/8	1637/9
Lloyd, William	Llanbedrycennin Cn	–	W Al	17 July 1640	1640/25

[1] Mary Lloyd, his sister and administratrix, described as being of Beaumaris.

[2] Will dated 4 March 1675 (28 Chas. II).

[3] See also Gaynor vch William Prees (endorsement on document M).

Name	Parish & County	Status	Docs. Filed	Date of Probate/Admon.	Ref. No.
Lloyd, William	Eglwys[-ael] *alias* Llangadwaladr (Bodgorgan) A	Gent.	W* B	13 April 1642	1642/10
Lloyd, William	Llandyrnog D	–	W I	11 Oct. 1662	1662/82
Lloyd, William	Llanbedr[-goch] (Rhose y Gad) A	Gent.	W I Rd	23 March 1665/6	1665/6
Lloyd, William	Salop[1]	–	B	18 Jan. 1666/7	1666/128
Lloyd, William	[Llanbadrig] (Clygyrog)[2] A	–	I	n.d.[3]	1669/10
Lloyd, William	Pentraeth A	Clerk	W	n.d.[4]	1670/56
Lloyd, William	[Deneio] (Pwllheli) Cn	Gent.	B*	28 March 1671	1671/59
Lloyd, William	Trawsfynydd Mr	–	I	n.d.[5]	1677/64
Looyd, William	Trawsfynydd (Bryn y llefrith) Mr	–	B	15 March 1680/1	1680/57
Lloyd, William	[Llandwrog] (Bodvan) Cn	Esq.	W I	n.d.[6]	1682/42
Lloyd, William	Llangwnnadl Cn	Gent.	W	26 Aug. 1684	1684/49
Lloyd, William	Llanfachreth (Blaenglin) Mr	–	B I R	7 June 1687	1687/99
Lloyd, William	Llandrygarn A	Gent.	W I Rd	30 Oct. 1696	1696/12
Lloyd, William	Beddgelert (Havod lwyfog) Cn	Esq.	W* I* Rd	[4 Sept. 1697]	1697/16
Lloyd, William David	Llanfachreth Mr	–	I/G	10 Aug. 1669	1669/128
Lloyd, William David	Bangor Cn	–	W I	12 May 1680	1680/20
Lloyd, William ap Ievan	Derwen D	–	W	n.d.[7]	1641/56
Lloyd, William John	Dolgellau Mr	Carpenter/ Yeoman	W I	10 June 1668	1668/83
Lowe, Richard	Llanwnnog Mg	Tucker	I/G	17 Sept. 1668	1668/142
Lowe, William	Llandinam Mg	Yeoman	W I	21 Oct. 1682	1682/96
Lucas, Hugh	Llanidloes Mg	Yeoman	B* I	1 Sept. 1677	1677/91
Lucas, John	Llangurig Mg	Yeoman	W I	19 March 1680/1	1680/77
Lucas, John	Llangurig Mg	–	W	[29 Dec. 1691]	1691/132
Lucas, Rees	Llangurig Mg	Yeoman	W I	5 July 1695	1695/105
Luke, Margaret	Caerhun Cn	Widow	W I*	22 April 1686	1686/34
Lunt, Thomas	Rhuthun D	–	B I*	21 Dec. 1685	1685/105

1 Endorsement on cover. B *Wm. Lloyd late within the Diocese of Bangor.* John Lloyd of Tyddyn-mawr, parish of Trawsfynydd, co. Merioneth, named as one of the obligors

2 Incorrectly endorsed *Clynnog*.

3 Inventory taken 16 Nov. 1669.

4 Will dated 14 March 1670.

5 Died 1 Jan. 1677.

6 Inventory taken 21 Oct. 1682.

7 Will dated 25 Nov. 1641.

Name	Parish & County	Status	Docs. Filed	Date of Probate/Admon.	Ref. No.
Madder *see* Mather					
Madockes, John	Llandyrnog D & Bodfari F	Gent.	W* Rd	21 Aug. 1662	1662/83
Madryn, Edward	Llanwnda Cn	Gent.	W I*	31 March 1671	1671/87
Madrynne, Owen	Llannor Cn	–	W	13 May 1636	1636/36
Mainwaring, Mannering *see* Maynwaringe					
Marpoole, George	Llandinam Mg	–	B I	24 Sept. 1661	1661/128
Marpoole, John	Llandinam (Dethienydd) Mg	Yeoman	W/I	5 July 1692	1692/111
Mersh *alias* Pue, Dorothy	Conway Cn	Widow	W Rd	21 July 1668	1668/47
Marsh *alias* Jones, Elizabeth	Conway Cn	Widow	W I M	25 Nov. 1666	1666/49
Marsh, Margery	Beaumaris A	Widow	W(2)	21 July 1665	1665/2
Massey, John ap William	Llanelidan D	Yeoman	W	n.d.[1]	1675/56
Madder (Mather), Dennis	Beaumaris A	Tanner	W I	3 Sept. 1672	1672/5
Madther *alias* Shawe, Margaret	Beaumaris A	Widow	W	26 April 1681	1681/2
Mathew, Evan	Llanwnnog Mg	–	B I	11 Nov. 1691	1691/136
Matthew, Evan	Llangurig Mg	–	B I	22 Oct. 1696	1696/131
Mathewes, William	Derwen D	–	W I	[27 May] 1664	1664/109
Maurice *see* Morris					
Maynwaringe (Mannering), Randulph	Holyhead A	Gent.	B I	26 Nov. 1667	1667/9
Meiricke *see* Meyricke					
Mellars, Elizabeth	Aber (Bodsilin) Cn	Widow	B I	25 Jan. 1676/7	1676/31
Mellers, John	[Llanbeblig] (Carnarvon) Cn	–	B(2)	22 July 1670	1670/76
Mellers, William	[Llanbeblig] (Caernarvon) Cn	Tanner	W Rd	25 Oct. 1637	1637/20
Mellars, William	[Llanbeblig] (Carnarvon) Cn	Tanner	W I	6 Nov. 1688	1688/37
Mercer, Richard	[Llanbeblig] (Carnarvon) Cn	Smith	B*	28 [ ] 1689	1689/35
Meredith, David	Tal-y-llyn (Ddolwen) Mr	Gent.	B I	7 April 1677	1677/63
Mredyth, Elin	Carnguwch Cn	Widow	W	[7 July 1674]	1674/15
Meredith, Elizabeth	Dolgellau Mr	–	W	12 June 1663	1663/80
Meredith, Evan	Llanidloes Mg	Corviser	B* I	1 Aug. 1697	1697/67
Meredith, Gaynor	Clynnog (Menaughty Gwyn) Cn	Widow	W I	22 April 1698	1698/26
Meredith, Griffith	Llanddaniel-fab A	–	B	22 Oct. 1641	1641/9
Meredyth, Gruffyth	Llanfihangel-y-traethau Mr	Yeoman	W I	25 May 1674	1674/49
Meredyth, Hugh	Clynnog (Manachty) Cn	Gent.	W Rd	15 March 1670/1	1670/84
Mredith, Humphrey	Llannor Cn	–	B	11 Oct. 1680	1680/35
Meredith, Jenkin	Llangurig Mg	Yeoman	W	[9 July 1674]	1674/60
Meredith, John	[Llanbeblig] (Carnarvon) Cn	–	B I	11 Sept. 1661	1661/48

[1] Will dated 3 June 1675.

Name	Parish & County	Status	Docs. Filed	Date of Probate/Admon.	Ref. No.
Meredith, John	Llandinam Mg	–	W I	3 June 1698	1698/72
Meredith, Lewis	Llandinam (Dethienydd) Mg	–	W/I	n.d.[1]	1687/129
Mredith, Lewis	Llangeinwen A	Yeoman	B I	24 Oct. 1699	1699/22
Mredith, Margarett	Tal-y-llyn Mr	Spinster	W I	[27 May 1681]	1681/80
Meredyth, Mary	Conway Cn	Wife of Ephraim Stodart	B	8 July 1686	1686/42
Meredith, Meredith	Llanwnda Cn	Gent.	W	16 May 1661	1661/82
Mredith, Morgan	Llanidloes Mg	Yeoman	W	3 May 1683	1683/103
Meredith, Owen	Tregaean A	–	B I	20 Feb. 1672/3	1672/35
Meredith, Owen	Llangurig Mg	–	B I	11 Feb. 1685/6	1685/114
Meredyth, Richard	Llanbedr Niwbwrch A	–	B	13 Oct. 1685	1685/13
Meredith, Richard	Clynnog (Bachwen) Cn	Gent.	W I	19 June 1699	1699/54
Mredyth, Robert	Caerhun Cn	–	W	20 Jan. 1637/8	1637/18
Meredith, Robert	Conway Cn	Gent.	B I R	3 Aug. 1691	1691/49
Meredith, Rowland (the younger)	Llechylched (Traffwl) A	–	W Rd	2 April 1642	1642/15
Meredith, Rowland	Trefdraeth A	Yeoman	W I	16 July 1677	1677/18
Mredith, Thomas	Llanddaniel-fab A	–	B I*	29 April 1682	1682/13
Meredith, Thomas	Llanwnnog Mg	–	B I	11 Nov. 1691	1691/137
Mredith *alias* Nailer, William	Dolgellau Mr	Miller	W	22 July 1638	1638/53
Meredyth, William	Trefdraeth (Trefdrayth destiniet) A	Yeoman	W	1 Dec. 1642	1642/16
Mredith, William	Llanedwen A	Tailor	W I	3 June 1664	1664/20
Mersh *see* Marsh					
Merton, Thomas	Llanrhaeadr-yng-Nghinmeirch D	–	I	n.d.[2]	1687/124
Meyricke, Ellin	Rhuthun D	Widow	W	26 Nov. 1644	1644/45
Meiricke, Gaynor	[Aberffraw] (Bullen) A	Widow	W*	27 March 1671	1671/1
Meiricke, Griffith	Llanelltud (Kaemabsivion) Mr	Clerk	W I	14 Aug. 1683	1683/69
Meyricke, Richard	Eglwys-ael *alias* Llangadwaladr (Boddgorgan) A	Esq.	W Cd	16 Jan. 1644/5	1644/12
Meuricke, Richard	[Llangadwaladr] (Bodgorgan) A	Esq.	W	10 Dec. 1669	1669/34
Michaell, Ellin	[Tudweiliog] (Brynodol) Cn	Widow	W Al	[c. 14 Oct. 1675]	1675/31
Michaell, Ellen	Llaneilian A	Widow	B	12 Feb. 1690/1	1690/20
Michaell, Griffith	Aberffraw (Rhosbadrick) A	Gent.	W I Al	22 Sept. 1682	1682/1
Michael, John	Cerrigceinwen A	–	B	23 Sept. 1662	1662/6
Michael, Rees	Llaniestyn (Penhwnllys) A	Gent.	W I R(2) B	21 July 1684	1684/18

1 Will dated 30 June 1687.

2 Inventory taken 25 April 1687.

Name	Parish & County	Status	Docs. Filed	Date of Probate/Admon.	Ref. No.
Michael, Richard	Llandegfan A	Yeoman	W I	16 July 1667	1667/15
Mycheall, Roger	Llanegryn Mr	–	W I	6 May 1686	1686/77
Michaell, Thomas	Llandegfan A	Labourer	I	n.d.[1]	1671/16
Michaell, Thomas	Llaneilian (Mayne y Drew) A	Esq./Gent.	W I B Rd	22 May 1683	1683/7
Midleton, John	Llandyrnog D	Gent.	I R	n.d.[2]	1684/89
Midleton, Margaret	Llanfwrog D	Widow	B I	13 Jan. 1665/6	1665/84
Myddelton, William	Llanrhaeadr-yng-Nghinmeirch (Klickiedig) D	–	W	9 Sept. 1671	1671/129
Miles, Lewis	Llanidloes Mg	–	B* I	24 Oct. 1662	1662/104
Miles, Mary	Llandinam Mg	–	B I	5 July 1692	1692/112
Mills, Richard	Llandinam Mg	Yeoman	W I	28 Sept. 1664	1664/129
Milles, Richard	Trefeglwys (Eskireth) Mg	Yeoman	W*	20 Dec. 1671	1671/148
Milles, Roger	Trefeglwys (Eskireth) Mg	–	I/G	5 June 1684	1684/121
Morgan, Catterine	Llanwnda Cn	Widow	W	5 March 1665/6	1665/51
Morgan, Katherine	Llangurig (Llanivyny) Mg	Widow	W I	22 March 1679/80	1679/64
Morgans, David	Llanddeiniolen (Dynorwicke) Cn	Clerk	W	17 April 1638	1638/41
Morgan, David	Trefeglwys Mg	–	W(2) M	31 July 1647	1647/55
Morgan, David	Penmachno (Cae r Moch) Cn	–	B I	5 July 1687	1687/81
Morgan, David	Tywyn Mr	–	B I	13 Feb. 1691/2	1691/102
Morgan, David	Llanidan A	Yeoman	W I Db	31 March 1692	1692/24
Morgan, David	Llanwnnog Mg	Yeoman	B I	14 Oct. 1693	1693/142
Morgan, Edward	Llanbedr[-goch] A	–	W Rd	7 Dec. 1661	1661/10
Morgan, Edward	Llanidloes Mg	–	B I	9 Jan. 1661/2	1661/139
Morgan, Edward	Llanberis Cn	Gent.	W*	20 June 1666	1666/59
Morgans, Edward	Llanidloes (Glynhaveren) Mg	Gent.	W I Rd	21 June 1676	1676/104
Morgans, Edward	Rhuthun D	–	I	n.d.[3]	1684/101
Morgan, Edward	Carno Mg	Yeoman	W I	7 Aug. 1690	1690/115
Morgan, Elizabeth	Llangurig Mg	Widow of David Jenkin Moris	B I	22 April 1678	1678/85
Morgan, Elizabeth	Llandwrog (Tythun David ddu) Cn	Widow	W Rd	24 March 1695/6	1695/39
Morgan, Evan	Dolwyddelan Cn	–	W	19 Sept. 1638	1638/40
Morgan, Evan	Llangurig Mg	Gent.	B I	31 Oct. 1682	1682/100
Morgan, Evan	Trefeglwys Mg	–	B I	17 Dec. 1687	1687/136
Morgans, Gabriel	Llangristiolus A	–	B	2 Aug. 1680	1680/10

[1] Inventory taken 10 Nov. 1671.
[2] Inventory taken 30 Sept. 1684; renunciation dated 5 Jan. 1684.
[3] Inventory taken 29 Nov. 1684.

Name	Parish & County	Status	Docs. Filed	Date of Probate/Admon.	Ref. No.
Morgan, George	Llanidloes Mg	Yeoman	W I	17 Sept. 1669	1669/171
Morgan, Gwen	Llanidloes Mg	Widow	B	16 June 1663	1663/144
Morgan, Hary	Llandanwg Mr	–	W(2) D	15 March 1676/7	1676/74
Morgan, Hugh	Caerhun Cn	–	W	3 April 1637	1637/19
Morgan *alias* Wood, Jane	[Amlwch] (Gwredogg) A	Widow	W Rd	11 Nov. 1647	1647/1
Morgan, John	[Llanbedrog] (Cefn Llanvair) Cn	–	B	25 Nov. 1661	1661/61
Morgan, John	Llanddyfnan A	Yeoman	W I R	24 June 1672	1672/17
Morgan, John	Llanfair Pwllgwyngyll A	–	B	24 Jan. 1676/7	1676/15
Morgans, John[1]	Trawsfynydd (Kelli Ierweth) Mr	Esq.	I	[20 Dec. 1676]	1676/83
Morgan, John	Llanedwen A	–	B I	5 Dec. 1687	1687/8
Morgan, John	Llandinam Mg	Yeoman	W I	19 June 1692	1692/113
Morgan, Katherine *see* Morgan, Catherine					
Morgan *alias* Thomas, Mahallt	Llangurig (Glynbrochan) Mg	Widow	B I	26 June 1692	1692/120
Morgan, Margarett	Betws-y-coed Cn	Widow	B	28 Dec. 1671	1671/47
Morgan, Margeret	Trefeglwys Mg	Widow	W I	19 Feb. 1696/7	1696/140
Morgan, Morris	Llangurig Mg	Yeoman	B I	24 Feb. 1699/1700	1699/151
Morgan, Moses	Llandinam Mg	–	I/G	[29 March 1677]	1677/89
Morgan, Owen	Llanbedr[?-goch] A	Yeoman	W	6 June 1648	1648/2
Morgans, Rice	Llanidloes Mg	–	B I	16 June 1663	1663/145
Morgan, Rees	Llanenddwyn Mr	Yeoman	W I	n.d.[2]	1670/147
Morgan, Richard	Llangeinwen A	Gent.	W I Rd	13 Dec. 1664	1664/31
Morgan, Richard	Llangurig Mg	Gent.	W*	13 May 1694	1694/121
Morgan, Rowland	Llandwrog (Llwun y gwalch) Cn	–	W	1 Aug. 1678	1678/27
Morgan, Thomas	Llanidloes Mg	–	B I	29 Sept. 1663	1663/146
Morgan, Thomas	Aberdaron Cn	–	W	29 Nov. 1672	1672/38
Morgan, Thomas	Llanfair Dyffryn Clwyd (Glascoed, Vaynol) D	Yeoman	W I	14 Aug. 1690	1690/106
Morgan, Ursula	Tywyn Mr	Widow	W I R	11 Nov. 1687	1687/108
Morgan, William	Clynnog Cn	–	B*	25 April 1662	1662/43
Morgan, William	Llanenddwyn Mr	Yeoman	I/G	17 Sept. 1669	1669/127
Morgan, William	[Llanbeblig] (Carnarvon) Cn	Tailor	W Rd	8 July 1670	1670/77
Morgan, William	Trefeglwys (Glyntrefnant) Mg	Yeoman	W I	28 Nov. 1689	1689/98
Morgan, William	Llangwyfan A	–	B I	8 May 1694	1694/26

[1] See also under Richard, Margaret, of Trawsfynydd (document L) for a reference to the administration of his goods.
[2] Inventory taken 3 Feb. 1670.

Name	Parish & County	Status	Docs. Filed	Date of Probate/Admon.	Ref. No.
Morgan, William	Dolbenmaen Cn	–	I	n.d.[1]	1699/57
Morgans *see* Morgan					
Morris, Aleth	Llandinam Mg	–	W I	25 March 1695	1695/102
Moris, Arthyr	Llanwnnog Mg	Gent.	B I	12 Jan. 1689/90	1689/96
Maurice, Athelstan	Llandinam (Pyllau) Mg	Gent.	W I	16 Jan. 1668/9	1668/132
Morris, Bridgett	Llandinam Mg	Spinster	W I	6 Aug. 1696	1696/128
Moris, Cadwalader	Dolgellau (Garthgynvor) Mr	Tailor	I/G	18 Nov. 1699	1699/99
Morris, Catherine	Llandecwyn Mr	–	B	18 Aug. 1688	1688/73
Morris, Catherine	Pennal (Pen-y-Bont) Mr	Widow	B I R	4 July 1692	1692/83
Morris, Daniel	Carno Mg	Yeoman	W	24 Jan. 1695/6	1695/99
Moris, David	Llandinam Mg	Gent.	W B	15 July 1636	1636/64
Moris, David	Trefeglwys Mg	–	W I	6 March 1678/9	1678/95
Morris, David	Llangurig Mg	–	B	17 May 1684	1684/114
Morris, David	Carno Mg	–	W I	16 Oct. 1688	1688/99
Moris, David	Llanegryn Mr	Gent.	W	28 June 1692	1692/76
Morris, David	Tal-y-llyn Mr	Yeoman	B I	26 April 1692	1692/86
Morris, David	Llanegryn (Penniarth) Mr	Gent.	B C	16 Feb. 1694/5	1694/81
Morris, Dorothy	Llandyrnog D	Widow	W	7 Jan. 1670/1	1670/166
Maurice, Edward	Llandyrnog D	Gent.	W I Rd	27 March 1665	1665/80
Morris, Edward	Llangurig Mg	Yeoman	I/G	17 Oct. [1683]	1683/101
Moris, Elein	Trefdraeth A	Widow	W I	5 Feb. 1678/9	1678/15
Morris, Ellen	Llanbeblig Cn	Widow	B I	9 Sept. 1699	1699/66
Morris, Ellis	Llanfihangel-y-Pennant (Ymwlch) Cn	Gent.	B* I* L	24 March 1662/3	1662/49
Morris, Ellis	Llanfrothen Mr	–	B	10 June 1668	1668/97
Moris, Ellis	Dolwyddelan (Penamnen) Cn	–	W	3 April 1676	1676/46
Morris, Ellis	Dolgellau (Garthgynvor) Mr	–	W	3 May 1693	1693/69
Moris, Elizabeth	Llanrug Cn	Widow	W* I	9 Dec. 1697	1697/35
Morris, Ellen *as* Morris, Elin					
Morris, Ellis *as* Morris, Elis					
Morris, Evan	Trefeglwys (Eskirieth) Mg	–	W I	27 Sept. 1667	1667/143
Moris, Evan	Llanidloes (Manleth) Mg	–	W I	21 July 1681	1681/106
Morris, Evan	Carno (Llyssin-Iscorvor) Mg	Yeoman	W* I* Al	23 Sept. 1697	1697/62
Mores, Hugh	Trewalchmai A	–	W	13 Feb. 1642/3	1642/18
Morris, Hugh	Aber-erch Cn	–	W	28 April 1673	1673/22
Morris, Hugh	Bangor (Bodelgynfor yssa) Cn	–	B I	7 Sept. 1689	1689/30
Morris, Humphrey	Llanaelhaearn Cn	–	B	4 March 1681/2	1681/40

[1] Inventory taken 11 Dec. 1699.

Name	Parish & County	Status	Docs. Filed	Date of Probate/Admon.	Ref. No.
Morris, Humffrey	Carno Mg	Yeoman	W I	n.d.[1]	1684/105
Morris, Humphrey	Llanystumdwy (Ynys Ely) Cn	–	B(2) I	4 Aug. 1687	1687/72
Morris, Jane	Llanenddwyn (Bron y foel) Mr	Widow	I/G	29 May 1667	1667/98
Maurice, Jane	Llanaber Mr	Widow	W/I Al	5 Aug. 1696	1696/93
Moris, Jeffrey	Beaumaris A	–	B	18 July 1661	1661/3
Moris, John	Clynnog Cn	–	B I	4 May 1663	1663/43
Morris, John	Llanystumdwy Cn	–	B	30 June 1668	1668/71
Maurice, John	Llanrhaeadr-yng-Nghinmeirch (Clickedig) D	Gent.	B I C	23 Nov. 1669	1669/155
Moris, John	Gyffylliog D	–	W	n.d.[2]	1670/163
Moris, John	Tal-y-llyn Mr	Yeoman	W*	31 July 1675	1675/49
Moris, John	Llanfihangel-y-Pennant Cn	Yeoman	W I	n.d.[3]	1677/39
Morris, John	Llanddeiniolen Cn	–	W I	7 April 1680	1680/30
Moris, John	Carno Mg	Yeoman	B I* C	7 June 1684	1684/106
Morris, John	Llan Sant Cathrin *alias* Cricieth Cn	–	B I	21 Oct. 1691	1691/54
Morris, John	Pistyll Cn	Yeoman	W I	2 June 1697	1697/39
Morris, John	Llanarmon Cn	Yeoman	B I	17 Jan. 1698/9	1698/31
Morris, John	Aber-erch Cn	Yeoman	B I	11 April 1699	1699/40
Maurice, Jonett	Llandyrnog D	Widow	W I	10 Sept. 1672	1672/105
Moris, Joyes	Llanwnnog Mg	Widow	W I B	17 Aug. 1683	1683/104
Morris, Lewis	Llanidan (Trefarthyn) A	Yeoman	B I	28 Feb. 1678/9	1678/13
Morris *alias* Jones, Lewis	Aberffraw A	–	B I	24 Feb. 1684/5	1684/1
Morris, Lowry	Llangybi Cn	Widow	B*	22 Jan. 1699/1700	1699/80
Moris, Marie	Cricieth Cn	–	W/L	10 Feb. 1672/3	1672/51
Maurice, Oliver	Pennal (Drayn Llwydion) Mr	Gent.	W I Db	n.d.[4]	1689/77
Morris, Owen	Ynyscynhaearn (Llannerch y Gest) Cn	Yeoman	W I	[24 March 1678/9]	1678/35
Morris, Owen	Llanarmon Cn	–	W I	24 Oct. 1682	1682/41
Morris, Rees	Llanidloes (Trevelin) Mg	Husbandman	B I	9 April 1666	1666/121
Morris, Richard	Llanwnnog Mg	–	W	[7 Aug. 1672]	1672/131
Morris, Richard	Dolwyddelan (Penamen) Cn	Yeoman	W I	[13 Oct. 1680]	1680/26
Morris, Richard	Trefeglwys Mg	Yeoman	I/G	30 June 1698	1698/83
Moris, Robert	Ffestiniog Mr	Yeoman	W I	24 Jan. 1665/6	1665/63

1 Inventory taken 29 Aug. 1684.
2 Will dated 24 Aug. 1670.
3 Inventory taken 21 Nov. 1677.
4 Inventory taken 5 March 1688.

Name	Parish & County	Status	Docs. Filed	Date of Probate/Admon.	Ref. No.
Morris, Robert	Llanaber Mr	Bachelor	B*	4 Aug. 1686	1686/73
Morris, Robert	[Llanbeblig] (Carnarvon) Cn	–	B*	27 April 1689	1689/36
Moris, Robert	Llanfair-is-gaer (Tyddyn Huskin) Cn	–	B I	12 Feb. 1690/1	1690/63
Morris, Robert	Llanllechid Cn	–	B	14 June 1695	1695/49
Moris, Robert	Llandanwg Mr	Yeoman	I/G	5 May 1696	1696/98
Morris, Robert	Llanfihangel-y-Pennant (Brithdir Bach) Cn	Gent.	W	16 Nov. 1699	1699/78
Morris, Roger	Betws-y-coed Cn	–	I	n.d.[1]	1699/46
Moris, Rowland	[Llanidan] (Gwydryn) A	Gent.	I	5 Nov. 1665	1665/19
Morris, Rowland	Llangaffo (Hendregadog) A	Gent.	W I	n.d.[2]	1676/18
Moris, Thomas	Llanaelhaearn Cn	Yeoman	W I	29 March 1672	1672/54
Morris, Thomas	Llangurig Mg	–	B	28 Nov. 1676	1676/100
Morres, Thomas	Bodedern A	–	B I	20 April 1682	1682/4
Morris, Thomas	Bryncroes Cn	Yeoman	W I C B	18 April 1691	1691/43
Maurice, Thomas	Llandinam Mg	–	B I	5 July 1695	1695/103
Morris, William	Bangor Cn	Gent.	B I	4 March 1664/5	1664/53
Morris, William	Llandinam Mg	Gent.	B I	28 July 1664	1664/130
Morris, William	Llanidan A	–	W	24 April 1667	1667/35
Morris, William	[Bangor] (Treborth vcha) Cn	Gent.	B I(3) Db R	19 June 1668	1668/33
Morris, William	[Llanbeblig] (Carnarvon) Cn	Gent.	B I	30 May 1670	1670/78
Morice, William	[Dolgellau] (Dolgleder) Mr	Yeoman	W	[31 Dec. 1675]	1675/35
Moris, William	Maentwrog (Cidnerth) Mr	Yeoman	W I	5 July 1680	1680/55
Morris, William	Llanaber Mr	–	W I Al B	2 July 1685	1685/71
Morris, William	Llanbeblig (Castellmay) Cn	–	B I	6 Dec. 1687	1687/54
Morrice, William	Llanddeiniolen Cn	Yeoman	W	6 Nov. 1689	1689/46
Moris, William	Maentwrog (Tyddun y garreg) Mr	Yeoman	W I B	10 May 1692	1692/80
Morris, William	Ffestiniog Mr	Yeoman	B I	10 July 1695	1695/66
Moris, William	Aber-erch Cn	Yeoman	W I	29 Dec. 1698	1698/18
Morris, William	Llanddeiniolen (Tŷ-mawr) Cn	Yeoman	B I	15 Aug. 1698	1698/32
Mortimer, George	Beaumaris A	Merchant	B I(2) R	[ ] March 1689/90	1689/6
Morton, David	Llandinam Mg	–	B I	11 Nov. 1691	1691/128
Mostyn, Kattrinn	Llanfair-yn-neubwll A	Widow	W G	23 April 1666	1666/18
Mostyn, Gaynor	Llanbeblig (Carnarvon) Cn	Spinster	W Al	19 May 1680	1680/21
Mostyn, Moses	Llanwnnog Mg	–	B I C	9 July 1661	1661/144
Myddelton *see* Middleton					

[1] Inventory taken 26 Dec. 1699.

[2] Inventory taken 5 Jan. 1676[/7].

Name	Parish & County	Status	Docs. Filed	Date of Probate/Admon.	Ref. No.
Nabbs, John	[Llanrwst] (Trewydder) Cn	Gent.	W	24 Nov. 1677	1677/45
Nailer *alias* Mredith, William	Dolgellau Mr	Miller	W	22 July 1638	1638/53
Nanney, Anne	[Dolgellau] (Dolychowgryd) Mr	Widow	B I	21 Nov. 1668	1668/78
Nanney, Anne	Tywyn (Dolegwyn) Mr	Widow	B I R	9 Jan. 1688/9	1688/86
Nanney, Catherine *see* Nanney, Margaret	Trawsfynydd Mr				
Nanney, Ellin	Dolgellau Mr	Widow	W	19 Dec. 1673	1673/46
Nanney, Hugh	[Dolgellau] (Dolychowgryd) Mr	Esq.	W Rd	11 March 1675/6	1675/36
Nanney, Hugh	Penmorfa (Gilfach) Cn	Gent.	B I	8 Sept. 1692	1692/65
Nanney, John	Llanfachreth Mr	Gent.	I C	25 March 1673	1673/56
Nanney, John	Tal-y-llyn (Perfeddnant) Mr	Gent.	B I*	[ ] 1681[1]	1681/81
Nanney, Lewis	Trawsfynydd (Kefn y ddauddwr) Mr	Gent.	B C	[14 Oct.] 1661	1661/108
Nanney, Margaret & Catherine	Trawsfynydd Mr	–	B(2)	17 Aug. 1685	1685/82
Nanney, Richard	Trawsfynydd (Cefen-dauddwr) Mr	Esq.	B I R	8 Aug. 1685	1685/83
Nanney, Robert	Dolgellau Mr	Gent.	B	12 June 1663	1663/81
Newall, Richard	Llanwnnog Mg	Yeoman	W I	15 Jan. 1666/7	1666/123
Newel, Thomas	Llanwnnog Mg	Yeoman	W*	28 Nov. 1676	1676/106
Nicholas, Ellyn	Deneio Cn	Widow	W[2]	n.d.[3]	1696/48
Nicholas, Hugh, & Jane vch John his wife	Conway Cn	–	B I	23 Sept. 1661	1661/51
Nicholas, Jane	Llanystumdwy Cn	–	W	4 April 1672	1672/80
Nicholas, John	Trawsfynydd Mr	–	W(2)	17 Oct. 1674	1674/54
Nicholas, John	Amlwch A	–	B I	21 May 1677	1677/2
Nicolas, John	Conway Cn	–	B	21 April 1692	1692/42
Nycolas, Rees	Llanfrothen Mr	Gent.	W B	15 Feb. 1637/8	1637/34
Oliver, Henrey	Llandinam (Dithenith) Mg	Yeoman	W I	25 Oct. 1685	1685/110
Oliver, Maurice	Llanwnnog Mg	–	B I	11 Nov. 1691	1691/138
Orne, James	Trefeglwys (Dol Gwyden) Mg	Weaver	W I	21 July 1681	1681/108
Owen, Alexander	Llaniestyn A	–	W I	15 April 1675	1675/8
Owen, Anne	Llanwnnog (Caersoos) Mg	Widow	W I	9 Jan. 1661/2	1661/145

1 Inventory taken 19 March 1680.

2 Note of administration *de bonis non* of Thomas Edwards of Llangybi endorsed on will.

3 Will dated 3 Nov. 1696; endorsed *non probat. fuit.*

Name	Parish & County	Status	Docs. Filed	Date of Probate/Admon.	Ref. No.
Owen, Anne	[Llangadwaladr] (Bodowen *alias* Bodeon) A	Widow	W*	9 Feb. 1663/4	1663/22
Owen *alias* Jones, Anne	Llangïan (Ty yn y Caye) Cn	Widow of John Jones	W I	24 Dec. 1668	1668/66
Owen, Anne	Llandegfan A	Widow	W I	13 Aug. 1669	1669/15
Owen *alias* Wynne, Anne	Clynnog (Tu yn y Coed) Cn	Widow of John Owen, gent.	W I M[1]	24 Jan. 1673/4	1673/28
Owen, Anne[2]	Llangelynnin Mr	–	B	28 Oct. 1686	1686/81
Owen, Kadwalader	Llandygái (Dyffryn Mymbyr) Cn	–	W I	30 March 1677	1677/38
Owen, Cadwalader	Aber-erch Cn	–	W I	[5 Nov. 1686]	1686/28
Owen, Cathrine	Llandrygarn A	Widow	W	27 Nov. 1645	1645/5
Owen, Catherin	Llanfairfechan Cn	–	B I	16 Nov. 1670	1670/110
Owen, Catherin	Rhoscolyn A	–	B I	22 Sept. 1670	1670/60
Owen, Katherine	Penmorfa (Gilfach) Cn	Spinster	W	12 March 1686/7	1686/67
Owens, Daniel	Llanwnnog Mg	Gent.	I/G	6 June 1668	1668/143
Owen, David	Llangurig Mg	–	I	27 Jan. 1678/9	1678/86
Owen, David	Llanrhaeadr-yng-Nghinmeirch D	Yeoman	W I	20 July 1680	1680/69
Owen, David	Aber Cn	Yeoman	B* I*	25 Jan. 1699/1700	1699/39
Owen, Edmund	Gyffin (Gwerodros) Cn	–	W I	8 Dec. 1693	1693/43
Owen, Edward	Dolgellau (Garth yn Arader, Dolgleder) Mr	Gent.	W* I	3 April 1671	1671/98
Owen, Edward	Llangristiolus A	Gent.	W I	16 May 1678	1678/12
Owens, Edward	Llanidloes Mg	–	B I Db	24 Jan. 1678/9	1678/89
Owen, Edward	Llanidan A	Gent.	W* I	17 May 1687	1687/23
Owen, Edward	Trawsfynydd Mr	–	I/G	n.d.[3]	1693/95
Owen, Ellin	Llanfair-iuxta-Harlech Mr	Widow	W	18 June 1645	1645/37
Owen, Ellin	Trefdraeth (Trevilir) A	Widow	W	8 March 1645/6	1645/14
Owen, Ellen *see* William ap Hugh ap William	Llanfechell A				
Owen, Ellen	Conway Cn	Widow	B I	6 Oct. 1663	1663/46
Owen, Ellin	Trefdraeth A	–	B G	19 Feb. 1664/5	1664/46
Owen, Elin	Cricieth (Ynysken) Cn	Widow	W I Rd	23 Sept. 1665	1665/39
Owen, Ellin	[Llanbedr Niwbwrch] (Brondêg) A	Spinster	W I R	20 July 1670	1670/15
Owen, Ellin	Llanddyfnan A	–	W	5 April 1670	1670/26

[1] Also relates to John Owen of Clynnog (q.v.).

[2] See also under Owen, John, of Dolgellau (document C).

[3] Inventory taken 1 April 1693.

Name	Parish & County	Status	Docs. Filed	Date of Probate/Admon.	Ref. No.
Owen, Ellin	Llandegfan A	–	B	7 April 1671	1671/17
Owen, Ellin	Penmorfa (Gilvach) Cn	Spinster	W* Al Ir D	[7 Feb. 1682/3]	1682/61
Owen, Ellis	Trawsfynydd Mr	Gent.	W	21 Oct. 1645	1645/39
Owen, Elis	Llandanwg Mr	–	W I	8 Jan. 1675/6	1675/41
Owen, Elizabeth	Pentraeth A	Widow	W	12 Nov. 1664	1664/44
Owen, Ellizabeth	Dolgellau (Garthgynvor) Mr	–	W I(2) Db	10 June 1668	1668/79
Owen, Elizabeth	Penmynydd A	Widow	W Rd	1 Feb. 1681/2	1681/19
Owen, Elisabeth	Holyhead A	Spinster	B I	20 Nov. 1690	1690/12
Owens *alias* Jones, Elizabeth	Pennal Mr	Wife of Robert Owen of Machynlleth, gent.	B C	8 March 1691/2	1691/97
Owen, Ellen/Ellin *see* Owen, Elin					
Owen, Ellis *see* Owen, Elis					
Owen, Evan	Llanfihangel-y-Pennant Cn	–	W	20 Aug. 1645	1645/29
Owen, Evan	Llanfflewin A	Yeoman	B* I G	19 May 1662	1662/21
Owen, Evan	Ffestiniog Mr	Yeoman	W I	[16 April 1676]	1676/71
Owen, Evan	Beddgelert Cn	–	B	15 Feb. 1677/8	1677/23
Owen, Evan	Ludlow S	–	W	[1 March 1678/9]	1678/96
Owen, Evan	Llanbeblig Cn	–	W I B	30 June 1679	1679/24
Owen, Evan	Llanaber Mr	Gent.	W I	18 Oct. 1681	1681/68
Owen, Evan	[Llandanwg] (Harleigh) Mr	–	W	13 Sept. 1682	1682/68
Owen, Evan	Llangurig Mg	–	W(2) I	4 May 1682	1682/101
Owen, Gaynor	[Llangadwaladr] (Llanfeirian) A	Widow	W	20 July 1664	1664/28
Owen, Grace	Beaumaris A	Widow	W	7 July 1665	1665/3
Owen, Grace	Llan-faes (Henllys) A	–	W	[28 March 1676]	1676/13
Owen, Grace	Llanfair Pwllgwyngyll A	Widow	W I Al	13 Feb. 1678/9	1678/8
Owens *alias* Sparrow, Grace	Llanddona (Cremlyn) A	Widow	B I	12 March 1690/1	1690/18
Owen, Griffith	Llanfihangel Ysgeifiog (Berow ucha) A	Yeoman	W I	30 May 1670	1670/38
Owen, Griffith	Llaniestyn Cn	–	B	21 Oct. 1681	1681/50
Owen, Gryffyth	Penmorfa Cn	–	W	6 Nov. 1682	1682/62
Owen, Gruffyth	Dolwyddelan Cn	Yeoman	W I	[15 March 1687/8]	1687/49
Owen, Griffith	Tywyn Mr	–	I/G	23 June 1696	1696/111
Owen, Gwen	Trefriw (Brin y pill) Cn	Widow	W	15 Jan. 1665/6	1665/55
Owens, Gwenn	Dolgellau Mr	Spinster	W I	22 June 1674	1674/36
Owens, Gwen	Llanddyfnan (Marian Heylyn) A	Widow	W I Rd	11 April 1693	1693/11
Owen, Gwen	Llandecwyn Mr	Widow	W* I*	23 Jan. 1699/1700	1699/111

Name	Parish & County	Status	Docs. Filed	Date of Probate/Admon.	Ref. No.
Owen, Harry	Llanfihangel-y-Pennant Cn	–	W I	24 March 1663/4	1663/61
Owen, Henry	Dolgellau Mr	Gent.	W	21 June 1671	1671/99
Owen, Henery	Llanfigel A	–	W I	10 April 1688	1688/18
Owen, Henry	Bryncroes (Cylliwicke) Cn	Gent.	W I	n.d.[1]	1689/33
Owen, Henry	Llandegfan A	–	W I	8 May 1690	1690/17
Owen, Harry	Llanddwywe Mr	–	I/G	26 May 1691	1691/85
Owen, Harrie	Llanynghenedl A	–	B I	27 Sept. 1699	1699/32
Owen, Hugh	Llanystumdwy Cn	–	W	31 July 1645	1645/35
Owen, Hugh	[Llangadwaladr] (Bodowen *alias* Bodeon) A	Esq.	W* C Rd	17 Jan. 1660/1	1660/6
Owen, Hugh	Beaumaris A	Slater	W M B	11 March 1666/7	1666/4
Owen, Hugh	Llanddyfnan A	Gent.	B I	10 March 1667/8	1667/17
Owen, Hugh	Trefeglwys Mg	–	W I	10 Feb. 1667/8	1667/144
Owen, Hugh	Ceidio Cn	Carpenter	W I	18 April 1671	1671/55
Owen, Hugh	Penmorfa (Gilfach) Cn	Gent.	I	n.d.[2]	1672/84
Owen, Hugh	Llangefni A	Gent.	W I Rd	[16 Feb. 1683/4]	1683/13
Owen, Hugh	Tregayan A	Smith	B I	17 April 1688	1688/29
Owen, Hugh	Tal-y-llyn (Llanerch goidog) Mr	Bachelor	B I	5 Oct. 1692	1692/87
Owen, Hughe	Trefdraeth A	–	B I	8 April 1692	1692/29
Owen, Hugh	Dwygyfylchi Cn	Clerk (Vicar of Dwygyfylchi)	B I	20 Jan. 1693/4	1693/41
Owen, Hugh	Llanidloes (Dôl y Llys) Mg	Gent.	W I	[12 June 1693]	1693/140
Owen, Hugh	Trawsfynydd (Dolgen) Mr	Gent.	W I	18 April 1693	1693/96
Owen, Hugh	Llanfihangel-y-Pennant (Caerberllan) Mr	Gent.	I/G R	6 Feb. 1695/6	1695/76
Owen, Humffrey	Llanegryn (Bron y Clydwr) Mr	Gent.	W R Rd	21 May 1647	1647/41
Owen, Humphrey	Trefeglwys Mg	–	I/G	12 April 1666	1666/125
Owen, Humphrey	Llanbedrog Cn	–	I	n.d.[3]	1670/97
Owen, Humphrey	Llanelltud (Cysilgwn mawr) Mr	Gent.	W Rd	28 April 1677	1677/57
Owen, Humphrey	Llandanwg (Garreg-Wenn) Mr	–	W I	7 Nov. 1699	1699/108
Owen, James	Llannor (Penprus) Cn	–	W I	18 March 1684/5	1684/52
Owen, Jane	Aberffraw A	Widow	W Rd	31 Oct. 1638	1638/1
Owen, Jane	Trefdraeth (Treveilir) A	Widow	B I	18 July 1668	1668/30
Owen, Jane	Llanrhaeadr-yng-Nghinmeirch D	–	W I	2 Aug. 1680	1680/70
Owen, Jane	Llangwyfan A	Widow	W I M	13 Jan. 1690/1	1690/29

[1] Inventory taken 2 June 1688; will endorsed *1689*.

[2] Inventory taken 3 July 1672.

[3] Inventory taken 29 Sept. 1670.

Name	Parish & County	Status	Docs. Filed	Date of Probate/Admon.	Ref. No.
Owen, Jane	Llanwnda Cn	Widow	B I	15 May 1695	1695/55
Owen, Jenkyn	Carno Mg	Yeoman	W	30 Sept. 1635	1635/50
Owen, John	Tywyn Mr	–	W*	11 July 1636	1636/51
Owen, John	Llanfachreth Mr	Bachelor	W	17 Feb. 1643/4	1643/34
Owen, John	Llanwnnog (Lloyn y Brayne) Mg	Gent.	W Rd	24 March 1647/8	1647/54
Owen, John	Aber-erch Cn	Weaver	W I C	19 April 1661	1661/37
Owen, John	Llanengan Cn	Gent.	W	7 Sept. 1661	1661/72
Owen, John	Llaneilian A	Weaver	W* I C	14 April 1662	1662/16
Owen, John	Llandinam Mg	Gent.	B I	2 April 1663	1663/134
Owen, John	Penrhos[llugwy A]	–	W I	7 Feb. 1663/4	1663/30
Owen, John	Llanfaethlu A	Esq.	B I G	9 Nov. 1667	1667/20
Owen, John	Cricieth Cn	–	B	15 Aug. 1670	1670/89
Owen, John[1]	Clynnog [Tu yn y Coed] Cn	Gent.	B I(2)	8 May 1673	1673/27
Owen, John	Llanfihangel-y-Pennant (Brithdir mawr) Cn	Gent.	W I	16 April 1677	1677/40
Owen, John	Llanfihangel-y-Pennant (Caerberllan) Mr	Gent.	B I	14 Nov. 1681	1681/76
Owen, John	Llanfihangel-y-Pennant (Cynnenfynydd) Cn	–	W	23 Feb. 1682/3	1682/48
Owens, John	Trefdraeth (Trefeylyr) A	Gent.	B I C	14 July 1682	1682/30
Owen, John	Dolgellau Mr	–	{B C[2] {B	28 Oct. 1686 31 Oct. 1687	1686/71 1687/90
Owen, John	Llangristiolus A	Clerk	W I	25 March 1686	1686/19
Owen, John	Llanidloes Mg	Yeoman	W R	[10 Feb. 1689/90]	1689/94
Owen, John	[Llanystumdwy] (Keven) Cn	Clerk	B I	15 Oct. 1690	1690/77
Owen, John	Llanwnnog Mg	Yeoman	B I	14 Oct. 1693	1693/143
Owen, John	Llanarmon (Plas du) Cn	Yeoman	W I B	30 Oct. 1694	1694/47
Owen, John	Llanenddwyn (Craig fforchog ucha) Mr	Yeoman	W I	24 April 1695	1695/75
Owen, John	Llanystumdwy Cn	Bachelor	B	9 May 1695	1695/57
Owen, John	Llaniestyn Cn	Gent.	W I	5 Aug. 1699	1699/81
Owen, Jonet	Caerhun (Pen y lan) Cn	Widow	W*	21 Jan. 1646/7	1646/13
Owen, Dame Jonett	Penmorfa (Clenneney) Cn	Widow	W I	12 Jan. 1674/5	1674/32
Owen, Jonnet	Dolwyddelan Cn	–	W	[27 April 1676]	1676/47
Owen, Jonett	Llanfachreth A	–	B	1 Aug. 1682	1682/17

1 See also under Wynne *alias* Owen, Anne, of Clynnog (document M).

2 Also relates to his sister, Anne Owen of Llangelynnin (q.v.).

Name	Parish & County	Status	Docs. Filed	Date of Probate/Admon.	Ref. No.
Owen, Kadwalader *see* Owen, Cadwaladr					
Owen, Katherine *see* Owen, Catherine					
Owen, Lewis	Llanddaniel-fab A	Yeoman	W B	14 May 1636	1636/8
Owen, Lewis	Ceirchiog A	Yeoman	W	21 Feb. 1645/6	1645/3
Owen, Lewis	Penrhos Cn	–	B I C	22 Feb. 1661/2	1661/86
Owen, Lewis	Llanbedr [Niwbwrch] (Abermeney) A	–	I	n.d.	1668/10
Owen, Lewis	Dolgellau (Havodtowyll) Mr	Gent.	W I	10 Oct. 1681	1681/63
Owen, Lewis	Tal-y-llyn (Cwm y gerwyn) Mr	–	B I	29 May 1688	1688/85
Owen, Lewis	Dolgellau (Garthgynvor) Mr	–	I/G R	18 Nov. 1699	1699/100
Owen, Lowry	Llanfihangel-y-traethau Mr	Widow	W	n.d.	1676/79
Owen, Lowry	Penmorfa (Kefn Côch) Cn	Widow	W*	26 April 1696	1696/84
Owen, Margaret	Llanddyfnan (Castell bulghewyn) A	Widow	W	17 Oct. 1637	1637/6
Owen, Margaret	Llanbedr[-goch] (Carrog) A	Widow	W* I	3 Jan. 1664/5	1664/12
Owen, Margaret	Llangurig Mg	Spinster	W	20 Feb. 1685/6	1685/115
Owen, Margerett	Trewalchmai A	Widow	W I	12 Dec. 1687	1687/30
Owen, Mary	[Penmynydd] (Dyffryn) A	Widow	W M B Rd	28 April 1666	1666/29
Owen, Mary	Llechgynfarwy (Ynus-Todyn) A	Spinster	W I	[ ] Jan. 1690/1	1690/33
Owen, Mary	Ceirchiog A	Widow	B I	4 Feb. 1692/3	1692/5
Owen, Mary	Llanllechid Cn	Widow	W* I*	3 June 1695	1695/50
Owen, Michaell	Llanddyfnan (Marian) A	Gent.	W I Rd	3 Nov. 1697	1697/8
Owen, Morris	Llanwnda Cn	–	B*	29 Dec. 1670	1670/125
Owen, Maurice	Llannor Cn	–	B I	14 April 1681	1681/53
Owen, Maurice	Llanllechid Cn	–	I	n.d.[1]	1691/64
Owen, Moris	Llanynghenedl A	–	B I	20 Jan. 1693/4	1693/25
Owens, Owen	Llandinam Mg	Gent.	B I	28 July 1664	1664/131
Owens, Owen	Llanystumdwy ([K]even) Cn	Gent.	W*	n.d.[2]	1675/30
Owens, Owen	[Rhoscolyn] (Bodiar) A	–	W	21 Aug. 1684	1684/23
Owens, Owen	[Llanddona][3] (Cremlyn) A	Gent.	W* I*	7 March 1693/4	1693/10
Owens, Owen	Llangristiolus A	Gent.	I(2)	28 Jan. 1695/6	1695/13
Owens *alias* Griffith, Penelope	Llanddwywe Mr	Widow	W I	6 Oct. 1675	1675/42
Owen, Philipp	Llanberis Cn	Yeoman	B	9 March 1696/7	1696/57

[1] Inventory taken 21 March 1690/1.
[2] Will dated 7 June 1675.
[3] Endorsed *Llandegvan*.

Name	Parish & County	Status	Docs. Filed	Date of Probate/Admon.	Ref. No.
Owen, Rees	Llaneilian A	Weaver	W I	20 July 1669	1669/23
Owen, Rodderch	Llanfrothen (Cay glase) Mr	–	W I	7 March 1691/2	1691/93
Owen, Richard	[Llechylched][1] (Kefnysgwyd) A	Gent.	W* Rd*	12 Oct. 1638	1638/22
Owen, Richard	Llanfrothen Mr	–	W	12 Jan. 1646/7	1646/26
Owen, Richard	Llanaelhaearn Cn	–	B I	24 Feb. 1661/2	1661/58
Owen, Richard (the elder)	Trefeglwys (Ebled) Mg	Gent.	W I	8 July 1665	1665/111
Owen, Richard	Llangelynnin Cn	–	I*	n.d.	1672/66
Owen, Richard	Llangristiolus (Kerrigwyddel) A	Gent.	W	25 April 1672	1672/25
Owen, Richard	[Llanfihangel-y-traethau] (Moel y Glo) Mr	–	W	4 Jan. 1675/6	1675/46
Owen, Richard	Llanffinan A	Yeoman	W I	29 Jan. 1678/9	1678/11
Owen, Richard	Llanddaniel-fab A	–	B* I	20 May 1685	1685/15
Owen, Richard	Amlwch A	–	B I	7 March 1691/2	1691/2
Owen, Richard	Bodedern A	–	B I	12 Aug. 1693	1693/4
Owen, Richard	Cerrigceinwen A	–	W*	25 April 1694	1694/8
Owen, Richard	Llandanwg (Harlech) Mr	–	W I	18 July 1695	1695/70
Owen, Richard	[Llanbeulan][2] (Trefeibion Meuricke) A	Yeoman	W I	27 Sept. 1699	1699/12
Owen, Richiart	Llangristiolus A	Yeoman	W I	7 July 1699	1699/24
Owen, Robert	Llangeinwen A	–	W Rd	30 April 1638	1638/19
Owen, Robert	Aberdaron Cn	–	W I	13 June 1661	1661/35
Owen, Robert	Clynnog Cn	–	W* I	31 May 1666	1666/48
Owen, Robert	Llanystumdwy Cn	Yeoman	W I	22 April 1666	1666/68
Owen, Robert	Llangeinwen A	–	W I	14 June 1669	1669/38
Owen, Robert	Llangelynnin Mr	Clerk (Rector of Llangelynnin)	W(3)*	5 Feb. 1672/3	1672/95
Owen, Robert	Llanystumdwy Cn	Yeoman	W I	[4 March 1674/5]	1674/30
Owen, Robert	Aber Cn	–	B I	24 Jan. 1676/7	1676/32
Owen, Robert	Beddgelert Cn	–	W* Al Ir* D	[23 March 1682/3]	1682/35
Owen, Robert	Llanfihangel-y-traethau Mr	–	W/R I	n.d.[3]	1683/73
Owen, Robert	Llanystumdwy Cn	–	B	29 June 1686	1686/62
Owen, Robert	Llanaelhaearn Cn	–	B I	26 Sept. 1688	1688/43
Owen, Robert	Llangefni (Pencraig) A	Gent.	W I	[22 Aug. 1689]	1689/18
Owen, Robert	Cricieth (Mynyddednyfed) Cn	Yeoman	B I	17 Sept. 1690	1690/51
Owen, Robert	Beaumaris A	Yeoman	W	2 Oct. 1691	1691/8

1 Rd *late of kefnysgwyd within the parish of Aberffrawe* (cf. will of William Owen *of Keven yscwyd of the parish of Llechylched*).

2 Endorsed *Llangristiolys*.

3 Renunciation dated 3–4 May 1683.

Name	Parish & County	Status	Docs. Filed	Date of Probate/Admon.	Ref. No.
Owen, Robert	Dolgellau (Tu gwyn) Mr	Gent.	W I(2)	14 June 1695	1695/63
Owen, Roger	Trefeglwys Mg	–	W I	16 Feb. 1664/5	1664/138
Owen, Roger	Penmorfa Cn	–	I/G	17 Sept. 1695	1695/59
Owen, Rowland	Llansadwrn (Ucheldref) A	Gent.	W B	3 July 1637	1637/10
Owen, Rowland	Tal-y-llyn Mr	–	B I*	17 June 1664	1664/102
Owen, Rowland	Aber-erch Cn	Yeoman	W I	9 April 1670	1670/66
Owen, Rowland	Aberffraw (Trefryw) A	–	B* I(2) Db(2)	3 April 1690	1690/1
Owen, Rowland	Aberffraw (Treiddon) A	Clerk	B I	7 Aug. 1691	1691/1
Owen, Symond	Llanfachreth Mr	–	B(2) I R	18 July 1661	1661/100
Owen, Symon	Dolgellau (Maes Angharad) Mr	Gent.	W	[7 Aug. 1691]	1691/76
Owen, Susanna	Llanfihangel[-y-Pennant] (Penmeini) Mr	Widow	I/G R	18 May 1694	1694/87
Owen, Thomas	Llangybi Cn	–	B I	17 Oct. 1667	1667/74
Owen, Thomas	Llanddyfnan A	Yeoman	W I	19 Jan. 1669/70	1669/21
Owen, Thomas	Llannor Cn	–	W I	5 April 1671	1671/83
Owen, Thomas	Gyffin Cn	–	B	16 Sept. 1672	1672/53
Owen, Thomas	Llanfrothen (Braich) Mr	Husbandman	W I	[ ] June 1676	1676/81
Owen, Thomas	Llandwrog (Grugan) Cn	Clerk	W	[9 Feb. 1683/4]	1683/34
Owen, Thomas	Llanaelhaearn Cn	–	W I	7 April 1685	1685/42
Owen, Thomas	Llanbedr Niwbwrch A	–	B I	6 Dec. 1692	1692/7
Owen, Thomas	Trefdraeth A	–	B	10 May 1692	1692/30
Owen, Thomas	Aber Cn	Yeoman	W I	25 Sept. 1694	1694/33
Owen, Thomas	Llanrug Cn	–	B I	30 April 1694	1694/58
Owen, Thomas	Llanddeiniolen (Rhyw-Goch) Cn	Yeoman	B I	26 March 1696	1696/62
Owen, Tuder	Dolgellau (Garthgynvawr) Mr	Gent.	W I Rd	18 July 1661	1661/89
Owen, William	Llandrygarn (Clegir gwynnion) A	–	W	16 Oct. 1643	1643/5
Owen, William	Beaumaris A	Cooper	B I	22 Feb. 1664/5	1664/4
Owen, William	Llechylched A	Gent.	W(2)	8 March 1664/5	1664/41
Owen, William	Llechylched (Keven yscwyd) A	Gent.	W	14 Sept. 1667	1667/38
Owen, William	Llanbedrycennin (Arthey) Cn	–	B I	7 April 1671	1671/62
Owen, William	Llanfair-yng-Nghornwy A	–	B L	6 June 1673	1673/8
Owen, William	[Trefdraeth] (Trefeilir) A	Gent.	W	13 Feb. 1676/7	1676/28
Owen, William	Amlwch A	–	W* I*	[11 April 1690]	1690/3
Owen, William	Beddgelert (Ffrithllwyn-llinon) Cn	Yeoman	B	6 July 1691	1691/42
Owen, William	Llanbedrycennin Cn	Slater	B I	20 Feb. 1695/6	1695/36
Owen, William	Aber-erch Cn	Yeoman	B I	29 Dec. 1698	1698/19
Owens *see* Owen					

Name	Parish & County	Status	Docs. Filed	Date of Probate/Admon.	Ref. No.
Parry, Ann	Trefdraeth A	Spinster	W	3 June 1680	1680/16
Parry, Anne	Rhuthun D	Widow	W(2) B	10 Aug. 1696 18 March 1696/7	1696/123
Parry, Anthony	Llangelynnin (Llwyngwril) Mr	Carpenter	B I	15 July 1695	1695/79
Parry, Blaynch	Conway Cn	–	B	11 Sept. 1675	1675/20
Parry, Catherine	Llanllyfni Cn	–	B	2 Feb. 1681/2	1681/52
Parrie, David	Llanynghenedl A	–	B I	21 Oct. 1669	1669/43
Parry, David	Llanrhaeadr-yng-Nghinmeirch (Tre r llech) D	–	B	3 Jan. 1678/9	1678/74
Parry, David	Llandwrog Cn	–	W	29 Oct. 1686	1686/49
Parry, Edward	Llanbedr Dyffryn Clwyd D	Yeoman	W I	n.d.[1]	1664/112
Parry, Edward	Llanelidan (Plas yr Escob) D	–	B I	3 Feb. 1693/4	1693/104
Parry, Ellis[2]	[Llanfachreth] (Mais-y-llech) & Dolgellau Mr	–	I[3] B	 25 Aug. 1676	1675/44 1676/67
Parry, Elizabeth[4]	Rhodogeidio A	Widow	B	29 Oct. 1685	1685/28
Parry, Elizabeth	Amlwch A	Widow	W I	14 Jan. 1691/2	1691/3
Parry, Elizabeth	Beaumaris A	Spinster	B	28 April 1691	1691/9
Parry, Ellis *as* Parry, Elis					
Parry, Foulke	Llangynhafal D	Weaver	W I	6 April 1698	1698/67
Parry, Francis	Llanaber Mr	Gent.	W I	22 April 1697	1697/43
Parry, Grace	Llanbedr Dyffryn Clwyd D	Widow of John Parry, esq.	W I	[5 April 1678][5]	1678/67
Parry, Grace	Rhuthun D	Spinster	W	3 Oct. 1699	1699/141
Parrie, Harrie	Llanegryn Mr	–	B I	26 June 1668	1668/90
Parry, Hugh	Bangor (Porthaythwy) Cn	Gent.	W I	22 June 1666	1666/39
Parry, Hugh	Aber-erch Cn	–	B I	25 Oct. 1667	1667/49
Parry, Hugh	Llanfaelog A	–	B	9 Aug. 1681	1681/9
Parry, Hugh	Dolgellau Mr	Yeoman	B I	10 Oct. 1693	1693/70
Parry, Humffrey	Llanffinan A	–	W	17 March 1670/1	1670/39
Parry, Jane	Llan-rhudd D	Widow	W	[ ] Feb. 1681/2	1681/100
Parry, Jane	Amlwch A	Widow	B I	22 Oct. 1691	1691/4
Parry, John	Llanbedr Dyffryn Clwyd D	Esq.	W*	30 June 1636	1636/54

1 Inventory taken 23 June 1664.

2 The will of Ellin Harry (q.v.) indicates that Ellis Parry of Mais-y-llech and Ellis Parry of Dolgellau are one and the same person.

3 Taken 29 June 1675.

4 Same person as Elyzabeth vch Harry of Bryngwallan (q.v.)?

5 Inventory taken 4 March 1661.

Name	Parish & County	Status	Docs. Filed	Date of Probate/Admon.	Ref. No.
Parry, John	[Llanbeblig] (Carnarvon) Cn	Gent./Esq.	B R	2 Sept. 1663	1663/41
Parry, John	Llanbedr[ycennin] Cn	Yeoman	W I	14 Dec. 1665	1665/42
Parrie, John	Beaumaris A	–	W	15 Jan. 1668/9	1668/5
Parry, John	Pennal Mr	–	B I	12 Dec. 1678	1678/49
Parry, John	Llanbedr Dyffryn Clwyd D	Gent.	W I	n.d.[1]	1681/87
Parry, John	Bangor Cn	–	W	10 Aug. 1683	1683/22
Parry, John	Llanfihangel-y-traethau Mr	Labourer	W I	16 Oct. 1688	1688/80
Parry, John	Llangeinwen (Clynnog) A	–	B I	1 June 1692	1692/20
Parry *alias* Williames, Margaret	Conway Cn	Widow	W	12 March 1690/1	1690/50
Parry, Magaret	[ ] D[2]	–	I	n.d.[3]	1691/125
Parry *alias* Wynne, Margaret	Bangor (Llanporthauthwy) Cn	Widow	W I	15 Jan. 1694/5	1694/40
Parry, Mary	Llangïan Cn	–	B	13 April 1672	1672/67
Parry, Michell	Llanbadrig (Pentre Heilin) A	–	W I	20 Aug. 1684	1684/8
Parry, Owen	Maenol Bangor Cn	Gent.	I	n.d.[4]	1679/17
Parry, Owen	Ceirchiog (Bodfeddan) A	Gent.	W(2) Rd*	11 April 1682	1682/5
Parry, Rice	Rhodogeidio (Bryngwallan Isa) A	Yeoman	W I	n.d.[5]	1669/51
Parry, Richard	Amlwch A	Gent.	B* I* C*	20 Dec. 1662	1662/1
Parry, Richard	Pentraeth A	Yeoman	B I	11 April 1667	1667/43
Parry, Richard	Llaniestyn Cn	–	W I	n.d.[6]	1671/81
Parry, Richard	Amlwch (Eskellog) A	Gent.	W B	20 July 1675	1675/1
Parry, Richard	Llanbeblig (Castellmay) Cn	Carpenter	W I	n.d.[7]	1681/44
Parry, Richard	Llanfwrog D	Tanner	W* I	19 Jan. 1683/4	1683/86
Parry, Richard	Llanrhwydrys A	–	B	30 Nov. 1687	1687/25
Parry, Richard	Ceidio Cn	Gent.	W* I*	[ ] Oct. 1690	1690/47
Parry, Robert	Llandygái Cn	–	B I	1 April 1669	1669/83
Parry, Robert	Amlwch A	–	B	28 March 1677	1677/3
Parry, Robert	Llanfwrog D	–	B	4 Aug. 1680	1680/68
Parry, Robert	Llanllyfni Cn	Yeoman	W* I*	7 May 1685	1685/56
Parry, Robert	Amlwch A	Esq.	W I Rd	23 Oct. 1689	1689/3
Parry, Robert	Llangïan (Caie) Cn	–	I	n.d.[8]	1690/67

1 Inventory taken 16 June 1681.

2 Endorsed *Duffryn Clwyd*.

3 Inventory taken 2 March 1690.

4 Inventory taken 15 Oct. 1679.

5 Inventory taken 3 Nov. 1668; endorsed *1669*.

6 Will dated 23 Feb. 1671/2; inventory taken 30 March 1672.

7 Inventory taken 27 Oct. 1681.

8 Inventory taken 10 July 1690.

Name	Parish & County	Status	Docs. Filed	Date of Probate/Admon.	Ref. No.
Parry, Robert	Llandyrnog (Rhybebyll) D	–	W I	15 Oct. 1691	1691/108
Parry, Robert	Derwen D	Yeoman	W I	4 Jan. 1693/4	1693/98
Parry, Rowland	Llanwnda Cn	–	B	21 Oct. 1669	1669/99
Parry, Samuel	Llanaber Mr	Yeoman	B I	10 July 1694	1694/76
Parrie, Thomas	Llanllyfni (Tregrwyn) Cn	Yeoman	W I	14 June 1665	1665/50
Parry, Thomas	Llanhychan D	Yeoman	W I	22 April 1676	1676/93
Parry, Thomas	Llanynys (Bachymbyd) D	–	W I	5 Jan. [1683/4]	1683/91
Parry, Thomas	Llangelynnin (Glyn) Cn	Gent.	W* I* Al Rd	26 March 1685	1685/53
Parry, Thomas	Llanynys D	–	B I	25 Sept. 1686	1686/102
Parry, Thomas	Llanfihangel-ym-mhenrhos *alias* Penrhosllugwy A	–	B I	6 June 1691	1691/35
Parry, William	Llanddaniel-fab A	–	W I	2 June 1673	1673/6
Parry, William	Gyffin Cn	–	W G	[29 Sept. 1675]	1675/21
Parry, William	Bryncroes Cn	–	R	n.d.[1]	1683/24
Parry, William	Llanengan Cn	–	B	26 June 1688	1688/50
Pary, William	Tywyn Mr	–	I	n.d.[2]	1688/87
Parry, William	Llanaber Mr	–	B I	4 Aug. 1696	1696/94
Parton, Anne	Llandinam Mg	Widow	W* I B	9 Jan. 1661/2	1661/129
Parton, Lewis	Trefeglwys Mg	Gent.	W I	15 Jan. 1684/5	1684/122
Parton, Lucie	Trefeglwys Mg	–	W	[28 Nov. 1673]	1673/73
Patric, Evan	Llangelynnin Mr	–	B I	6 June 1665	1665/71
Peate, William	Carno Mg	Yeoman	B I	29 Aug. 1661	1661/124
Peirce, Peirs *see* Pierce					
Penry, James	Llanwnnog Mg	Gent.	B I	26 Sept. 1667	1667/140
Persol (Piersol), Jeremy	Llandinam Mg	Yeoman	W I	[26 April 1693]	1693/133
Phersol, Richard	Llandinam Mg	–	W I	29 June 1665	1665/98
Peters, Katherine	Llandyrnog (Corvedwen) D	Widow of Peter Thomas, yeoman	B I	1 June 1682	1682/83
Petterson, Abraham	Tywyn (Aberdovi) Mr	Merchant	W	20 April 1645[3]	1645/40
Pettonson, John	Beaumaris A	Yeoman	B I	16 July 1673	1673/3
Phersol *see* Persol					
Phillip, Hugh	Aber-erch (Brinllaith) Cn	–	W(2) I	10 May 1686	1686/29
Philip, Jane	Aber-erch Cn	–	W	11 March 1669/70	1669/56
Phillipps, Roberte	Llanwnnog Mg	Yeoman	W/I	6 April 1665	1665/108
Phillipps, Thomas	Llandinam (Gwernerin) Mg	–	W I	17 Oct. 1683	1683/97

1 Renunciation dated 27 April 1683.
2 Inventory taken 10 May 1688.
3 *20 March 1645* in endorsement on back of will.

Name	Parish & County	Status	Docs. Filed	Date of Probate/Admon.	Ref. No.
Phillips, Thomas	Llandinam Mg	–	B I	1 June 1694	1694/118
Phillip, William	Llanaber Mr	Gent.	I*	n.d.[1]	1670/139
Phillips *see* Phillip					
Peirs, David	Derwen D	–	W I	25 Feb. 1678/9	1678/63
Peirce, David	Gyffylliog D	Yeoman	B I	30 Jan. 1696/7	1696/119
Pierce, Edward	Llanfwrog (Bodyngharad) D	–	W I	21 April 1669	1669/148
Peirce, Edward	Llanfwrog ([Galchog], Keel-y-Groes Llwyd) D	Yeoman	W I	4 Sept. 1699	1699/127
Piers, Gabriel	Nefyn Cn	–	I/G	4 May 1669	1669/103
Perse, Griffith	Llanfairfechan Cn	Clerk	W* I	2 April 1690	1690/61
Pierce, Hugh	Llanfwrog (Bodyngharad) D	Gent.	W I	15 Feb. 1688/9	1688/91
Pierce, Hugh	Llanrhychwyn Cn	Yeoman	B[2]	19 May 1699	1699/83
Peirs, John, *alias* John Owen Peirs	Beddgelert Cn	–	W/I	14 April 1637	1637/17
Piers, John	Llandyrnog (Banker) D	Husbandman	W*	9 Feb. 1662/3	1662/84
Pvrs, Owen	Bedd[gelert] Cn	–	W*	15 Jan. [1638/9]	1638/35
Pierce, Robert	Llanfaelrhys Cn	Clerk	W	26 Oct. 1671	1671/71
Pierce, Roger	Carno Mg	Yeoman	W*	12 April 1641	1641/67
Piers, William	Llandygái (Coydhowel) Cn	Yeoman	B I	28 Nov. 1671	1671/67
Peerce, William	Llanberis Cn	Clerk (Rector of Llanberis)	I/G	5 June 1672	1672/57
Piersol *see* Persol					
Pilston, Hugh	Llanrhuddlad A	Yeoman	W I B	20 Nov. 1663	1663/29
Pilliston (Pulston), John	Llanfwrog D	Glover	B I R	27 June 1693	1693/111
Pilston, Robert	Pentraeth A	Yeoman	B I	28 March 1690	1690/37
Poole, Anthony	[Llanbedr] (Caer nest) Mr	–	I	n.d.[3]	1669/122
Poole, Humffrey	Llanbedr Mr	–	W*	31 May 1638	1638/57
Poole *alias* Lloyd, Jonett	Botwnnog Cn	Widow	W L	10 Jan. 1693/4	1693/33
Poole, Margaret	Llanfair-iuxta-Harlech Mr	Widow	W*	14 July 1641	1641/53
Poole, Margerett	Llanegryn Mr	Widow	W* I	[ ] June 1664	1664/90
Poole, Samuel	Llanfair-iuxta-Harlech (Argoed) Mr	Gent.	W I Rd	13 April 1665	1665/67
Pott, John	Llangurig Mg	Yeoman	W/I	[21 May 1673]	1673/69
Pott, Thomas	Llangurig Mg	Yeoman	W* I*	30 Sept. 1661	1661/135
Powel, Ann *see* Thomas ap Robert					

1 Inventory taken 30 May 1670.

2 Being also a bond to administer the goods of his father, Piers William (q.v.).

3 Inventory taken 25 March 1669.

Name	Parish & County	Status	Docs. Filed	Date of Probate/Admon.	Ref. No.
Powell, David	Llanaber Mr	Yeoman	W* I	19 Aug. 1678	1678/41
Powell, David	Clocaenog D	Gent.	W I	[9 July 1684]	1684/85
Powell, David	Llandinam Mg	–	W I	2 July 1685	1685/111
Powell, Edward	Heneglwys (Glan-y-Llyn) A	–	B* I	[ ] 1686[1]	1686/7
Powell, Ellis	Dolgellau (Brithdyr) Mr	Yeoman	B I	1 [ ] 1690	1690/84
Powell, Elis	Clocaenog D	–	B I*	5 Feb. 1696/7	1696/112
Powell, Elizabeth	Llandinam (Trewythen) Mg	Widow	B I	18 June 1679	1679/63
Powell, Elizabeth	Llandinam Mg	Widow	W I	4 May 1682	1682/97
Powell, Ellis *see* Powell, Elis					
Powell, Griffyth	Deneio (Pwllheley) Cn	Tanner	B I	6 Nov. 1693	1693/39
Powell, Henry	Llandyrnog D	–	B I(2)	19 Nov. 1672	1672/106
Powell, John	Trawsfynydd Mr	–	W I	[28 Oct. 1678]	1678/54
Powell, John	Llangïan Cn	Miller	W I	16 March 1687/8	1687/66
Powell, John	Llangurig Mg	–	W I	5 July 1692	1692/121
Powell, Lewis	Llechylched A	Gent.	W*	n.d.[2]	1662/31
Powell, Margarett	Llanwnnog Mg	Widow	B I	16 May 1681	1681/107
Powell, Meredith	Llandinam Mg	–	W I	[1 Aug. 1661]	1661/130
Powell, Moris	Llanddaniel-fab A	–	W*	19 May 1647	1647/8
Powell, Morris	Llanwnnog (Uchllawrcoed) Mg	Gent.	W I	6 May 1680	1680/81
Powell, Richard	Llangeinwen A	–	B I	22 Sept. 1663	1663/23
Powell, Thomas	Llandinam (Dithenith) Mg	–	B I	4 July 1699	1699/145
Powell, William	Conway Cn	Burgess	W I G	1 Dec. 1668	1668/46
Powell, William	Llangefni A	–	W I	3 April 1673	1673/11
Powell, William	Llanwnnog Mg	–	W I Rd	7 March 1691/2	1691/139
Prees *see* Price					
Prees, Anne	Llanfechell A	–	B	17 Jan. 1666/7	1666/19
Prys, Anne[3]	Llanfihangel-ym-mhenrhos *alias* Penrhosllugwy A	Widow	B I	30 June 1699	1699/37
Price, Antony	Rhuthun D	Tailor/Almsman	W I	17 Aug. 1676	1676/95
Price, Catheringe	Gyffylliog (Nilig) D	–	W(2) I	27 April 1681	1681/85
Price, Catherine	Llanrhuddlad A	Spinster	Rd	n.d.[4]	1693/21
Price, David	Llanfair Dyffryn Clwyd (Vaynol) D	–	B	24 June 1687	1687/119

1 Inventory taken 19 Nov. 1686.

2 Will dated 30 Aug. 1662.

3 See also Bangor Probate Records for 1700 (bond to administer goods remaining unadministered).

4 Will proved but not filed; bond for its redelivery dated 30 Jan. 1693.

Name	Parish & County	Status	Docs. Filed	Date of Probate/Admon.	Ref. No.
Price, David	[ ]	–	I	n.d.[1]	1692/130
Price, Edmund	Llanfechell A	Clerk (Rector of Llanfechell)	W	8 Jan. 1643/4	1643/8
Price, Edward	Llanfair Dyffryn Clwyd (Ffynnoggion) D	Gent.	W	18 July 1642	1642/37
Price, Edward	Llanwnnog (Stredfaylog) Mg	–	B I	16 June 1663	1663/149
Price, Edward	[Llanidan] (Bodowir) A	Esq.	I	n.d.[2]	1672/27
Prees, Edward	Bangor Cn	–	W Al	[11 Nov. 1675]	1675/15
Price, Edward	Llanaber Mr	–	I/G	[26 July 1679]	1679/37
Price, Edward	[Llandyfrydog] (Llwydiarth-escob) A	Clerk	B	31 March 1682	1682/11
Price, Edward	Llanddaniel-fab (Rhose-bothon) A	Gent.	W Al Ir D Rd	[13 Nov. 1683]	1683/4
Prys, Edward	Llanfair-y-Cwmwd A	Yeoman	W I	4 July 1687	1687/12
Price, Edward	Llangynhafal D	–	W I	[21 June 1687]	1687/121
Price, Edward	Llanwnnog Mg	Gent.	B	22 April 1697	1697/70
Price, Ellin	Beaumaris A	Widow of Edward Price, gent.	W	21 April 1681	1681/1
Price, Elinor	Llanelidan (Caerddinan) D	Widow	W	2 Jan. 1676/7	1676/89
Price *alias* Roberts, Elizabeth	Bodwrog (Eriannell) A	Widow/ Gentlewoman	B I	5 Dec. 1667	1667/5
Price, Evan	Carno Mg	Gent.	I/G	2 Dec. 1669	1669/157
Price, Griffith, *alias* Gruffyth ap Richard	Aber-erch Cn	–	W*	30 March 1640	1640/21
Price, Henry	Llanrhuddlad A	Gent.	W*	28 March 1645	1645/9
Price, Harry	Pennal Mr	Gent.	I G R	1 Sept. 1669	1669/134
Price, Hugh	Tywyn Mr	Gent.	W I	25 Oct. 1666	1666/98
Price, Hugh	Llanidan (Glas-ynus) A	–	W	25 April 1681	1681/15
Prees, Hugh	Llanallgo A	Fisherman	W	23 June 1691	1691/15
Price, Hugh	Llandyrnog D	–	B I	1 Feb. 1699/1700	1699/122
Pryse, Sir James	Tywyn (Ynysymaengwyn) Mr	Knight	W B Rd	20 Dec. 1644	1644/37
Price, Jane	Llanelidan D	Widow	I	n.d.[3]	1683/83
Price *alias* Roberts, Jane	Rhuthun (the Kinges Armes) D	Widow	B I	10 Feb. 1692/3	1692/106
Price, John	Llanrhaeadr-yng-Nghinmeirch D	–	W R B	2 Jan. 1641/2	1641/62
Price, John	Llangynhafal D	–	B	20 Aug. 1661	1661/118

[1] Inventory taken 29 June 1692.
[2] Inventory taken 2 May 1672; exhibited 14 May 1673.
[3] Inventory taken 20 July 1683.

Name	Parish & County	Status	Docs. Filed	Date of Probate/Admon.	Ref. No.
Price, John	Beddgelert Cn	–	B	17 Dec. 1667	1667/53
Price, John	Penrhos[llugwy] (Brynlys) A	Gent.	W(2) I Rd	29 May 1667 1 Sept. 1668	1667/41
Price, John	Rhuthun D	Vintner	W I	7 April 1671	1671/138
Pryce, John	Llanfair Dyffryn Clwyd D	Clerk (Vicar of Llanfair Dyffryn Clwyd)	B I*	6 Nov. 1672	1672/110
Price, John	Llanddaniel-fab (Rhosbothan) A	Gent.	B I	15 Aug. 1682	1682/14
Price, John	Rhuthun D	Mercer	I	n.d.[1]	1684/102
Price, John	Llangynhafal D	–	B I	10 March 1685/6	1685/97
Prees, John	Llantrisant A	–	B I	17 Dec. 1686	1686/23
Prees, John	Llan-faes A	–	W I	17 Oct. 1692	1692/13
Price, John	Rhuthun D	Innkeeper	W I R	2 Jan. 1693/4	1693/124
Prees, John	Llangwyllog (Cerrig ddewi) A	Yeoman	W I	8 April 1698	1698/11
Preese, John	Llanberis Cn	Yeoman	W I	16 Oct. 1699	1699/69
Price, Lewis	Llangeinwen (Penrin) A	–	W(2) I R	n.d.[2]	1688/22
Prise, Littleton	[Tal-y-llyn] (Maesypandy) Mr	Gent.	W	27 Aug. 1684	1684/75
Price, Lowry	[Llanenddwyn] (Taltreuthyn) Mr	Widow	W	21 March 1660/1	1660/21
Price, Margarett	Llandyrnog D	Spinster	B I	27 Aug. 1670	1670/167
Prise, Owen	Llangelynnin Mr	–	W	25 April 1670	1670/156
Price, Owen	Llan-rhudd D	Yeoman	W I	7 Nov. 1691	1691/120
Prees, Owen	Penmynydd A	Yeoman	W I B	7 March 1691/2	1691/34
Pryce, Philippe	Llangwyfan D	–	W	n.d.[3]	1660/27
Price, Richiard	Gyffylliog D	–	W	26 Sept. 1643	1643/43
Price, Richard	Llanwnnog Mg	Yeoman	I*	n.d.[4]	1662/106
Prees, Richard	Bangor Cn	–	W	n.d.[5]	1666/40
Prees, Richard	Llanrhuddlad A	Yeoman	W I	6 June 1688	1688/24
Pryse, Robert	Llanfair-iuxta-Harlech (Gerddi Bluog) Mr	Gent.	W I	16 Jan. 1661/2	1661/101
†Prees, Robert	Betws-y-coed Cn	–	W*	6 May 1663	1663/36
Price, Robert	Llanfair Dyffryn Clwyd (Derwen Llanerch) D	Gent.	W I	9 Jan. 1670/1	1670/168
Price, Robert	[Llanbeblig] (Carnarvon) Cn	Gent.	W	n.d.	1683/26

1 Inventory taken 2 April 1684.
2 Inventory taken 26 March 1688.
3 Will dated 27 July 1659.
4 Inventory taken 1 Oct. 1662.
5 Will dated 11 Jan. 1666.

Name	Parish & County	Status	Docs. Filed	Date of Probate/Admon.	Ref. No.
Prees, Robert	Llanrhuddlad (Botteth) A	–	W I Al D	[30 April 1689]	1689/24
Prees, Robert	Llanllechid Cn	Yeoman	B I	15 Feb. 1696/7	1696/77
Price, Rowland	[Clocaenog] (Bryngwrgi) D	Yeoman	W I	28 Feb. 1688/9	1688/88
Price, Samuel	Dolgellau Mr	–	W	[2 July 1673]	1673/47
Pryce, Thomas	Llanrhaeadr-yng-Nghinmeirch (Postney Parke) D	Gent.	W I	[5 March 1677/8]	1677/82
Price, Thomas	Gyffylliog D	–	B I	2 March 1685/6	1685/91
Prees, William	Llechylched A	Yeoman	W*	22 Jan. 1660/1	1660/8
Price, William	Llanfechell A	–	W I B	25 July 1663	1663/19
Prees, William	Llanfair Pwllgwyngyll A	–	B	14 Oct. 1665	1665/14
Price, William	Llanrhaeadr-yng-Nghinmeirch (Prion) D	–	W I Rd	27 July 1665	1665/85
Prees, William	Llanrug Cn	–	I Ac M	n.d.[1]	1673/41
Prees, William	Llanaber Mr	Yeoman	B I	24 May 1682	1682/66
Preese, William	Trawsfynydd Mr	Yeoman	W	22 Sept. 1685	1685/84
Price, William	Llandrygarn A	–	W	n.d.[2]	1686/10
Price, William	Llanfaelog A	–	W Rd	12 Jan. 1691/2	1691/20
Price, William	Llangelynnin (Bronyfoil) Mr	–	B I(2)	9 Oct. 1694	1694/90
Prees, William	Aber Cn	–	B	4 June 1695	1695/20
Prees, William	Beaumaris A	Yeoman	W I*	7 March 1697/8	1697/2
Prichard, Bartholomew	Llangelynnin Cn	–	W	12 Dec. 1682	1682/49
Prichard, David	Aber-erch Cn	–	B I	11 Nov. 1687	1687/35
Prichard, David	Llanrhychwyn Cn	Yeoman	B I R	6 Jan. 1693/4	1693/61
Prichard, Ellis	Treflys Cn	–	B I	24 Oct. 1676	1676/60
Prichard, Evan	Llangwnnadl Cn	–	W I	n.d.[3]	1672/69
Prichart, Harry	Llanllechid Cn	–	I	n.d.[4]	1669/93
Prichard, Harry	Llannor (Hendre) Cn	Gent.	W I	31 May 1688	1688/55
Prichard, Henry	Llanynghenedl A	Yeoman	B I	29 July 1698	1698/14
Prichard, Henry	Pistyll Cn	Yeoman	W I	26 July 1699	1699/90
Prichard, Hugh	Llanfihangel-y-traethau Mr	–	W	23 April 1686	1686/79
Prichard, Hugh	Llangelynnin (Llanvendiged) Mr	–	B I	1 Sept. 1687	1687/101
Prichard, Hugh	Amlwch A	–	B	18 Feb. 1694/5	1694/5
Prichard, Humffrey	Llandanwg Mr	Gent.	I/G*	4 Oct. 1667	1667/90
Prichard, Humphrey	Tal-y-llyn Mr	Yeoman	B I	26 April 1692	1692/88

[1] Inventory exhibited 17 May 1665; account exhibited 15 Jan. 1673.
[2] Will dated 18 June 1686.
[3] Inventory taken 5 July 1672.
[4] Inventory taken 21 Sept. 1669.

Name	Parish & County	Status	Docs. Filed	Date of Probate/Admon.	Ref. No.
Prichard, John	Aberffraw A	Clerk (Curate of Aberffraw)	W	9 March 1639/40	1639/1
Prichard, John	[Llanbeblig] (Carnarvon) Cn	Weaver	W B	28 Dec. 1676	1676/39
Prichard, John	Bangor Cn	Gent.	B	26 Aug. 1680	1680/19
Prichard, John	Llanrhaeadr-yng-Nghinmeirch (Prion) D	Yeoman	W* I	n.d.[1]	1683/89
Prichard, John	Llandwrog / Llanllyfni Cn	–	B I	14 June 1684	1684/42
Prichard, John	[Amlwch] (Hafod y Gors) A	Joiner	W I	[ ] July 1692	1692/1
Prichard, John	Llanllyfni Cn	Yeoman	B	14 June 1697	1697/34
Prichard, John	Clynnog Cn	Yeoman	B I	11 Dec. 1699	1699/55
Prichard, John	Dolbenmaen Cn	Gent.	W I Rd	7 July 1699	1699/58
Prichard, Lewis	Llanfachreth [A/Mr]	Smith	I	n.d.[2]	1689/13
Prichard, Morgan	[Bodwrog] (Cors-r- Eira) A	–	W	n.d.[3]	1675/2
Prichard, Rhytherch	Llaniestyn (Nant) Cn	Yeoman	W	[1 March 1674/5]	1674/25
Prichard, Robert	Llaneilian A	Labourer/Yeoman	W I	28 March 1665	1665/11
Prichard, Robert	Aber-erch Cn	–	B I	25 June 1687	1687/36
Prichard, Thomas	Bangor (Pentre ucha) Cn	Labourer	W I	26 Oct. 1689	1689/31
Prichard, William	Heneglwys (Kerrig dûon) A	Drover	W	11 Feb. 1640/1	1640/1
Prichard, William	Llanllechid Cn	–	W(2)	10 Feb. 1645/6	1645/33
Prichard, William	Llanfachreth Mr	–	B I	1 Feb. 1660/1	1660/23
Prichard, William	Llanddyfnan (Hendrehowe[l]) A	–	B* I*	13 Feb. 1662/3	1662/15
Prichard, William	Dolwyddelan Cn	–	W I	6 May 1665	1665/41
Prichard, William	Dolgellau Mr	Yeoman	I	1 June 1666	1666/76
Prichard, William	Llansadwrn A	Gent.	W* I*	14 Nov. 1670	1670/52
Prichard, William	Llanllechid (Cae mawr) Cn	Yeoman	W I B Ac(2)	19 Feb. 1674/5	1674/26
Prichard, William	Caerhun Cn	Yeoman	W	14 March 1675/6	1675/19
Prichard, William	Llanrhuddlad (Bottedd) A	Yeoman	W I	5 Feb. 1675/6	1675/9
Prichard, William	Gyffylliog (Ffrithoedd) D	Yeoman	W I B	21 Feb. 1678/9	1678/66
Prichard, William	Clocaenog D	Gent.	W I Rd	21 July 1683	1683/80
Prichard, William	Llanfair-iuxta-Harlech (Llwin Hulkin) Mr	–	W I	22 June 1683	1683/72
Prichard, William	Llanbedrycennin (Arddey) Cn	Yeoman	W Al D	21 April 1685	1685/44
Prichard, William	Llanfrothen Mr	–	B I	22 May 1689	1689/74
Prichard, William	Llanrhychwyn Cn	–	B L	21 May 1689	1689/57
Prichard, William	Llandwrog Cn	Yeoman	W I B	5 Feb. 1690/1	1690/55

1 Inventory taken 1 May 1683.
2 Died 4 Nov. 1688.
3 Will dated 14 March 1675.

Name	Parish & County	Status	Docs. Filed	Date of Probate/Admon.	Ref. No.
Prichard, William	Llanfwrog D	Glover	W I	25 April 1695	1695/92
Prichard, William	Llanbeulan (Ddrydwy) A	Yeoman	W I	12 May 1696	1696/10
Prichard, William	Llanfwrog A	Labourer/Yeoman	W	[ ] 1699	1699/21
Probert, Hugh	Clynnog Cn	–	B	23 Nov. 1685	1685/37
Probert, John	Llanfihangel [Bachellaeth] Cn	Yeoman	I	n.d.[1]	1676/54
Probert, William	Llanynghenedl A	–	B R	2 Feb. 1669/70	1669/44
Probert, William	Llandwrog Cn	Gent.	W* I* Rd	28 Oct. 1670	1670/103
Probert, William	Llanaber Mr	–	W I	20 Feb. 1682/3	1682/67
Probert, William	Clocaenog D	Yeoman	I/G	26 March 1683	1683/81
Probert, William	Llanfwrog (Pen y Coed) D	Cooper	W I	10 July 1699	1699/128
Prowdly, Evan	Penystrowed Mg	–	W	10 July 1637	1637/53
Proudley, Mary	Llanidloes (Hengynwyd) Mg	Spinster	W	[1 Sept. 1669]	1669/172
Pryce, Prys, Pryse *see* Price					
Prytherch, David	Penmachno Cn	–	G	4 Sept. 1666	1666/70
Prytherch, Evan	Ffestiniog Mr	Bachelor	B I	11 Nov. 1663	1663/84
Prytherch, Henry	Llanbedrycennin Cn	–	B I	18 March 1666/7	1666/57
Prydderch, Hugh	Llanrhwydrys A	–	W*	7 Jan. 1636/7	1636/19
Prytherch, Humffrey	Heneglwys A	Gent.	B I	17 Aug. 1667	1667/6
Prytherch, John	Tregaean A	Gent.	B	5 Aug. 1692	1692/31
Prydderch, John	Llanwenllwyfo (Llys-dylas) A	Gent.	W I Rd	14 April 1693	1693/23
Prytherch, Lewis	Llanrhuddlad A	–	W B	9 Dec. 1647	1647/18
Prytherch, Martha	Llanidan A	Widow	W*	10 Dec. 1662	1662/28
Prytherch, Robert	Llanfechell A	Mercer	W	10 May 1648	1648/4
Prytherch, William	[Llanbeblig] (Carnarvon) Cn	Yeoman	W I	27 June 1673	1673/25
Prythergh, William	Conway Cn	Gent.	W Rd	3 May 1680	1680/22
Pugh, Kadwalader	Llaniestyn Cn	Yeoman	B I	23 Nov. 1697	1697/30
Pue *alias* Mersh, Dorothy	Conway Cn	Widow	W Rd	21 July 1668	1668/47
Pugh, Elizabeth	Caerhun (Varchwell) Cn	Widow	W I	23 Nov. 1691	1691/44
Pugh, Evan	Llanfachreth Mr	–	W I	10 Oct. 1693	1693/83
Pugh, Griffith	Llanddwywe Mr	Gent.	W I	[ ] 1697[2]	1697/46
Pugh, Hugh	Llanbedr Dyffryn Clwyd D	Clerk (Rector of Llanbedr)	W	n.d.[3]	1681/88
Pugh, Hugh	Tal-y-llyn Mr	–	W I	20 May 1682	1682/77
Pugh, Hugh	Llanfechell A	–	B*	7 Dec. 1685	1685/19
Pugh, Hugh	Beaumaris A	Vintner	W I	23 July 1696	1696/2

1 Died 20 Dec. 1676.
2 Inventory taken 5 May 1697.
3 Will dated 1 Nov. 1681.

Name	Parish & County	Status	Docs. Filed	Date of Probate/Admon.	Ref. No.
Pugh, Jane	Llandrygarn A	Widow	W	10 March 1680/1	1680/6
Pugh, Jane	Llanbadrig (Rhydgroys) A	Spinster	W I B	22 Oct. 1696	1696/6
Pughe, John	Llanfihangel-y-Pennant Mr	Gent.	B I	9 April 1677	1677/60
Pugh, John	Aber-erch Cn	–	I	n.d.[1]	1681/24
Pugh, Kadwalader *as* Pugh, Cadwaladr					
Pugh, Lewis	Dolgellau (Dolgleder) Mr	Yeoman	W I	10 Oct. 1693	1693/71
Pugh, Mary	Dolgellau Mr	Widow	W I	25 Dec. 1683	1683/60
Pugh, Rice	Llanrhaeader-yng-Nghinmeirch D	Clerk	W Rd	9 March 1647/8	1647/48
Pugh, Rice	Llandrygarn A	Gent./Major	W(2) I Rd	17 Sept. 1666	1666/11
Pugh, Rice	Llanrhychwyn Cn	–	I/G	5 Sept. 1692	1692/60
Pugh, William	Llanfachreth Mr	–	B	12 June 1663	1663/97
Pue, William	Ceirchiog A	Yeoman	W I	9 May 1688	1688/7
Pugh, William	Trawsfynydd (Cae yn y Cefn) Mr	Gent./Yeoman	B I(2) C	7 April 1691[2]	1691/100
Pugh, William	[Llanrwst] (Trewydder) Cn	–	W I	11 Jan. 1693/4	1693/60
Pulston *see* Pilston					
Purscell *alias* William, Elizabeth	Llangurig Mg	Widow [of George Pursel]	W I	13 July 1699	1699/153
Pursel, George	Llangurig Mg	Yeoman	W I	12 Feb. 1693/4	1693/138
Randolph *see* Rondolph					
Rees, David	Tal-y-llyn Mr	–	W	26 April 1665	1665/73
Rees, David	Trefeglwys Mg	Yeoman	W I	[25 Nov. 1690]	1690/122
Rees, David	Trefeglwys Mg	–	W I	[9 Feb. 1692/3]	1692/129
Rees, David	Trefeglwys Mg	Yeoman	B I	23 Sept. 1697	1697/76
Rees, Edward	Llandinam (Carnethe) Mg	Husbandman	W	26 April 1637	1637/49
Rees, Elizabeth	Llanwnnog Mg	–	W I	23 Oct. 1665	1665/109
Rees, Evan	Llanwnnog (Weeke) Mg	Yeoman	W I	26 Sept. 1667	1667/141
Rhees, Evan	Llanidloes (Hengynwydd) Mg	Yeoman	W	[17 Nov. 1692]	1692/125
Rees, Gwenn	Carno Mg	Widow	W I	[9 Feb. 1692/3]	1692/108
Rees, Hugh	Carno Mg	Yeoman	B I	20 Jan. 1693/4	1693/128
Rees, Jenkine	Llandinam (Trellan) Mg	Weaver	W I	16 Oct. 1688	1688/101
Rees, John	Llangelynnin (Bodgadvan) Mr	Yeoman	W I	30 May 1665	1665/72
Rhice, John	Llannor Cn	–	W	17 Oct. 1666	1666/65

1 Inventory taken 20 Jan. 1681.

2 B *1690*; recte *1691* on the evidence of the other documents.

Name	Parish & County	Status	Docs. Filed	Date of Probate/Admon.	Ref. No.
Rees, Lewis	Llanfihangel-y-Pennant Mr	–	B	28 Sept. 1663	1663/102
Rees, Margaret	Trefeglwys Mg	Widow	I	n.d.[1]	1688/105
Rees, Morgan	Llanidloes Mg	–	W	28 June 1638	1638/89
Rees, Morgan	Trefeglwys Mg	Single man	W I	24 Jan. 1695/6	1695/115
Rees, Moris	Llanidloes Mg	–	B I	16 Feb. 1694/5[2]	1695/109
Rees, Owen	Llangurig (Llanyfyny) Mg	Yeoman	W I	26 June 1697	1697/64
Rees, Richard	Llangurig Mg	–	I/G	10 Feb. 1667/8	1667/133
Rees, Richard	Llandinam Mg	Yeoman	W	1 May 1669	1669/163
Rees, Robert	Dolgellau Mr	–	B C	29 Aug. 1670	1670/136
Rees, Robert	Pennal Mr	Shoemaker	W I C	17 Jan. 1686/7	1686/83
Rhees, Roger	Trefeglwys (Kevenbarach) Mg	–	B* I*	6 Aug. 1697	1697/77
Rees, Rowland	[Dolgellau] (Dyffrydan) Mr	–	W	n.d.[3]	1674/37
Rees, Thomas	Llangurig Mg	–	W I	6 Feb. 1670/1	1670/184
Rees, Thomas	Llanidloes Mg	–	B I	8 Dec. 1693	1693/141
Reinalld, Edward	Llangaffo A	–	W I	12 Sept. 1667	1667/26
Reynallt *alias* Ellis, Elizabeth	Llanystumdwy Cn	–	B	16 May 1688	1688/57
Reynelds, Jane	Llanwnnog Mg	–	B I	16 June 1692	1692/127
Reignallt, John	Llanfwrog A	Gent.	W	22 July 1638	1638/14
Rinalds, John	Llanwnnog Mg	Gent.	W I C	17 April 1686	1686/107
Reignald, John	Penmachno (Dulasse) Cn	Yeoman	B I	26 Jan. 1698/9	1698/47
Rynald, Stephen	Llanfwrog (Pen y Coed) D	Gent.	W I	25 March 1699	1699/129
Reignald, Thomas	Llangïan Cn	Mercer	W Cd	31 Aug. 1696	1696/71
Reynald, William	[Deneio] (Pwllhely) Cn	Mercer	W	27 May 1676	1676/45
Reynallt, William	Llanfaglan Cn	Yeoman	B I	4 May 1696	1696/67
Rhydderch, Elizabeth	Dolgellau Mr	–	W I	n.d.[4]	1688/67
Rhydderch, Richard	Tal-y-llyn Mr	–	B I*	28 Feb. 1681/2	1681/82
Richard, Katherine	Llanfairfechan Cn	–	W	7 Feb. 1683/4	1683/41
Richard, David	Llangurig Mg	–	W B	13 April 1641	1641/73
Richard, David	Trefeglwys (Cwm-biga-ycha) Mg	Yeoman	W I	6 Aug. 1696	1696/141
Richard, Ellin	Llanfachreth Mr	–	W I	n.d.[5]	1682/73
Richard, Francis	Dolgellau Mr	–	B I	2 July 1695	1695/64
Richard, Howell	Llanwnnog Mg	Weaver	B I	6 May 1695	1695/113
Richard, Hugh	Tywyn (Garthmor) Mr	Yeoman	W	6 May 1685	1685/87

1 Inventory taken 7 Aug. 1688.
2 Inventory taken 13 Feb. 1695 with memorandum endorsed of swearing administratrix on 16 Feb. 1695 (new style reckoning?).
3 Will dated 25 June 1674.
4 Will dated 14 April 1688.
5 Inventory taken 16 Jan. 1682.

Name	Parish & County	Status	Docs. Filed	Date of Probate/Admon.	Ref. No.
Richards, John	Beaumaris A	Tailor	W	23 Feb. 1673/4	1673/4
Richard, John	Llanfachreth (Tyddyn Mawr) Mr	–	W I	5 Feb. 1684/5	1684/71
Richard, John	Trefeglwys Mg	Gent.	W I	[26 April 1693]	1693/145
Richard, John	Llandanwg Mr	Yeoman	I/G	5 May 1696	1696/99
Richard, Katherine *as* Richard, Catherine					
Richard, Lewis	Pennal (Dyffryn Caer) Mr	Yeoman	B I R	26 April 1692	1692/84
Richard, Margaret	Trawsfynydd Mr	Widow	W I L[1]	[16 Dec. 1676]	1676/84
Richard, Mary	Trawsfynydd Mr	Wife of Hugh Owens	B	6 July 1680	1680/58
Richards, Owen, *alias* Owen ap Richard ap Hugh ap John	Llangristiolus A	–	W(2) I Rd	24 Feb. 1664/5	1664/34
Richard, Owen	Llanberis Cn	–	B I	9 Oct. 1668	1668/53
Richard, Owen	Llanddaniel-fab A	–	W I	28 Oct. 1670	1670/21
Richard, Owen	Llandygái (Dyffryn Mymbir) Cn	–	B I	7 March 1676/7	1676/52
Richard, Owen	Llanbeblig Cn	Yeoman	W* I*	3 Aug. 1697	1697/22
Richard, Rhees	Llanidloes Mg	–	W	[5 June] 1695	1695/110
Richard, Rowland	Llangeinwen A	–	W I	7 July 1663	1663/24
Richard, Thomas	Llanwnnog (Treuchlawrcoed) Mg	Gent.	B I	21 June 1664	1664/135
Richard, Thomas	Llangurig (Llanivyny) Mg	–	W I	14 April 1692	1692/122
Richards *see* Richard					
Ridge, William	Llandyrnog D	Gent.	W I	17 Jan. 1687/8	1687/115
Robert *see* Roberts					
Robertes, Alice	Llanffinan A	Widow	W	10 April 1647	1647/14
Roberts, Anne	Llanrhaeadr-yng-Nghinmeirch (Prion) D	Spinster	W	17 March 1679/80	1679/56
Roberts, Anne	Llanrhaeadr-yng-Nghinmeirch D	Widow	B I	13 Oct. 1692	1692/100
Roberts, Katharine	Llandyrnog D	Widow	I*	n.d.[2]	1686/92
Roberts, Catherine	Beaumaris A	–	B	9 Nov. 1692	1692/2
Robert, Catherine	Llanelltud Mr	–	W/I	4 Aug. 1696	1696/103
Roberts, David	Llandinam Mg	Clerk (Vicar of Llandinam)	Rd[3]	n.d.	1670/182
Robert, David	Pennal Mr	Miller	W I(2)	[ ] 1694/5[4]	1694/92
Roberts, David	Llandinam Mg	–	B I	5 July 1695	1695/104

1 Also relates to the administration of the goods of John Morgans of Trawsfynydd (q.v.).

2 Died c. 28 Aug. 1686.

3 Filed with the will of Theophilus Roberts (q.v.). Will, dated 20 April 1668, mentioned but not filed.

4 Inventory exhibited 14 Jan. 1694[/5].

Name	Parish & County	Status	Docs. Filed	Date of Probate/Admon.	Ref. No.
Robert, Edward	Llanaber Mr	–	I	n.d.[1]	1693/74
Roberts, Ellyn	Bangor Cn	Widow	W	n.d.[2]	1664/54
Roberts, Ellin	[Llanbeblig] (Carnarvon) Cn	–	W	n.d.[3]	1670/79
Roberts, Ellen	[Llandyfrydog] (Llwydiart Escob) A	Widow	W	5 Sept. 1691	1691/17
Roberts, Ellis	Cricieth Cn	Gent.	B I*	6 Nov. 1680	1680/23
Roberts, Ellis	Clynnog Cn	–	W I D M	n.d.[4]	1687/45
Roberts *alias* Price, Elizabeth	Bodwrog (Eriannell) A	Widow/ Gentlewoman	B I	5 Dec. 1667	1667/5
Robertes, Elizabeth	Llanrhaeadr-yng-Nghinmeirch D	–	I	n.d.[5]	1680/71
Roberts, Elizabeth	Bangor Cn	Widow	W I	n.d.	1682/32
Roberts, Elizabeth	Llanfihangel-y-traethau (Tyddun tege) Mr	Widow	B I	16 May 1693	1693/86
Roberts, Ellen/Ellin *as* Roberts, Elin					
Roberts, Ellis *as* Roberts, Elis					
Robert, Evan	Llangelynnin Mr	–	W	7 Oct. 1669	1669/131
Robert, Evan	Llanenddwyn Mr	–	W I	1 May 1671	1671/106
Roberts, Evan	Holyhead A	–	W Rd	26 Feb. 1694/5	1694/10
			B I	7 Nov. 1696	1696/5
Roberts, Gaynor	Llangybi Cn	–	B	5 Aug. 1668	1668/67
Roberts *alias* Lewis, Gaynor	Llanrhwydrys A	–	W	[12 March 1672/3]	1672/28
Robert, Gryffith *see* Gryffith Sir Robert	Llanfrothen (Clarken-well) Mr				
Roberts, Gryffyth	Llangwnnadl (Trefgraig) Cn	Gent.	W* Rd	19 June 1644	1644/27
Roberts, Griffith	Botwnnog Cn	Clerk	W*	6 Aug. 1668	1668/36
Roberts, Griffyth	Llan Sant Catherin *alias* Cricieth (Bach y saynt) Cn	Gent.	W I	[23 March 1673/4]	1673/31
Roberts, Gryffyth	Holyhead A	Gent.	W I	[ ] 1676[6]	1676/8
Roberts, Griffith	Clynnog Cn	–	B I	28 May 1688	1688/38
†Roberts, Gruffudd	Penmorfa Cn	Yeoman	W Al D	[ ] Feb. 1696/7	1696/85

1 Inventory taken 20 Feb. 1692/3.
2 Will dated 5 Feb. 1664.
3 Will dated 23 June 1670.
4 Will dated 25 Jan. 1687[/8].
5 Inventory taken 29 March 1680.
6 Date of swearing executors – 21 May 1676 – incorrect? Codicil dated 28 Nov. 1676 and inventory taken 12 Dec. 1676.

Name	Parish & County	Status	Docs. Filed	Date of Probate/Admon.	Ref. No.
Roberts, Henry	Llanrhaeadr-yng-Nghinmeirch (Parke) D	Yeoman	W I	12 June 1682	1682/85
Roberts, Henry	Llanfwrog D	Glover	W I	13 March 1685/6	1685/95
Roberts, Henery	Llangwyfan D	–	B	19 July 1690	1690/108
Roberts, Hugh	Llanfwrog (Bodyngharad) D	Yeoman	W I	21 April 1669	1669/149
Roberts, Humffrey	Llanfairfechan Cn	Gent.	W Rd	16 Feb. 1646/7	1646/20
Roberts, Immanuel	Ysbyty [Ifan] (Blaen y Coed) Cn	Yeoman	W I	25 Jan. 1689/90	1689/62
Roberts, Jane	Llanllyfni Cn	Widow	W I	11 March 1670/1	1670/119
Robert, Jane	Llandecwyn Mr	Spinster	W	n.d.[1]	1679/38
Roberts *alias* Price, Jane	Rhuthun (the Kinges Armes) D	Widow	B I	10 Feb. 1692/3	1692/106
[Roberts, John]	[Llanrhuddlad] A	–	W*	3 May 1636	1636/18
Robert, John	Trawsfynydd Mr	–	W B	17 Sept. 1661	1661/109
Robert, John	Llanidloes Mg	Carpenter	W/I	3 Aug. 1665	1665/106
Roberts, John	Nefyn Cn	Yeoman	W	19 Feb. 1677/8	1677/48
Robert, John	Caerhun (Brynn gwenyth) Cn	Yeoman	B I	1 June 1678	1678/20
Roberts, John	Llanrhaeadr-yng-Nghinmeirch D	Clerk	W	[3 May 1678]	1678/75
Roberts, John	Aber-erch Cn	–	W I	24 Feb. 1680/1	1680/17
Robert, John	Llanrwst (Gwyddir) Cn	–	W	20 Sept. 1681	1681/55
Robert, John	Pennal Mr	–	W I	13 June 1682	1682/76
Roberts, John	[Llangwnnadl] (Treigwraig [issa]) Cn	Gent.	W I	[27 Oct. 1683]	1683/44
Roberts, John	Llanystumdwy (Coet kay) Cn	–	B I	13 Jan. 1687/8	1687/73
Roberts, John	Llanystumdwy (Chwilog) Cn	–	B I	17 Nov. 1688	1688/58
Roberts, John	Aber-erch Cn	–	B I	27 Aug. 1690	1690/40
Roberts, John	Holyhead A	Widower	W	16 Jan. 1691/2	1691/14
Robert, John	Llanllechid Cn	Yeoman	W I	[19 Jan. 1691/2]	1691/65
Roberts, John	Edern Cn	–	W B	2 Aug. 1692	1692/45
Robert, John	Llanrhaeadr-yng-Nghinmeirch (Brun hokin, Trevibychain) D	–	W I*	15 Feb. 1693/4	1693/115
Roberts, John	Llangeinwen A	Yeoman	W I	28 May 1695	1695/12
Roberts, John	Llanelidan D	–	B I	25 May 1697	1697/57
Roberts, John	Trawsfynydd (Gilvachwen) Mr	–	I*	n.d.[2]	1697/54
Roberts, John	[Llanbeblig] (Carnarvon) Cn	Corviser	B I	22 Nov. 1699	1699/52
Roberts, Katharine *see* Roberts, Catherine					
Roberts, Lewis	Llangefni A	Gent.	W I	21 Nov. 1693	1693/16

[1] Will dated 2 Aug. 1679.
[2] Inventory taken 9 June 1697.

Name	Parish & County	Status	Docs. Filed	Date of Probate/Admon.	Ref. No.
Robert, Lowry	Llanenddwyn Mr	–	W I	7 May 1680	1680/50
Robert, Margeret	Pennal Mr	Widow	W I	21 Jan. 1678/9	1678/50
Roberts, Margaret	Llanfair-yng-Nghornwy A	–	B	11 July 1683	1683/9
Roberts, Methanwy	Llanbeulan A	Widow	B	9 Oct. 1667	1667/14
Roberts, Morgan	Bangor Cn	Clerk	W	29 April 1684	1684/29
Roberts, Morgan	Llanrug Cn	Yeoman	W* I	4 March 1697/8	1697/36
Roberts, Nicholas	Llanfihangel-y-traethau Mr	Gent.	W I	9 Oct. 1685	1685/78
Roberts, Osmond	[Llanbeblig] (Carnarvon) Cn	Corviser	W I	7 June 1698	1698/24
Roberts, Owen	Ceirchiog (Bodveddan) A	Gent.	W I	23 Feb. 1663/4	1663/6
Robert, Owen	Clynnog (Henbant) Cn	Yeoman	W I	2 April 1668	1668/42
Roberts, Owen	Llandwrog (Gilwerne) Cn	Gent.	W(2)	1 March 1669/70	1669/80
Robert, Owen	Dolgellau Mr	Yeoman	W I	19 March 1684/5	1684/66
Robert, Owen	Llannor Cn	–	B I	17 Sept. 1684	1684/53
Roberts *alias* Wynne, Peter	Efenechtid D	Gent.	W	27 Oct. 1684	1684/88
Roberts, Richard	Treflys (Bron y foyle) Cn	Gent.	B I	28 Sept. 1661	1661/87
Robert, Richard	Llanaber Mr	Yeoman	W I	13 June 1670	1670/140
Roberts, Richard	Aberffraw (Rhosepadricke) A	Gent.	W	21 May 1672	1672/1
Roberts, Richard	Caerhun (Biart) Cn	Gent.	W I C B	12 Oct. 1677	1677/26
Roberts, Richard	Nefyn (Cerniog) Cn	–	W I	24 May 1690	1690/79
Roberts, Robert	Llandyrnog D	Gent.	B I	27 Feb. 1684/5	1684/90
Roberts, Robert	Conway Cn	Clerk (Rector of Llanfairfechan & vicar of Conway)	W	16 March 1697/8	1697/20
Roberts, Simonnt	Llandyrnog D	–	W	29 March 1638	1638/75
Roberts, Simon	Llanrhaeadr-yng-Nghinmeirch D	–	I	n.d.[1]	1661/119
Roberts, Susan	Mellteyrn Cn	Widow	W I	24 April 1694	1694/60
Roberts, Theophilus	Llanerfyl & Llandinam Mg	Gent.	W Rd[2]	2 March 1670/1	1670/182
Roberts, Thomas	Llangybi Cn	Gent.	W I B	22 June 1671	1671/79
Roberts, Thomas	Llanaber Mr	Gent.	W I	10 July 1694	1694/77
Roberts, William	Bodwrog A	Gent.	W*	31 May 1643	1643/3
Roberts, William	Llanfechell (Cefen Coch) A	Gent.	W(2) I	29 Oct. 1666	1666/20
Roberts, William	Rhuthun D	Gent.	B I	22 Aug. 1666	1666/110
Roberts, William	Llanllyfni (Llwyn dû, Ethinog) Cn	Gent.	W I Rd	27 April 1668	1668/69
Roberts, William	Cricieth Cn	–	W	[21 Dec. 1674]	1674/19

1 Died 25 Sept. 1661.

2 Being also a bond for the redelivery of the will of his father, David Roberts of Llandinam, clerk.

Name	Parish & County	Status	Docs. Filed	Date of Probate/Admon.	Ref. No.
Roberts, William	Llanfair-yng-Nghornwy (Caerae) A	Gent.	W* Cd I Rd	n.d.[1]	1683/10
Roberts, William	Llanfihangel-y-Pennant (Isaullt) Cn	–	W	[24 May 1683]	1683/43
Roberts, William	Llanfrothen (Brondanwg) Mr	Gent.	W I	26 Oct. 1693	1693/87
Robyns, Elizabeth	Llandwrog (Bryn r Odyn) Cn	Widow	W I	9 March 1687/8	1687/58
Robyns, Herbert	[Llanbeblig] (Castellmay) Cn	Gent.	W	n.d.[2]	1669/71
Robins, John	Llandysilio A	Gent.	B R	8 June 1697	1697/5
Robins, William	Llanfair Pwllgwyngyll A	Weaver	I/L	24 Feb. 1636/7	1636/13
Robyns, William	Llanbeblig (Castellmay) Cn	Gent.	W I Al Rd	20 June 1678	1678/26
Robins, William John	Llanfair Pwllgwyngyll A	Yeoman	B I	1 May 1693	1693/12
Robinson, George	Llanfigel A	–	W I	[12 Oct. 1672]	1672/20
Robinson, Mary	Conway Cn	Widow	W I	6 May 1694	1694/44
Robinsonne, Robert	[Llanbeblig] (Caernarvon) Cn	Tanner	W	8 July 1636	1636/25
Roe, Jane	Beaumaris A	Widow	B I C(2)	21 April 1691	1691/10
Roe, Peter	Beaumaris A	–	B	27 Jan. 1686/7	1686/5
Roger, David	Llanfihangel Ysgeifiog (Rhydgeint) A	Gent.	W I	29 Oct. 1694	1694/21
Roger, Evan	Trefdraeth A	–	B G	13 Feb. 1664/5	1664/47
Roger *alias* Heynes, Evan	Carno Mg	–	I/G	17 Feb. 1665/6	1665/89
Roger, Jonett	Aberffraw A	Widow	W I	7 Feb. 1688/9	1688/2
Rogers, Lewis	Llanfair Dyffryn Clwyd D	–	W	16 June 1636	1636/56
Roger, Margaret	[Llanbeblig] (Carnarvon) Cn	Widow	W I	1 Aug. 1665	1665/37
Rogers, Thomas	Llanbadrig A	–	B	10 Nov. 1682	1682/7
Rogers, Thomas	Llanynys D	–	B	30 July 1699	1699/139
Rogers *see* Roger					
Rondolph, Harry	Llanrug Cn	–	B* I*	[ ] June 1683	1683/50
Rothwell, Hugh	Beaumaris A	–	W*	5 Jan. 1636/7	1636/1
Rowland, Alce	Llansadwrn A	Widow	W	13 Feb. 1691/2	1691/31
Rowland, Anne	Amlwch (Llechog) A	Widow	W I	1 April 1661	1661/2
Rowland, Kadwallader	Llandysilio A	Gent.	W Cd I Rd	3 July 1665	1665/10
Rowland, Kadwalader	Ffestiniog (Bryn y bige) Mr	Yeoman	B I(2)	28 Dec. 1696	1696/92
Rowland, Katherin	Bodedern A	–	B	8 Feb. 1670/1	1670/3
Rowland, Catherine	Llanddeiniolen Cn	Widow	B R	26 March 1695	1695/45
Rowlands, Catherine	Beaumaris A	Widow	W I* Al C B	20 June 1699	1699/4
Rowland, David	Llangïan Cn	–	B	24 Feb. 1689/90	1689/51

1 Proved by 15 June 1683 according to bond for redelivery of will.
2 Will dated 31 Dec. 1669.

Name	Parish & County	Status	Docs. Filed	Date of Probate/Admon.	Ref. No.
Rowland, David	Llanddeiniolen Cn	Yeoman	B I	12 Jan. 1696/7	1696/63
Rowland, Edward	Llanbadrig A	Yeoman	W I	31 May 1694	1694/11
Rowland, Ellenor	Aber-erch Cn	Spinster	B*	2 June 1662	1662/35
Rowland, Elizabeth	Pennal (Cwmkadian) Mr	Widow	W	n.d.[1]	1675/48
Rowland, Evan	Llanwnda Cn	Pedlar	B* I	21 Aug. 1662	1662/53
Rowland, Grace	Llan-faes A	Widow	W* Rd	14 Dec. 1643	1643/7
Rowland, Griffith	Llandygái (Kelly r Menŷch) Cn	–	B I G	9 Dec. 1665	1665/44
Rowland, Gruffyth	Clynnog Cn	Yeoman	W	11 Dec. 1668	1668/43
Rowland, Griffith	Llanfair-iuxta-Harlech Mr	–	W	[8 Aug. 1672]	1672/94
Rowland, Griffith	Llaniestyn Cn	Yeoman	W I	10 June 1692	1692/54
Rowlands, Henry	Llanedwen A	–	W* Rd*	30 April 1640	1640/8
Rowland, Henry	Llanwnda Cn	Gent.	W Rd	10 July 1643	1643/29
Rowland, Hugh	Llandegfan A	–	B I	28 Jan. 1667/8	1667/16
Rowland, Hugh	Llandrygarn A	–	W(2) I	17 Dec. 1669	1669/16
Rowland, Hugh	Llanddaniel-fab A	Yeoman	W	7 June 1670	1670/22
Rowland, Hugh	Aber-erch Cn	Clerk (Rector of Llanaelhaearn and vicar of Aber-erch)	W	1 March 1672/3	1672/39
Rowland, Hugh	Llanfaglan Cn	Yeoman	B I Db	2 Dec. 1682	1682/46
[Row]land, [Hugh]	[ ] [?Cn][2]	–	B*	30 Oct. 1699	1699/161
Rowland, Humffrey	Llanfechell A	–	B	23 Feb. 1660/1	1660/5
Rowland, Humphrey	Llangeinwen A	–	W	23 May 1663	1663/25
Rowland, John	Llanddeiniolen Cn	–	W	1 May 1643	1643/19
Rowland, John	Llanbedr[-goch] (Carrog) A	Yeoman	W* I* Rd*	29 June 1661	1661/11
Rowland, John	Llanfachreth Mr	–	B I* C	23 Sept. 1662	1662/63
Rowland, John	Llanbedr Niwbwrch A	–	W I	27 Nov. 1666	1666/9
Rowlants, John	Aber-erch Cn	Weaver	W	2 Oct. 1690	1690/41
Rowland, John	Dolgellau (Brithdir) Mr	Gent.	W I Rd	5 Oct. 1692	1692/67
Rowland, John	Aber-erch Cn	Gent.	W	17 April 1696	1696/33
Rowland, John	Llangeinwen A	Yeoman	B I(2)	1 Dec. 1696	1696/17
Rowland, Kadwalader *as* Rowland, Cadwaladr					
Rowland, Katherin *see* Rowland, Catherine					

[1] Will dated 15 April 1675.

[2] Rowland Hughes, gent., of the parish of Llanddeiniolen described as administrator.

Name	Parish & County	Status	Docs. Filed	Date of Probate/Admon.	Ref. No.
Rowland, Morgan	Llangefni (Tregarnedd) A	Yeoman	W	12 Sept. 1667	1667/27
Rowland, Morgan	Llanwnnog Mg	Yeoman	W I	13 Oct. 1693	1693/144
Rowland, Moris	Penmorfa Cn	–	I	n.d.[1]	1669/109
Rowland, Morris	Llechylched A	–	W	n.d.[2]	1670/53
Rowland, Owen	Llangristiolus A	–	B	23 March 1664/5	1664/35
Rowland, Owen	Bangor (Aber y pwll) Cn	Smith	B(2)	13 Dec. 1671	1671/44
Rowland, Pierce	Llandygái Cn	Yeoman	B I R	9 June 1686	1686/50
Rowland, Rees	Heneglwys A	Yeoman	W	22 Aug. 1647	1647/5
Rowland, Rees	[Llangwyllog] A	–	B*	9 May 1683	1683/14
Rowland, Richard	Ynyscynhaearn Cn	–	W	14 Nov. 1641	1641/46
Rowland, Richard	Trefdraeth A	–	B	19 Dec. 1664	1664/48
Rowland, Richard	Llandrygarn A	Yeoman	B I	13 May 1672	1672/14
Rowland, Richard	Penmynydd A	–	B I	23 April 1689	1689/25
Rowland, Richard (the younger)	Beaumaris A	Corviser	W I Rd	21 Jan. 1690/1	1690/7
Rowland, Richard	Aberffraw A	Clerk (Rector of Aberffraw)	B I	15 June 1694	1694/2
Rowland, Richard	Llanberis Cn	–	W I Al	1 Aug. 1695	1695/38
Rowland, Robert	Llanllechid (Tu Gwyn) Cn	–	B I	31 May 1683	1683/46
Rowland, Robert	Llanrug Cn	Yeoman	B I	20 June 1698	1698/43
Rowland, Thomas	Llangwyllog (Treskaven) A	Yeoman	W*	[ ] 1643[3]	1643/10
Rowland, Thomas	Llanidan A	–	B	13 Aug. 1662	1662/29
Rowlands, Thomas	Aberdaron Cn	–	W	13 Nov. 1669	1669/55
Rowland, William	Holyhead A	Joiner	W Db B	2 Sept. 1661	1661/8
Rowland, William	Llanfair-iuxta-Harlech Mr	–	W	16 Aug. 1670	1670/152
Rowland, William	Llanddaniel-fab A	–	B I	25 April 1681	1681/7
Rowland, William	[Rhodogeidio] (Bryngwallan) A	Gent.	W I	23 April 1683	1683/17
Rowland, William	Llangybi Cn	Yeoman	W I	28 March 1690	1690/69
Rowland, William	Llanllechid Cn	Yeoman	B I	28 Sept. 1693	1693/54
Rowlands *see* Rowland					
Rownson, James	[Deneio] (Pwllhely) Cn	Saltman	W I	22 May 1674	1674/20
Ruffe, Paul	Llandinam (Chappell Banhadlogge) Mg	–	B I R	13 March 1683/4	1683/98
Ruff, Paul	Llandinam Mg	Yeoman	W I Al D	13 July 1699	1699/146

1 Inventory taken 16 Dec. 1669.

2 Will dated 1 Dec. 1670.

3 Will dated 11 Sept. 1643.

Name	Parish & County	Status	Docs. Filed	Date of Probate/Admon.	Ref. No.
Saethon *see* Saython					
Salesbury, Salisbury *see* Salusbury					
Salmon, Jane	Beaumaris A	–	B	7 June 1686	1686/6
Salesbury, Ellisabeth	Llanfwrog (Pool Park) D	Widow	W Cd I	17 July 1693	1693/112
Salisbury, Harry ap Hugh	Clocaenog D	Gent.	W I Rd	16 Nov. 1691	1691/103
Salesbury, Hugh	Clocaenog D	–	W I	6 May 1661	1661/111
Salusbury, John	Llanrhaeadr-yng-Nghinmeirch (Llech) D	–	W	16 May 1637	1637/44
Salisbury, John	Llandyrnog D	Yeoman	B I	21 March 1694/5	1694/102
Salusbury, John Pierce	[Llanrhaeadr-yng-Nghinmeirch] (Astrad) D	Yeoman	W* I	14 Dec. 1685	1685/99
Salusbury, Richard	Llanrhaeadr-yng-Nghinmeirch (Llan) D	Yeoman	W I	21 Jan. 1678/9	1678/76
Salesbury, Richard	Llanfair Dyffryn Clwyd (Derwen Llannerch) D	Gent.	W* I Rd	[23 Oct. 1686]	1686/96
Salesbury, Richard ap Hugh	Gwyddelwern[1] (Boteulog) Mr	Yeoman	W	17 Aug. 1696	1696/142
Salisbury, Robert	Llanrhaeadr-yng-Nghinmeirch (Pen y bryn) D	Yeoman	W I R	1 Oct. 1670	1670/173
Salesbury, Robert ap Hugh	Clocaenog D	–	W	27 May 1665	1665/77
Sampson, Katherine	Llangynhafal D	Widow	W	20 Nov. 1662	1662/88
Sampson, John	Llanfwrog D	–	W	12 May 1698	1698/65
Sampson, Robert	Llangynhafal D	Gent.	W I	9 Oct. 1672	1672/114
Sandar, David	Llanrhaeadr-yng-Nghinmeirch D	–	I	n.d.[2]	1695/94
Savage, John	Trefeglwys Mg	–	B	5 Nov. 1685	1685/122
Savage, Thomas	Llanwnnog Mg	–	W I	31 July 1668	1668/144
Savage, Thomas	Trefeglwys Mg	Yeoman	B I	10 Jan. 1699/1700	1699/160
Saython, Ellis	[Mellteyrn] (Bodnithoedd) Cn	Gent.	B	5 Oct. 1672	1672/82
Saython, Evan	Llanfihangel Bachellaeth (Saython) Cn	Esq.	W Rd	12 March 1638/9	1638/42
Saython, Evan	[Llanfihangel Bachellaeth] (Saython) Cn	Gent.	W I	[28 Aug. 1683]	1683/42
Shawe *alias* Madther, Margaret	Beaumaris A	Widow	W	26 April 1681	1681/2
Shawe, Samuell	Carno Mg	–	I/G	16 Jan. 1664/5	1664/125

[1] Normally within the jurisdiction of the St. Asaph Consistory Court. Testator bequeaths property in the parish of Derwen, co. Denbigh, within the jurisdiction of the Bangor Consistory Court.

[2] Inventory taken 3 Dec. 1695.

Name	Parish & County	Status	Docs. Filed	Date of Probate/Admon.	Ref. No.
Shelmerdine, Elizabeth	Beaumaris A	Widow	W	4 Aug. 1666	1666/5
Shelmardine, Robert	Beaumaris A	Gent.	W	24 Jan. 1645/6	1645/2
Shurlock, Hugh	Rhuthun D	–	B I	13 April 1668	1668/126
Shurlocke, John	Rhuthun D	Gent.	W I	24 April 1693	1693/125
Simond, Cadwalader	Llanbedrycennin Cn	–	B I	18 March 1666/7	1666/58
Symond, Griffith	Dolgellau (Garthgynvor) Mr	–	W(2) I	[7 June 1679]	1679/35
Symon, Griffith	Dolgellau Mr	Yeoman	B* I*	27 Sept. 1699	1699/101
Symon, John	Dolgellau Mr	–	B	6 July 1680	1680/46
Simond, Robert	[ ] Mr	–	W I	8 Feb. 1667/8	1667/114
Symond, Robert	Llanfwrog (Bodyngharad) D	–	B I	10 May 1699	1699/131
Sims, Peter	Llandinam (Dethienidd) Mg	Yeoman	W I	29 Dec. 1676	1676/98
Smith, Katherine	Llanidloes (Glinne havren) Mg	Widow	W I	7 Dec. 1678	1678/90
Smith, David	Llanidloes Mg	Yeoman	W I B	21 June 1676	1676/105
Smyth, John (the elder)	[Llanbeblig] (Carnarvon) Cn	Gent.	W Db	9 Aug. 1645	1645/20
Smith, Katherine *as* Smith, Catherine					
Smyth, Richart	Llanidloes Mg	Yeoman	W I	[24 March 1695/6]	1695/111
Smith, Robert	Rhuthun D	–	W*	20 May 1636	1636/61
Smyth *alias* Ellis, Trephena	Llanarmon Cn	Widow[1]	W M	3 May 1689	1689/41
Smith, William	Beaumaris A	Smith	B	22 July 1681	1681/3
Southal, Francis	Tywyn (Bryn Glas) Mr	–	W I Rd	3 Oct. 1662	1662/75
Sparks, Jane	Llanynys D	Widow	W I C	[22 Feb. 1660/1]	1660/30
Sparrow, Anne	Beaumaris A	Spinster	W	1 July 1698	1698/1
Sparrow *alias* Owens, Grace	Llanddona (Cremlyn) A	Widow	B I	12 March 1690/1	1690/18
Sparrow, Henry	[Bodwrog] (Bodychan) A	Esq.	I	n.d.[2]	1695/1
Sparrow, Richard	Beaumaris (Ffordd deg) A	Gent.	B I(3)	25 Jan. 1674/5	1674/2
Spencer, Arthur	Conway Cn	Gent.	W I*	26 May 1666	1666/50
Spencer, George	Conway Cn	Gent.	W*	2 Nov. 1671	1671/56
Spicer, Jane	[Llanbeblig] (Caernarvon) Cn	Spinster	W	17 Oct. 1638	1638/36
Spicer ,William	[Llanbeblig] (Caernarvon) Cn	Gent.	W	17 Aug. 1641	1641/25
Spicer, William	[Llanbeblig] (Carnarvon) Cn	Gent.	W I Rd	20 July 1684	1684/34
Steele, Anne	Rhuthun D	Widow [of John Steele]	W	n.d.[3]	1670/176
Steele, John	Rhuthun D	Feltmaker	W I	5 April 1670	1670/177
Stephen *see* Stephens					

1 W *spinster*, although it contains a reference to *my Late Husband's goods*.
2 Inventory taken 18 June 1695.
3 Will dated 10 Oct. 1670.

NAME	PARISH & COUNTY	STATUS	DOCS. FILED	DATE OF PROBATE/ADMON.	REF. NO.
Stephens, Edward	Llangurig Mg	–	B I	28 Dec. 1699	1699/152
Stephens, Evan	Llangurig Mg	–	B I	7 Nov. 1696	1696/132
Stephen, Gabriel	Llanfwrog (Pen y coed) D	Yeoman	W I	3 July 1699	1699/130
Stephens, John	Holyhead A	–	B	18 Jan. 1686/7	1686/8
Stodart *alias* Kyffin, Grace	Conway Cn	Widow	W	15 June 1691	1691/48
Stodart *alias* Wynne, Mary	Gyffin Cn	Widow	B G	4 Jan. 1666/7	1666/53
Swancott, John	Trefeglwys Mg	Gent.	W	14 Oct. 1680	1680/84
Swancott, Phillippe (the elder)	Llanidloes (Pen y Castle, Treflyn) Mg	Gent.	W I	12 Dec. 1672	1672/128
Swancotte, Phillipp	Llanwnnog Mg	Cooper	W I	20 Jan. 1695/6	1695/114
Swancott, Richard (the elder)	Trefeglwys Mg	Gent.	W	[21 May 1673]	1673/74
Swancott, Richard	Trefeglwys (Argoed) Mg	Gent.	B I	15 Jan. 1686/7	1686/108
Swayne, John	Tywyn Mr	Clerk (Vicar of Tywyn)	B I	12 June 1663	1663/113
Swift *alias* Carre, Margaret	Holyhead A	Widow	W	14 May 1664	1664/11
Sydenham, Catherine	[Llantrisant] (Chwaen gôch) A	Widow	W I	14 July 1681	1681/18
Sydenham, John	Llantrisant (Chwaen Gogh) A	Gent.	W I(2) Ac	25 May 1672	1672/29
Symon(d) *see* Simond					
Tabias, Hugh	Llanddyfnan A	Yeoman	W I	26 June 1683	1683/6
Teage, David	Llanwnnog Mg	–	W* I	22 Nov. 1683	1683/105
Thelwall, Ambrose	[Llanfair Dyffryn Clwyd] (Bacherrig) D	Gent.	W*	[ ] 1698/9	1698/63
Thelwall, Anne	Rhuthun D	Widow	W* I	[6 April 1678]	1678/80
Thellwall, Dorothy	Llanynys D	Spinster	B I	17 Jan. 1677/8	1677/85
Thelwall, Edward	Llanbedr Dyffryn Clwyd D	Gent.	W	11 June 1669	1669/144
Thelwall, Gaynor	Llanfwrog D	Widow of Symon Thelwall, clerk	W I	4 June 1669	1669/150
Thelwall, Magdalen, *alias* Magdalen vch Rees *Wynne*	Llanynys (Maesmaen Cymro) D	Widow [of Thomas Thelwall]	W Al D B[1]	17 Jan. 1677/8	1677/86
Thelwall, Thomas	Llanynys (Maesmynkymro) D	–	W I	16 May 1677	1677/87
Thomas, Adam	[Llanbeblig] (Carnarvon) Cn	–	B	21 Feb. 1670/1	1670/80
Thomas, Anne	Llanidan A	–	B	16 Aug. 1677	1677/16
Thomas, Anne	Llandinam Mg	Widow	W* I	[5 April 1699]	1699/147
Thomas, Anthoney	Llangelynnin (Hendre) Mr	Esq.	W I	20 April 1695	1695/80
Thomas, Arthur	Trefriw Cn	–	W*	27 May 1640	1640/37

[1] This could also be a bond for the administration of the goods of Magdalen Thelwall, spinster, daughter of Magdalen Thelwall, widow.

Name	Parish & County	Status	Docs. Filed	Date of Probate/Admon.	Ref. No.
Thomas, Cadwalader	Llanaelhaearn Cn	Yeoman	W	24 June 1686	1686/45
Thomas, Katherin	Dolgellau Mr	–	B I	5 April 1666	1666/77
Thomas, David	Carno Mg	–	W	12 April 1641	1641/68
Thomas, David	Llanfair Dyffryn Clwyd (Coed y Talwrn) D	Yeoman	W Rd	24 March 1670/1	1670/169
Thomas, David	Llangurig (Rhywlas) Mg	Husbandman	W I	6 Feb. 1670/1	1670/185
Thomas, David	[Pentir] (Glasinfrin) Cn	–	W Al*	29 June 1671	1671/94
Thomas, David	Llangurig (Llan[ ]) Mg	–	I/G	16 Dec. 1680	1680/78
Thomas, Davidd	Llanfairfechan Cn	Yeoman	B I* Ac	16 Dec. 1691	1691/61 1693/51
Thomas, David	Llangeinwen (Clynog Vechan) A	Yeoman	W I	5 Feb. 1694/5	1694/24
Thomas, David	Llandwrog Cn	Yeoman	W I	20 March 1695/6	1695/40
Thomas, David	Llanynys (Esceibion) D	–	W	25 June 1695	1695/97
Thomas, Edward	Llanbedr Dyffryn Clwyd D	–	W Db	4 Aug. 1635	1635/42
Thomas, Edward	Llanfair-iuxta-Harlech Mr	Labourer	W	6 Feb. 1667/8	1667/102
Thomas, Edward	Llanfihangel-y-traethau (Meeneffordd) Mr	Yeoman	W	[12 Dec. 1674]	1674/50
Thomas, Edward	Llangurig (Glynbrochan) Mg	Gent.	W* I*	n.d.[1]	1689/91
Thomas, Ellen	Llanfihangel-ym-mhenrhos *alias* Penrhosllugwy A	Spinster	W*	28 Feb. 1641/2	1641/21
Thomas, Elin	Llanfihangel Ysgeifiog A	Widow	W	16 Jan. 1664/5	1664/26
Thomas, Elice	Llanwnnog Mg	Gent.	W B	27 June 1638	1638/91
Thomas, Ellis	Ynyscynhaearn Cn	–	B I G	7 Oct. 1699	1699/96
Thomas, Elizabeth	Llanfair Dyffryn Clwyd (Keelan) D	Widow	W B Rd	31 May 1661	1661/115
Thomas, Elizabeth	[Llanbeblig] (Carnarvon) Cn	Widow of Gruffyth Thomas, esq.	W	15 Dec. 1662	1662/42
Thomas, Elizabeth	Llangurig Mg	Widow	W I	16 June 1663	1663/140
Thomas, Elizabeth	[Llanwnnog] (Caersoos) Mg	Widow	W	[26 Oct. 1699]	1699/158
Thomas, Ellen *see* Thomas, Elin					
Thomas, Ellis *see* Thomas, Elis					
Thomas, Ievan	Llanelltud Mr	–	W	18 June 1645	1645/36
Thomas, Evan	Llanfihangel Ysgeifiog (Berw ycha) A	Yeoman	W I	13 April 1665	1665/17
Thomas, Evan	Ffestiniog Mr	–	I R	n.d.[2]	1683/62

1 Inventory taken 12 Aug. 1689.

2 Renunciation dated 3 March 1683/4.

Name	Parish & County	Status	Docs. Filed	Date of Probate/Admon.	Ref. No.
Thomas, Evan	Llanwnnog Mg	Labourer	B I	7 Aug. 1696	1696/138
Thomas, Gaynor	[Llanbeblig] (Carnarvon) Cn	Spinster	W	28 Aug. 1699	1699/53
Thomas, Gruffith	[Llanbeblig] (Caernarvon) Cn	Esq.	W B	8 Dec. 1647	1647/22
Thomas, Gryffith	Llanenddwyn Mr	Alehouse keeper	W	29 July 1668	1668/95
Thomas, Griffith	Aber Cn	Esq.	W* I* D	n.d.[1]	1676/33
Thomas, Griffith	Llandwrog / Betws Garmon Cn	Tailor	W I Rd	n.d.[2]	1690/56
Thomas, Griffith	Penmachno Cn	Yeoman	B I	19 May 1698	1698/48
Thomas, Henry	Cerrigceinwen A	–	B	10 Nov. 1671	1671/9
Thomas, Henery	Llandysilio A	–	B I	2 Jan. 1693/4	1693/9
Thomas, Howel	Llandysilio A	–	B	5 June 1671	1671/18
Thomas, Howel	Penrhos[llugwy] A	–	B	1 March 1685/6	1685/27
Thomas, Howell	Llanddwywe (Ganllwyd) Mr	Yeoman	W I	13 Sept. 1692	1692/75
Thomas, Hugh	Dolgellau Mr	Yeoman	I/G	16 July 1669	1669/114
Thomas, Hugh	Amlwch A	Smith	W* I*	19 June 1671	1671/3
Thomas, Hugh	Llangelynnin Mr	Gent.	B I	12 June 1688	1688/84
Thomas, Hugh	Llangïan Cn	Yeoman	W I	23 July 1690	1690/68
Thomas, Hugh	Llanbedr Niwbwrch (Cefn Bychan) A	Yeoman	W I Rd	29 Aug. 1692	1692/8
Thomas, Hugh	Llangelynnin (Tu Cerrig, Bodgadfan) Mr	Yeoman	W/I	6 Jan. 1697/8	1697/50
Thomas, Humphrey	Llangïan Cn	Yeoman	W	1 Aug. 1687	1687/67
Thomas, Ievan *see* Thomas, Evan					
Thomas, James	Llandinam Mg	–	W	14 April 1646	1646/31
Thomas, Jane	Llanrhaeadr-yng-Nghinmeirch (Astrad, Segrwyd) D	–	W I	14 Oct. 1682	1682/86
Thomas, Jane	[Llanbeblig] (Carnarvon) Cn	Widow of William Thomas, esq.	W I	1 June 1685	1685/34
Thomas, Jane	Llanbedr Niwbwrch A	–	B	8 Sept. 1692	1692/9
Thomas, Jasper	Holyhead A	Mariner	W I	2 June 1684	1684/7
Thomas, Jenkin	Llangurig Mg	–	B	6 Aug. 1685	1685/116
Thomas, John	Llandinam Mg	–	W	12 April 1641	1641/71
Thomas, John	Penmynydd A	Labourer	W	n.d.	1641/20
Thomas, John	Aber Cn	Clerk (Parson of Aber)	W Rd	15 March 1642/3	1642/19
Thomas, John	Llaniestyn Cn	–	W	17 Feb. 1642/3	1642/26

[1] Inventory taken 1 Feb. 1676 (29 Chas. II); depositions dated 2 Feb. 1681–22 June 1682.
[2] Inventory exhibited 28 Jan. 1689; bond for redelivery of will dated 23 May 1690.

Name	Parish & County	Status	Docs. Filed	Date of Probate/Admon.	Ref. No.
Thomas, John	Llangaffo A	–	B I	12 Feb. 1661/2	1661/19
Thomas, John	Llanfair Dyffryn Clwyd (Coed y talwrn) D	–	W*	n.d.[1]	1662/86
Thomas, John	Clocaenog D	–	W I	27 May 1664	1664/107
Thomas, John	Llaneilian (Berrech) A	Husbandman/ Yeoman	W* I	1 Oct. 1666	1666/14
Thomas, John	Llantrisant A	Yeoman	W	28 Dec. 1668	1668/24
Thomas, John	Clynnog Cn	–	W	25 Feb. 1669/70	1669/65
Thomas, John	Llanfihangel-y-Pennant Cn	–	I/G	19 Aug. 1673	1673/39
Thomas, John	Aber Cn	–	B I	26 March 1677	1677/20
Thomas, John	Llanbedr Dyffryn Clwyd D	–	W I	5 March 1677/8	1677/73
Thomas, John	Llangwyfan D	Weaver	W I	29 July 1678	1678/70
Thomas, John	Llandyrnog D	–	B	25 Feb. 1679/80	1679/52
Thomas, John	Llanllyfni (Eithinog) Cn	Weaver	W I Al	n.d.[2]	1683/49
Thomas, John	Beaumaris A	Gent.	W I B	10 Oct. 1684	1684/4
Thomas, John	Llanystumdwy Cn	–	B	23 Sept. 1686	1686/63
Thomas, John	Llandinam Mg	Yeoman	W I	23 July 1691	1691/129
Thomas, John	Trawsfynydd Mr	–	W I	28 July 1691	1691/101
Thomas, John	Llanynghenedl A	Yeoman/ Shoemaker	B I Db	28 March 1692	1692/26
Thomas, John	Dolgellau Mr	Yeoman	B I	11 July 1699	1699/102
Thomas, Katherin *as* Thomas, Catherine					
Thomas, Lewis	Llandudno Cn	Yeoman	W I*	4 Jan. 1669/70	1669/76
Thomas, Lewis	Llanidan (Myfyrian) A	–	W	27 Sept. 1671	1671/31
Thomas, Lewis	Llanfaelog A	Weaver	W*	15 Feb. 1676/7	1676/12
Thomas, Lewis	[ ]	–	I	n.d.[3]	1682/108
Thomas, Lewis	Llanidloes Mg	–	W I	[11 Nov. 1692]	1692/126
Thomas, Lewis	Dolgellau Mr	Miller	W I	14 Sept. 1694	1694/70
Thomas, Lewis	Llangelynnin Mr	–	R	n.d.[4]	1698/56
Thomas, Lowry	Llanfechell A	Widow	W I	20 May 1673	1673/9
Thomas, Magdalen	Bodedern A	–	I	n.d.[5]	1699/7
Thomas *alias* Morgan, Mahallt	Llangurig (Glynbrochan) Mg	Widow	B I	26 June 1692	1692/120

1 Will dated 20 Dec. 166[2].
2 Inventory taken 8 Feb. 1683[/4].
3 Inventory taken 22 July 1682.
4 Renunciation dated 25 May 1698.
5 Inventory taken 27 Dec. 1699.

Name	Parish & County	Status	Docs. Filed	Date of Probate/Admon.	Ref. No.
Thomas, Margaret	Caerhun Cn	Widow	W Al D	2 March 1687/8	1687/42
Thomas, Margerie	Llanbedrycennin Cn	Widow	W	15 July 1670	1670/99
Thomas, Marie	Llangristiolus A	Widow	W	9 Feb. 1671/2	1671/30
Thomas, Mary	Llangoed A	–	B	3 Nov. 1692	1692/22
Thomas, Mathanwy *see* Lewis, William	Llaneilian A				
Thomas, Meredith	Llanidloes (Manleth) Mg	–	W I	2 Aug. 1665	1665/107
Thomas, Michael	Trewalchmai A	Yeoman	B* I*	3 June 1699	1699/38
Thomas, Morgan	Llanegryn (Peniarth) Mr	Yeoman	W(2)	18 July 1667	1667/95
Thomas, Moris	Llandinam Mg	–	I/G	21 Sept. 1665	1665/99
Thomas, Maurice	Llanrhaeadr-yng-Nghinmeirch (Segroit) D	–	W I	24 April 1671	1671/130
Thomas, Oliver	Tywyn (Tyno) Mr	Yeoman	W I C	12 May 1685	1685/88
Thomas, Owen	Llanrug (Bodruall) Cn	–	W	19 Aug. 1645	1645/34
Thomas, Owen	Mellteyrn Cn	Miller	W I	28 March 1663	1663/73
Thomas, Owen	Llangelynnin Cn	Yeoman	W B Rd	1 Aug. 1670	1670/113
Thomas, Owen	Llanddeusant A	Fuller	W	27 June 1677	1677/9
Thomas, Owen	Llanfechell A	Labourer	B I	1 Jan. 1694/5	1694/19
Thomas, Rees	Llandygái Cn	–	W	20 Oct. 1641	1641/35
Thomas, Rees	Llandudno Cn	–	W B	26 Jan. 1645/6	1645/25
Thomas, Rees	Llandinam (Dethienidd) Mg	–	W I	16 June 1663	1663/135
Thomas, Rees	Dolwyddelan Cn	Yeoman	I	n.d.[1]	1682/39
Thomas, Rees	Llandinam Mg	Miller	W I	21 March 1693/4	1693/134
Thomas, Richard	Llantrisant A	–	W B	4 March 1642/3	1642/14
Thomas, Richard	Gyffin Cn	Yeoman	W B	26 Dec. 1646	1646/17
Thomas, Richard	Beaumaris A	Gent.	W	11 July 1662	1662/3
Thomas, Richard	Aber Cn	Esq.	W	21 Feb. 1664/5	1664/51
Thomas, Richard	Llangristiolus A	–	B	3 Sept. 1667	1667/34
Thomas, Richard	Llantrisant A	Yeoman	W	23 March 1669/70	1669/42
Thomas, Richard	Penmynydd A	–	B	3 Jan. 1670/1	1670/54
Thomas, Richard	Amlwch A	Yeoman	B I	16 July 1690	1690/4
Thomas, Richard	Llanddeiniolen Cn	Servant	W I	25 March 1692	1692/50
Thomas, Richard	Llanrug Cn	Yeoman	B I	1 Sept. 1693	1693/57
Thomas, Richard	Llanddeiniolen Cn	Yeoman	W I	22 Dec. 1698	1698/33
Thomas, Robert	Llanelidan D	–	B I	5 June 1665	1665/82
Thomas, Robert	Clynnog Cn	–	W* I[2]	19 Nov. 1670	1670/85

1 Inventory taken 2 Nov. 1682.

2 The inventory was loose in the 1670 bundle. It could belong to either the above Robert Thomas or to Robert ap Thomas of Llanfair Dyffryn Clwyd (q.v.).

Name	Parish & County	Status	Docs. Filed	Date of Probate/Admon.	Ref. No.
Thomas, Robert	Bangor Cn	–	B	6 Sept. 1672	1672/41
Thomas, Robert	Ffestiniog (Teilie bach) Mr	Yeoman	W I	19 May 1676	1676/72
Thomas, Robert	Rhuthun D	Feltmaker	W* I*	21 Jan. 1680/1	1680/72
Thomas, Robert	Pentir Cn	–	W I	23 Sept. 1681	1681/61
Thomas, Robert	Llanrhychwyn Cn	–	I	n.d.[1]	1683/52
Thomas, Robert	Beddgelert Cn	Yeoman	B I	21 April 1685	1685/33
Thomas, Robert	Trawsfynydd Mr	Gent.	W I	5 Oct. 1692	1692/91
Thomas, Robert	Llanfair-is-gaer Cn	–	B I	11 May 1694	1694/54
Thomas, Robert	Llanaber (Fridd ddû) Mr	–	W/I	8 Nov. 1696	1696/95
Thomas, Roger	Conway Cn	Smith	B I	4 April 1691	1691/50
Thomas, Rowland	Aber Cn	–	W I B	4 April 1662	1662/32
Thomas, Rowland	Llansadwrn A	–	B I	14 June 1673	1673/15
Thomas, Rowland	Aberdaron (Hendre) Cn	–	W I C	[23 Feb. 1691/2]	1691/39
Thomas, Samuell	Llanwnnog Mg	Fuller/ Clothworker	W I*	[19 Sept. 1662]	1662/107
Thomas, Stephen	Llanfwrog D	Gent.	W I	30 Oct. 1691	1691/110
Thomas, William	Llanfihangel-y-Pennant Cn	–	W*	11 Oct. 1638	1638/43
Thomas, William	[Llangeinwen] (Quyrt grange) A	Esq.	W B	28 July 1638	1638/20
Thomas, William	Heneglwys A	Gent.	W Rd	10 Sept. 1667	1667/7
Thomas, William	Clynnog Cn	–	I L	15 June 1668	1668/44
Thomas, William	Llanfwrog D	–	W	19 March 1669/70	1669/151
Thomas, William	Llanelidan (Bryn Cymme) D	–	W	30 July 1677	1677/77
Thomas, William	Llanfihangel Tre'r-beirdd A	Yeoman	B I	16 May 1682	1682/21
Thomas, William	Llanfair [ ][2] Cn	–	B	22 Jan. 1684/5	1684/46
Thomas, William	Llanrhychwyn (Ardde) Cn	–	B I	15 May 1688	1688/56
Thomas, William	Clynnog Cn	Clerk	B	27 April 1691	1691/47
Thomas, William	Llansadwrn A	Gent.	W I	28 Sept. 1692	1692/25
Thomas, William	Llan-faes A	–	W I	25 May 1694	1694/17
Thomas, William	Llanfechell A	–	B I	28 Feb. 1699/1700	1699/19
Thompson *see* Tompson					
Tibbots *see* Tybbots					
Tickons, Elizabeth	Beaumaris A	Widow of Thomas David, tailor	W I	23 July 1663	1663/4
Tilsley, Ellnor	Trefeglwys Mg	Widow	W	16 June 1663	1663/154
Tylsley, John	Llandinam Mg	–	W I	29 Nov. 1693	1693/135
Tobias *see* Tabias					

1 Inventory taken 19 Sept. 1683.
2 Llanfair-is-gaer or Llanfairfechan.

Name	Parish & County	Status	Docs. Filed	Date of Probate/Admon.	Ref. No.
Tompson, John	Llanynys (Trevechan) D	Gent.	I/G	14 April 1671	1671/134
Tompson, Richard	Llanynys (Trevechan) D	Gent.	W I	5 Dec. 1692	1692/103
Tomsonne, Robert	Llanynys (Trevechan) D	Gent.	W B	22 June 1638	1638/86
Trygan, Herbertt	Bryncroes Cn	Gent.	B	16 Feb. 1664/5	1664/55
Trygarn, Jane	Tudweiliog [Hirdre] Cn	[Widow of Francis Jones, gent.]	W	19 Oct. 1683	1683/57
Trygarne, Richard	Bryncroes (Trygarne) Cn	–	W	17 June 1667	1667/54
Trygarn, Richard	[Bryncroes] (Trygarne) Cn	Gent.	W	[1 Aug. 1683]	1683/25
Tudur, Catherine	Llanfwrog D	–	W* I	20 Nov. 1661	1661/116
Tudeyr, Hugh	Llanaber (Egryn) Mr	Gent.	W Rd	9 July 1644	1644/32
Tudor, Madam Jane	Llanaber Mr	–	B	1 Sept. 1687	1687/96
Tudyre, Thomas	Rhuthun D	Yeoman	W I	16 May 1693	1693/126
Tydder, William	Llanaber (Egrin) Mr	Gent.	W	23 Nov. 1669	1669/118
Turbridge, Anne	Llanbedr Dyffryn Clwyd D	–	W	8 June 1682	1682/82
Turbridge, John	Aberffraw A	Gent.	B I	8 Jan. 1693/4	1693/1
Turner, Edward	Llandinam Mg	Yeoman	B I	11 Nov. 1691	1691/130
Turner, Richard	Llandinam Mg	–	W I	23 June 1674	1674/59
Turner, Thomas	[Llanrwst] (Gwyder) Cn	Student & Practitioner of Physic	W*	17 May 1673	1673/42
Twisleton, Marie	Clynnog (Llyar) Cn	Widow	W* I	3 Aug. 1676	1676/41
Twiston, Katherine	Llandyrnog D	–	B	25 Sept. 1686	1686/93
Tybbots, Richard	Tywyn Mr	Husbandman	W* I	29 Sept. 1680	1680/60
Tyrer, Anne	Beaumaris A	Widow	W Rd	7 May 1662	1662/4
Vaughan, Anne	Llanbeblig (Carnarvon) Cn	Widow	W I(2) Db* Al* D	21 July 1686	1686/39
Vaughan, Arthur	Ysbyty [Ifan] (Pennant) Cn	Gent.	W I C	7 Nov. 1672	1672/85
Vaughan, Kadwalader	[Llanbeblig] (Carnarvon) Cn	Gent.	B	6 March 1670/1	1670/81
Vaughan, Catherine	[Llanffinan] (Hirdrevaig) A	Widow	W	n.d.	1692/16
Vaughan, Katherine vch Gruffith	Llanrhaeadr-yng-Nghinmeirch (Trevibychen) D	Widow	W	9 March 1647/8	1647/49
Vaughan, David	Carno Mg	Gent.	I/G	10 May 1665	1665/90
Vaughan, David	Rhuthun D	Mercer	W R L	28 Dec. 1669	1669/156
Vaughan, David	Carno Mg	Gent.	W	11 April 1684	1684/107
Vaughan, Edward	Conway Cn	Gent.	B	4 Sept. 1696	1696/45
Vaughan, Ellen	Llanystumdwy (Aberkin) Cn	Widow	W I	31 July 1680	1680/40
Vaughan, Ellice	Llandinam [Maesmawre] Mg	[Yeoman]	I/G	17 May 1669	1669/164

Name	Parish & County	Status	Docs. Filed	Date of Probate/Admon.	Ref. No.
Vauchan, Elisabeth	Ynyscynhaearn Cn	Widow	W B	27 July 1663	1663/77
Vaughan, Evan	Carno Mg	Gent.	I/G	10 May 1665	1665/91
Vaughan, Gruffyth	Llanllyfni (Pant Dû) Cn	Gent.	W I	23 March 1663/4	1663/68
Vaughan, Henry	Aber Cn	Gent.	R	n.d.[1]	1672/36
Vaughan, Howell David	Carno Mg	Gent.	B I	6 June 1661	1661/126
Vaughan, John	Aber-erch Cn	–	B*	17 Jan. 1662/3	1662/36
Vaughan, John	[Llangybi][2] (Glasfryn) Cn	Gent.	B I M	2 Dec. 1664	1664/72
Vaughan, Jonnett vch Griffith	Llangristiolus A	Widow	W* Al*	10 Feb. 1636/7	1636/15
Vaughan, Juan	Llandinam (Maesmawre) Mg	Widow of Ellis Vaughan, yeoman	W I	28 Sept. 1669	1669/165
Vaughan, Kadwalader *as* Vaughan, Cadwaladr					
Vaughan, Martha	[ ]	–	I	n.d.[3]	1669/177
Vaughan, Moris	Carno Mg	–	B I	26 Jan. 1696/7	1696/126
Vaughan, Owen	Beaumaris A	Gent.	W	13 July 1643	1643/2
Vaughan, Owen	Llanystumdwy (Aberkain) Cn	Gent.	W I	[21 March 1673/4]	1673/43
Vaughan, Richard	[Llandudwen] (Nyffryn) Cn	Gent.	W	9 April 1648	1648/11
Vaughan, Richard John	Trawsfynydd (Brynclynnog) Mr	Gent.	W* I	1 Aug. 1662	1662/74
Vaughan, Robert	Llanystumdwy Cn	–	B	6 Jan. 1671/2	1671/89
Vaughan, Rowland	Pennal Mr	Gent.	B*	17 April 1678	1678/51
Vaughan, Theoder	Dolgellau (Caerunwch) Mr	Gent.	W* I	n.d.[4]	1672/86
Vauchan, Vespatian	[Llanbeblig] (Carnarvon) Cn	–	B	20 April 1670	1670/82
Vaughan, William	[Llanddwywe] (Corsygedol) Mr	Esq.	B*	20 [ ] 1670	1670/144
Vaughan, William	Tywyn (Cathley) Mr	Esq.	W(2) I R(2) B(2) Rd(2)	23 Sept. 1678	1678/58
Vaughan, William John	Bryncroes Cn	–	W I	28 June 1661	1661/47
Vaughan, Ynner	Dolgellau Mr	Gent.	B I	28 July 1691	1691/77
Wageworth, Griffith	Rhuthun D	Tanner	W	23 Oct. 1685	1685/106
Walley *alias* Bulkley, Elen	Llanddona (Cremlin) A	Widow	W*	13 Jan. 1669/70	1669/20
Walter, Thomas	Llanwnnog Mg	Husbandman	B I	6 April 1663	1663/150
Warley, Anne	Llanidloes Mg	Widow	W I	2 Aug. 1682	1682/106

[1] Renunciation dated 26 April 1672.

[2] Endorsed *Llanarmon*.

[3] Inventory taken 5 Nov. 1669.

[4] Will dated 11 Nov. 1672; inventory taken 14 June 1673.

Name	Parish & County	Status	Docs. Filed	Date of Probate/Admon.	Ref. No.
Warley, Richard	[Llanidloes][1] Mg	–	I/G	17 Sept. 1689	1689/95
Warmincham, William	Llanfechell A	–	W I	27 Oct. 1661	1661/15
Watkin, David	Llanbedr[-goch] A	Yeoman	W I	18 May 1696	1696/7
Watkin, Harry	Rhodogeidio/Llannerch-y-medd A	Gent.	W(3)	4 Dec. 1665	1665/25
Watkin, John	[Llanbadrig] (Clygyrog) A	Widower	W/I* B*	15 Oct. 1670	1670/13
Watkin, John	Rhosbeirio A	Yeoman	B* I	24 May 1698	1698/16
Watkin, William	Llanaber Mr	–	B I	17 April 1677	1677/53
Watckin, William	Llanbedr[-goch] A	–	W I	17 Aug. 1688	1688/10
Watkin, William	Llanfechell A	–	B	2 Nov. 1699	1699/20
Watts, Juan	Llandinam Mg	Spinster	W	12 April 1641	1641/72
Watts, Thomas	Maenol Bangor Cn	Gent.	B I	17 July 1690	1690/43
Whyte, Barbara	Llanedwen A	Spinster	W Cd I	8 Jan. 1689/90	1689/10
White, Ellin	Llandygwnning Cn	–	B G	30 Jan. 1672/3	1672/62
White, Hannah	Llandygwnning Cn	–	B	30 Jan. 1672/3	1672/63
White, John	Llandygwnning Cn	Gent.	B	28 May 1661	1661/68
Whyte, John	Llandygwnning (Neugwl) Cn	Gent.	W I Rd	15 May 1696	1696/61
Whyte, Magdalen	Llan-faes A	Spinster	W	4 Sept. 1647	1647/10
White, Robert	Llangwnnadl (Trefgraig) Cn	Gent.	B I	10 Feb. 1667/8	1667/73
Whittington, Joan	Llanwnnog Mg	Widow	B I	3 May 1677	1677/92
Whittington, Richard	Llanwnnog (Weeg) Mg	Gent.	W I M	23 Oct. 1672	1672/132
Wiggin *alias* Williams, Jane	[Llanbeblig] (Carnarvon) Cn	Widow	B I	18 Feb. 1694/5	1694/43
Wiggin, Richard	[Llanbeblig] (Carnarvon) Cn	–	W* I	2 May 1671	1671/53
William *see* Williams					
William, Annes	Llanfachreth Mr	Spinster	W/I	22 Sept. 1697	1697/47
Williams, Alice, *alias* Alice vch John	Pentraeth A	Widow	B I	23 Jan. 1666/7	1666/33
Williams, Alls	Llanbadrig A	–	W	7 Oct. 1668	1668/9
Williams, Ales	Llangynhafal D	Widow	W I	n.d.[2]	1683/87
William, Ales	Dolgellau Mr	Widow	W	15 Sept. 1687	1687/91
Williams, Amydas	Llechgynfarwy A	Weaver	W I	[28 Sept. 1676]	1676/26
Williams, Anne	Llanrhaeadr-yng-Nghinmeirch D	Widow	W* I* B	10 May 1694	1694/109
Williams, Anne	Llantrisant (Chwaen) A	Spinster	B	1 March 1694/5	1694/28
William, Annes *as* Williams, Agnes					

1 Supplied from the bishops transcripts of the parish register of Llanidloes, 1689.

2 Inventory taken 27 Sept. 1683.

Name	Parish & County	Status	Docs. Filed	Date of Probate/Admon.	Ref. No.
Williams, Arthur	Bryncroes (Bron y llwyd) Cn	Gent.	W I Rd	16 March 1667/8	1667/55
Williams, Beniamin	Clynnog Cn	Yeoman	W	12 Feb. 1677[1]	1677/28
William, Cadwalader	Llanfachreth (Tyddyn Mawr) Mr	–	I/G	11 Feb. 1683/4	1683/70
William, Cadwalader	Penmachno Cn	–	W I	27 April 1687	1687/82
Williams, Catharine	Conway Cn	Widow	W	8 Aug. 1674	1674/17
Williams, Katherine	[Caerhun] (Biart) Cn	Wife of William Williams, gent.	B	18 Jan. 1686/7	1686/35
William *alias* Lewis, Catherine	Llanidloes Mg	–	B	11 Oct. 1697	1697/68
Williams, Cuningsby	Trefriw Cn	–	B	26 April 1689	1689/61
Williams, David	Rhuthun D	–	W*	9 April 1664	1664/120
Williams, David	Conway Cn	Gent.	W I Rd	3 July 1677	1677/29
William, David	Trefriw (Ardde) Cn	–	B I	23 July 1677	1677/50
William, David	Carno Mg	Yeoman	W I	n.d.[2]	1686/104
Williams, David, *alias* David William ap Evan	Aberffraw A	Labourer	W	17 Aug. 1689	1689/1
William, David	Llangelynnin Mr	–	B	30 June 1693	1693/89
William, David	Llandinam (Dethienydd) Mg	Yeoman	W I	9 Feb. 1694/5	1694/119
Williams, Edmond	Llangeinwen A	–	W	14 April 1664	1664/32
Williams, Edmund	Caerhun (Penylan) Cn	Gent.	W I	19 April 1672	1672/46
Williams, Edward	Llanynys D	–	B	30 May 1665	1665/87
Williams, Edward	Llanfairfechan Cn	–	B	12 Aug. 1668	1668/63
Williams, Ellen	Trefdraeth A	Widow	B	19 Dec. 1664	1664/49
Williams *alias* Hughes, Ellin	Beaumaris A	Widow	B I	18 Feb. 1669/70	1669/2
Williams, Ellin	Bryncroes (Bron y llwyf) Cn	Spinster	W Rd	12 Oct. 1669	1669/60
Williames, Ellen	Llanfaelrhys (Millionyth) Cn	Widow	W(2)	[4 Aug.] 1669	1669/88
Williams, Elin	[Llanddyfnan] (Hendrehowel) A	–	B	13 June 1670	1670/27
Williams, Elis	Llandecwyn (Coetu) Mr	–	W I	16 Jan. 1670/1	1670/143
Williams, Ellis	Dolwyddelan (Penamme) Cn	–	W I	9 Oct. 1685	1685/40
Williams, Elyzabeth	Llanbedrycennin Cn	Widow	W*	15 Oct. 1661	1661/62
Williams, Elizabeth	Llandwrog Cn	Widow	B	19 Aug. 1665	1665/43
Williams, Elizabeth	Aberffraw A	–	B	18 July 1668	1668/1
Williams, Elizabeth	Llanllechid Cn	Widow	W I	[13 Dec. 1690]	1690/70
Williams, Elizabeth	Llanbeblig Cn	Spinster	B	9 May 1699	1699/67
William *alias* Purscell, Elizabeth	Llangurig Mg	Widow [of George Pursel]	W I	13 July 1699	1699/153

[1] *1676/7* or *1677/8*? Will dated 10 Jan. 1677; executrix sworn 12 Feb. 1676.

[2] Endorsed *1686/7*; inventory taken 29 Aug. 1686.

Name	Parish & County	Status	Docs. Filed	Date of Probate/Admon.	Ref. No.
Williams, Ellen/Ellin *see* Williams, Elin					
Williams, Ellis *see* Williams, Elis					
Williams, Emme	Llantrisant (Nantanogg) A	Widow	W	n.d.	1682/27
William, Evan	Carno Mg	Yeoman	W*	11 Jan. 1671/2	1671/140
William, Evan	Trefeglwys Mg	–	W I	[9 June 1674]	1674/66
William, Evan	Llanaber Mr	–	B I	21 Oct. 1677	1677/54
William, Evan	Trawsfynydd Mr	–	W	[29 March 1677]	1677/65
Williams, Evan	Llanystumdwy (Glan y llynnai) Cn	Yeoman	W I	15 Nov. 1689	1689/59
Williams, Foulk	Caerhun Cn	Yeoman	W*	n.d.[1]	1681/33
Williams, Frances	Llanenddwyn Mr	Spinster	W	24 July 1691	1691/90
Williams, Frederick	Llangybi Cn	–	W I	27 Feb. 1684/5	1684/50
Williams, Gaynor	Llanfechell (Groes fechan, Caerdegog) A	Widow	W I G	24 April 1665	1665/15
Williams, Gaynor	Gyffin (Llechen-uchaf) Cn	Spinster	W I Al S	11 March 1696/7	1696/51
Williams, Grace	[Caerhun] (Biart) Cn	Widow	B I	18 Jan. 1686/7	1686/36
Williams, Griffith	Llanfairfechan Cn	–	W	29 Dec. 1645	1645/27
Williams, Gryffyth	Llannor (Tu yn y Coed) Cn	Gent.	W Cd C	26 March 1661	1661/81
William, Griffith	Llanenddwyn Mr	Gent.	W* I Al*	[27 Oct.] 1664	1664/95
William, Griffith	Llanaber Mr	Gent.	W Rd	n.d.[2]	1666/82
Williams, Sir Gruffyth	[Bangor] (Vaynol) Cn	Baronet	B I	2 Aug. 1669	1669/59
William, Gryffyth	Llanenddwyn Mr	Weaver	W* I*	28 Jan. 1675/6	1675/43
William, Griffith	Llanddwywe Mr	Gent.	B I	16 June 1676	1676/75
William, Griffyth	Bodfean Cn	–	W I	7 July 1688	1688/35
Williams, Gruffyth	Llanrug Cn	Yeoman	W I B	24 Oct. 1690	1690/76
Williams, Gwen, *alias* Gwen vch William Prees Wynne	[Llanfechell] (Bottenniel) A	Widow [of Griffith John Griffith]	W	3 Dec. 1670	1670/11
William, Gwen	Pennal Mr	–	B	18 June 1684	1684/74
Williams, Henery	[ ]	–	I	n.d.[3]	1681/110
Williams, Henry	Llanfaglan Cn	–	B	9 Nov. 1683	1683/40
Williams, Henry	Llanfairfechan Cn	Yeoman	W I	19 May 1685	1685/50
Williams, Henry	Clynnog Cn	Apothecary	B I* C	18 March 1690/1	1690/49
Williams, Henry	Llangoed A	Gent.	W I	17 Aug. 1691	1691/28

1 Will dated 9 Feb. 1681[/2]; endorsed *1680/1*.

2 Will dated 14 Feb. 1666.

3 Inventory taken 8 May 1680; exhibited 1681.

Name	Parish & County	Status	Docs. Filed	Date of Probate/Admon.	Ref. No.
Williams, Henry	Llanbedr Niwbwrch (Abermenai) A	Ferryman	B I	31 Jan. 1692/3	1692/10
Williams, Henry	Llanaber Mr	Gent.	W I	12 July 1694	1694/78
Williames, Henery	Bodewryd A	–	B I	21 July 1698	1698/2
Williames, Harry	Penllech Cn	Yeoman	W I	7 July 1699	1699/87
William, Howell	Llanegryn Mr	Yeoman	W I	13 Feb. 1683/4	1683/67
William, Howel	Llanddwywe Mr	–	W I	n.d.[1]	1687/98
Williams, Hugh	Caerhun (Byart) Cn	Gent.	W I	4 March 1660/1	1660/11
William, Hugh	Llanbedr Mr	–	B	27 Aug. 1664	1664/88
Williams, Hugh	Llanfairfechan Cn	Gent.	W I	9 Nov. 1667	1667/70
Williams, Hugh	Llangoed A	Gent.	W I*	12 Nov. 1672	1672/24
Williams, Hugh	Llanfair Mathafarn Eithaf A	–	B	18 April 1681	1681/10
Williams, Hugh	Aber Cn	–	B I	11 June 1684	1684/25
Williams, Hugh	Llanddaniel-fab A	–	B*	20 May 1685	1685/16
Williams, Hugh	Llangaffo A	Gent.	W I* C	20 Dec. 1686	1686/16
Williams, Hugh	Llantrisant (Chwaen) A	Esq.	W R	1 March 1694/5	1694/29
Williams, Hugh	Llandygái Cn	–	B	11 June 1695	1695/44
Williams, Hugh	Tudweiliog (H[i]redre) Cn	Gent.	B I	2 March 1695/6	1695/60
William, Humphrey	Llanfihangel-y-Pennant (Keninvonidd) Cn	Labourer	W I	8 March 1678/9	1678/32
Williams, Humphrey	Llannor Cn	–	W	14 Oct. 1692	1692/58
Williams, Humphrey, *alias* Humphrey ap William Humphrey	Llanddeiniolen Cn	Yeoman	W I	30 Sept. 1696	1696/64
William, Humphrey	Dolgellau Mr	Tailor/Yeoman	W I	4 Jan. 1699/1700	1699/103
William, Humphrey	Dwygyfylchi Cn	–	B	21 June 1699	1699/59
Williams, Jane	Llandyrnog D	Widow	W Rd	31 May 1662	1662/85
Williams, Jane	Trefdraeth A	Widow	B L	15 Feb. 1672/3	1672/34
William, Jane	Llandinam Mg	Widow	W I	15 Jan. 1677/8	1677/90
Williams, Jane	Llandrygarn (Tryfill) A	Widow	W	8 May 1682	1682/10
Williams *alias* Wiggin, Jane	[Llanbeblig] (Carnarvon) Cn	Widow	B I	18 Feb. 1694/5	1694/43
Williams, Jane	Llanengan Cn	Widow	W	17 Aug. 1699	1699/76
Williams, Jeffrey	Pentir Cn	Gent.	W(2)	n.d.[2]	1669/111
William, Jenkin	Llanidloes Mg	Glover	W I	1 Dec. 1669	1669/173
William, John	Llanegryn Mr	–	W	10 July 1640	1640/43
Williams, John	Llantrisant (Chwaen) A	Gent.	W I	20 Aug. 1661	1661/25

[1] Will dated 4 Aug. 1687.
[2] Will dated 28 Feb. 1669[/70].

Name	Parish & County	Status	Docs. Filed	Date of Probate/Admon.	Ref. No.
William, John	Llanllyfni Cn	–	B I*	22 Aug. 1662	1662/52
William, John	Aber-erch Cn	–	B	30 Sept. 1663	1663/33
Williams, John	Llanfaelrhys Cn	–	G(2)	11 July 1664	1664/67
Williams, John	Dolgellau Mr	–	W	4 April 1666	1666/78
Williams, John	[Llanfaelrhys] (Meillionydd) Cn	Esq.	W C Rd	10 July 1666	1666/63
Williams, John	Bangor (Maes y Keirchie) Cn	Gent.	W Rd	6 Nov. 1668	1668/34
Williams, John	Llanrug Cn	–	B I	10 Dec. 1668	1668/70
William, John	Llanfaglan Cn	Yeoman	W I	14 Jan. 1669/70	1669/89
William, John	Llanrhuddlad A	–	W*	16 Feb. 1670/1	1670/51
William, John	[Ynyscynhaearn] (Garreg-velen) Cn	–	I	n.d.[1]	1670/130
Williams, John	Gyffin (Merchlyn) Cn	Corviser	B I Db	7 Feb. 1671/2	1671/60
Williams, John	Derwen D	–	W	16 Jan. 1673/4	1673/60
Williams, John	Betws [Cedewain][2] Mg	–	W R B	11 Feb. 1675/6	1675/72
Williams, John	Clynnog Cn	Yeoman	B I	24 Feb. 1681/2	1681/36
Williams, John, *alias* John ap William Hughes	Llanarmon / Llanystumdwy Cn	–	B* I	2 Feb. 1681/2	1681/43
Williams, John	Llannor Cn	–	B I	14 April 1680[3]	1681/54
Williams, John	Llanrhaeadr-yng-Nghinmeirch (Cader) D	–	W I	25 Nov. 1681	1681/99
Williams, John	Nefyn Cn	–	W	[27 Jan. 1681/2]	1681/59
Williams, John	[Llangadwaladr] (Llanfeirian) A	–	W I Al	26 Oct. 1682	1682/22
Williams, John	Llandyrnog (Spethyd) D	Yeoman	W I B	26 July 1687	1687/116
William, John	Trawsfynydd Mr	Yeoman	W I B	1 Sept. 1687	1687/103
Williams, John	Llanfihangel-y-Pennant (Llecheiddior) Cn	Gent.	W Rd	25 Oct. 1688	1688/53
Williames, John	Penmachno (Bwlch y maen) Cn	Gent.	W*	11 Oct. 1693	1693/66
Williams, John	Llanllechid Cn	Yeoman	B I	29 Jan. 1696/7	1696/78
Williams, John	Penrhos[llugwy] (Bodafon) A	Gent.	B* I R	29 June 1696	1696/25
William, John	Maentwrog Mr	–	W I R	22 June 1698	1698/58
William, John	Ffestiniog Mr	Yeoman	B I(2)	27 Nov. 1699	1699/106
Williams, John	Llangristiolus A	Gent.	W I	9 Aug. 1699	1699/25
Williams, Jonett	Llangefni A	Spinster	W I	2 May 1685	1685/22
Williams, Katherine *see* Williams, Catherine					

1 Inventory taken 5 Oct. 1670.

2 Normally within the jurisdiction of the St. Asaph Consistory Court.

3 Recte *1681*? Endorsed *1680* and *1681*; inventory taken 7 April 1681.

Name	Parish & County	Status	Docs. Filed	Date of Probate/Admon.	Ref. No.
Williams, Lewis	Llanidan A	Clerk	W I	25 May 1666	1666/27
Williams, Lewis	Llanddeiniolen Cn	–	B I	2 Feb. 1685/6	1685/48
Williams, Lewis	Rhiw Cn	Yeoman	B I	19 June 1690	1690/82
Williams, Lewis	Llanfechell[1] (Cavnan) A	Gent./Carpenter	W I Al	3 June 1692	1692/15
William, Lewis	Llandinam Mg	–	W I	29 March 1698	1698/73
William, Lowry	Llanaber Mr	Widow	B I	10 March 1663/4	1663/86
Williams, Lowry	Gyffylliog D	Widow	W	18 April 1693	1693/99
Williams, Margaret	Beaumaris A	Widow	W*	25 May 1636	1636/2
Williames, Margarett	Bangor Cn	–	W	14 Aug. 1665	1665/34
Williams *alias* Jones, Margarett	[Llanbeblig] (Carnarvon) Cn	Widow	W* Rd	17 Jan. 1671/2	1671/52
Williams, Margarett	Penmynydd A	Wife of Coningsby Williams, esq.	B	21 Nov. 1678	1678/14
Williams, Margaret	Llanfair-yng-Nghornwy A	Widow	B I	17 June 1687	1687/14
Williames *alias* Parry, Margaret	Conway Cn	Widow	W	12 March 1690/1	1690/50
William, Margery	Llandinam Mg	Widow	B I	22 July 1681	1681/105
Williams, Mary	Penmorfa (Cessylgyfarch) Cn	Spinster	W	27 May 1673	1673/44
Williams, Mary	Llanfihangel Ysgeifiog (Glan y Gors) A	Spinster	W C	21 Feb. 1686/7	1686/14
Williams, Mary	Llanbeblig (Carnarvon) Cn	Widow	W Rd	[14 March 1691/2]	1691/46
William, Mary	Llandrygarn A	–	B	14 Oct. 1692	1692/11
William, Mary	Llangelynnin Mr	Widow	I/G	18 Jan. 1693/4	1693/90
Williams, Mathew	Llanidloes Mg	Glover	B I*	7 Aug. 1690	1690/119
William, Morgan	Llanfihangel-y-Pennant Mr	–	B I	23 Oct. 1662	1662/66
Williams, Morgan	Llanllechid Cn	Gent.	W I	22 Feb. 1667/8	1667/78
William, Morgan	Llanidan A	Yeoman	B* I*	1 Dec. 1696	1696/19
Williames, Moris	[Llanbeblig] (Carnarvon) Cn	Gent.	W I	3 July 1635	1635/21
Williams, Morris	Beaumaris A	–	W	9 June 1648	1648/1
Williams, Moris	Gyffylliog D	–	B I	22 June 1663	1663/117
Williams, Maurice	Beddgelert (Havodgregog, Nanmore) Mr	Esq.	W(2) Rd	26 Oct. 1676	1676/37
Williams, Morris	[Llanrwst] (Caeawr, Gwydr) Cn	–	I	n.d.[2]	1683/51
Williams, Moris	Trawsfynydd (Llwyncrwn) Mr	Gent.	W I* C	21 March 1684/5	1684/77
William, Moris	Carno Mg	–	W I	[20 Jan. 1691/2]	1691/126
William, Maurice	Llanddeiniolen (Vachwen) Cn	Yeoman	B I	16 Nov. 1699	1699/74
Williams, Nicholas	Conway Cn	Tanner	W* I	21 Feb. 1666/7	1666/51
William, Owen	Llanynghenedl A	Yeoman	W I G	14 May 1661	1661/27

[1] I, Al *Llanrhwydrys*.
[2] Inventory taken 12 Nov. 1683.

Name	Parish & County	Status	Docs. Filed	Date of Probate/Admon.	Ref. No.
Williams, Owen	Llangeinwen A	Clerk	W* I	12 June 1671	1671/26
William, Owen	Llangwyfan A	Yeoman	W	29 Jan. 1672/3	1672/26
Williams, Owen	Llanfechell (Groes-fechan) A	Esq./Gent.	B I	18 May 1681	1681/12
Williams, Owen	Pentraeth A	Gent.	W	n.d.[1]	1681/20
Williams, Owen	Llaneilian A	Clerk (Rector of Llaneilian)	W I Al D Rd	[1 June 1687]	1687/9
William, Owen	Llanddwywe Mr	Labourer	W	21 May 1691	1691/86
William, Owen	Dwygyfylchi Cn	–	W I	15 Dec. 1693	1693/42
Williams, Owen	Llandwrog Cn	–	I/G	16 July 1695	1695/41
William, Owen	Caerhun (Tyddyn-croes) Cn	Yeoman	W*	3 Jan. 1697/8	1697/18
William, Owen	Llangybi Cn	Yeoman	B	25 Nov. 1697	1697/29
Williams *alias* Bulkeley, Dame Penelope	[Bangor] (Vaynol) & [Eglwys Rhos] (Bodescallan) Cn	Wife of Hugh Wynne, esq.	W	[28 May 1673]	1673/23
Williams *alias* Jones, Penelope	Llanfaelog A	Widow	W I	15 June 1687	1687/10
William, Peirce	Llandygái (Cappell Cerrig) Cn	Yeoman	B I	31 March 1699	1699/72
William, Piers[2]	Llanrhychwyn (Lledwigan) Cn	–	W I	[19 May] 1699	1699/84
William, Rice	Llanenddwyn Mr	–	B I	20 March 1661/2	1661/97
Williams, Reece	Llangoed A	Smith	W I Rd B	23 Feb. 1666/7	1666/24
Williams, Rice	Llandwrog Cn	Clerk (Rector of Llandwrog)	B	19 May 1671	1671/64
Williams, Rees	[Llangeinwen] (Quirt) A	Gent.	I(2)	n.d.[3]	1672/22
Williams, Rinalld	Llangristiolus A	Clerk (late curate of Llangristiolus)	W*	3 Jan. 1638/9	1638/21
Williams, Richard	Llandyrnog (Bankar) D	Gent.	W Rd	21 Sept. 1641	1641/60
Williames, Richard	Beaumaris A	–	B	23 M[ay] 1661	1661/4
Williams, Richard	Llanarmon (Rhoskill) Cn	Yeoman	W I	23 Jan. 1667/8	1667/64
William, Richard	Llanbedr Mr	–	I/G	9 Oct. 1667	1667/87
William, Richard	Llandanwg (Wmwlch) Mr	–	W	28 April 1668	1668/87
Williams, Richard	Llanllechid Cn	–	W* I*	13 Dec. 1678	1678/34
Williams, Richard	Dolgellau Mr	–	B	6 July 1680	1680/47
William, Richard	Tal-y-llyn Mr	–	B	18 May 1680	1680/56
Williams, Richard	Llanbedr Dyffryn Clwyd D	–	W/I	5 April 1687	1687/114
Williams, Richard	Llanllechid Cn	–	I	n.d.[4]	1688/54

1 Will dated 8 Sept. 1681.
2 See also under Pierce, Hugh, of Llanrhychwyn (document B).
3 Inventory exhibited 10 April 1672.
4 Inventory taken 15 June 1688.

Name	Parish & County	Status	Docs. Filed	Date of Probate/Admon.	Ref. No.
Williams, Richard	[Llanbeblig] (Carnarvon) Cn	Tanner	W I Rd	n.d.[1]	1690/46
William, Richard	Llanllyfni [Tythyn Kynverch fawr] Cn	Yeoman	W	n.d.[2]	1691/67
Williams, Richard	Clynnog Cn	Yeoman	B I	24 April 1693	1693/36
Williams, Richard	Caerhun Cn	Gent.	B	22 Jan. 1696/7	1696/38
Williams, Richard	Llangefni A	Gent.	W I	9 Oct. 1696	1696/16
Williams, Richard	Llandwrog Cn	Yeoman	B I	16 Aug. 1699	1699/70
William, Robert	Llanddwywe Mr	–	W	10 July 1640	1640/42
Williames, Robert	Llandrygarn A	Gent.	W	8 Sept. 1643	1643/6
William, Robert	Llandwrog Cn	–	B I	10 J[an.] 1661/2	1661/64
Williams, Robert	Rhuthun D	–	W Rd	23 June 1663	1663/130
Williams, Robert	Beaumaris A	Tailor	W I	7 Oct. 1669	1669/4
Williams, Robert	Llanfechell A	–	I	n.d.[3]	1669/28
Williams, Robert	Llanfairfechan Cn	Gent.	W R B	19 April 1671	1671/73
Williams, Robert	Llannor Cn	–	B	16 Feb. 1671/2	1671/84
Williams, Robert	Rhuthun D	Butcher	W I	25 Jan. 1672/3	1672/122
Williams, Robert	[Llanfaelrhys] (Mellionyth) Cn	Esq.	W Rd	14 Aug. 1673	1673/38
Williams, Robert	Llanllechid Cn	–	B	25 Oct. 1683	1683/47
William, Robert	Llanfrothen Mr	Yeoman	W	24 April 1684	1684/73
Williams, Robert	Llandwrog Cn	Labourer	W I	[28 April 1687]	1687/59
Williams, Robert	Llanelltud Mr	–	B I	16 July 1689	1689/71
William, Robert	Llangybi Cn	–	B I	29 April 1689	1689/54
William, Robert	Carno (Derowloyne) Mg	Yeoman	W* I	[20 Jan. 1691/2]	1691/127
Williams, Robert	Llanfairfechan Cn	–	B* I*	25 Jan. 1691/2	1691/62
Williams, Robert	Llanynys D	–	B	23 Nov. 1691	1691/123
William, Robert	Llanrhychwyn Cn	Yeoman	W I	29 April 1692	1692/61
Williams, Robert	Llangynhafal D	Yeoman	B I	20 July 1694	1694/108
William, Robert	Penmynydd A	Smith	B	27 June 1694	1694/31
William, Robert	Llanarmon Cn	Yeoman	W* I	17 April 1695	1695/34
Williams, Roger	Llanrhaeadr-yng-Nghinmeirch (Llewesog) D	–	B I	14 Aug. 1679	1679/57
Williams, Roger	Llanllechid Cn	Clerk (Rector of Llanllechid)	W	26 April 1693	1693/55
Williams, Rowland	Llanengan Cn	Clerk (Curate of Llanengan)	W	9 Dec. 1642	1642/24

1 Proved by 24 Jan. 1690[/1] according to bond for redelivery of will.
2 Will dated 6 June 1691.
3 Inventory taken 31 May 1669.

Name	Parish & County	Status	Docs. Filed	Date of Probate/Admon.	Ref. No.
William, Rowland	Llanbedrycennin Cn	–	B	7 Oct. 1669	1669/74
Williams, Rowland	Llanaber Mr	–	B I	21 Jan. 1678/9	1678/42
Williams, Rowland	Llanfechell A	Gent.	W	2 Jan. 1678/9	1678/10
Williams, Rowland	Llanfair-is-gaer Cn	–	B I	19 May 1682	1682/47
Williams, Rowland	Llanfachreth A	–	B	5 Aug. 1691	1691/19
Williams, Rowland	Llanllechid (Glanllugwy) Cn	Yeoman	B I	24 March 1698/9	1698/37
Williams, Rowland	Llangwyfan A	Yeoman	W I	21 Nov. 1699	1699/26
Williams *alias* Brwynog, Sarah	Llantrisant A	Widow	W	25 Sept. 1671	1671/34
William, Thomas	Caerhun Cn	–	B*	7 Feb. 1662/3	1662/39
Williams, Thomas	Llanelidan (Bryngole) D	Gent.	B I	22 June 1663	1663/120
Williams, Thomas	[Llangefni] (Tregarnedd) A	Clerk	W I	31 Dec. 1664	1664/29
Williams, Thomas	Rhuthun D	Innholder	W* I Rd	4 Jan. 1664/5	1664/121
Williams, Thomas	Ynyscynhaearn Cn	–	B I	25 Nov. 1665	1665/57
Williams, Thomas	Beaumaris A	Gent./Tanner	W* I	29 Jan. 1666/7	1666/6
Williams, Thomas	Llangeinwen (Quirt) A	Gent.	I G	12 Dec. 1667	1667/30
Williams, Thomas	Llanfwrog (Bodyngharad) D	–	W I	14 Sept. 1668	1668/112
William, Thomas	Llangelynnin (Tre r morva) Mr	Yeoman	I/G	n.d.[1]	1670/157
Williams, Thomas	Aberffraw (Grigor) A	–	W*	[13 Sept. 1671]	1671/2
Williams, Thomas	Llanbedr Niwbwrch A	–	B	25 May 1671	1671/14
Williams, Thomas	Llandyrnog D	Smith	W	29 Dec. 1675	1675/53
William, Thomas	Trawsfynydd Mr	Yeoman	I	n.d.[2]	1678/55
Williams, Thomas	[Deneio] (Pwllhelie) Cn	Mercer	W I	11 Jan. 1681/2	1681/38
Williams, Thomas	Gyffin Cn	Labourer/Yeoman	W I Al	24 April 1684	1684/41
Williams, Thomas	Caerhun (Bryn y Pin) Cn	–	W I* Db* Al	[6 June 1689]	1689/34
Williams, Thomas	Llanrug Cn	Gent.	B	3 April 1693	1693/58
Williams, Thomas	Llanrhaeadr-yng-Nghinmeirch (Garth, Segroit) D	Labourer	W I	23 March 1695/6	1695/95
Williams, Thomas	Llanrhaeadr-yng-Nghinmeirch (Trevybychyn) D	Yeoman	W I	n.d.[3]	1699/136
Williams, William[4]	Llandygwnning Cn	Gent.	W I	10 Sept. 1668	1668/60
Williams, William	Conway Cn	Esq.	W(2)	12 Aug. 1673	1673/29
Williams, William	Clynnog Cn	–	B I	30 Jan. 1676/7	1676/42
Williams, William	Llandwrog Cn	–	W	6 April 1680	1680/28
Williams, William	[Holyhead] (Treyarddur) A	Gent.	W Rd	24 Nov. 1681	1681/5

1 Inventory taken 10 Oct. 1670.
2 Inventory taken May 6 1678.
3 Inventory taken 25 Nov. 1698; endorsed *1699*.
4 See also under David, Robert, of Llandygwnning (document M2) for a reference to a citation to prove his will.

Name	Parish & County	Status	Docs. Filed	Date of Probate/Admon.	Ref. No.
Williams, William	Llanbeblig (Castellmay) Cn	Gent.	W	n.d.[1]	1683/32
Williams, William	[Llanbeblig] (Carnarvon) Cn	Mariner	W I	28 Aug. 1685	1685/35
Williams, William	Llanidan A	–	R	n.d.[2]	1687/24
Williams, William	Edern Cn	Clerk (Rector of Edern)	B I	21 Sept. 1689	1689/39
Williams, William	Llanfaelog A	Yeoman	W I	12 May 1690	1690/23
Williams, William	Rhoscolyn A	–	B I	18 Feb. 1690/1	1690/38
Williams, William	Llanfair-is-gaer Cn	Gent.	B I	14 Dec. 1692	1692/51
Williams, William	Llanelidan D	Yeoman	B* I R	19 July 1699	1699/123
Williams, William Price	Pennal Mr	–	I/G	16 April 1694	1694/94
Williamson, Robert	Beaumaris A	Gent.	B I R	17 June 1667	1667/3
Willott, George	Llanwnnog Mg	–	B I	4 July 1664	1664/136
Wilson, Hugh	Trefeglwys Mg	Clerk (Vicar of Llangurig and Trefeglwys)	W I	9 Nov. 1687	1687/137
Wilson, Humphrey	Llandinam Mg	Yeoman	W	[3 July 1672]	1672/126
Wilson, Joan	Llanidloes Mg	Widow	W	29 May 1667	1667/137
Wilson, Lucy	Llandinam Mg	–	B	2 Jan. 1662/3	1662/97
Wilson, Mary	Trefeglwys (Ffinant) Mg	Widow of Hugh Wilson, clerk	W	17 July 1688	1688/106
Willson, Richard	Llandinam (Henginwydd) Mg	–	W I	27 Sept. 1667	1667/130
Wilson, Richard	Llandinam Mg	Yeoman	B I M	7 Feb. 1670/1	1670/183
Wilson, William	Llanwnnog Mg	–	I/G	29 Nov. 1683	1683/106
Wood, Elizabeth	Holyhead A	Spinster	W I B	6 May 1685	1685/10
Wood, Hugh	Holyhead (Isallt) A	Gent.	W	8 Feb. 1680/1	1680/4
Wood *alias* Morgan, Jane	[Amlwch] (Gwredogg) A	Widow	W Rd	11 Nov. 1647	1647/1
Woods, Owen	Llanallgo A	Clerk (Rector of Llaneugrad)	W	n.d.[3]	1668/8
Wood, Thomas	Llangwyfan (Rhosmore) A	Esq.	W*	17 Nov. 1670	1670/47
Woolla, Richard	Llandinam Mg	Yeoman	I/G	[2 March 1675/6]	1675/63
Woosencraft, Thomas	Llandinam Mg	–	B I	28 July 1664	1664/132
Wosenam, Nicholas	Llandinam Mg	–	I/G	20 Oct. 1665	1665/100
Woosnam, Robert	Llandinam Mg	–	I/G	14 Dec. 1689	1689/88
Worsley, John	Beaumaris A	Merchant	W	7 Sept. 1664	1664/5

[1] Will dated 21 May 1683.
[2] Renunciation dated 4 Feb. 1687.
[3] Will dated 30 Dec. 1668.

Name	Parish & County	Status	Docs. Filed	Date of Probate/Admon.	Ref. No.
Worthinton, Mathew	Llandinam Mg	–	B	15 Aug. 1661	1661/131
Worthington, Richard	Trefeglwys (Bodaioch) Mg	–	W I	[12 Jan.] 1664/5	1664/139
Worthington, William	Trefeglwys Mg	Yeoman	W I	[20 June 1687]	1687/138
Wright, Thomas	Rhuthun D	–	B I	27 Jan. 1661/2	1661/122
Wenne, Anne	Llanrhaeadr-yng-Nghinmeirch (Drws bythel) D	Widow	W Rd	27 July 1665	1665/86
Wynne *alias* Owen, Anne	Clynnog (Tu yn y Coed) Cn	Widow of John Owen, gent.	W I M[1]	24 Jan. 1673/4	1673/28
Wynne, Anne	[Deneio] (Pwllhely) Cn	Spinster	W C	12 Nov. 1685	1685/38
Wynne, Anne vch John	Aberffraw A	Widow	W I	5 Nov. 1667	1667/1
Wynne, Arthur	Beaumaris A	–	B	12 March 1684/5	1684/5
Wynne, Cadwaladr	Llanbedr Dyffryn Clwyd D	–	B	19 March 1664/5	1664/113
Wynne, Kadwaleder Thomas	Aber (Hafod gelŷn) Cn	Gent.	W	14 Jan. 1646/7	1646/10
Wynne, Katherin	Llanystumdwy (Gwern y vach) Cn	Widow	B I	14 Feb. 1666/7	1666/69
Wynne, Catherine	[Llanbedr] (Cwm) Mr	–	W I	[16 Oct. 1676]	1676/73
Wynne, Cathrine	Penllech Cn	Widow	W* I	[21 March 1682/3]	1682/59
Wynne, Catherine	Llanystumdwy Cn	–	B I	13 Oct. 1691	1691/71
Wynne, Katheryn vch [ ]	[Clynnog] (Bryn y grô) Cn	Widow of Robert ap Rees Wynne	W*	2 July 1646	1646/14
Wynne, Cicely	Beaumaris A	Widow	W	29 March 1644	1644/2
Wynne, Edward	Llangynhafal D	–	W M	15 April 1635	1635/44
Wynne, Edward	Bodewryd A	Esq.	W*	25 Oct. 1638	1638/5
Wynne, Edward	Llanenddwyn (Tall y trithyn) Mr	–	B R	16 March 1660/1	1660/22
Wynn, Edward	Bodewryd A	Clerk	W I	21 April 1681	1681/4
Wynne, Edward	Rhuthun D	Innholder	W	11 Sept. 1688	1688/97
Wynne *alias* Foulkes, Edward	Llanrhaeadr-yng-Nghinmeirch (Llewesog) D	Gent.	B I	14 March 1691/2	1691/112
Wynn, Edward John	Llanynys (Rhŷd-onnen) D	–	B I	6 Dec. 1672	1672/120
Wynne *alias* Bulkley, Elen	[Trewalchmai] (Bodwiney) A	Widow	W* I	17 March 1666/7	1666/36
Wynne, Ellen	[Llandudwen] (Madryn issa)[2] Cn	Widow	W(2)*	21 Jan. 1689/90	1689/43
Wynne, Ellin vch Robert	Derwen D & Gwyddelwern (Beyarth) Mr	Widow	W I(2)	10 Dec. 1680	1680/62
Wynne, Ellice	Beaumaris A	Gent.	W*	9 March 1636/7	1636/3
Wynne, Ellis	[Penmorfa] (Llystyn-rhyn) Cn	Gent.	W(2) I*	9 Feb. 1666/7	1666/71
Wynne, Ellis	Llanbedr Mr	Gent.	I/G	27 Feb. 1667/8	1667/88

1 Also relates to John Owen of Clynnog (q.v.).

2 W *late of Bodgadle*, [Llanfihangel Bachellaeth].

Name	Parish & County	Status	Docs. Filed	Date of Probate/Admon.	Ref. No.
Wynne, Ellis	Beddgelert Cn	Gent.	W I Rd	27 Nov. 1672	1672/45
Wynne, Ellis	Llanfihangel-y-traethau (Glynne) Mr	Gent.	W I(2) B	23 Feb. 1690/1	1690/95
Wynne, Elizabeth	Llanedwen A	Widow of John Wynne, gent.	W Rd	25 Nov. 1684	1684/11
Wynne, Elizabeth	Llangwnnadl Cn	Widow	W I	30 July 1696	1696/72
Wynne, Evan	Llanedwen A	Gent.	W M	14 Feb. 1664/5	1664/21
Wynne, Evan	Penmorfa (Werne) Cn	G[ent.]	W	22 Dec. 1670	1670/128
Wynne, Frances	Llanfihangel-y-Pennant (Brynkir) Cn	Spinster	W I Ir	21 Oct. 1675 15 Feb. 1676/7	1675/27
Wynne *alias* Brereton, Frances	Llandegfan A	–	W	26 April 1694	1694/14
Wynne, Grace	Llanfihangel Tre'r-beirdd (Trewyn) A	Widow	W I	8 March 1668/9	1668/16
Wynne, Griffith	[Llanbeblig] (Carnarvon) Cn	Mercer	W I	22 Jan. 1672/3	1672/49
Wynne, Griffith (junior)	Llanfwrog (Keel-y-groeslwyd) D	Gent.	B I	28 Jan. 1698/9	1698/66
Wyne, Gwen vch John	Llangïan Cn	Widow	W	2 May 1638	1638/44
Wynne, Henry	[Llansadwrn] (Penheskin) A	Gent.	W Rd	26 June 1661	1661/23
Wynne, Henry	Llanarmon Cn	–	B	[ ] 1686	1686/47
Wynne, Henry	Llansadwrn (Penheskin) A	Gent.	B I	27 Dec. 1698	1698/13
Wynne, Hugh	Bodedern (Treyerwarth) A	Gent.	W I	5 March 1669/70	1669/6
Wynne, Hugh	Bangor Cn	Gent.	B(2) R	25 June 1679	1679/18
Wynne, Hugh	[Llanfechell] (Cromlech) A	Esq.	W B	25 Sept. 1691	1691/24
Wynne, Humphrey	Llanenddwyn Mr	–	I/G*	4 June 1694	1694/85
Wynne, Jane	Llanrhuddlad A	Widow	B	5 April 1665	1665/22
Wynne, Jane	Beaumaris A	Spinster	W B Rd	1 April 1667	1667/4
Wynne, Jane	Bangor Cn	Widow	B R	3 Sept. 1678	1678/17
Wynne, Jane	[Llanystumdwy] (Gwnfrin) Cn	Widow	B I	4 Oct. 1681	1681/58
Wynne, Jane vch Thomas	Derwen D	Widow	W B	4 Aug. 1640	1640/51
Wynne, John	Llanllechid Cn	Gent.	W*	4 May 1641	1641/40
Wynne, John	Llanfair-iuxta-Harlech (Kil y bronnydd) Mr	–	B	25 April 1661	1661/102
Wynne, John	Maentwrog Mr	Gent.	W I	19 Oct. 1666	1666/94
Wynne, John	Bodewryd A	Esq.	W	28 Oct. 1671	1671/7
Wynne, John	[Llanbeblig] (Carnarvon) Cn	Gent.	B R	7 Nov. 1678	1678/23
Wynne, John	Llanedwen A	Gent.	W(2)* Rd*	20 June 1678	1678/7
Wynne, John	Llanystumdwy (Gwnfrin) Cn	Gent.	B I R C	5 June 1679	1679/29
Wynne, John	[Llandwrog] (Plâs newydd) Cn	Gent.	W	[21 June 1682]	1682/43
Wynne, John	Conway Cn	Gent.	B	10 Jan. 1684/5	1684/37

Name	Parish & County	Status	Docs. Filed	Date of Probate/Admon.	Ref. No.
Wynne, John	Efenechtid D	Gent.	W I*	n.d.[1]	1686/88
Wynne, John	Llanelidan D	–	W I	21 Feb. 1686/7	1686/94
Wynne, John	[Penllech] (Berthaure) Cn	Esq.	I	n.d.[2]	1695/58
Wynne, John	Llanrhaeadr-yng-Nghinmeirch (Drwsbythel, Segwroit ucha) D	Gent./Yeoman	W I	5 Feb. 1699/1700	1699/137
Wynne, John Thomas	Amlwch A	–	W Rd	18 Jan. 1646/7	1646/1
Wynne, Jone(t)	Llanedwen (Glan r rhafon) A	Widow of Henry Wynne of Penheskin, gent.	W I	24 Aug. 1663	1663/17
Wynne, Katherin *see* Wynne, Catherine					
Wynne *alias* Gwynne, Lewis	Dolgellau Mr	Gent.	B I*	24 Oct. 1662	1662/57
Wynne, Lowry	Llanfihangel-y-traethau Mr	Spinster	W C	11 Jan. 1665/6	1665/68
Wynne, Magdalen vch Rees *see* Thelwall, Magdalen					
Wynne *alias* Lloyd, Margaret	Llanedwen A	Widow	W I	28 March 1671	1671/19
Wynne, Margaret	Bodewryd A	Widow [of Edward Wynne]	W C	27 Feb. 1676/7	1676/3
Wynne *alias* Parry, Margaret	Bangor (Llanporthauthwy) Cn	Widow	W I	15 Jan. 1694/5	1694/40
Wynne, Margarett	Beddgelert Cn	Widow	W* I C B	2 Jan. 1699/1700	1699/45
Wynn, Margarett vch Robert	Clocaenog (Bryngwrgi) D	Widow	W	17 April 1638	1638/70
Wynn, Mary	[Penmorfa] (Ceselgyfarch) Cn	Spinster	W*	[3 Feb.] 1664/5[3]	1664/81
Wynne *alias* Stodart, Mary	Gyffin Cn	Widow	B G	4 Jan. 1666/7	1666/53
Wynne, Mary	Llanrhaeadr-yng-Nghinmeirch (Llewesog) D	–	W I	24 April 1668	1668/122
Wynne, Maurice	Llangynhafal D	Gent.	I/G*	21 Feb. 1662/3	1662/89
Wynne, Maurice	Llandanwg Mr	Esq.	W I	25 Sept. 1673	1673/51
Wynne, Maurice	Deneio (Pwllhelie) Cn	Grocer	W L/R B(2)	20 Aug. 1692	1692/43
Wynn, Owen	Llanddeiniolen (Glascoed) Cn	Esq.	W I Rd	23 Dec. 1670	1670/104
Wynne, Owen	Bangor Cn	–	W	10 Feb. 1681/2	1681/28
Wynne *alias* Roberts, Peter	Efenechtid D	Gent.	W	27 Oct. 1684	1684/88
Wynn, Rees	Aber (Gorddinock) Cn	Gent.	W* Cd	25 Feb. 1640/1	1640/19
Wynne, Rees	Llanelidan D	–	W	6 June 1644	1644/43
Wynne, Richard	Llansadwrn (Penheskin) A	Esq.	W* I* R(2)* Rd	19 [ ] 1671/2	1671/33
Winne, Richard	Aberffraw (Tinllwden) A	Gent.	W	21 April 1684	1684/2

[1] Inventory taken 6 May 1686.
[2] Inventory taken 30 May 1695.
[3] Proved at the Prerogative Court of Canterbury.

Name	Parish & County	Status	Docs. Filed	Date of Probate/Admon.	Ref. No.
Wynne, Richard	Conway Cn	–	B	10 Jan. 1684/5	1684/38
Wynne, Richard	Llansadwrn (Treffos) A	Gent.	W I Rd	19 May 1699	1699/29
Wynne, Robert	Conway Cn	Esq.	W* I	19 June 1665	1665/38
Wynne, Robert	Llanfihangel-y-traethau (Glynn) Mr	Esq.	W I	6 Dec. 1670	1670/153
Wynne, Robert	Penllech Cn	Gent.	W I(2)	[13 March 1674/5]	1674/31
Wynne, Robert	Llannor Cn	Clerk (Rector of Llanddeiniolen and Llaniestyn)	B I R	10 March 1679/80	1679/28
Wynne, Robert	Llannor Cn	–	B	5 Jan. 1682/3	1682/53
Wynne, Robert	Llanfihangel-y-traethau (Maes y nyoedd) Mr	Esq.	W I	30 April 1692	1692/79
Wynne, Robert John	Holyhead A	Gent.	W I Db	21 April 1677	1677/6
Wynne, Robert ap Rees	Llanelidan D	Gent.	W I	17 Jan. 1684/5	1684/92
Wynne, Robert William	Llanaber Mr	–	B* I(2)	9 Oct. 1694	1694/79
Wynne, Rowland	Clocaenog D	Gent.	I/G	[7 Oct. 1668][1]	1668/103
			B	23 March 1695/6	1695/84
Wynne, Thomas	Llanfwrog D	–	W B	17 Feb. 1636/7	1636/57
Wynn, Thomas	Llansadwrn (Treffos) A	Gent.	W Rd	5 Nov. 1641	1641/17
Wynne, Thomas	Llangynhafal D	Gent.	W I	n.d.[2]	1668/117
Wynne, Thomas	[Llanbeblig] (Carnarvon) Cn	Gent.	B* I	28 July 1671	1671/54
Wynne, Thomas	Llanrhaeadr-yng-Nghinmeirch (Llewesog) D	Gent.	W* I	7 July 1691	1691/117
Wynne, Thomas	Llanbedr [Mr]	–	I	n.d.[3]	1695/69
Wynne, Thomas ap Rees	Llanelidan (Garthneuodd) D	Yeoman	W I	[28 June] 1663	1663/121
Wynne, Tydyr ap Robert	Llanynys (Maesmonkymro) D	Yeoman	W	7 July 1682	1682/93
Wynne, William	Rhuthun D	Gent.	W	5 April 1641	1641/66
Wynne, William	Llandyfrydog A	–	B*	4 Sept. 1662	1662/13
Wynne, William	Llanystumdwy Cn	–	B	13 July 1665	1665/53
Wynn, William	Llanddwywe (Llwyngriffrey) Mr	Esq.	W I*	23 Jan. 1668/9	1668/88
Wynne, William	[Llanarmon] (Pennarth) Cn	Gent.	W I	3 Sept. 1669	1669/70
Wynne, William	Beaumaris A	–	B	4 April 1685	1685/8
Wynne, William	Derwen D	Gent.	W* Rd	23 July 1688	1688/89
Wynne, William, ap John ap Humffrey	Ffestiniog Mr	–	B	3 June 1661	1661/94

1 Date of exhibiting inventory.
2 Endorsed *1668*; will dated 27 June 1668 and inventory taken 22 May 1669.
3 Inventory taken 26 Oct. 1694; endorsed *1695*.

Name	Parish & County	Status	Docs. Filed	Date of Probate/Admon.	Ref. No.
Wyn, William John ap Rees	Aberffraw A	–	W	11 Aug. 1638	1638/3
Wynne, William Owen	Llanbedr Niwbwrch A	–	B* I	23 Oct. 1685	1685/14
Wynne, William Probert ap John	Clocaenog (Llannerch Gronn) D	–	W I	5 June 1677	1677/70
[ ][1]	[ ]	–	B	20 June 1668	1668/148
[ ][2]	[ ] [?A]	–	B	9 Aug. 1680	1680/45
[ ][3]	[?Llanddyfnan A]	–	B	3 May 1687	1687/31
[ ][4]	[?Dolgellau Mr]	–	B	28 Sept. 1689	1689/63

1 Thomas Lloyd of Llanddoged (D) and John Thomas of Llanbedr[ycennin] (Cn) named as administrators.

2 Richard Wynne of Tinllwyden, [Aberffraw], gent., Hugh Johnson, clerk, and Henry Parry named as administrators.

3 Thomas Jones of Llanddyfnan, yeoman, and Jane Jones *alias* Williams named as administrators.

4 Howell Lewis of Gwanas, parish of Dolgellau, named as administrator.

APPENDIX

NAMES LISTED IN THE OLD MS. INDEX FOR WHICH NO DOCUMENTS WERE TRACED

Year	Name	Place of Abode	Doc. Listed
1641	David ap William	Llechylched A	W
,,	Evan Thomas John	Llandudno Cn	B
,,	John ap Robert	Llanaelhaearn Cn	W
,,	William ap Howel Griffith	Llanbeulan A	W
,,	Mary James	Heneglwys A	W
,,	Humphrey Jones	Llangïan Cn	I
,,	John Parry	Pwllheli Cn	B
,,	Hugh Prise	Llanallgo A	I
,,	Jane Pugh	Coedyffynnon Cn	W
,,	Jane Wynne *alias* Bold	Heneglwys A	I
1667	Richard Parry	Penystrowed Mg	B
1680	Elinor vch Edward	—	I
1684	Simon Parry	Rhuthun D	I
1691	Ellis Rowland	Caernarfon Cn	W
1692	Owen Rowland	Llanrug Cn	B
1694	Robert Humphrey	Rhuthun D	W
,,	Robert Jones[1]	Dolgellau Mr	B
1695	Judith Edmund	Aber Cn	B
,,	Griffith Parry	Perfeddgoed	W
1696	Anne Parry[2]	Pistyll Cn	W
1698	Owen Morris	Clynnog / Llangwnnadl Cn	W
,,	William Rowland	Llanbeblig Cn	W
1699	John Williams	Trefeglwys Mg	W

[1] Possibly a reference to the inventory of Robert John Gryffith of Dolgellau (1694/73) not listed in the old index.

[2] Possibly an error for Anne Parry of Rhuthun who is listed once in the old index while two copies of her will, together with an administration bond, are filed (1696/123).

INDEX OF PARISHES

An asterisk indicates more than one reference on the page.

INDEX OF TRADES AND CONDITIONS

An asterisk indicates more than one reference on the page.